ISBN 978-0-265-82746-8
PIBN 10095428

HISTORY OF ENGLAND

FROM THE

DEATH OF CHARLES I. TO THE BATTLE OF DUNBAR.

HISTORY

OF THE

OMMONWEALTH OF ENGLAN

FROM THE DEATH OF CHARLES I. TO THE EXPULSION

OF THE LONG PARLIAMENT BY CROMWELL:

BEING

OMITTED CHAPTERS OF THE HISTORY OF ENGLAND.

BY ANDREW BISSET.

IN TWO VOLUMES—VOL. I.

LONDON:

JOHN MURRAY, ALBEMARLE STREET.

1867

In the course of a somewhat minute investigation, continued for a good many years, of the records of English history during the 17th century, I found when I reached the period immediately succeeding the death of Charles I., that, while the printed sources of information were scanty, there existed in the State Paper Office a vast number of MSS. relating to the period of English history called, in the State Paper Office classification, "The Interregnum." Among others are the MS. volumes which contain the original minutes of all the proceedings of the Council of State as long as the government called the Commonwealth lasted. On a careful perusal of some of the volumes, and a more cursory examination of others, I resolved to attempt to write, by their aid, a history of England during the period extending from the death of Charles I. to the restoration of Charles II. Of this history I now offer to the public the first volume, bringing the narrative down to the battle of Dunbar towards the end of the 2nd year of the Interregnum, or of the Commonwealth, according to the prevalent, and, in my opinion, inaccurate designation of the government of England after the death of Charles I.

CONTENTS.

CHAPTER I.

CHAPTER II.

CHAPTER III.

CHAPTER IV.

THE TRIAL OF LIEUT.-COL. JOHN LILBURNE.

CHAPTER V.

CHAPTER VI.

HISTORY OF ENGLAND.

CHAPTER I.

THE political condition of England upon the death of King Charles presented a phenomenon at once anomalous and complicated. It consequently presented to those who were to carry on the English government a practical ——.

ERRATA.

Page 2, Note, *for* Leeds Journals, *read* Lords' Journals.
Page 7, Note 2, 9th line, *for* Magna Chartas, *read* Magna Charta.
Page 21, bottom line but two, *for* executed, *read* exacted.

ment of the Great Rebellion, a vital change had taken place. At the former time there were, as Raleigh has observed, "many earls who could bring into the field a thousand barbed horses; many a baron five or six hundred barbed horses; whereas now (at the beginning of the 17th century) very few of them can furnish twenty fit to serve the king. The force, therefore, by which our kings in former times were troubled, is vanished away." [1] In the list of the Peers summoned to the Long Parliament,

[1] Birch's edition of Raleigh's Works, vol. i. p. 206.

CONTENTS.

HISTORY OF ENGLAND.

CHAPTER I.

THE political condition of England upon the death of King Charles presented a phenomenon at once anomalous and complicated. It consequently presented to those who were to carry on the English government a practical problem proportionally difficult of solution. In order to furnish even an approximation to an accurate view of the elements that entered into that problem, it will be necessary to place before us the principal elements of the English Government in the early part of the 17th century.

The power of the ancient English kings had been limited, not merely by the parchment provisions of the Great Charter, but by the swords of the Anglo-Norman barons and their vassals. But, between the commence. ment of the wars of the Roses, and the commence. ment of the Great Rebellion, a vital change had taken place. At the former time there were, as Raleigh has observed, "many earls who could bring into the field a thousand barbed horses; many a baron five or six hundred barbed horses; whereas now (at the beginning of the 17th century) very few of them can furnish twenty fit to serve the king. The force, therefore, by which our kings in former times were troubled, is vanished away." [1] In the list of the Peers summoned to the Long Parliament,

---

[1] Birch's edition of Raleigh's Works, vol. i. p. 206.

may be observed, indeed, a few names of families which had levied war against the Plantagenets. But the names are but shadows—*nominum umbræ*. Besides these, there were titles in that list that sounded like those which had once formed the Norman war-cry; but they were only mock titles; bought by money, or earned by baseness and indelible infamy, from those who had debased both nobility and knighthood in England.

A glance at the state of the peerage at the time of the meeting of the Long Parliament is nearly as suggestive of the effect of the government of the Stuarts upon the ancient institutions of England, as the cruellest acts of oppression they had exercised upon the humblest and poorest of their subjects. The list of the peers consists of 1 duke, 1 marquis, 63 earls, 5 viscounts, and 54 barons; in all 124. Now, the list of peers summoned to the first Parliament of James, consists of 1 marquis, 19 earls, 1 viscount, and 21 barons; in all 42. And the list of all the peers summoned to the first Parliament of Charles the First, consists of 1 duke, 1 marquis, 37 earls, 11 viscounts, and 47 barons; in all 97. And the list of all the peers at the opening of the fifth Parliament of Charles, the Long Parliament, consisting of 124; while the number of peers created or advanced in peerage, between the opening of the Long Parliament in 1640, and the battle of Naseby in 1645, amounted to 43; it appears that James more than doubled the number of peers during his reign of some twenty years; and that Charles in the space of twenty years, again nearly doubled them.[1] Of the peers made by James, it may be said with truth, in the words of Mrs. Hutchinson, "the nobility of the land was utterly debased

[1] State of the Peerage, in Parl. Hist., vol. ii. pp. 591–597, extracted from the Leeds Journals, Dugdale's Baronage, and other authorities.

by setting honours to public sale, and conferring them on persons that had neither blood nor merit fit to wear, nor estates to bear up their titles, but were fain to invent projects to pillage the people, and pick their purses for the maintenance of vice and lewdness." [1] Even the peerage of Francis Bacon was conferred, not for his merits, but for his demerits, for acts of servile baseness to that hideous court that have left behind them a stain as immortal as his name.

"My seat," said Queen Elizabeth on her deathbed, " is the seat of kings, and I would have none but a king fill it after me." If the spirit of the great queen could have beheld what these Stuarts had been doing in that royal seat of hers for the last forty years, the spectacle would have provoked no ordinary amount of indignation, as well as astonishment—the spectacle of that ancient monarchy, which, for 600 years, had been, on the whole, supported with so much wisdom and valour, fallen into such a depth of decrepitude and dishonour. In all history there could hardly be found a contrast more striking than that between Queen Elizabeth and her immediate successors.

Of the English peerage at the opening of the Long Parliament in 1640, since two-thirds could not date their nobility farther back than the accession of James, that is, thirty-seven years ; and, of the remaining third, hardly one-half could date their nobility as far back as the time of the Plantagenets, the English nobility must certainly be con-

---

[1] Memoirs of Col. Hutchinson, p. 78, Bohn's edition, London, 1854. This statement is borne out fully by other contemporary evidence. Thus, in a letter dated March 21, 1628, in the Sloan MSS., and cited in Mr. Forster's Life of Sir John Eliot, p. 57, note, the writer says :—"The House of Commons was, both yesterday and to-day, as full as one could sit by another ; and they say it is the most noble and magnanimous assembly that ever these walls contained. And I heard a lord intimate they were able to buy the Upper House (his Majesty only excepted) thrice over, notwithstanding there be of lords temporal to the number of 118. And what lord in England would be followed by so many freeholders as some of these are ?"

sidered to have been at that time a new nobility. But
there was a class in England, known by the name of
"gentry," and composing a considerable portion of the
House of Commons, which, from the great length of time
that many of their members had held their lands, by free
and military tenure, must be considered not new, but
ancient in lineage, as well as in rank and position. This
class, besides many who had never belonged to the great
barons or peerage, but had held their lands, if not so long
as the heralds assert, still, a very long time, comprehended
also many of the younger branches of the great Norman
families, the elder branches of which had become extinct.
And yet, it is not unimportant to remark that while many
members of this class might represent counties in the
House of Commons, and were, in that character, denominated knights of the shire, others might represent boroughs,
and were, in that capacity, denominated burgesses; though
strictly, the burgess for any town was understood to be
one of the burgesses or burghers of that town, sent by
them as their representative in the House of Commons.
And not unfrequently they really were so, being men who
were, or had been engaged in trade in that town. Such
men might still be connected with, or descended from, the
class of gentry as Oliver Cromwell, the burgess for
Huntingdon, was. There were, also, undoubtedly many
men of humble birth, and who had been of humble occupa-
tion, among the eminent officers of the Parliament. Denzil,
Lord Holles, describes them as being "all of them from
the general (Sir Thomas Fairfax), except what he may have
in expectation after his father's death, to the meanest sen-
tinel, not able to make a thousand pound a-year lands, most
of the colonels and officers mean tradesmen, brewers,
tailors, goldsmiths, shoemakers and the like; a notable

dunghill, if one would rake into it to find out their several pedigrees."[1]　I have not the least wish to prove that these men were not what Denzil Holles and other Presbyterian and royalist writers have represented them as being; but I wish to ascertain the truth, if possible, whatever it may be; and it is well known to any one who has studied this period of English history, that to find out the truth in these matters is extremely difficult, if not altogether impossible, since writers that have been cited by some modern historians as good or sufficient authorities, such as Walker, Bates, Noble, and the author or authors of "The Mystery of the Good Old Cause," are all violent royalist or Presbyterian partizans.　And I believe that the pedigrees of many of the Ironsides, even the humblest born of them, would bear "raking into" quite as well as those of the Stuart peers.　The pedigree of Oliver Cromwell, whom Lord Holles classes among "mean tradesmen," because he was a brewer, was at least better, though Oliver cared little for such things, than that of Lord Holles, whose father's nobility went no farther back than James's reign of infamy.

It is, however, beyond a doubt, that in the earlier stages of the struggle between the King and the Parliament, it was to members of the class of gentry, such as Hampden and Fairfax,[2] that the nation looked with confidence, as the men best fitted to lead her councils and command her armies.　Such men, with the ancient lineage,

[1] Holles's Memoirs, p. 149. London, 1699.

[2] The fact of Sir Thomas Fairfax's father having, in 1627, been created a Scotch peer can hardly be considered as taking the Fairfaxes out of the class of gentry to which they had belonged for so many ages. Indeed, Ferdinando, Lord Fairfax, the father of Sir Thomas Fairfax, sat in the Long Parliament for Yorkshire; as Lucius Carey, Viscount Falkland, also a Scotch peer, sat for the borough of Newport—sat, therefore, in Parliament as a burgess, and in that character was strictly included in the designation "Goodman Burgess," which the doorkeeper of the House of Lords, to be mentioned presently, probably, however, meant to apply to the whole House of Commons.

inherited also a large portion of the territorial wealth, the military character, and the high spirit of that old Norman aristocracy, which had so often resisted the encroachments of their kings, and had once filled Europe and Asia with their victories and their renown.   In looking over the list of the House of Commons, at the opening of the Long Parliament, we are struck with many indications, from the names of the members in connection with the counties or places they represent, of the ancient establishment of this class in England, and even of its continuance down to our own times—for some of the places are represented in 1860 by men bearing the same names as those who sat for them in 1640.   There are the ancient names of Hampden, of Godolphin, of Trevanion, of Percy, of Montague, of Basset, of Glanville, of Grenville, associated with places which had known them for twenty generations.

To the class of gentry also belonged the lawyers, at least the members of the Inns of Court; who, in England, did not, as in France, constitute a nobility of the gown, distinct from, and inferior to, the nobility of the sword, but were, upon all fitting occasions, able and ready to prove themselves men of the sword as well as men of the gown; and furnished, indeed, almost all the best officers of the Parliamentary armies.   Ireton, Lambert, Ludlow, Michael Jones,[1] were members of the Inns of Court ; and though Oliver Cromwell's name is certainly not to be found now in the books of Lincoln's Inn, it appears to be beyond a doubt that he was sent up to London for the purpose of being entered as a member ; and that whether or not his name was ever actually entered on the books of that society, he occupied chambers

---

[1] Whitelock's speech in favour of lawyers being elected members of Parliament, in Parl. Hist., vol. iii. p. 1341.

in Lincoln's Inn for some time.[1] The insolence of the modern military despotisms, which have, throughout Europe, risen up on the ruins of the feudal system, changing their old title, "suzerain," into "sovereign," and to establish a despotism similar to which in England was the aim of the Stuarts,[2] has attempted to affix a word of contempt on all men who are not soldiers by profession, that is, *soldati*, and with that object they have used the word *robin,* and more recently *péquin*. Among nations who have not been trampled under the heel of a despot, the greatest men are those who graft the character of a man of the sword upon that of a man of the gown. Such men were the greatest Roman generals, including Julius Cæsar himself; and such men were Cromwell and his best officers. Among the earlier Norman lawyers and judges we find the

---

[1] It is possible that even contemporary writers may have been mistaken; but it appears impossible that the official inscription over the bed of state after his death should have described him as "educated in Cambridge, afterwards of Lincoln's Inn," if he had not actually lived in Lincoln's Inn, although he had not entered his name on the books : since there were many persons living at the time, to whom the fact was distinctly known, and who would have had the inscription corrected if it was inaccurate in that particular. The steward of Lincoln's Inn, in showing me the entry of Richard Cromwell on the books of the Inn, observed that if at that time it was customary, as it is now, to describe a member as the son of a member, provided the father had been a member, the absence of such description in the case of Richard Cromwell, who is only described as "filius et heres apparens, Oliv. Cromwell de Ely de insula Ely in com. Cantab. Ar.," would prove that Oliver Cromwell had not been a member of the society. But we found that this proved nothing, as the same omission occurs in the case of the entry of the son of Thurloe, Cromwell's secretary, who was undoubtedly a member of Lincoln's Inn.

[2] Every one who knows anything of the constitutional laws of England knows that the word "sovereign" cannot be constitutionally or correctly applied to the king or queen of England. In the debates in Parliament on the Petition of Right, Lord Chief Justice Coke used these memorable words :— "Magna Chartas is such a fellow that he will have no sovereign." (Rushworth, vol. i. p. 568. Parl. Hist. vol. ii. p. 357.) Those persons who mislead constitutional princes by teaching them to use words that are at once inaccurate and dangerous are their enemies. The "sovereign" of England consists at present of the queen, lords, and commons. Each of these separately forms only a limb of the sovereignty.

names of the most warlike and powerful feudal families. And the union in early times of the civil with the military character in the highest judicial functionary is particularly observable among the Normans and Anglo-Normans.

It is to be borne in mind that the Chief Justiciary was an officer whose functions by no means corresponded with those of the modern Chief Justice. In order to comprehend the functions of the Chief Justiciary, it is necessary to know those of the grand seneschall, or Senescallus Angliæ ; in modern language the Lord High Steward. This officer was the highest in the State, after the King; executing all the chief offices of the kingdom, as the king's representative ; and being thus chief administrator of justice, and leader of the armies in war. This is proved to have been the case in France, by Ducange and other high authorities, as well as by the public records of the kingdom ;[1] and in England by the *Dialogus de Seaccario*, written in the time of Henry II., and published by Madox, from the black and red books of the Exchequer,[2] and likewise by certain MSS. preserved in Sir Robert Cotton's collection in the

---

[1] Ducange, Gloss. ad voc. Dapifer et Senescallus. See also the Grand Coustumier de Normandie, c. X. "Solebat autem antiquitus quidam justiclarius prædictis superior per Normaniam discurrere qui senescallus principis vocabatur."

[2] Madox, Hist. Exchequer. See Co. Litt. 61a, for some account of the judicial part of the office of seneschal or steward, and some attempt at the etymology of the word, not much more successful than such attempts usually are. Madox is in error when he says (Hist. Excheq. p. 28) that, in the reign of William I., William Fitz Osbern was the King's constable, because he is called *magister militum* ;

whereas in the very same passage (of Orderius Vitalis) he is called *Normanniæ Dapifer*, in virtue of which office he would be *magister militum* as well as *capitalis justiciarus*. The constable was not originally *magister militum*, but was an officer subordinate to the *senescallus*, or *dapifer*. The feudal system was the same in its application to a manor and to a kingdom. The steward of every manor held the lord of the manor's court, and, in his absence, led his vassals to battle, as Scott has accurately described it, in "Marmion :"—

"There fight thine own retainers too, Beneath De Burg, thy steward true."

British Museum, particularly an old MS. intituled "Quis sit Senescallus Angliæ, et quid ejus efficium."[1] All these concur in the extensive and paramount nature of the authority originally wielded by the Lord High Steward, but none of them explain the anomaly of the co-existence of such an officer as the High or Chief Justiciary. I will shortly state here the substance of an explanation of this, which I had occasion to give elsewhere.

By the nature of the feudal system everything had a tendency to be given in fief. Among other things the office of seneschal was given in fief, too, and became hereditary among the Franks, Normans, and Anglo-Normans. In France, under the Merovingian dynasty, the office was in the family of Charles Martel, from whom sprung the Carlovingian dynasty. Afterwards the Plantagenets, Counts of Anjou were hereditary seneschals of France.[2] In England this high office was granted by William the Conqueror to the Grantmesnils, and thence came by marriage to the Earls of Leicester. After the attainder of the family of Montfort, Earls of Leicester, the office was given to Edmund, the second son of King Henry III. It then remained in the royal family till its abolition; Thomas Plantagenet, second son of King Henry IV., being the last permanent high steward,[3] and the office being conferred afterwards only *pro unicâ vice.*

---

[1] Cotton MSS., Vespasian, b. vii. fo. 99b. It will also be found in the Harl. MSS. 305, fo. 48, transcribed in a modern hand by D'Ewes, who supposed it to be of the age of Edward II. See also Cotton MSS., Titus C. *passim.* There is also, a tract intituled "Summus Angliæ Senescallus," in Somers' Tracts, vol. viii. Barrington says (Observations on the Statutes, p. 286, note b, 5th edition, London, 1796),

"Mr. Petyt hath copied a treatise upon the office of the High Steward of England from a manuscript in the Cotton Library (Vespasian, b. vii. fo. 99b), which he says is '*dangerous to be printed.*'" *Pet. MSS.* vol. xix. p. 293.

[2] The eldest son of Henry II. is said to have actually performed the duties of the office to the French king.

[3] For a list of the High Stewards, see Harl. MSS. 2194.

In France, when the office became hereditary in the family of the Counts of Anjou, it became necessary to have another seneschal or dapifer besides the hereditary one; and this officer, as the representative of the hereditary seneschal, still took precedence—as appears from the charters of the French kings—of all the other great officers of state.   In England, also, something of the same kind took place, but with this difference: that the various functions of the original grand seneschal, or *senescallus Angliæ*, were divided into two parts, and committed to two distinct officers as his representatives; the judicial functions being committed to an officer styled the chief justiciary; the administrative functions to an officer styled, not the *seneschallus* or *dapifer Angliæ*, but the *seneschallus* or *dapifer regis*.   This view of the subject would, if it needed it, be corroborated by the high powers of the officer created in later times, *pro hâc vice*, to preside in the House of Lords at state trials, which officer is not styled " high justiciary," but " lord high steward," that is, *seneschallus Angliæ*.   This explanation also removes the difficulty of accounting for the extraordinary powers of the lord high steward's court, which some English lawyers have attempted to get over by assuming that the lord high steward succeeded to some of the powers of the high or chief justiciary, whereas he merely exercises powers which had been delegated to the high justiciary.[1]

The chief justiciary, even in those times when a special

---

[1] Mr. Amos, in a disquisition on the office of Lord High Steward in Phillips's State Trials, Appendix, vol. ii., falls into the usual error of supposing that the judicial authority of the Lord High Steward grew out of that which appertained to the chief justiciary at the period when the latter office was abolished. Madox, whom Blackstone and others, both lawyers and historians, follow on this subject, has fallen into strange confusion, although even the documentary evidence contained in his own book furnished the means of extricating himself.

education was not considered absolutely necessary to fit a man for the judicial office, was usually a person who had given particular attention to the study of jurisprudence. As the representative of the judicial portion of the grand seneschal's powers, his authority extended over every court in the kingdom, except the court of the lord steward of the king's household. What Blackstone says[1] of the court of the marshalsea, that is, the court of the lord steward of the king's household, having never been subject to the jurisdiction of the chief justiciary, and no writ of error lying from it to the King's Bench, confirms what has been said, and merely amounts to this : that the court of the steward was, in fact, originally the court of the lord high steward, and in that court that one of his representatives, who was called the lord steward, pre-sided. That the functions of the *senescallus,* or *dapifer regis,* as the representative of the administrative portion of the grand seneschal's authority, were political, and not merely, like those of the present lord steward of the household, confined to matters connected with the king's household, is proved by the constant appearance of his name in the charters and other important public documents of the time. His relative position with regard to the earl marshal appears from the following passage of Britton :— "We ordain also that the Earl of Norfolk (marshal) shall, either by himself or his deputy (being a knight), be atten-dant upon us and our steward, to execute our commands, and the attachments and executions of our judgments, and those of our steward throughout the verge of our palace, so long as he shall hold his office of marshal." [2]

The chief justiciary not only presided in the king's court and the exchequer, but was, by virtue of his office, regent

---

[1] 3 Bl. Com. 76.   [2] Britton, fo. 1. b.

of the kingdom during the king's absence ; and, at those times, writs ran in his name and were tested by him.[1]   In this light the chief justiciary is regarded as having been the greatest subject in England.   One of the most distinguished of those who held this high office was Ranulph de Glanville, who is usually regarded as the author of the "*Tractatus de Legibus et Consuetudinibus Angliæ*," the oldest book extant on English law.[2]   The last who held the office and bore the title of *capitalis justitiarius Angliæ* was Philip Basset, the third of his family who held that high office—a family of which there were at one time six barons in England ; and the first who held the office of *capitalis justiciarius ad placita coram rege tenenda*, i. e. chief justice of the King's Bench, was Robert de Bruis, appointed in the fifty-second year of Henry III.[3] Sir Edward Coke was fond of indulging his vanity by bestowing the same title, "chief justice of England," upon himself whom a court insect such as Buckingham, the minion of James I., could crush ; and on the grand justiciary, the *capitalis justitiarius Angliæ*, the principal representative of the high functionary who had been at once chief administrator, supreme judge, and leader of the armies of England and Normandy.   This proceeding on the part of Coke was noticed by Lord Chancellor Ellesmere in his address to Sir Henry Montague, Coke's successor, upon his being sworn chief justice, in these words :—" Instead of containing himself within the words of the writ to be the chief justice, as the king called him '*ad placita coram nobis tenenda*.' "

[1] Madox, Hist. of the Exchequer, p. 17.

[2] Madox, p. 35.   Beames's Glanville, Introd. p. 12.   The two offices of Chief Justiciary and Dapifer seem to have been sometimes filled by the same person ; Ranulph de Glanville seems to have been at the same time Chief Justiciary and Dapifer.

[3] Dugd. Orig. 38.

I will here add an observation which will make apparent the vast power anciently attached to this high office of seneschal, dapifer, or steward.   To two of the most illustrious royal lines of modern Europe, the Carlovingians and Plantagenets, it served as a stepping-stone to the throne. It was for fear of its again doing the same thing to the house of Montfort, earls of Leicester, that the office was first taken into the royal family, and afterwards abolished in England.   The very name of the House of Stuart came from their holding the office of steward of Scotland.

The English nobility of that time (as distinguished from the class called gentry), though, as we have seen, thus new and thus humble in their origin, to use no stronger word, had displayed, instead of humility, all the insolence of a conquering caste in their demeanour towards their fellow-subjects.   Many examples might be given of this insolence ; but one which rests on unimpeachable authority will be sufficient.   One day, in March, $160\frac{3}{4}$,[1] Sir Herbert Croft, and some other members of the House of Commons, offering to enter the House of Lords, a yeoman of His Majesty's guard, keeping one of the doors of the Upper House, repulsed them, and shut the door in their faces with these words, " Goodman burgess, you come not here."[2]   The demeanour of the doorkeeper may be assumed to be a measure by no means inaccurate of the estimate formed by those within the Upper House of the power and dignity of those without it.   But between March, $160\frac{3}{4}$, and February, $164\frac{8}{9}$, a change had come over the scene. " Goodman Burgess " had shown by unmistakeable signs that he could do now what the " Upper House " could do

---

[1] It is necessary to bear in mind that before September, 1752, the legal year began on the 25th of March, and that according to that reckoning James succeeded to the throne of England on the last day of the year 1602, namely, the 24th of March.   In this history I will write all the dates between Jan. 1st and Mar. 25th thus—24th Mar. $160\frac{3}{4}$.

[2] Com. Jour. Lunæ, Martii 19, $160\frac{3}{4}$.

no longer ; that he could do those deeds of which a great authority has truly said that they "are great things, for empires lie beyond them."

The men who did these things proved incontestably that they possessed talent for efficient action of the highest kind ; but they unfortunately did not show that they possessed a still more rare and valuable quality of states-manship. They proved themselves so far sure-footed, but they did not prove themselves far-sighted statesmen. They had effectually shown that they knew how to destroy at a time when the work of destruction seemed the work impe-ratively demanded. But construction must follow destruc-tion, and in their work of construction they committed errors leading to some most fatal consequences.

On the 1st of February, $164\frac{8}{9}$, the House of Lords met, and it was moved to take into consideration the set-tlement of the Government of England and Ireland in the present conjunction of affairs on the king's death. A committee of nine Lords was appointed to join with a pro-portionate number of Commons, and a message to that effect was sent to the Commons' House. On the following day the messenger sent by the Lords the day before to the Commons acquainted their lordships that they went to that House and waited long, but were not admitted. The Lords thereupon ordered that they should go again, and desire that the committee of both Houses might meet the next morning, at the same hour as before appointed. On the 3rd of February, the Lords being informed that their messengers to the House of Commons were not yet ad-mitted, expressed not the least resentment, but ordered them to go again that day, being Saturday, and desire that the Committee for settling the Government might meet on the Monday next. But on Monday the Lords still found there was no admittance either for their messengers or their message : whereupon, it was once more ordered to send another message for a meeting next morning ; only the messengers were changed.[1]

During this time, in the Commons' House there had been a long and sharp debate on the subject of the Lords' House. The words used by Whitelock,—who was present and took a prominent part in the debate—" the debate was long and smart concerning the Lords' House," and, " after a long and quick debate," they passed the vote for abolishing the office of king,[2]—show that there were several Members of the House of Commons of sufficient weight to command a hearing who were opposed to the design of sweeping away what had always been considered as essential parts of the English Constitution. Yet the majority, more impressed with the result of their own personal experience than with those of records, or histories, or law-books, had come to the settled conclusion that the House of Peers was " useless and dangerous," and that " the office of a king in this nation was unnecessary, burthensome, and dangerous," and they voted accordingly the abolition of the House of Peers and of the office of king.[3]

Before we pronounce judgment on the judgment these men pronounced on these two parts of the old English Constitution, we ought to take into consideration the experience they had had of them. Lawyers like Coke and Selden, who were familiar with the records of the past, could remember how much, in the times of the Plantagenets, the great barons had done, in securing their own independence, for the security of the independence of all English freemen ; and, even without entering into the arguments philosophers might advance, founded on the corrupting

---

[1] Parl. Hist. vol. iii. pp. 1282, 1283, 1284.

[2] Whitelock's Memorials, p. 377. Folio. London, 1732.

[3] Whitelock's Memorials, *ibid.* Commons' Journals, Die Mart., 7 Feb., 164⅜. Parl. Hist., vol. iii. p. 1292.

influence of undivided power, would be apt to vote against the abolition of such an order as had once consisted of those brave and energetic men.   But men who looked more to the present than to the past, and whose experience of royalty and nobility was such as theirs, saw no good and much evil in a king such as James or Charles Stuart; and saw, if no danger, at least no use in a House of Lords, which contained neither great statesmen, great soldiers, nor great lawyers.   For it is impossible to obtain any approximation to an adequate conception of the thoughts and feelings by which those men were actuated without bearing in mind that those years of the lives of all of them in which the faculties of observation and reflection are most active were the years, or a part of them, during which the Stuarts had occupied the throne of England; that during a portion of those years they had seen sitting in the seat of their ancient kings a king who had carried his vices, his misgovernment, and his baseness to such an extent that the ambassadors of foreign powers resident in England repeatedly expressed their astonishment that the English nation submitted to such oppression and disgrace, and did not rise in insurrection and depose their king and hang his favourites, as the English barons had done in the case of Edward II., and Archibald Bell-the-cat in the case of James III. of Scotland,—calling it cowardice in the English people, and some of them even going so far as to say that there were " no men in England: " [1] that, when this king died, his son who succeeded him, instead of treating his father's favourite as Edward III. had treated the minions of Edward II., actually made him his own favourite, and gave up to him the government of England at

[1] The Count de Gondemar, the Spanish Ambassador, who used this expression, and to whose hostility Raleigh was sacrificed by the base cur which then sat on the English throne, probably thought that the last *man* in England perished with Raleigh.

home and the command of her armies in the discreditable wars into which he drew his country; that defeat and dishonour followed wherever this minion led, till England had sunk so low that her ambassadors were insulted at foreign courts, her merchant-ships could not sail the sea in safety, and her very coasts were ravaged by the Barbary pirates, who plundered the villages and carried off many of the inhabitants into slavery; that, therefore, this king's attempts to govern without parliaments and without laws had not about them anything of the illusion of a great or splendid tyranny, which, however bitter in itself, might have presented the spectacle of a coherent system, carried out with an ability and courage which, were its object good or bad, rendered it great and formidable; that, in short, all these men had lived for a considerable portion of their lives under the teasing, exasperating tyranny of a man of whose mental constitution the weakness is described by those who knew him as exceeding all imagination;[1] and that the patience with which they had submitted to all this can hardly be conceived without the evidence of their own words.

"My Lords," said Sir Henry Martyn, in his speech at the conference with the Lords against the addition made by the Lords to the Petition of Right —"My Lords, we are not ignorant in what language our predecessors were wont to express themselves upon lighter provocation; and in what style they framed their petitions. No less amends

---

[1] Count Tillieres to the King of France, August 28 and 31, 1625, in Raumer's History of the 16th and 17th centuries, vol. ii., p. 294.—At Paris, Madrid, and the Hague, the English ambassadors were repeatedly insulted. When Sir Thomas Edmunds went as ambassador to France, the Frenchmen sent to meet him at St. Denis pretended to excuse the smallness of the attendance on the ambassador by saying that "his Excellency should not think it strange that he had so few French gentlemen to attend on this service and to accompany him to the Court, in regard there were so many killed at the Isle of Rhé."—*Howell's Letters*, p. 210, 8vo, London, 1678.

could serve their turn than severe commissions to inquire upon the violation of their liberties ; banishment of some, execution of other offenders ; more liberties, new oaths of magistrates, judges, and officers ; with many other provisions written in blood.   Yet from us there hath been heard no angry words in this Petition ; no man's person is named ; we say no more than what a worm trodden upon would say (if he could speak), 'I pray tread upon me no more.' " [1]

These remarkable words in the speech of a Member of the Commons in the Parliament of Charles, which passed the Petition of Right, taken together with the not less remarkable language used by the French ambassadors, prove that the Lords had abdicated their office of being a bulwark of protection to the nation against the encroachments of the Crown ; that they were not virtually, as they were not lineally, the representatives of the warlike and high-spirited barons who had set their seals to the Great Charter, but truly, as well as lineally, the representatives of the creatures of the Tudors—the pettifoggers to make whom gentlemen,[2] to borrow the words of Raleigh, that enormous mass of national property taken from the Church by Henry VIII., about one-third of the land of England, was diverted from its legitimate use ; and of the still baser minions of the Stuarts.   It was not to be expected that, when the trodden worm had changed into the deadly adder, when "goodman burgess" had started up into an armed man, and gone forth conquering and to conquer, such kings and such Houses of Lords should appear either very useful or very worshipful institutions.

There were still, however, some members of the House of Commons, mostly constitutional lawyers, such as White-

[1] Parl. Hist. vol. ii. p.   [2] Birch's edition of Raleigh's Works, vol. i. p. 227.

lock and Widdrington, two of the Commissioners of the Great Seal, who argued, and justly, that the question was not what Government might be best in the abstract, but what was most conformable to the habits and feelings of the people, and, therefore, likely to be both stable and practicable ; that monarchy would be more in accordance with the general sentiments and old associations, and that the election of a king from one of the late king's younger sons, being a deviation from the ordinary rules of succession, would put an end to the Divine-right pretensions, and stamp him and his successors as holding their place by Act of Parliament, and not by Divine right ; while the continuance of the Crown in the same family, under certain limitations, strictly and clearly marked out and settled by the national will, would form a safeguard against the ambition of private men.

Some even named King Charles's third son, the Duke of Gloucester ;[1] others may have thought of the Prince Elector, the king's nephew, who remained in England till March, and to whom the House paid the arrears of his pension ;[2] and the latter scheme, if adopted and carried out with judgment and prudence, might have been attended with many advantages to the nation, might have saved it from many evils, from much suffering, much oppression, and much disgrace.   I only say " might have saved it," for, when we consider the tenacity with which not only the Stuarts themselves, but many other persons in England, Scotland, and Ireland, clung to the notion that the islands of Great Britain and Ireland were those Stuarts' private property, in the disposal of which the inhabitants had no voice whatever ; and that, when a settlement of the crown on a

[1] Whitelock's Memorials, p. 364,   [2] Whitelock, pp. 382, 386.
Dec. 23, 1648, folio, London, 1732.

basis somewhat similar to that mentioned above was made forty years after, even then nearly sixty years more elapsed before the Stuarts finally ceased from troubling, it would be rash to pronounce any scheme that could have been adopted perfectly free from objections and difficulties.

Nevertheless, there were some matters of detail, in regard to which I think it can be shown conclusively that the ruling men of the Long Parliament committed errors of the most deplorable, if not fatal, nature. I do not mean, however, matters of administration, for their administrative ability was very conspicuous on most occasions ; but matters of legislation. At the same time many of their legislative measures were undoubtedly good, and formed the basis of nearly all the law reforms of the next generation. But while the parliaments of Charles the Second adopted what was good in the legislation of the Long Parliament, it was not to be expected that they would shun what was bad, particularly if that which was bad was beneficial to the majority who voted for it, however hurtful, and even fatal, it might be to the English nation, not only of that, but of all succeeding ages.

During the first thirty years of the seventeenth century, the English Parliament had the great advantage of being led by two or three of the greatest constitutional lawyers, such as Coke and Selden, that have appeared in England. All through the reign of James I. the question of getting rid of the oppressive part of the feudal tenures very much occupied the attention of Parliament. In the conference in July, 1610, with the Lords, on the subject of the abolition of the Court of Wards, an assurance on the part of the Commons was placed on record, that in raising the revenue to be substituted for the revenue arising from the Court of Wards, and the feudal dues, "nothing shall be levied upon the people's ordinary victual; videlicet, bread, beer, and corn, nor upon their handy labours : " and on the part of the Lords that " the manner of levying it should be in such sort as may be secure to his Majesty, and in the most ease-ful and contentful sort to the subject that by both Houses of Parliament can be devised." [1]   And in the eighteenth year of the reign of James, a motion was made in Parlia-ment for commuting the feudal payments into a " compe-tent yearly rent, to be assured to his Majesty, his heirs, and successors." [2]   The amount of the proposed rent-charge was equal to nearly one-half of the whole revenue of the kingdom at that time ; [3] and as the value of the land would increase with the wealth of the kingdom, the pro-portion would continue the same.   In order, however, to make this rent-charge correspond in beneficial effect with the feudal tenure, it must have been so constructed as to rise in time of war, and fall in time of peace, thus furnishing the truly and only efficient check which the old English Con-stitution had placed upon unnecessary and expensive wars.

Unmindful of or disregarding all these most important considerations, the Long Parliament, by a vote or ordinance passed on the 24th of February, 1646, [4] had abolished the Court of Wards and Liveries, and all tenures by knight service, without any compensation or equivalent whatever to the State.   This ordinance seems, however, not to have been acted upon at the time.   The dues of wardship, and all the other feudal dues, with the exception of purveyance, continued to be rigorously executed till 1656, when one of Cromwell's Parliaments passed an Act " for the further establishing and confirming" the ordinance above men-

---

[1] Journals of the House of Lords, 23rd July, 1610.

[2] To this motion Coke has affixed the stamp of his approbation. . See

4 Inst. 202, 203.

[3] Sinclair, Hist. Reven., vol. i. pp. 233, 244.

[4] Parl. Hist., vol. iii. p. 440.

tioned. This Act was in substance re-enacted by a majority
of 2 (the number being 149 against, and 151 for it) in
the convention parliament in 1660, and the excise, in direct
contravention of the assurance of the Commons stated
above, and placed on record on the Lords' Journals, was
substituted as an equivalent for the revenue arising from
the Court of Wards. After a debate, in which one member
said that if this bill was carried, every man who earns his
bread by the sweat of his brow, must pay excise to excuse the
Court of Wards, which would be a greater grievance upon
all, than the Court of Wards was to a few; and another,
one of the most learned of English lawyers, spoke strongly
against the gross injustice of making those who had no
lands pay an equivalent for the rent-charge, which was the
condition on which the land of England had originally been
granted to be held as private property.[1]

As the House of Commons, or the body which called
itself the House of Commons, was now the sole governing
power in England, it would be desirable to ascertain the
exact number of members composing that assembly at this
time. But that, I apprehend, is impossible, for the following reason. Immediately after the king's execution certain
of the secluded members were permitted, on certain conditions, to resume their seats in the House. But while
the journals contain the entries of the orders for the re-ad-
mission of six of those secluded members, namely, of
Colonel Bingham, Mr. Edward Ashe, and Mr. Armyne, on
the 2nd of February; of Mr. Gould, and Mr. John Ashe,
on the 3rd of February; and of Sir William Masham, on
the 8th of February; there is ground for believing that at
the same time several other members were re-admitted, and
took their seats. For immediately before the entries of

---

[1] Commons' Journals, Nov. 21, 1660. Parl. Hist., vol. iv. pp. 148, 149.

the orders for the readmission of Colonel and Mr. Edward Ashe, there are two entries erased, and in the margin is written "Obliterated by order of Feb. 22, 1659." And between the entries of the order for the readmission of Mr. Edward Ashe and of that for the readmission of Mr. Armyne, there are several entries erased.[1] Again, immediately before the order for the admission of Mr. Gould, there are three entries erased, and in the margin is written "Nulled, by order of Feb. 22, 1659;" and immediately after the order for the admission of Mr. John Ashe, there is also an entry erased.[2] There are, moreover, in other places, several entries erased, and the words written in the margin "Nulled, by order of Feb. 22, 1659."[3]

But though, for this reason, the number of members cannot be exactly ascertained, a very close approximation to it may be obtained in this way. When there was a contest for power and place, the number of members present, which, upon other occasions when the business of the nation only was to be done, very seldom exceeded 50, and very often fell below 40, amounted to more than 100, the highest number being 122. This contest for power and place was the greatest when the annual elections of a new Council of State took place. Thus, at the election of a new Council of State in February, $16\frac{49}{50}$, there was a House of 98[4] members; at the same election in $165\frac{0}{1}$ there was a House of 121 members;[5] in $165\frac{1}{2}$, there was a House of 120;[6] in $165\frac{2}{3}$, there was a House of 122.[7] We may therefore conclude that 122 was the

---

[1] Commons' Journals, Die Veneris, 2 Feb., $164\frac{8}{9}$.

[2] Commons' Journals, Die Sabbati, 3 Feb., $164\frac{8}{9}$.

[3] Commons' Journals, Die Lunæ, 5 Feb., $164\frac{8}{9}$; Die Jovis, 8 Feb, $164\frac{8}{9}$.

[4] Commons' Journals, Die Mercurii, 20° Februarii, $16\frac{49}{50}$.

[5] Commons' Journals, 7 Feb., $165\frac{0}{1}$.

[6] Commons' Journals, 24 Nov., 1651.

[7] Commons' Journals, 24 Nov., 1652.

greatest number the House could assemble ; and that the ordinary business of the government was carried on by a number not exceeding 50 on an average, though often falling below 50.   It is evident that a government con- sisting of this number of men, who, as we shall see, shrunk from any appeal to the general sense of the nation, and retained their power by means of an army, had about the same title to call itself the commonwealth of England, that the three celebrated tailors of Tooley Street had to style themselves the people of England.

On the 7th of February, the House " ordered that the Committee of Safety, and the Committee at Derby House, and the powers to them and either of them given by any order or ordinance of Parliament, be absolutely dissolved and taken away." [1]   On the same day it was ordered, " that there be a Council of State erected to act and proceed according to such instructions as shall be given to this House." [2]   At the same time, Mr. Lisle, Mr. Holland, Mr. Scott, Colonel Ludlow, and Mr. Robinson, were ap- pointed to present to the House instructions to be given to the Council of State ; and likewise the names of such persons as they conceived fit to be of the Council of State, not exceeding the number of 40 ; and power was given to them to send for papers and writings from Derby House, or elsewhere.

On the 8th of February Sir Thomas Widdrington and Mr. Whitelock, two of the commissioners for the Great Seal, brought the Great Seal into the House, and delivered it into the hands of the Speaker, the House then sitting. The House then ordered the Great Seal to be broken ; and a workman was brought into the House with his tools,

---

[1] Commons' Journals, Die Mercurii,   [2] *Ibid.*
7° Februarii, 164⅞.

who, in the face of the House, upon the floor, broke the seal in pieces. The House then ordered the several pieces of the said seal thus broken and the purse to be delivered to Sir Thomas Widdrington and Mr. Whitelock, to be disposed of at their pleasure.[1] After this, the House passed an Act for establishing the new Great Seal to be the Great Seal of England; and Whitelock, L'Isle, and Keeble were appointed Lords Commissioners of the Great Seal.[2] The Commons also published, on the 21st of March, a long elaborate declaration, in English, Latin, French, and Dutch, stating their reasons for establishing what they called a republic or commonwealth.[3] But names have not the power of changing the nature of things. Nevertheless, the bold and able men who then ruled England have so far succeeded in getting their names accepted for realities that histories have actually been written of their doings under the title of histories of the commonwealth of England, meaning of the republic of England; for commonwealth was used formerly to express the established form of government, and is thus used by Sir Thomas Smith,[4] one of the principal secretaries of state to King Edward VI. and Queen Elizabeth, and by Queen Elizabeth herself in her speeches to her parliaments. However, if these men imagined that by abolishing the king and House of Lords, and constituting themselves the sole governing power in England, they thereby established that form of government which the Greeks called a democracy, and the Romans a republic, they committed a great error. Whether, if they had been so minded, they could have established a republic, is, at least, very doubtful; but they never tried. They

---

[1] Commons' Journals, Die Jovis, 8 Feb., 164⅞. Whitelock, p. 378.
[2] *Ibid.*

[3] Parl. Hist. vol. iii. pp. 1292-1304.
[4] The English Commonwealth, in three books, first published in 1584.

perhaps supposed that if, in accordance with the requisitions of the writing intituled "An Agreement of the People of England and the places therewith incorporated,"[1] being, in fact, a draft of a parliamentary reform bill drawn up chiefly by Ireton, they had dissolved themselves on the last day of April, 1649, to make room for the election of a new parliament, and that if every reasonable degree of freedom of election had been permitted, all that they had done would have been undone at once, and they themselves hanged for doing it. But this could not have happened while the victorious army, from the officers of which proceeded the petition accompanying "The Agreement of the People," existed. It might be said, indeed, that elections made under the protection of this army could not be reckoned free elections. At the same time, there is, undoubtedly, a great show of fairness in the proposal to tender the agreement to the people throughout the whole country, to be subscribed by those who should approve of it, as petitions of a voluntary nature are ; and that it may be carried into effect if, upon the amount of subscriptions, to be returned by commissioners to be appointed for that purpose in April next, there should appear a general reception of it among the people, or the well-affected of them. Now, at least in the neglect of this fair and reasonable proposal, the treatment of this document by the Parliament appears not quite honest ; and if it be said, in defence of the Parliament, that not only the principle of policy, but the still more powerful instinct of self-preservation dictated imperatively the course they pursued, it may be answered that they would have taken a

[1] Parl. Hist., vol. iii. pp. 1267–1277. The first article of this "Agreement," is—"That to prevent the many inconveniences apparently arising from the long continuance of the same persons in supreme authority, this present Parliament end and dissolve upon the last day of April, 1649."

more sound and far-sighted view of their own ultimate advantage by at least giving the above-mentioned plan a trial. They might then have said that they had, at least, attempted to establish a republic. Whitelock has expressed their view of the matter in a very few words, saying, "It was much pressed to set a time for dissolving this Parliament. Most of the House disliked to set a time, as dangerous; but agreed that when the business of the kingdom would permit, that then it should be dissolved." [1]

It is needless to go through the clauses and enter into the details of Ireton's draft. Some of its leading features may, however, be shortly stated. It proposed that the number of representatives should be 400, to be elected by men above twenty-one years of age, assessed to the relief of the poor, not servants to, and receiving wages from, any particular person; and according to a fair and equal proportion of numbers throughout England and Wales; that a Parliament should be chosen once every two years; that the persons to be chosen shall be men of courage, fearing God, and hating covetousness; and in case any lawyer shall be chosen into any representative or Council of State, that he shall be incapable of practice as a lawyer during that trust; and that 150 members at least be always present in each sitting of the representative at the passing of any law or doing of any act whereby the people are to be bound, but that sixty may make a house for debates or resolutions preparatory thereunto.[2] It may, I think, be truly said of it that whatever objections this draft may be open to, it bears all the marks of having been framed with perfectly honest intentions. The clause respecting the exclusion of practising lawyers renders Whitelock's appa-

[1] Whitelock's Memorials, p. 389, folio, London, 1732. [2] Parl. Hist. vol. iii. pp. 1267-1277.

rently candid criticism of this bill of Ireton's sufficiently intelligible. "The frame of this Agreement of the People," he says, "was thought to be, for the most part, made by Commissary-General Ireton, a man full of invention and industry, who had a little knowledge of the law, which led him into the more errors." [1] The bill is evidently the work of an able and ingenious man, and contains, amid some of a questionable character, many provisions of the highest practical value. There were undoubtedly at that time certain reforms wanted in the distribution of the representatives of the people in Parliament. For instance, the single county of Cornwall elected forty-four; while Essex and other counties, each having as great a share in the payment of taxes, sent no more than six or eight each. In some instances, moreover, as in carrying measures with a House of only forty members, there was a clear departure from the fundamental constitution of Parliament. In proposing to reform such abuses as these, the framers of the draft did well. And as statesmen-soldiers they occupied the same position, and had acquired the same experience, as

---

[1] Whitelock's Memorials, p. 356. It is remarkable that Whitelock, in his speech in the House in November, 1649, in favour of lawyers being elected members of Parliament in answer to the argument of a member who called the lawyers "gownmen, who had not undergone the dangers and hardships that martial men had done," said :— "The ancient Romans · were soldiers though gownmen; nor doth that gown abate either a man's courage or his wisdom, or render him less capable of using a sword when the laws are silent or you command it. You all know this to be true by the great services performed by Lieut.-Gen. Jones, Commissary Ireton, and many other lawyers; who, putting off their gowns when you required it, have served you stoutly and manfully as soldiers, and undergone almost as many and as great dangers and hardships as the gentleman who so much undervalues all of them."—*Parl. Hist.* vol. iii. p. 1341. But then it will be observed that the cases of Jones, Ireton, and others did not come under the clause proposed in Ireton's draft, which only objected to lawyers *practising* while they were members of Parliament, which Ireton and the others certainly did not do. The clause is the more remarkable as coming from an able man who had received the education of a lawyer.

that great statesman-soldier, Simon . de Montfort, who did
so much towards the introduction of the most important
discovery ever made in the science and art of government.   It may be a lesson of humility to the pride of philosophy to reflect that the principle of representative
government, for want of which all the ancient experiments
in government were failures, after eluding the search of the
greatest philosophers and legislators of antiquity, was discovered by a comparatively unlettered but practically saga-
cious baron of the dark ages ; and that the Petition of
Right, and even Magna Charta itself, with a great number
of other most important constitutional statutes, were but
declaratory and in affirmation of that body of laws and
customs which had sprung from the healthy mental activity
and conscious responsibility of free men managing their
own affairs, public and private, and surpassed, in the practical ingenuity of adapting means to ends, the most subtle
devices of the greatest philosophers.

It is due to Ireton, and those who acted with him in
the drawing up of that petition and agreement, to cite
their own account of the ends they set before themselves
and offered to their fellow-countrymen.   The petition which
accompanied the draft of a constitution, entitled " An
Agreement of the people of England," was couched in
terms guardedly respectful and courteous :—" While your
time," say the armed petitioners, " hath been taken up in
other matters of high and present importance, we have spent
much of ours in preparing and perfecting such a Draught
of Agreement, and in all things so circumstantiated, as to
render it ripe for your speedier consideration, and the
kingdom's acceptance and practice if approved, and so we
do herewith humbly present it to you.   Now, to prevent
misunderstanding of our intentions therein, we have but

this to say, that we are far from such a spirit, as positively
to impose our private apprehensions upon the judgments of
any in the kingdom that have not forfeited their freedom,
and much less upon yourselves : neither are we apt in any-
wise to insist upon circumstantial things, or aught that is
not evidently fundamental to that public interest for which
you and we have declared and engaged; but, in this
tender of it, we humbly desire :—1. That, whether it shall
be fully approved by you and received by the people, as it
now stands or not, it may yet remain upon record before
you, a perpetual witness of our real intentions and utmost
endeavours for a sound and equal settlement; and as a testimony whereby all men may be assured what we are
willing and ready to acquiesce in; and their jealousies
satisfied or mouths stopt, who are apt to think or say, we
have no bottom.   2. That, with all the expedition which
the immediate and pressing great affairs will admit, it
may receive your most mature consideration and resolutions
upon it; not that we desire either the whole, or what you
shall like in it, should be by your authority imposed as a
law upon the kingdom, for so it would lose the intended
nature of ' An Agreement of the People ; ' but that, so far as
it concurs with your own judgments, it may receive your
seal of approbation only.   3. That, according to the
method propounded therein, it may be tendered to the
people in all parts, to be subscribed by those that are
willing, as petitions and other things of a voluntary nature
are ; and that, in the meanwhile, the ascertaining of those
circumstances which are referred to commissioners in the
several counties, may be proceeded upon in a way preparatory
to the practice of it : and if, upon the account of subscriptions (to be returned by those Commissioners in April next)
there appears a general or common reception of it amongst

the people, or by the well-affected of them, and such as
are not obnoxious for delinquency, it may then take place
and effect, according to the tenor or substance of it." [1]

The deputation, consisting of Lieut.-Gen. Hammond,
Col. Okey, and other officers appointed by the general and
his council of officers to present the petition, having withdrawn, the Commons ordered the petition but not the
agreement to be read; the reason of which, according to
Whitelock, was the great length of it. The Commons
then ordered their Speaker to return their thanks to the
petitioners; which he did accordingly.[2]

The persons who now called themselves the Parliament
of England, and who owed not only all their present power
and importance, but their very existence, not to any merit
of their own, or to anything they had done, but solely to
the great deeds of the men who had drawn up and presented this petition and agreement to their consideration,
do not appear to have taken any further notice of the
"Agreement of the People," which had been prepared with
so much pains, and so respectfully presented to them.
Instead of putting an end to their sitting on or before the
last day of April, 1649, in the "Agreement" proposed, or
taking any steps towards obtaining the opinion of the
nation on the subject, they continued to sit till April 20,
1653, when Cromwell turned them out by force.

I think it may be concluded from all this, that whatever they might say of the dishonesty of Cromwell's proceedings their own conduct was at least questionable: we
might almost say not that of honest men, were there not
other parts of their proceedings that bear strongly the
marks of honest intentions. If, however, the turning them

---

[1] Parl. Hist., vol. iii. pp. 1265,
1266, 1267.

[2] Parl. Hist., vol. iii. p. 1277.

out by force was a necessary step towards the establishment of a really constitutional government, the best thing under the circumstances for the nation at that time would have been for Fairfax and Ireton to have turned them out, when they found by their treatment of the " Agreement of the People," that they were not inclined to act an honest part.

But Fairfax and Ireton were men of the strictest and most punctilious honour. It was from this Parliament, at least from a parliament of which they still considered this residue as the representative, that they had received their commissions, and they knew that when the generals of an army seek to corrupt their soldiers and to win their favour in order to use them against those to whom they have sworn allegiance, they become degraded to the condition of robbers or pirates. The difference between them and Cromwell was the difference between the Roman generals while Roman generals were men of honour, and the Roman generals when Rome had become thoroughly corrupt. The former, as Plutarch observes,[1] were men of kingly souls, and moderate in their living, and satisfied with a small fixed expenditure, and they thought it baser to attempt to win the soldiers' favour than to fear their enemies. But the generals in the time of Sulla acted the demagogue, while they were in command, for their own aggrandizement and their country's ruin; and by purchasing the services of the soldiers by the money they distributed among them, they made the Roman State a thing for bargain and sale, and themselves the slaves of the vilest wretches, in order that they might domineer over honest men.

This character would not apply to the English army

[1] Life of Sulla, c. 12.

under Fairfax, but we shall see as we proceed how Fairfax's successor changed the character of that army by weeding out the citizen element and substituting for it men who fought not for a principle, civil or religious, but simply for pay.

As this remnant of the Long Parliament thus declined even to take the sense of the part of the English people who were well-affected to themselves as to the form and nature of their government, the government of England at the time cannot, according to any intelligible meaning attached to that word, be called a republic, democracy, or commonwealth, in the sense in which that last word was used by them. What form of government was it then? It is easier to say what it was not, than what it was. It was not a monarchy, and it was not a democracy: neither was it an oligarchy, nor an aristocracy according to Aristotle's definition of those forms of government. But as it held its power not at all from or at the will of the nation, but from and at the will of a victorious army, composed indeed of citizen soldiers and not of mere mercenaries, it may be described as a close, able, and well-obeyed military oligarchy, or rather aristocracy, which by the very fact of calling itself a commonwealth recognized popular rights and wants, and kept in view great national objects to such an extent as was consistent with its own very critical and difficult position, and which might perhaps, by dexterous management and undeviating integrity and single-mindedness in its members, have developed itself ultimately into an actual commonwealth or republic. But the conditions necessary for such a result are so rarely found among mankind that the chances of its ultimate failure, either from external or internal enemies, were greater than the chances of its ultimate success. Besides,

D

those who now were at the head of affairs in England had already taken a step which, although some of them might have thought it conducive to their safety, was one ultimately leading to the destruction not only of their republic but of themselves.

If there ever existed a chance for those who really wished to establish a republic, they threw that chance away when they determined on the king's execution. As Charles could not be amenable to the English law of treason, his execution was not only a most unjust, but a most impolitic act on the part of the republican party. There was a time when they might perhaps really have established a republic, and a time when, I am inclined to think, even Cromwell would have co-operated heartily in the work. It was, I think, with a view to defeat the views of the more violent fanatics in the army with regard to bringing Charles to a violent death, that Cromwell brought about the king's escape from Hampton Court. I think that he meant that Charles should make his escape to France. Perhaps Cromwell did not know all the difficulties in the way of that. However the plan failed, and then Cromwell's own safety might compel him to go along with the army fanatics. But probably even Cromwell, with all his sagacity and foresight, had not calculated all the wonderful effects of the king's trial and execution—of the public spectacle of a king, the representative of a long line of kings, first patiently submitting to the interruptions and to the sentence of his judges, and then kneeling at the block like a common malefactor, and dying quietly and bravely. Charles thus obtained by his death a posthumous reputation, which his life could never have obtained for him ; for the whole course of that life had exhibited him as a man of a soft head, and a hard but not a brave heart, forming a marked contrast to the hard head and soft yet brave heart, which, " despite some passing clouds of crime," formed the character of Cromwell.

If Charles had escaped to France, and had succeeded in making an attempt to recover his power, and to execute his purpose of doing for England what his wife's brother had done for France by the help of a French army, the parliamentary army of England might have established Cromwell's family firmly on the throne, or set up a republican government, which would have had at least some chance of success.   But the day of that execution in front of Whitehall, which the republican party hailed as the commencement of their beloved republic, was instead of that the total destruction of any chance that had existed for the establishment of a real republic. Henceforth the character of Charles assumed a new aspect, shaped and coloured from his death, and not from his life.

It appears that Ireton's draft embodying his honest, able, and, as far as we have now the means of forming a judgment, practicable scheme for reforming and settling the representative system and government of . England, not only met with no acceptance, but exposed its author to the ill-will and hostility of this remnant of the Long Parliament, which styled itself the parliament of the Commonwealth of England.   This hostility was signally manifested in the debate on the election of members of the Council of State, when the name of Ireton was rejected.   Besides the clause excluding practising lawyers from being eleceed as members of Parliament, there were other expressions in the " Agreement," of which the consciences of many members would feel the force and justice, and which on that very account would be the more disagreeable ; " and we desire and recommend it to all men, that, in all times, the persons to be chosen for this great trust may be men of courage, fearing God, and hating covetousness."

On the 13th of February, Mr. Scott reported from the committee, appointed to nominate a Council of State, the instructions for the Council of State, fourteen in number, which were read and assented to.[1] Whitelock has stated concisely that their powers were, 1st. To command and settle the militia of England and Ireland. 2nd. To set forth such a navy as they should think fit. 3rd. To appoint and dispose magazines and stores. 4th. To sit and execute the powers given them for a year.[2] Mr. Scott also reported a list of the names of persons to be of the Council of State. On the 14th of February, the House took up the debate upon the names of persons to be of the Council of State. They first passed a resolution that some of the officers of the army should be of the Council of State. The names proposed were then adopted without a division, except in the case of Philip, Earl of Pembroke, when the yeas were 50, and the noes 25, and in the case of William, Earl of Salisbury, when the yeas were 23, and the noes 20, and in the cases of Ireton and Harrison who were rejected. The two following entries in their own journals throw more light on the character of this assembly than all the pamphlets written against them by their most deadly enemies. "The question being propounded, that Henry Ireton,

[1] Commons' Journals, Die Martis, 13 Feb., 164⅞.

[2] Whitelock's Memorials, p. 381, folio, London, 1732.

Esquire, be one of the Council of State; it passed with the negative. The question being propounded, that Colonel Harrison be one of the Council of State; it passed with the negative." [1]

The House then proceeded to nominate the following lords and gentlemen as the persons who were to constitute the Council of State; Basil, Earl of Denbigh, Edmund, Earl of Mulgrave, Philip, Earl of Pembroke, William, Earl of Salisbury, William, Lord Grey of Werke, Henry Rolle, lord chief justice of the upper bench, Oliver St. John, lord chief justice of the common bench, John Wylde, lord chief baron of the exchequer, John Bradshaw, serjeant at law, Thomas, Lord Fairfax, Thomas, Lord Grey of Groby, Oliver Cromwell, Philip Skippon, Henry Martin, Isaac Pennington, Sir Gilbert Pickering, Rowland Wilson, Anthony Stapeley, Sir William Masham, William Heveningham, Bulstrode Whitelock, Sir Arthur Haselrig, Sir James Harrington, Robert Wallop, John Hutchinson, Sir Henry Vane, Jun., Dennis Bond, Philip, Lord Lisle, Alexander Popham, Sir John Danvers, Sir William Armyne, Valentine Wauton, Sir Henry Mildmay, William Purefoy, Sir William Constable, John Jones, John Lisle, Edmund Ludlow, Thomas Scott. It had been before ordered that the number of persons who were to compose the Council of State should not exceed 40. On the 15th of February, it was ordered that the persons to be of the Council of State shall not exceed the number of 41. It was then resolved that Cornelius Holland, Esquire, be one of the Council of State; and that Luke Robinson, Esquire, be one of the Council of State. These two added to those before

---

[1] Commons' Journals, Die Mercurii, 14 Feb., 164$\frac{8}{9}$.

chosen made up the number of 41. It was then resolved " that the number of nine of those persons, who
are named to be of the Council of State, and not under,
shall constitute the said Council of State " [1] The
question being propounded " that there shall be a Lord
President of the Council of State, it passed in the
negative by 22 against 16. [2] The Council of State
accordingly for some weeks appointed a president at each
meeting, who signed warrants and other papers in this form :
" signed in the name and by order of the Council of
State, appointed by authority of Parliament." For
instance, on the 22nd of February, certain warrants are
signed in this form with the name of Oliver Cromwell,
" preses pro tempore." [3] But on the 10th of March, the
Council made an order " that Mr. Sergeant Bradshaw,
shall be the president of this Council," and a further
order, " that when any nine of the Council shall meet in the
place of the Council, though the president be not there,
yet they will act as a Council." [4] On the 17th of
February, the House made an order for the Council of
State to sit, and the members that desired it to have
lodgings in Whitehall. [5] On the same day, the Act,
constituting the Council of State, the title of which was,
" An Act of this present Parliament for constituting a
Council of State for the commonwealth of England,"
was read and agreed to. At the same time it was
ordered that the Council of State do prepare two seals,
a greater and a less, for the use of the Council, each of

[1] Commons Journals, Die Jovis, 15
Februarii, 164⅞.

[2] Commons Journals, Die Jovis, 15
Februarii, 164⅞. Here, though the
question was important, the number
who voted was only thirty-eight.

[3] Order Book of the Council of
State, 22 Feb., 164⅞. MS. State Paper
Office.

[4] Ibid., 10 March. MS. State Paper
Office.

[5] Whitelock's Memorials, p. 382.

them to have for impression the arms of England and Ireland; the impression to be " the seal of the Council of State, appointed by the Parliament of England." It was also ordered that Whitehall be prepared for the Council of State.[1]

Walter Frost, who had before been secretary to the committee of Derby House, was appointed secretary to the Council of State,[2] and his appointment, like that of the members of the Council, was for one year. For we find him re-elected formally for another year, at the next election of the Council of State.[3]

There is preserved in the State Paper Office a vast number of volumes of original papers relating to the period of English history called in the State Paper Office classification the Interregnum. Among others are those volumes which contain the original minutes of all the proceedings of the Council of State, as long as the Government called the Commonwealth lasted, forming a historical document of such value that I doubt whether one of equal value and importance could be found in the archives of any nation that ever existed. It is fortunate that Hugh Peters, who proposed the burning of all the old records of England,[4] did not lay his hands on these minutes. Of most of the volumes of minutes there are, besides the original drafts, fair copies in handwriting of the same period; for the Council of State have shown by various minutes that they were very far from being of the opinion of Hugh Peters, mentioned above, and have, on the contrary, evinced a most anxious care for the preservation in good order and

---

[1] Commons' Journals, Die Sabbati, 17 Februarii, 164⅚.

[2] Commons' Journals, 15 Feb. 164⅚.

[3] Commons' Journals, 13 Feb. 16⁴⁹⁄₅₀.

[4] Good Work for a Good Magistrate, 1651, p. 96, cited by Prynne in the Introduction to the first volume of his Parliamentary Writs.

condition of all the papers that contained a record of their proceedings. In an order of 12th Ootober, 1649, they direct "that it be referred to the Committee for Whitehall to take care that the Paper Office may be put into good repair, that the papers may not suffer, and that they take care to provide some other convenient room or rooms, wherein some other papers may be disposed which are to be put into order." And it appears from another order that we are partly indebted for the good condition in which those valuable papers have come to our hands, to the care of John Milton, the secretary for foreign tongues to the Council of State. I think the Council of State are entitled to the benefit of whatever evidence this anxious care for the preservation of the exact minutes of their proceedings may be considered to afford of the honesty of their intentions.

The first meeting of the Council of State took place at Derby House, which was situated in Cannon Row, between the river and the present Parliament Street, which did not then exist ; King Street serving the purpose of a thoroughfare between Whitehall and Westminster Abbey and Hall. I transcribe the minutes of the first meeting which, it will be seen, was a short one.

"Derby House, Die Saturni, 17 Februarii, 164$\frac{8}{9}$. At the Council of State, present—

Lt.-Gen. Cromwell.	Sir Wm. Constable..
Sir John Danvers.	Sir Wm. Masham.
Lord Grey of Groby.	Col. Purefoy.
Col. Martyn.	Col. Ludlow.
Col. Wauton.	Mr. Scott.
Mr. Robinson.	Mr. Holland.
Mr. Stapeley.	Mr. Heveningham.

" Ordered

1. " That this Council do meet on Monday morning next, by the hour of nine, at Derby House.

2. " That the several lords and gentlemen, nominated by the Act of Parliament to be of the Council, be desired to meet at Derby House on Monday morning, by nine of the clock." [1]

On the 13th of February, when Mr. Scott had brought up from the Committee the instructions for the Council of State, he had also reported the form of an obligation or engagement to be entered into by such persons as should be of the Council of State. This engagement was read and assented to ; and a resolution was passed, " That this engagement shall be signed and subscribed by every person appointed to be of the Council of State, before he sit therein." [2]　But this engagement gave rise to a difficulty ; for although, at the meeting of the Council on Saturday evening, 13 out of the 14 members present subscribed, and at the meeting on Monday morning six more subscribed, making the whole number who subscribed 19, one of the first entries on the minutes at the meeting on Monday, the 19th of February, consists of the names of the members who declined to subscribe the engagement. [3]　And it is particularly worthy of note that these amounted to more than half of the whole Council.

The answer of the Earl of Denbigh for not subscribing, appears to turn chiefly on an objection to the retrospective effect of the engagement, which would make those subscribing it express approbation of all that had been done, of the death of the King, and the force put upon the Parlia-

---

[1] Order Book of the Council of State, 17th Feb. 164⅞. MS. State Paper Office.

[2] Commons' Journals, Die Martis, 13th Februarii, 164⅞.

[3] Order Book of the Council of State, 19 Feb. 164⅞. MS. State Paper Office.

ment. And in substance, though not in words, the Earl of Denbigh's true reason was probably much the same as Whitelock's, that he did not approve of all that had been done, and particularly "excepts the court of justice." [1] But they were both willing to accept the present Government, without a King or House of Lords, as a Government *de facto*. To meet this difficulty, the original engagement, which a majority of the members of the Council of State refused to subscribe was altered; and on the 11th of October, 1649, a resolution was made by the House, "That every member that now doth or shall at any time hereafter sit in this House, shall subscribe his name to this engagement, viz., "I do declare and promise that I will be true and faithful to the commonwealth of England, as the same is now established, without a King or House of Lords" : and that subscription shall begin to-morrow morning : and that every person that shall be chosen to sit in Parliament shall subscribe the same engagement, before he be admitted to sit in the House." [2]

On the 23rd of February, a resolution of the House was passed, "That this House do begin to sit on Mondays, Wednesdays, and Fridays only in every week : and that the House be adjourned and do not sit on Tuesdays, Thursdays, and Saturdays in every week." [3] But this resolution does not seem to have been strictly acted on, at least for some time. It was further ordered "that the several committees of the members, now sitting in this House, do and be enjoined to sit, notwithstanding the said adjournment, upon the days when the House is adjourned. [4]

[1] Order Book of the Council of State, Die Lunæ, 19 Feb. 164⅗. MS. State Paper Office.

[2] Commons' Journals, Die Jovis, 11° Octobris, 1649.

[3] Commons' Journals, Die Veneris, 23 Feb. 164⅗.

[4] *Ibid.*

As the Council of State consisted of forty-one members, and the average number of members that met in the House of Commons now was not above fifty, a majority of whom were also members of the Council of State, it might be inferred that the House was now little else than an instrument, like the French Parliament before the revolution, to register the acts of the Council of State; and the form of many of the orders of the Council of State would seem to support such an inference.[1] But, again, there are other orders of the Council of State which show that the Council did refer matters of importance to the House. The following order, while it shows this, shows also the great care and deliberation with which both the Parliament and the Council performed their work. "That it be reported to the House that, in pursuance of their order of the 9th of March, concerning the modelling of the forces that are to go into Ireland, they have conferred with the lord-general about it, who hath since consulted with his council of war, and returned their opinion that those forces would best be modelled with advantage of the service of the commonwealth if the commander-in-chief for those forces were first named, which this Council, taking into serious consideration and finding it a business of weight, have thought fit to represent the same to the House, to desire them to declare their pleasure concerning the nomination of the commander-in-chief, which being determined, the rest of the work will proceed with more effect and expedition."[2] This order was made on the 13th of March. On the 15th the Council

---

[1] The following is an example:— "That it be reported to the House that there may be an Act passed for the making of saltpetre, the ordinance being out the 25th of this month by which it was made,"—*Order Book of* *the Council of State*, 6 March, 164⅚. MS. State Paper Office.

[2] Order Book of the Council of State, à Meridie, 13 March, 164⅚. MS. State Paper Office.

of State, having received the answer of the Parliament, made the following order. "That Lieutenant-General Cromwell shall be the person who shall command in chief the twelve thousand horse and foot which are to go over into Ireland in pursuance of an order of the Parliament of the 14th day of this instant."[1]

In other orders of the Council of State, as well as in the Commons' Journals, the words are "twelve thousand horse, foot, and dragoons;" words which are used to this day in the annual Mutiny Act.[2] It is necessary for any approach to a clear understanding of the military operations of that period, to explain the meaning attached at that time to the term "dragoon." When the musket, or portable fire-arm, was first introduced in war, it was usual to mount muske-teers on horseback, for the purpose of being speedily con-veyed to different points, and then acting either on horse-back or on foot. In every expedition of any importance, a body of dragoons was always considered a necessary adjunct to what were called the "horse." Thus, in this expedition to Ireland, to the five or six regiments of horse selected, *one* regiment of dragoons was added. As it was not essential to the original service of the dragoons that they should be mounted on the best or strongest horses, their horses were of an inferior description to those of the "horse" or "cavalry." One of their uses at that time was to perform the duty of outposts and detachments. Another was to dismount and line the hedges, or thickets, and do the "rough and ready" work of the attack on a difficult pass, a bridge, or any stronghold that was not strong

---

[1] Order Book of the Council of State, à Meridie, 15 March, 164⅜. MS. State Paper Office.

[2] "Resolved, that out of the forces now in being in England and Wales, there shall be added to the establish-ment twelve thousand horse, foot, and dragoons, to be forthwith sent into Ireland." — *Commons' Journals*, Die Martis, 6 Martii, 164⅜.

enough to require a regular and protracted siege with the use of heavy artillery. The dragoons at that time, though very useful in the way mentioned, were not usually troops of equal military qualities with either the horse or pike-men.[1] The arms of the dragoons, both offensive and defensive, were totally different from those of the horse. The dragoons wore only a buff coat, with deep skirts, and an open head-piece, with cheeks; whereas the horse were armed with back, breast, and head-piece, or pot, as it was then called. These are sufficiently proved to have been at that time the defensive arms of the cavalry by the following resolution of the House of Commons, of 12th April, 1649: —"Resolved, that such backs, breasts, and pots, as shall be wanting, shall be provided for every trooper that shall be employed in the service (in Ireland): and these to be transported to such places as the commander-in-chief shall direct."[2]   And while the troopers' weapons were a good sword,[3] "stiff-cutting and sharp-pointed," and pistols, the dragoons' weapon was at this time a fire-arm shorter and lighter than the musket.   This shorter piece was at first

---

[1] It is remarkable that Sir Walter Scott, in Old Mortality, constantly uses the term "dragoon" in a sense which it did not bear at the time of which he writes, applying it to the Scottish Life Guards, who would have considered it an affront to be styled "dragoons." And yet Claverhouse, in his dispatch written on the evening of the day of the skirmish of Drumclog, to the Earl of Linlithgow, commander-in-chief of Charles II.'s forces in Scotland, distinguishes the dragoons from his own regiment of horse (the Life Guards) thus :— "I saved the standarts, but lost on the place 8 or 10 men, besides wounded; but the dra-goons lost many mor."

[2] Commons' Journals, Die Mercurii, 12 Aprilis, 1649.

[3] On the 4th of July, 1649, a warrant was issued by the Council of State "to try all swords for the service of Ireland before their delivery into the public stores."—Order Book of the Council of State, 4th July, 1649. MS. State Paper Office. And on the 5th June, there is an order "that Browne of Manchester make good the 600 musquets that proved unserviceable that were delivered to Colonel Tothill's regiment, or that otherwise a course must be taken against him."—Ibid., 5 June, 1649.

called "the dragon," from which the French troops of this description had originally received their name. In the warrants in the order book of the Council of State "dragoon arms" are specified separately; and "troop saddles with furniture" are distinguished from "dragoon saddles."[1] As pistols are usually mentioned by pairs, as thus, "fifty pairs of pistols with holsters,"[2] it may be inferred that the Parliament's troopers were each provided with a pair, or, as the phrase now is, a brace of pistols.

This force of twelve thousand horse, foot, and dragoons was exclusive of certain regiments of horse and foot, which were dispatched beforehand as fast as they could be got ready to the assistance of the English forces at that time in Ireland, under the command of Colonel Michael Jones, Sir Charles Coote, and Colonel Moncke.[3]

On the 13th of March, the Council of State also made the following order:—"That Mr. Whitelock, Sir Henry Vane, Lord Lisle, the Earl of Denbigh, Mr. Martyn, Mr. Lisle, or any two of them, be appointed a committee to consider what alliances this Crown hath formerly had with foreign States, and what those States are, and whether it will be fit to continue those alliances, or with how many of the said States, and how far they should be continued, and upon what grounds, and in what manner, applications and addresses shall be made for the said continuance."[4]

It is a remarkable and interesting coincidence that on the same two days on which the orders I have here transcribed were made, orders were made by the Council of State respecting another man whose name has also become

---

[1] Order Book of the Council of State, 6th July, 1649.

[2] *Ibid.*

[3] The name is thus spelt in the Order Book of the Council of State.

[4] Order Book of the Council of State, à Meridie, 13th March, 164⅞. MS. State Paper Office.

famous over the world. "That it be referred to the committee for foreign alliances to speak with Mr. Milton to know whether he will be employed as secretary for the foreign tongues and to report to the Council."[1] And on the same day on which Oliver Cromwell was appointed commander-in-chief of the army destined for Ireland, John Milton, was appointed secretary for foreign tongues to the Council of State. For on the 15th of March, at their morning meeting, the Council made the following order :—" That Mr. John Milton be employed as secretary for foreign tongues to this Council, and that he have the same salary which Mr. Werkherlyn formerly had for the said service."[2]

It appears from the order book that Milton's salary as secretary for foreign tongues to the Council of State was £300 a-year.[3]

On the 5th of February Whitelock says that letters from Scotland mentioned that "the Parliament and priests there were at variance ; that the latter brought all to the stool of repentance that were in the last invasion of England, yet they are now as much as ever enemies to the proceedings of the House and of the High Court of Justice ; that they talk big of raising an army, in revenge of the king's blood, and all will join unanimously against the sectaries of England, and ground themselves upon breach of the covenant."[4]

On the 2nd of February divers members of the Parliament, of the army, of the city, and private gentlemen, in all to the number of sixty, were by Act of Parliament

[1] Order Book of the Council of State, à Meridie, 13th March, 164⅞. MS. State Paper Office.

[2] Order Book of the Council of State, à Meridie, 15th March, 164⅞. The latter words of the order have reference to the "Committee of both Kingdoms," of which the Council of State was in some sense a continuation.

[3] Milton's salary, when he had an assistant, was £200 a-year.

[4] Whitelock's Memorials, p. 377, folio, London, 1732.

made a High Court of Justice for trial of Duke Hamilton, the Earl of Holland, and others.[1]

On the 6th of March, the president of the High Court of Justice, Bradshaw, " in his scarlet robes, spoke many hours in answer to the pleas of the prisoners, the Duke of Hamilton, the Earls of Holland, and Norwich (Goring), Lord Capel, and Sir John Owen." [2]

Hamilton had escaped from prison, but was again taken and arraigned as Earl of Cambridge. He demurred to the jurisdiction of an English Court, as being a native of Scotland, arguing that the title of Earl of Cambridge did not constitute him a subject of England. But it was held that as he had sat as an English peer in the House of Lords, and claimed and exercised all the privileges of a peer of England, he had necessarily subjected himself to English jurisdiction ; and his plea was overruled. Sentence was given against them all, " that their heads should be severed from their bodies, yet with relation to the mercy of Parliament." [3]

The Parliament by vote reprieved Lord Goring and Sir John Owen ; but Duke Hamilton, the Earl of Holland, and Lord Capel, were beheaded. The executioner struck off each of their heads at one blow. The Speaker's single vote saved the life of Lord Goring, and he said he did it because he had formerly received some civilities from Lord Goring.[4] The House being also equally divided in the case of the Earl of Holland, the Speaker's vote might have saved him : but, as the same reason for voting in his favour did not exist, the vote was given against him.

<hr />

[1] Whitelock's Memorials, p. 377, folio, London, 1732.

[2] Whitelock, p. 386.

[3] Whitelock, p. 386.

[4] Whitelock, pp. 386, 387.

I have mentioned that ' one of the powers and instructions of the Council of State was to set forth such a navy as they should think fit. In accordance with this instruction they appear to have applied themselves with indefatigable diligence to the affairs of the navy. That their labours in this matter were not fruitless their naval victories sufficiently prove. As such victories are, however, immediately due to the valour of the men by whom the ships are manned and fought and the skill of their commanders, it is often difficult to determine what precise portion of the result belongs to those who selected and sent forth the conquerors. Now, in this case the order books preserved in the State Paper Office show with the most minute detail with what unwearied diligence, and with what consummate ability, the Council of State executed the charge committed to them, of setting forth an efficient navy. With regard to the amount of time which the Council of State devoted to their business, their order book shows that they usually met at eight o' clock in the morning, sometimes at seven,[1] and again in the afternoon at three.

On the third day on which the Council of State met, namely, the 20th of February, an order was made "that it be reported to the House as the opinion of the Council that the Ordinance of Parliament constituting the Earl of Warwick Lord High Admiral be repealed."[2]

---

[1] It is necessary to bear in mind the distinction between the Committee of the Navy and the Commissioners of the Navy. The former were the supreme ruling body, consisting of members of the Council of State ; the latter were paid officials, subordinate to the former.

[2] Order Book of the Council of State, 20th Feb. 164⅘. MS. State Paper Office. On the same day it was resolved by the House " that the House doth agree with the Council of State as to the repeal of the ordinance constituting the Earl of Warwick Lord High Admiral ;" and at the same time it was ordered " that the Council of State shall have and exercise all such power and authority as any Lord Admiral or Commissioners of the Admiralty have had or ought to have had and exercised."—*Commons' Journals, Die Martis,* 20th Feb. 164⅘.

On the 21st of February it was resolved by the House that it be referred to the Council of State to consider of and report to the Parliament some reasonable increase of the salaries to officers in the fleet whereby they may be enabled to maintain themselves without abuse to the State in wilful embezzlement of the stores or goods committed to them.

On the 24th of February it was resolved by the House that the commissioners appointed for the command of the fleet shall have the salary of £4 per diem formerly allowed to the general of the fleet, and also the sum of £5 per diem more ; in regard the profits belonging to the place of High Admiral are reserved from them for other uses of the commonwealth ; both the said sums amounting in total to £9 per diem, to be equally divided amongst them ; and that the secretary and the commissioners appointed for the command of the fleet have the sum of £150 per annum allowed unto him for his salary. " And this House doth declare that the secretary shall take no fees for any commissions of such persons as had commissions granted the last summer." [1]

One of the first acts of the Council of State was, as has been seen, to supersede the Earl of Warwick as Lord High Admiral. On the 26th of February, 164$\frac{8}{9}$, the Council of State ordered "That the names of the commissioners who are appointed to command at sea shall be ranked in this order, viz.—Colonel Popham, Colonel Blake, and Colonel Deane.[2]

On the 24th of March Colonel Wauton reported to the House from the Council of State a table of the rates of the increase of wages of the various officers of the navy.

---

[1] Commons' Journals, Die Sabbati, 24th Feb. 164$\frac{8}{9}$.

[2] Order Book of the Council of State, 26th Feb. 164$\frac{8}{9}$. MS. State Paper Office.

It appears from this table that the difference between a naval captain's and lieutenant's pay was at that time very great. In this table it is proposed to raise the pay of a captain of a first-rate from 10s. to 15s. per diem, and the pay of a lieutenant of a first-rate from 2s. 6d. to 3s. per diem : and a like proportion prevails through all the rates from a first-rate to a sixth-rate.[1]

Whatever virtues fasting may possess or produce, it will be difficult to prove that it is likely to make men either work or fight better. It would appear that although England might in 1649 be said to have been a Protestant country, for about a century, the fasting prescribed by the Romish ritual had been up to this time kept up in the English navy, at least as regarded serving out short allowances to the men on certain days, and in Lent.

On the 20th of March, the Council of State made the following minute, which shows that whatever Vane's notions might be respecting the quantity and quality of food meet for the saints over whom he was to reign a thousand years, he did not imagine that English seamen would fight better on half rations. "That an order be given to the Commissioners of the Navy that the observation of Lent may not for the future be any more kept amongst the mariners in the fleet either at sea or in harbour—as likewise the half-allowance on Friday nights—and that in both the said cases victuals may be allowed unto them as at other times." [2]

Provision is also made in the Order Book with exact minuteness for furnishing every ship with a sufficient number of hatchets and pistols for the better

---

[1] Commons' Journals, 24 Martii, 1648⅞.

[2] Order Book of the Council of State, 20th March, 164⅞. MS. State Paper Office.

enabling the mariners to board such ships as they shall attempt.

The Council of State having used their best judgment in the selection of the commanders of their fleet, wisely leave to them the selection of officers who are to serve under them, as appears from the following minute : " That an order be sent to the Commissioners of the Navy, to enter such officers into the ships as shall be recommended to them by the generals at sea." [1] " That directions be given to the Commissioners of the Navy to obey such orders as the generals for the command of the fleet at sea shall give them, concerning the particulars herewith sent unto them for the setting out of the fleet to sea appointed for the summer's service." [2] The powers entrusted to the commanders at sea, or the " Commissioners " as they are sometimes styled, are further shown by such minutes as the following : " Whereas the commissioners that are to command in chief at sea have informed the Council that the *Triumph*, the *George*, and the *Andrew* are appointed to go to sea for the summer's service, it is ordered that the Committee of the Navy be desired to give orders that they may be fitted out with all possible expedition."

Their care for the protection of commerce and of person and property generally is shown by many minutes, of which the following are examples : " That a letter be written to Vice-Admiral Moulton to convoy the ships that are going to Newfoundland to fish,—off beyond Ireland, till they shall be out of the danger of pirates." [3] " That a letter be written to Vice-Admiral Moulton to let him know that a post barque was lately taken by the Irish rebels

[1] Order Book of the Council of State, à Meridie, 26th March, 1649.

[2] Order Book of the Council of State, 5th March, 164⅞, à Meridie.

[3] Order Book of the Council of State, à Meridie, 24th Feb. 164⅞. MS. State Paper Office.

passing between England and Ireland, and to desire him that he would beat up and down upon that sea, so they may be kept in from attempting anything upon those barques." [1] "That a letter be sent to Capt. Moulton, to let him know that the merchants who are owners of the *Rye*, bound for Dublin, do not conceive the ship *Satisfaction* to be a sufficient convoy for their ship, to desire him therefore that a strong and sufficient convoy be appointed." [2] "That a letter be written to Capt. Moulton to send about into the Irish seas such ships as shall be necessary for the convoying over a regiment of foot, which is to be transported from Chester water into Ireland." [3] "Memorandum.—That Mr. Frost is to enquire to whom a letter may be written into Turkey, who may be as an agent there to the Grand Seignior in the behalf of the prisoners at Algiers." [4] The prisoners at Algiers, however, had to wait for a more effective mission in their behalf than a letter, a mission in the shape of that fleet with Blake for its admiral, which made the name of England "famous and terrible over the world."

In the next volume of this history I shall have occasion to enter into some details respecting the energetic measures adopted by the Council of State for the manning of the navy. But I would here take the opportunity of correct-

---

[1] Order Book of the Council of State, à Miridie, 24th Feb., 164⅞. MS. State Paper Office.

[2] Order Book of the Council of State, à Meridie, 27th Feb. 164⅞. Present — Lt.-Gen. [Fairfax], Lieut.- Gen. Cromwell, &c. MS. State Paper Office.

[3] Order Book of the Council of State, à Meridie, 6th March, 164⅞. MS. State Paper Office.

[4] Order Book of the Council of State, 13th April, 1649. MS. State Paper Office. The ravages committed by the Barbary pirates are further shown by the following minute :—

"That the petition of the prisoners at Sallee be recommended to the Committee of the Navy, and they desired to take into their consideration to give them a relief as speedily as they may." — *Ibid.*, 16th May, 1649. "That the petition of the prisoners at Sallee be recommended to the House, and that the House be desired to appoint a collection in such places as they shall think fit for the redemption of these poor men from their miserable captivity, and that it be reported by Col. Wauton." — *Ibid.* 23rd May, 1649.

ing a grave error, which has been adopted by historians on the authority of an assertion of Roger Coke, that the Long Parliament never pressed either soldiers or seamen in all their wars.[1]   In pursuance of this error, some modern writers have described the preamble of the 16 Car. I., c. 28, which is nothing more than a recital or declaration of the common law that, "none of his Majesty's subjects *ought* to be impressed or compelled to go out of his county to serve as a soldier in the wars, except in case of necessity of the sudden coming in of strange enemies into the kingdom, or except they be otherwise bound by the tenure of their lands or possessions" (the Act being "to raise, levy, and impress soldiers, gunners, and chirurgions" on the occasion of the Irish rebellion), as *an Act* passed by the Long Parliament *against* impressment.

The above-cited preamble very accurately expresses the state of the case with regard to the pressing of soldiers, when it declares that "none of his Majesty's subjects *ought* to be impressed or compelled to go out of his county to serve as a soldier," seeing that there could be no question as to the existence of the *practice* of impressment, "even of soldiers (whatever the common law might be), from very early times," which if it be to be considered as an encroachment on the common law, must be admitted to be an encroachment of long continuance.   The Honourable Daines Barrington in his "Observations on the More Ancient Statutes,"—a work not only of the most profound learning in the laws of England, but so rich in the learning of the laws, the literature, and the philosophy of all nations, ages, and tongues—states, on the authority of the Petyt MSS.[2] that, in the 47th year of Henry III., an order issued to

[1] Detection of the Court and State of England, vol. ii. p. 30, 4th edition, London, 1719.

[2] Petyt MSS., vol. ix. p. 157, in the library of the Inner Temple.

the sheriff of every county, that, taking to his assistance the *Custos Pacis,* he should collect out of every township at least four able-bodied men, who were to repair to London on a particular day.[1]   And, even so late as 1596, Stowe mentions that a thousand men were pressed for the land service, though they were afterwards discharged instead of being sent to France, as intended.[2]   And the last clause of an ordinance of the 22nd of Feb. 164$\frac{8}{9}$, intituled " for encouragement to mariners and impresting [3] seamen," shows that the exemption of seamen and watermen from land service was then deemed a privilege :— " And, lastly, for the better encouragement of seamen and

---

[1] Barrington on the Statutes, pp. 337, 338, 5th edition, London, 1796.

[2] Stowe, pp. 709, 769 ; and see Stat. 5 Eliz. c. 5, s. 41.   "If one might be allowed," says Barrington, "to cite Shakespeare on a point of law, it may be supposed that in the time of Queen Elizabeth, shipwrights as well as seamen, were thus forced to serve :—

"Why such impress of seawrights ?"
                    Hamlet, Act I. sc. i.

If it be said that the scene of this play lies in Denmark, it must be recollected that Shakespeare generally transfers English manners and customs to every part of the globe in which he chooses his characters should act.   Sir John Falstaff, in the first part of Henry the Fourth, says, " I have misused the king's *press* damnably," speaking of it as a known practice.   In the second part of this play, indeed, when Falstaff brings his recruits before Justice Shallow, it should seem that there were sometimes temporary laws for raising men, as has been not unusual of late years.   Rastel's statutes, however furnish no such instance during the reign of Henry the Fourth."—*Obser-*

vations on the Statutes, pp. 335, 338, notes, 5th edition.

[3] "This word," says Barrington, "being derived from the French *em-prester,* seems to imply a contract on the part of the seaman, rather than his being compelled to serve.   The first use that I have happened to meet with of the term *press,* as applied to mariners, is in a proclamation of the 29th March, in the fourth year of Philip and Mary, which recites that "divers shipmasters, mariners, and seafaring men, lately prested and reteyned to serve her Majesty, had withdrawn themselves from the said service," &c.—*Coll. Procl.,* vol. ii. p. 144, *Penes Soc. Antiq.*   The penalty by this proclamation is death.   By a proclamation of the 15th of May, 1625, the word *prested* is applied to soldiers in the king's service ; and by another of the 18th of June, 1626, the expression is " every mariner receiving *press money* to serve the king."   By a proclamation, likewise, of the 17th Feb. 1627, pressed seamen are ordered to be billeted in the neighbourhood of *Limehouse, Blackwall,* &c. — *Ibid., Observations on the Statutes,* p. 334 [m].   5th edition.

watermen to apply themselves the more willingly to this service, it is further enacted and ordained that all mariners, sailors, and watermen, who have served an apprenticeship of seven years, shall hereby be exempted and freed *from being pressed to serve as soldiers in any land service.*" [1]

With regard to the power of pressing mariners, Barrington observes that, "as it was the intention of the Legislature to circumscribe the admiral's jurisdiction by the 5th chapter of the statute 13 Ric. II., the total silence of the preamble with regard to the warrants for pressing mariners, seems very remarkable, as well as that of the judges in their arguments with the civilians, before James the First in Council." He adds, "I do not mean to intimate that the pressing of mariners is not supported by usage and precedents, as far back in our history as records can be found, many of which are referred to in the case of *Alexander Broadfoot*, who was indicted for murder at the gaol delivery for the city of Bristol in 1743. Mr. Justice Foster, who at that time was Recorder of Bristol, has published a very elaborate argument on this head, and has supported the opinions which he then gave by authorities chiefly from Rymer's most valuable collection." [2]

Nathaniel Bacon, in his chapter on the Admiral's Court, says that "the lord admiral hath power not only over the

---

[1] Scobell's Collection, part ii. p. 4 ; and see Commons' Journals, 20th and 22nd Feb. 164⅜. I give the following minute from the Order Book in illustration : — "That the militia of the hamlets be sent unto to send to the Council the names of such seamen, shipwrights, and chirurgians as plead exemption from bearing and finding of arms, together with what they plead for it."—*Order Book of the Council of State, Die Lunæ*, 20 Augusti, 1640. MS. State Paper Office.

[2] Observations on the Statutes, p. 335, 5th edition. Barrington says that he has happened to meet with some authorities relative to the power of pressing, which have escaped the learned judge, and adds, in a note, that the most general pressing warrant which he has met with is in Carte's Rolles Gascognes, tom. ii. p. 151.

seamen serving in the ships of the State, but over all other seamen, to arrest them for the service of the State." [1] On the other hand Rushworth gives the following account of the resolution of the House of Commons with reference to the temporary acts [2] of Charles I., for the purpose of manning the fleet. "The House being informed that ships were ready to be put to sea, but that mariners could not be got, it was the same day (May 8, 1641) resolved that a Bill should be drawn to enable the pressing of mariners for a certain time, the House being very tender of bringing the way of pressing into example." [3] As already mentioned, the Long Parliament, after the execution of the king, and the abolition of the House of Lords, passed an ordinance for pressing seamen, on the 22nd of February 164$\frac{8}{9}$. This ordinance was continued by subsequent acts or ordinances, which are printed in Scobell's Collection. [4] And when Cromwell had usurped the power of the Parliament, and an order of his

---

[1] Historical Discourse of the Uniformity of the Government of England, part ii. p. 44, by Nath. Bacon, of Gray's Inn, Esq. The First Part, from the first times till the reign of Edward III., London, 1647; the Second Part or continuation until the end of the reign of Queen Elizabeth, London, 1651. It has been said, on the authority of Lord Chief Justice Vaughan, one·of Selden's executors, that "the grounds of this book were laid by that eminent person." A fifth edition of this book was published in 1760.

[2] 16 Car. I. ss. 5, 23, 26. These acts, empowering the Lord Admiral to impress seamen, make no mention of the 1s press-money, ordered afterwards by the Council of State, but all of them allow conduct-money, at the rate of 1d. per mile, from the place where

the man shall be impressed to the ship or place to which he shall be appointed to make his repair, and the like sum from the place of his discharge to the place of his abode.

[3] Rushworth, vol. iv. p. 261.

[4] Scobell's Collection, part ii. p. 4. The following entries in the Commons' Journals refer to this Act :—"Die Martis, 20 Feb. 164$\frac{8}{9}$. Commissary-General Ireton reports some amendments to an Act for impressing of seamen and mariners for the next summer's fleet, which were twice read, and, upon the question, committed." "Die Jovis, 22 Feb. 164$\frac{8}{9}$. — An Act for the encouragement of officers and mariners and impressing seamen was this day read the third time, and, upon the question, passed."

Council of State had become equivalent to an act of Parliament, I find under date March 15, 1654, in the "Order Book of the Council of State," preserved in the State Paper Office, an order that the "Act for impressing be continued."[1]

The same valuable and curious record, while it was the Order Book of *the* Council of State, and not merely of Oliver Cromwell's Council of State, contains various warrants for impressing seamen, as well as commissions for the same purpose to the vice-admirals of the maritime counties of England, particularly at the time when the Dutch war presented the most formidable aspect, and the Parliament of England was fighting for its very existence against the greatest naval power at that time in the world. It certainly was then no time for a government, however devoted it might be to abstract justice, to discuss the question of the legality or illegality of press warrants. Accordingly warrants were issued for impressing seamen "that are outward bound as well as inward, so as you do not take out of each ship above the fourth part of the number of seamen in the ship."[2] And commissions were issued on the 24th of May, 1652, in the height of the Dutch war, to the vice-admirals of Essex, Norfolk, Suffolk, Kent, Sussex, Hants, "to summon before them all the seamen and mariners in their counties, from 15 to 50 years of age, and to acquaint them with the State's emergence of service, and the want of seamen to man a fleet, and withal to press for the service so many able seamen as they can possibly get," with an allowance of one shilling press money, and one penny per

---

[1] Order Book of the Council of State, 15th March, 1654. MS. State Paper Office.

[2] Order Book of the Council of State,

May 19, 1652. See also, Dec. 3, 1652, January 11, 1653. MS. State Paper Office.

mile from the place where they shall be impressed to Deptford, in Kent.[1]

It is to be carefully noted here, that although the "State's emergence of service" compelled them to have recourse to impressment, they nevertheless direct the vice-admirals, to whom the commissions are issued, to make an appeal to the seamen and mariners, as to free men about to fight for their honour, their freedom, and place among the nations. The anxiety of the Parliament, which was manifested in all these wars, to obtain troops of superior quality both as to character and intelligence, is strikingly confirmed and illustrated by the following order of the Council of State, under date 14th April, 1649 : "That a letter be written to Dr. Hill, Master of Trinity College, in Cambridge, that such students of that society as are willing to go to sea in this summer's fleet, may not be prejudiced in their elections to fellowships which are to be made about Michaelmas." [2]

On the 5th of March the Council of State ordered " that a letter be written to the Commissioners of the Navy, to make haste out with the fleet appointed for this summer's service, in regard of many advertisements they have received ;" [3] and on the 20th of March, " that Sir Henry Vane be desired to report to this Council from the Committee of this Council, appointed for the

---

[1] Order Book of the Council of State, 24th May, 1652. MS. State Paper Office. The assertion that they never pressed men is still further disproved by the fact of their seamen sometimes deserting, as appears by such minutes as the following :—" That it be recommended to the Committee of the Admiralty to take into consideration what punishment may be inflicted upon such seamen as run away from the service of the navy, and that those men apprehended by some of Col. Berksted's regiment be secured until further order."—*Ibid*, 30th April, 1649. MS. State Paper Office.

[2] Order Book of the Council of State, 14th April, 1649. MS. State Paper Office.

[3] Order Book of the Council of State, 5th March, 164$\frac{8}{9}$, à Meridie.

affairs of the navy, in what readiness the fleet is to go out to sea."[1]

On the 8th of May, the Council ordered "that one thousand pounds out of the tenths of the Admiralty be laid up for making chains and medals, for rewards of officers and mariners, that should do eminent service at sea."[2]

While the Council of State thus applied themselves to the affairs of the navy, they by no means neglected the land forces. On the same day on which the last-mentioned order was made, namely, the 5th of March, the Council made the following minute :—

"That it be reported to the House that the Council of State hath taken their order for the 2nd of March into consideration concerning the forces of the nation, and they find that there are in being of

Horse and foot	44,373
Besides those fit to be presently disbanded .	2,500."

"That it is necessary to have so many kept up for the service of England and Ireland."

"That of this number 12,000 horse and foot to be sent to Ireland."

"That for the maintenance of these forces, viz. the 44,373 there must be the monthly sum of

	£81,633	per mensem.
And for general officers the train and incidencies	18,367	
In all .	£100,000	"
For the relief of the forces already in Ireland	20,000	"
In all .	£120,000	"

[1] Order Book of the Council of State, 20th March, 164 8/9.

[2] Order Book of the Council of State, 8th May, 1649.

" That it be offered to the House for the raising of this money that the £60,000 per mensem by tax be continued as now it is, for the army of England, and the £20,000 per mensem for Ireland.

" That for the other £40,000 per mensem, it be raised out of the revenue of the Crown by sale, lease, or other disposing of it, as it shall seem good to the House ; and by the sale or otherwise disposing of the lands that are now by ordinance of Parliament at the disposing of the Commissioners at the Star Chamber, which lands are now for security for raising of £50,000 for Ireland.

" That there be a course taken by the House to charge the anticipations of the receipts at Goldsmiths' Hall upon some other visible security that the payments there may be made use of for carrying on of the public service." [1]

In accordance with this minute, the Parliament having resolved that £120,000 per mensem be provided for six months for maintaining the forces in England and Ireland, to the end free quarter might be taken off; and that, towards raising this sum, a tax of £90,000 per mensem, to begin from the 25th of March instant, be levied upon lands and goods, passed an Act for that purpose : and this being the first instance of a tax laid upon the subjects of England, by authority of the Commons only, the Speaker was ordered to write a circular letter to the Commissioners appointed in every county for levying the tax.[2] Notwithstanding the Speaker's circular this weight of taxation was

---

[1] Order Book of the Council of State, 5th March, 164⅞, à Meridie. MS. State Paper Office. On the same day is this minute :—" That the House will be pleased to set rules for the Committee at Goldsmiths' Hall to proceed upon for the composition with such delinquents as were in the last year's war." There is a large number of MS. volumes in the State Paper Office filled with the proceedings of this committee at Goldsmiths' Hall respecting these compositions in regard to delinquents' estates.

[2] Commons' Journals, Die Jovis, 8 Martii, 164⅞. Parl. Hist., vol. iii. p. 1304.

found to be very oppressive by the country at large, and the tax was levied with difficulty. Nothing could more strikingly show that, though England had got rid for a time of the ignoble tyranny of the Stuarts, it had to pay somewhat dear for the privilege of calling itself a commonwealth, than the following order of the Council of State of 16th June, 1649 :—"That the lord general be desired to appoint parties of horse to be aiding and assisting with the agents and collectors of the money upon the ordinance of £20,000 per mensem for Ireland in the several counties of England and Wales."[1]

It is no discredit to those clear-headed and strong-willed statesmen, that they were ignorant of a science which had not then dawned upon the world; but it may be not uninstructive to mark some of the errors they committed from ignorance of the natural laws that regulate trade, and which no statesman can violate with impunity. Immediately after the last-quoted minute, they make the following order :—"That for the more ready sale of such lands as are to be sold for the use of the commonwealth, the interest of money may be brought to six pounds per cent."[2] In accordance with this order, it was, on the 12th of March, resolved by the House that the interest of money should be brought down from eight per centum to six per centum from and after the 29th of September next; and an Act was ordered to be brought in for that purpose.[3] The following minute further shows their ignorance of those natural laws of trade which, in the time of a dearth or scarcity of corn, by raising the price enforce a more economical consumption, and which can only come

---

[1] Order Book of the Council of State, 16th June, 1649. MS. State Paper Office.

[2] Order Book of the Council of State, 5th March, 164⅘, à Meridie. MS. State Paper Office.

[3] Commons' Journals, Die Lunæ, 12 Martii, 164⅘.

into full operation under a complete freedom of the corn-trade—" the only effective' preventive of a famine, as it is the best palliative of the inconveniences of a dearth : " [1] " That the Ipswich petition against Robert Green, merchant, for engrossing of corn, be recommended to Mr. Attorney, to prosecute him according to law, and to take information from Wm. Hanby, attorney for that town, to proceed against the said Green, to the end the poor people may see that care is taken of them in the time of dearth." [2] And on the 5th of April an Act for abating the price of victuals and corn was read the first and second time, and committed. [3]

Lieutenant-General Cromwell having been appointed, as has been before mentioned, to the command in chief of the forces destined for Ireland, the Council of State proceeded to hasten as much as possible the dispatch of that important business.

Some new regiments were raised about this time for the service of Ireland. The case of one regiment may be selected to show the Council of State's mode of proceeding. On the 6th of March there is a minute for the payment of £400 to Colonel Tothill for a regiment of foot for Ireland now fully ready, near Chester, according to contract with the late committee at Derby House. Colonel Tothill was to receive the rest of his money for the said regiment upon the transporting of them, out of the £50,000 for Ireland out of the lands of delinquents. " The late committee being dissolved, that the House be moved to give power for the disposing of the said money, whereby the contract by which a very good regiment is actually ready for the service of Ireland may be speedily

---

[1] Smith's Wealth of Nations, vol. ii. pp. 398, 399, M'Culloch's edition.
[2] Order Book of the Council of State,
2nd May, 1649. MS. State Paper Office.
[3] Commons' Journals, 5th April, 1649.

furnished, and the said regiment transported." [1]   After
granting a warrant for the payment to Colonel Tothill of
£400, the Council order " that the rest of the money which
is to be paid to Colonel Tothill for the transporting of his
regiment into Ireland be transmitted to Chester to Mr.
Walley for that service."   On the 27th of March there is
a minute, "That a letter be written to the Governor of
Chester to let him know that sixpence per diem is ordered
for the payment of Colonel Tothill's regiment, and that
money is now in Mr. Walley his hands to defray it ; that,
therefore, free quarter is not to be demanded by them : "
and another minute, " That a letter be written to Mr.
Walley to desire him to take care that the quarters of
Colonel Tothill's regiment may be paid from the time of
their muster, that the people in the country be not bur-
thened by them more than of necessity, and that he do not
pay the money into the hands of the soldiers, but to the
people themselves." [2]

Now, it is to be observed that sixpence at that time was
equivalent to eighteenpence, or, rather, two shillings at
present, and the care of the Council of State in this important matter sufficiently distinguishes them from some of
the governments that went before, as well as from some
that came after them in this country.   It was one of the
worst features of the government of Charles I. that he
billeted his troops in private houses, and made them live
at free quarter.   But the sturdy English yeomen were not
people to submit quietly to such an outrage.   There is in
the State Paper Office a letter, dated 1st March, 1628, from
Captain John Watts, and other officers of the regiment of
Sir Thomas Fryer, stationed in the county of Dorset, to

[1] Order Book of the Council of State, 6th March, 164⁸⁄₉. MS. State Paper Office.

[2] Order Book of the Council of State, 27th March, 164⁸⁄₉. MS. State Paper Office.

Sir Thomas Fryer, in which it is stated that divers officers of his regiment met the Commissioners at Blandford to complain of their soldiers being turned out of their billets by violence, the billeters alleging that they would not provide any billets, but that the soldiers must shift for themselves. " The soldiers," the writers of the letter continue, " are thus enforced either to steal or starve.   The Commissioners say they have no order for anything.   The gentry contemn the deputy-lieutenants' warrants for billeting and are ill precedents to the commonalty.   If some speedy course be not taken, the greatest part of the men will run from their colours." [1]

Such is an example of the difference between the Council of State and some of the preceding Governments. I will now give an example of the difference between that Council and some of the succeeding Governments—an example which is a little startling from its being found so late as the middle of the nineteenth century.   When the militia was called out during the Crimean war, the practice which, with similar indulgences, cost Charles I. his crown, of billeting soldiers on private houses was not only still kept up in Scotland, but the whole burden of billeting the militia of the two counties of Forfar and Kincardine was thrown upon the town of Montrose alone, thus exempting not only the whole of the inland landed proprietors and farmers of those counties, but also the towns of Dundee, Arbroath, Forfar, Brechin, Stonehaven and others.   Such were the principles on which the billeting-tax was levied that persons who were too poor to be assessed to the poor-rate were subjected to the billeting-tax for the militia of these counties, while other persons with an income of £20,000 and even £40,000 a year

[1] 1628, March 1.   MS. State Paper Office.

were exempt' from it.   There were even cases in which
the poor people on whom soldiers were billeted were compelled to give up their only bed to two militiamen and
themselves lie on the floor.   In a petition from the inhabitants of the royal burgh of Montrose to the Secretary for
War it is stated that " while non-resident proprietors with
incomes of several hundreds a year each, are exempt from
billeting, and consequently from the payment into which
it is now commuted, a working-man, being a householder,
is subjected to the tax ; and assuming his income at £40
per annum, at the present rate of billeting soldiers in
Montrose, or what it will shortly arrive at, he has upwards
of £4 of his hard-earned income taken from him to provide billets for the militia—an exaction to which there is no
parallel in Her Majesty's dominions, except in some of the
other billeting towns in Scotland.   The oppressive nature
of the burden may be estimated when it is considered that
the householders in Montrose, on whom soldiers are
quartered, are, after deducting the present Government
allowance, compelled to pay £35 per week for billet-
money, which sum, there is reason to believe, will in a few
weeks be raised to £45 per week, or at the rate of £2340
per annum."

The orders for arms for the regiment of Col. Tothill
show more exactly than appears from any authority I have
before met with the proportion which the musketeers at
that time bore to the pikemen.   It may be convenient to
remind the reader that the foot regiments at that time
were composed partly of musketeers, partly of pikemen,
and that though the musketeers formed a larger proportion
of each regiment than the pikemen, the work, in consequence of the inefficiency of the muskets, a large proportion
of which were matchlocks, not flintlocks, and the want of

the bayonet, was mostly done by the pikemen who were the tallest and strongest men ; the pikes from their length, from fifteen to eighteen feet, and weight, requiring men of some strength and height to handle them efficiently.[1] I had an impression from all the authorities I had before consulted that the pikemen formed only about a third part of every regiment of foot : but it appears from the two following minutes that the pikemen in a regiment of foot 1000 strong were to the musketeers as 400 to 600, or as two-fifths to three-fifths : "That 600 musquets now at Liverpool be presently issued out for the arming of the regiment of Col. Tothill." "That Mr. Webster be sent unto to be here to-morrow in the afternoon to speak with the Council concerning the furnishing of 400 pikes for the arming of Col. Tothill's regiment."[2]

What, in addition to the want of the bayonet, rendered the musket a particularly ineffective weapon at that time, was the fact that, the use of wadding for the ball not being understood, the soldier could not shoot effectually with his piece inclined below a horizontal position. Gustavus Adolphus indeed had introduced the use of the cartridge, but it was not adopted generally till near a century after.[3] That the cartridge was not introduced during this war appears from one of the usual articles of the surrender of places, by which it is stipulated that the soldiers may depart " with their arms and baggage, with drums beating and colours flying, matches lighted at both ends, and *ball in their mouths, as they usually are wont to march.*"

---

[1] Mémoires de Montecuculi, i. 2, 16 ; Grove's Military Antiquities, vol. i. pp. 132, 133.

[2] Order Book of the Council of State, 13th March, 164⅚. MS. State Paper Office.

[3] Historical Record of the First Regiment of Foot, in Records of the British Army, printed by authority, compiled by Richard Cannon, Esq., Adjutant-General's Office, Horse Guards, London, 1847.

This clearly shows that cartridges were not used, and that the ball was put loose or separately into the gun ; in which case the mouth was found a convenient magazine. And at the time of which we write, about one in sixty-eight was the proportion of flintlocks to matchlocks, as appears from a despatch of Cromwell from Linlithgow, in 1651, in which he states that they have left in store " 2030 muskets, whereof 30 snaphances," or flintlocks.[1] Under such circumstances it is manifest that nearly all the work had to be done by the cavalry and pikemen.

[1] Cromwell to the Lord President of the Council of State, 26th July, 1651.

CHAPTER II.

THE Council of State occupied themselves a good deal in regard to what they termed "divers dangerous books printed and published;"[1] the multitude and constant succession of which "dangerous books," implied a spirit of discontent existing of a kind and degree which whether really formidable to their power or not was at least sufficient to render them uneasy. They appear to have been as much afraid of what they call "libellous books" as Archbishop Laud and the High Commission were some ten years before. And not without cause, for though the government of the Council of State was, as compared with the government of Laud and Charles's council—an able, a great, and a formidable tyranny, it was a tyranny still, that would not tolerate opposition, or even criticism; not merely in regard to its acts but also to its opinions. The Council of State were in this but the representatives of the body to which they owed their existence, the Long Parliament, which from an early period had evinced an abundantly intolerant and tyrannical spirit. In a paper indorsed by Lord Clarendon "Skippon's Relation of some of the Extravagances of the Parliament," it is related that about the month of August 1646, at Henley-on-Thames a woman having taken notice of the unwonted taxations imposed on her and others by the Parliament, expressed

---

[1] Order Book of the Council of State, 7th May, 1649. MS. State Paper Office.

some dislike thereof yet in civil terms; which being made known to a committee there, she was by them ordered to have her tongue fastened by a nail to the body of a tree by the highway side on a market day. This was accordingly done; and a paper in great letters, setting forth the heinousness of her offence, was fixed to her back to make her the more notorious.[1] Another instance of the cruel intolerance of the Long Parliament is the case of James Naylor, who was condemned by the Parliament to have his tongue bored as a blasphemer.[2] Several members were for passing sentence of death upon him. The Protector interested himself in Naylor's favour. " The conduct of the House of Commons," says Mr. Orme, " was as unconstitutional, as its sentence was brutal and unmerited." [3]

But there were other cases where the Parliament and Council may appear to have done no more than their situation imperatively demanded in imprisoning and bringing to trial the authors of pamphlets which raised up mutiny in their army and threatened their very existence. On the 27th of March 1649 it was resolved by the House " That the printed paper intituled ' The Second Part [4] of England's New Chains Discovered, &c.,' doth contain much false scandalous and reproachful matter; and it is highly seditious, and destructive to the present Government, as it is now declared and settled by Parliament, tends to division and mutiny in the army, and the raising of a new war in the Commonwealth, and to hinder the present relief of Ireland, and to the continuing of free quarter." [5] On the same day the Council of State made the following orders:

[1] Appendix to Clarendon's State Papers, vol. ii.

[2] See Baxter's Autobiography, part i. pp. 102, 103; and Burton's Diary, vol. i.

[2] Orme's Life of Baxter, p. 91, note.

[4] The First Part of England's New Chains consisted of Lilburne's Objections to the Agreement of the People, as put forth by the Council of War.

[5] Commons' Journals Die Martis 27 Martii 1649.

"That Sergeant Dendy," who was on the same day appointed
"Sergeant-at-Arms to this Council," "be appointed to make
proclamation of the order of the House this day against
the authors of the book called the 'New Chains;' and
that he do proclaim it in Cheapside, at the new Exchange,
in Southwark, and at the Spittle.   That the Lord General
be desired to give order that Sergeant Dendy may be furnished with a guard drum and trumpets for proclaiming
the order of the House against the authors of the book
called the 'New Chains.'   That a warrant general be issued
for the apprehension of all such as have been publishers of
the book called the 'New Chains.'   And that the posts
may that night be searched for the said book, and that
Mr. Sergeant Dendy do make that search." [1]   They also, on
the same day, issued a warrant for the apprehension of
John Lilburne, Mr. Walwyn, Mr. Overton and Thomas
Prince, as being "the authors or publishers of a scandalous
and seditious book printed intituled 'The Second Part of
England's New Chains Discovered.'" [2]   On the following
day the 28th of March the Council made an order "That
Mr. Milton be appointed to make some observations upon
the complication of interest which is now amongst the
several designers against the peace of the Commonwealth:
and that it be made ready to be presented with the papers
out of Ireland which the House hath ordered to be
printed." [3]   On the 28th of March the Council appointed
a committee to examine Lt.-Col. John Lilburne and the
others concerning the matters contained in the declaration
of the Parliament of the 27th of March: and also made an

---

[1] Order Book of the Council of State,
27th March, 1649.   MS. State Paper
Office.

[2] Order Book of the Council of State,

27th March, 1649.   MS. State Paper
Office.

[3] Order Book of the Council of State,
28th March, 1649.   MS. State Paper
Office.

order "That Lt.-Col. John Lilburne be committed prisoner
to the Tower upon suspicion of high treason for being the
author of a scandalous and seditious book intituled
'England's New Chains Discovered.'" [1]

In order to have some insight into the character of John
Lilburne as well as into that "complication of interest"
upon which "Mr. Milton" was appointed by the Council
of State to make some observations, it will be necessary to
go back for a few years to the time when Cromwell first as
a captain of a troop and then as a colonel of a regiment of
horse beat up his drums [2] for the ardent and energetic
souls lodged in strong and active bodies who had long been
groaning under a most grievous spiritual as well as civil
tyranny.   In the beginning of his career one of his
officers was James Berry, who had been a clerk of ironworks, [3] and was an old and dear friend of Richard Baxter.
When Cromwell lay at Cambridge with "that famous
troop which he began his army with," Berry and his other
officers proposed, says, Baxter, "to make their troop a
gathered church, and they all subscribed an invitation to

---

[1] Order Book of the Council of State,
28th March, 1649. MS. State Paper
Office.

[2] This was the official phrase of that
time — thus : "That George Lyon,
ensign to Capt. Anthony Stampe
have a warrant issued out unto him
for the beating up of drums for the
gathering recruits for the said captain's
company, and that Mr. Walley be
ordered to ship such men as the said
Lyon shall conduct to the waterside
to Derry to the rest of his company."
—Order Book of the Council of State,
6th July, 1649. MS. State Paper Office.

[3] Some modern writers say that Berry
had been a gardener, but Baxter, who
had known him well, and in whose
house he had lived, says that Berry,

at the Restoration, was imprisoned in
Scarborough Castle, "but being released, he became a gardener, and lived
in a safer state than in all his greatness."
—The Life of the Rev. Mr. Richard
Baxter, faithfully published from his
own original MS., by Matthew Sylvester,
folio, London, 1696, part i. p. 58.   In
another place Baxter says, "James
Berry was made Major-General of Wor-
cestershire, Shropshire, Herefordshire,
and North Wales ; the counties in which
he had formerly lived as a servant (a
clerk of ironworks).   His reign was
modest and short; but hated and
scorned by the gentry that had known
his inferiority : so that it had been
better for him to have chosen a stranger
place."—Ibid., pp. 97, 98.

me to be their pastor, and sent it to me at Coventry: I sent. them a denial." Baxter then says that afterwards meeting Cromwell at Leicester, Cromwell expostulated with him for refusing their proposal; and adds: "These very men that then invited me to be their pastor were the men that afterwards headed much of the army, and some of them were the forwardest in all our changes; which made me wish that I had gone among them, however it had been interpreted, for then all the fire was in one spark." [1]

Baxter heard nothing more of Cromwell and his old friend Berry for about two years. After the battle of Naseby he paid a visit to the army of the Parliament and he then found that Cromwell's chief favourites among the officers held opinions both political and religious which greatly shocked him. "What," they said, "were the lords of England but William the Conqueror's colonels? or the barons but his majors? or the knights but his captains?" [2] They most honoured the Separatists, Anabaptists, and Antinomians; but Cromwell and his Council joined themselves to no party, but were for the liberty of all. Baxter says he perceived that those they did commonly and bitterly speak against were the Scots, and with them all Presbyterians but especially the ministers, and also the committees of the several counties. There were, however, some officers who were still orthodox according to Baxter's

---

[1] Baxter's Autobiography, p. 51.

[2] Hobbes says, "The levelling soldiers, finding that instead of dividing the land at home they were to venture their lives in Ireland, flatly denied to go." — *Behemoth*, part iv., p. 266, London, 1682. But Baxter was much better informed on this matter than Hobbes; and we see that, according to Baxter, those who were for dividing the land among them were Cromwell's chief favourites among the officers, and not the men upon whom Cromwell fixed the name of Levellers. At the same time, I do not think that Ireton, Ludlow, Blake, Harrison, are to be reckoned in this class.

notion of orthodoxy; and partly from them, partly from the mouths of the leading sectaries themselves, Baxter informed himself of the state of the army.[1]

Baxter now blamed himself for having before rejected the invitation to be chaplain to Cromwell's regiment, and after taking two days to deliberate upon the matter accepted an invitation to be chaplain to Whalley's regiment several troops of which had belonged to Cromwell's old regiment.[2] Evanson a captain of Whalley's regiment had prevailed over Baxter's reluctance to leave his studies and friends and quiet at Coventry by telling him that their regiment though the most religious, most valiant, most successful of all the army was in as much danger of falling from orthodoxy as any regiment whatsoever; and Whalley the colonel, who like Evanson was according to Baxter orthodox in religion but engaged by kindred and interest to Cromwell, invited him to be chaplain to his regiment. The county committee were so angry with Baxter for proposing to leave them to go to the army that he was fain to tell them all the truth of his motives and design, what a case he perceived the army to be in, and that he was resolved to do his best against it. Whatever difference of opinion there may be as to Baxter's judgment, his statements respecting what he saw and heard may be accepted as generally truthful and even where from a slip of memory inaccurate, not intentionally so. It would appear from what followed Baxter's statement of his case to the committee, that Cromwell and his confidants did not wish just at that time, 1645, to make any public parade of the opinions religious and political, which Baxter imputed

---

[1] Baxter's Autobiography, p. 51.

[2] Baxter says (p. 54), "Cromwell, at the battle of Langport, bid Whalley send three of his troops to charge the enemy, and he sent three of the general's regiment to second them, all being of Cromwell's old regiment."

to them.   Baxter did not know till afterwards that Colonel
William Purefoy, a member of the committee and also a
member of Parliament, was a confidant of Cromwell's.
Purefoy, as soon as Baxter had spoken what he did of the
army, answered him in an imperious manner with the
following remarkable words which give a more striking
picture than anything I have anywhere else met with
of the terms in which Cromwell's officers spoke of him and
of the terrible promptitude with which he repressed any
symptom of insubordination :—" Let me hear no more of
that : if Nol Cromwell should hear any soldier speak but
such a word, he would cleave his crown.   You do them
wrong ; it is not so." [1]

" As soon as I came to the army," continues Baxter,
" Oliver Cromwell coldly bid me welcome, and never spake
one word to me more while I was there ; nor even all that
time vouchsafed me an opportunity to come to the head-
quarters where the councils and meetings of the officers
were, so that most of my design was thereby frustrated.
And his secretary gave out that there was a reformer come
to the army to undeceive them, and to save Church and
State, with some such other jeers ; by which I perceived
that all I had said but the night before to the committee
was come to Cromwell before me, (I believe by Colonel
Purefoy's means :) but Colonel Whalley welcomed me, and
was the worse thought on for it by the rest of the cabal." [2]

" All those two years that I was in the army," continues
Baxter, " my old bosom friend, who had lived in my house,
and been dearest to me, James Berry, then captain, after
colonel and major-general, then lord of the Upper House,
who had formerly invited me to Cromwell's troop, did never
once invite me to his quarters, nor ever once came to visit

[1] Baxter's Autobiography, p. 52.   [2] *Ibid.*, p. 52.

me, nor saw me save twice or thrice that we met acciden-
tally." [1] Of this change in his old friend's behaviour
towards him Baxter gives the following modest and candid
explanation. " He (Berry) was a man, I verily think, of
great sincerity before the wars, and of very good natural
parts, especially mathematical and mechanical; and affec-
tionate [well affected, or rather zealous] in religion, and he
carried himself as a very great enemy to pride. But when
Cromwell made him his favourite ; and his extraordinary
valour was crowned with extraordinary success, and when
he had been a while most conversant with those that in
religion thought the old puritan ministers were dull, self-
conceited men of a lower form, and that new light had
declared I know not what to be a higher attainment, his
mind, his aim, his talk and all was altered accordingly." [2]
" After a little time Colonel Walley," Baxter further
says, " though Cromwell's kinsman and commander of the
Trusted regiment, grew odious among the sectarian commanders at the head-quarters for my sake ; and he was
called a Presbyterian, though neither he nor I were of that
judgment in several points." [3]

Even among the orthodox of Walley's regiment however there were sectarians. Major Bethel's troop in particular consisted, according to Baxter, of very vehement
and dangerous sectaries. One characteristic or mark to
detect a sectary, in Baxter's opinion, was the disposition to
dispense with vicarious preaching and prayer and thereby
to encroach upon his professional functions. Great preachers
were those military saints, and the parliamentary army
exhibited scenes such as would be sought for in vain in any
other age or nation. Of one of those scenes Baxter has
preserved a sketch in outline. While he was in Walley's

---

[1] Baxter's Autobiography, p. 57. [2] *Ibid.*, p. 57. [3] *Ibid.*, p. 55.

regiment, and when they were quartered at Agmondesham, in Buckinghamshire, some sectaries of Chesham had appointed a public meeting as for conference; "and this in the church, by the encouragement," says Baxter, "of an ignorant sectarian lecturer, one Bramble, whom they had got in (while Dr. Crook, the pastor, and Mr. Richardson, his curate, durst not interrupt them)." When this public talking day came, Bethel's troopers (then Captain Pitchford's), and other sectarian soldiers, mustered strong in the church. Baxter thought it his duty to be there also, and took "divers sober officers" with him. Baxter took the reading pew, and Pitchford's cornet and troopers took the gallery. There was a crowded congregation. The leader of the Chesham men began, and was followed by Pitchford's troopers. Baxter then took up the argument, if such it could be called, in answer to what he designates "the abundance of nonsense which they uttered," and alone disputed against them from morning until almost night.[1]

Another type of those strange military saints was the gallant soldier and wild enthusiast Thomas Harrison, who has come in for almost as great a share of the Royalist calumny and scurrility as Cromwell himself. For the royalist and later Jacobite writers designate Harrison "that butcher's dog," or "brood of a butcher's mastiff," because he was the son of a grazier, and "bloody," when in fact he was a most humane as well as an honourable man; as they have styled Pride "a drayman" because he was a brewer, and Hewson "a cobbler" because he was a shoe-maker. Harrison was a favourite with Cromwell for the same reason that Berry was; because Cromwell naturally esteemed men who were thoroughly fit for their work—

[1] Baxter's Autobiography, p. 56.

men who never turned back from the sword or feared the face of a mortal enemy. But Harrison's religious enthusiasm was of a far wilder flight than Berry's, whose mind was naturally inclined to mathematical studies. Harrison's imagination like Vane's loved to dwell on the vision of a time when "Christ's saints fitted by Him to sit upon the throne of the same glory with Him, shall likewise be found prepared to bring forth magistracy itself in its right exercise, exactly answering the end for which it was set up by God ; and so shall be acknowledged by all the nations of the world, during the thousand years' reign of Christ on earth."[1] Harrison's military life naturally led him more than Vane was led to contemplate the attainment of his millenial paradise through deadly strife with the powers of evil, at the great battle of Armageddon, where the kings of the earth and their armies shall be gathered together to make war against him that sitteth on the white horse, and against his army, and shall be slain with the sword ; and the angel standing in the sun shall call all the fowls that fly in the midst of heaven to feed on the flesh of kings and captains, of the war-horse and his rider. To men who revelled in such visions as these the dust of battle was the breath of life ; and the "iron scourge and torturing hour" of the barbarians' law of treason were the keys that unlocked the gates of an everlasting Paradise.

Baxter describes Harrison as so far differing from the disputatious troopers last mentioned that he would not dispute at all, at least with him. "But he would in good

---

[1] The Retired Man's Meditations, or the Mystery and Power of Godliness shining forth in the living Word, to the unmasking the mystery of iniquity in the most refined and purest forms. In which old light is restored, and new light justified. Being the witness which is given to this age. By Henry Vane Knight, 4to, 1655, p. 392.

discourse very fluently pour out himself in the extolling of
free grace which was savoury to those that had right
principles, though he had some misunderstandings of free
grace himself. He was a man of excellent natural parts
for affection and oratory; [1] but not well seen in the principles of his religion : of a sanguine complexion, naturally
of such a vivacity, hilarity, and alacrity as another man
hath when he hath drunken a cup too much ; but naturally
also so far from humble thoughts of himself, that it was
his ruin." [2] This vivacity and this cheerfulness never
deserted Harrison, not even on the scaffold, with a death of
torture before him ; and combined with his religious enthusiasm they made him fearless and even exulting to
the last. He told the sheriff on the day of his execution
that he looked upon this as a clear answer to his prayers ;
"for many a time," said he, "have I begged of the Lord
that if he had any hard thing, any reproachful work or
contemptible service to be done by his people, that I
should be employed in it ; and now blessed be the name
of God who accounteth me worthy to be put upon this service for my Lord Christ." He told the people round the
scaffold, with respect to a shaking in his hands and knees,
which being observed gave rise to scoffing in some abject
spirits, that the shaking was not from fear of death, but by
reason of many wounds he had received in battle and
much blood he had lost, "This," added he, "causeth the
shaking and weakness in my nerves : I have had it these
twelve years ; I speak this to the praise and glory of God ;
He hath carried me above the fear of death : and I value
not my life, because I go to my Father, and am assured I
shall take it up again. Oh ! I have served a good lord and

---

[1] "Affection" seems to be here used   [2] Baxter's Autobiography, p. 57.
in the sense of zeal.

master, which hath helped me from my beginning to this day, and hath carried me through many difficulties, trials, straits, and temptations, and hath always been a very present help in time of trouble ; He hath covered my head many times in the day of battle. . By God I have leaped . over a wall, by God I have run through a troop, and by God I will go through this death, and He will make it easy to me. Now into thy hands O Lord Jesus I commit my spirit."

Harrison may be more correctly described as a Fifth Monarchy man than as Baxter describes him, when he says that his opinions were for Anabaptism and Antinomianism. Baxter also says that Cromwell had by degrees headed the greatest part of the army with Anabaptists, Antinomians, Seekers, or Separatists, and tied all these together by the point of liberty of conscience as the common interest in which they united ; and that, though Cromwell did not openly profess what opinion he was of himself, the most that he said for any was for Anabaptism and Antinomianism. [1] To apply the name of Anabaptists and Antinomians to Harrison and Cromwell is to do precisely what Baxter objects to Cromwell for doing, in calling certain men Levellers. The Church of Rome called those who differed from it "heretics ; " the Church of England, under Laud, called those who differed from it " schismatics ; " the Presbyterians, who succeeded Laud in power, called those who differed from them " sectaries." And worthy Mr. Baxter called Harrison and Cromwell " Antinomians," because they did not adopt all his theological views, to read which, as set forth in some twenty odd thick volumes, would be a labour to which that of reading Guicciardini would be light. And yet the story

---

[1] Baxter's Autobiography, p. 57.

says that the criminal, who was offered Guicciardini or the galleys, having chosen the history and tried to read it, changed his mind and went to the galleys.

The change that had taken place in the character of Cromwell in the interval between the time when he invited Richard Baxter to be chaplain to his troop of horse at Cambridge in 1643 and the time, two years later and after the battle of Naseby, when he gave Baxter a cold welcome to the army of the Parliament, is at least in part explained by Baxter when he says of Cromwell :—" I think that having been a prodigal in his youth, and afterwards changed to a zealous religiousness, he meant honestly in the main, and was pious and conscionable in the main course of his life, till prosperity and success corrupted him ; that at his first entry into the wars, being but a captain of horse, he had a special care to get religious men into his troop." [1]   But though Baxter might be able to understand the characters of ordinary enthusiasts such as Berry and Harrison, there were depths in the character of Cromwell which his plummet could not fathom, which perhaps no human plummet can ever fathom.   There were combined in him qualities apparently the most incompatible, the most fervent enthusiasm, the most adventurous courage, the calmest and keenest judgment.   One leading characteristic of Cromwell was the union of craft with bluntness and with a fiery temper, whereas crafty men are usually understood to be of a cold temper and smooth manner ; though craft under a cloak of bluntness and irascibility has the advantage of apparent openness and simplicity and thus of throwing off their guard those with whom it has to deal.

There are some well-authenticated facts in the history of Cromwell's life which may perhaps help to throw some

---

[1] Baxter's Autobiography, p. 98.

G

light on those parts of the character both of him and of other great men of the same type, which have been said to render such characters "the wonders of history—characters inevitably misrepresented by the vulgar, and viewed even by those who in some sense have the key to them, as a mystery, not fully to be comprehended, and still less explained to others."[1]

The early years of Cromwell's life appear to have been particularly darkened by those fits of mental gloom,[2] which, whether they be viewed as arising from physical or from religious and moral causes, seem strangely at variance with the daring and energetic character of the men in whom they are sometimes found. The names given in most languages to this temper of mind attribute it to a physical cause connected with the digestive organs. But the cause is probably also associated with the nervous system and the brain. And what appears strange or paradoxical is that men, to whom vulgar language assigns "nerves of iron," should have a nervous system apparently so delicate, as such susceptibility to derangement would seem to imply. Yet even if we retain that common metaphor, may not iron chords be so formed as to vibrate easily? But there is a certain class of minds in which, though generally under the control of a most powerful and acute understanding, the imagination at times exercises almost unbounded dominion. And if to the physical causes of disturbance referred to, religious enthusiasm be added, in such minds at such times ideas assume a force and vividness which give them the power and enable them to exercise the tyranny of sensations. Then in such men "thoughts, like masterless hell-hounds," rise to torture them. Then the

[1] Arnold's History of Rome, vol. iii. p. 386.   [2] Sir Philip Warwick's Memoirs of the Reign of King Charles I., p. 249.

phantoms of the brain assume the forms of fiends, to which they fancy themselves compelled to give battle even with a mortal weapon. There are fanatics in all times. But extraordinary times produce extraordinary fanatics, men of whose clear, strong and masculine minds the ordinary tenor seems strangely at variance with fanaticism. Laud and Strafford were the precursors, in the way of cause and effect, of Vane and Cromwell. And the persecution of such bigots and tyrants as Laud and Strafford may be regarded as having produced, among many other effects, the strange spectacle of Vane's dark and wild theology,[1] and of Cromwell's brainsick fancies[2] and hysterical tears.

Though Cromwell and many of his officers were great preachers, more influence was exercised on the minds of the soldiers by pamphlets than by preaching. And for a reason which is well put by Baxter who describes what he actually witnessed. The soldiers he says, " being usually disperst in their quarters," that is, scattered so that it was difficult to get together a large congregation of them at a time to hear a sermon, " they had such books to read when they had none to contradict them."[3]   Now as long as it was the object of Cromwell and his party to put down prelacy and presbyterianism they " abundantly dis-

---

[1] Clarendon's assertion (History, vol. vi. pp. 695, 696) that Vane "did at some time believe he was the person deputed to reign over the saints upon earth for a thousand years" (though Clarendon's testimony regarding Vane must be admitted with caution) is not unsupported by the evidence of Vane's own writings. See particularly the chapter on "The Thousand Years' Reign of Christ," in "The Retired Man's Meditations;" also, pp. 390,

392–395 of that work of Vane, a small quarto, published in 1655.

[2] Sir Philip Warwick was told by Cromwell's physician, Dr. Simcott, that his patient had "phansyes about the cross in that town," and that he, the doctor, had been very many times "called up to him at midnight and such unseasonable hours, upon a strong phansy, which made him believe he was then dying."

[3] Baxter's Autobiography, part i. p. 53.

persed such pamphlets as R. Overton's Martin Mar-Priest, and more of his, and some of J. Lilburne's."[1] But Cromwell and his friends learned in time that such pamphlets might become a two-edged sword which might be turned against themselves as well as against the prelatists and presbyterians. Then of course the pamphlets were to be put down as " dangerous books " and " scandalous and seditious libels." I do not impute blame to Cromwell and his friends for warring against presbyterians. Such war was in fact a necessity, if to put down the tyranny of the Stuarts and ultimately save the English constitution was a necessity. It was a necessary step in the process by which England was saved from the fate of the other European nations; for the presbyterian party had most clearly shown that they either could not or would not save the nation from the talons of the Stuart tyrants. And if the pamphlets of Overton and Lilburne were useful in that work, Cromwell did right to encourage them. But then comes the further question concerning the Agreement of the People, of which I have given a short account in the preceding chapter. It is admitted, I believe, on all sides that this Agreement of the People, which must be carefully distinguished from the Agreement of the People by John Lilburne bearing date May 1st 1649, was the work of men who were both able and honest. It may be objected to it that it was impracticable; that it was a piece of machinery that could not be worked. But then the experiment of working it was never tried; and, assuming for argument's sake, the absence of all selfish motives, the remnant of the Long Parliament were of opinion that England could at that time only be governed by an able oligarchical despot-

---

[1] Baxter's Autobiography, part i. p. 53.

ism in their persons, and Cromwell was of opinion that it could only be governed by an able monarchical despotism in his own person. So difficult has it always been found to get rid of one tyranny without having another set up in its place—so difficult that the exceptions may be called the wonders of history.

I have stated that on the 28th of March, the Council of State made an order for the committal to the Tower, of Lilburne, Walwyn, Overton, and Prince. On the 30th of March a petition signed by 10,000 persons was presented to the House in their behalf. This petition is ably and temperately drawn, and, from various expressions in it, those who framed it evidently believed that even at that time Cromwell had formed designs against the nation's liberties. The petitioners say that "the hostile seizure by the Council of State, and their examinations apart upon questions against themselves, no accuser appearing face to face, no friends allowed to be present, and thereupon committed prisoners to the Tower, being all directly contrary to Magna Charta, the Petition of Right, and to your own declarations of the 8th February and 17th March last; we are inforced to believe that some eminent persons, whose particular interests our said friends may have opposed, have surprised this honourable House." The petition then refers to their frequent motions and petitions, especially their "Agreement of the People, wherein are comprised such clear fundamentals of just government." The framers of the petition would here seem to claim for Lilburne and Overton the authorship of the "Agreement of the people;" a claim which can hardly be just, though they may have been consulted by Ireton in the framing of that document. The petitioners then charge "some eminent persons in the army" with hatred

towards their friends for their endeavours to keep the
military power subordinate to the civil, and for standing
betwixt the absolute domination of such "eminent
persons of the army" and the freedom of the people; for
which their friends have been long aspersed by them
as "*Levellers*, Atheists, Jesuits, &c." The petitioners
further say they are credibly informed that Lieut.-Gen.
Cromwell declared in the Council "that they must
break this party into pieces or they would break them:
that, if they did not do it, they would render themselves
the most silly, low-spirited men in the world, to be
routed by so contemptible and despicable a generation of
men." The petition then complains that the Declaration
of Parliament reflecting upon them as "persons seditious,
destructive to the present Government, mutineers, hinderers
of the relief of Ireland, and continuers of free quarter,
hath so forespoken them, that, whensoever they come to
trial, they are likely to fall under abundance of prejudice;
besides the influence those eminent persons (who now
visibly appear their particular adversaries) have upon all
persons in office, and upon all the present forces in being."
The petitioners say they cannot "discern how it can be
just to try men on a Declaration made after the fact pretended;" and earnestly intreat the House that they
will first make strict inquiry into the cause of that force
of soldiers used against the prisoners contrary to law,
enlarge them from their present imprisonment in the
Tower; and then, if any person hath wherewith to accuse
them, that they may be proceeded against, as by law they
ought, by warrants from a justice of the peace to be
served by constables not soldiers, and, if the fact
be bailable, to be allowed bail; if not, to be secured
in that legal prison appointed for that place and fact not

in a prerogative prison as the Tower is ; and then in an ordinary way to have the benefit of a trial by a jury of twelve sworn men in the neighbourhood, not overawed by soldiers: "a trial which we conceive, cannot in justice, in any circumstance, be denied to the worst of thieves, murderers, and traitors ; and which was our real intention in our late petition presented to you concerning them." The petition after praying that the execution of civil affairs may be wholly freed from the interposition of the sword, and that martial law may not be exercised in time of peace, thus concludes : "Lastly, we intreat that there may be some general encouragement from you, to proceed to a speedy settlement, by way of an "Agreement of the People," upon the grounds of an equal and just government ; and so that all discord, enmity and dissatisfaction amongst former friends, may finally receive a speedy end, by and with this Parliament ; and that the end of this may be the beginning of a new and equal representative."[1]

The petition being read gave so high offence to the House, that they resolved "that the petitioners should have a sharp reprehension for it." A Committee was also appointed to withdraw immediately, and prepare an answer to be given to the petitioners by the Speaker ; which, upon their being called in, he delivered to them in the following terms : "Gentlemen, the House hath read your petition ; and, lest I should mistake as you have done, hath commanded me to give you this answer ; that the four persons in your petition are, upon just and mature consideration, appointed to be brought under a legal trial for crimes against law preceding the fact, and not after, as suggested ; at which trial they will have free liberty to offer what-

[1] Parl. Hist. vol. ii. pp. 1306–1310.

oever they shall have to say in their own defence : and to such proceedings the Parliament do expect that all persons in England should submit, and in the judgment of Parliament acquiesce. That the contrivers of this petition have therein taken a liberty of scandalous and seditious suggestions, not allowable nor justifiable in any persons whatsoever, under pretence of petitioning; and do so far countenance the imprisoned persons, in the offences for which they are questioned, as might render them justly suspected of the like crimes. But the Parliament will yet exercise patience towards you, conceiving that divers well-meaning men may, by false yet specious pretences, be deluded into this miscarriage; and hoping that, by this forbearance, such may come to see their own errors." [1]

The petition of the men having thus failed, the women took up the case of Lilburne and his associates, and presented a petition to the House in terms, according to Whitelock, "almost scolding." [2] But the women did not improve the case of the prisoners by their interference, for the House ordered that the following answer be given them by their serjeant-at-arms: "That the matter they petitioned about was of an higher concernment than they understood; that the House had given an answer to their husbands; and therefore desired them to go home and look after their own business, and meddle with their housewifery." [3]

I have said that the Government called the Commonwealth was in fact a strong and able military oligarchy, supported by ability and courage indeed, but without that stability which a broad basis alone can give. If the Parliament had felt that their power was based on public

---

[1] Parl. Hist. vol. iii. pp. 1310, 1311.

[2] Whitelock's Memorials, p. 379, April 23, 1649, folio, London, 1732.

[3] Whitelock, p. 398, April 25, 1649. Parl. Hist., vol. iii., pp. 1310, 1311.

opinion, they would not have been so afraid of adverse pamphlets as their acts and deeds showed them to be. They are constantly recurring to this grievance. On the 16th of June we find these orders made by the Council of State —"That a letter be written to the lord mayor to pursue according to ordinance of Parliament all such persons as sell or make pamphlets;" "That the act for pamphlets be brought in on Wednesday next."[1] Not content with silencing the press they resolved to silence the pulpit also as far as regarded any expression of opinion respecting themselves. On the 28th of March it was ordered by the House that it be referred to a committee to bring in an act forbidding ministers in London or any part of England or Wales, in their pulpits, in preaching or praying, to meddle with matters of government on the transactions of State; and it was ordered that this act be brought in on Friday morning.[2]

The account given in the petition before mentioned of the origin of the term Levellers is not unsupported by the evidence of contemporary writers of some authority. Thus Richard Baxter in his Autobiography says that there arose a party who adhered to the principles of the Agreement of the People; "which suited not with Cromwell's designs: and to make them odious he denominated them Levellers, as if they intended to level men of all qualities and estates".[3]

[1] Order Book of the Council of State, 16th June, 1649. MS. State Paper Office. They had before, namely on the 14th of May, made the following order, which did not prevent them from answering pamphlets in the way tyrants answer :—"That Mr. Hall shall be employed by this Council to make answer to such pamphlets as shall come out to the prejudice of this Commonwealth, and that he shall have £100 per annum for his labour, with an assurance given him from this Council that they will take further care of him."—Ibid, 14th May, 1649, à Meridie. It appears from subsequent orders that a part of Mr. Hall's duties was to write answers to some of Prynne's pamphlets. Thus "That 500 of the copies of Mr. Hall his answer to Mr. Prynne be printed in Latin and that the charge of it be defrayed by the Council."—Ibid., 17th October, 1649.

[2] Commons' Journals, 28 Martii, 1649.

[3] Baxter's Life, by Himself, part i. p. 61.

It is to be observed here however that Baxter is not strictly accurate in describing the persons called Levellers as adhering to the principles of the Agreement of the People, as drawn by Ireton ; inasmuch as on the 26th of February, 164$\frac{8}{9}$, John Lilburne delivered a paper to the House signed by many of the Levellers proposing several alterations in the "Agreement of the People." A summary of these proposals of which some are reasonable and sensible enough while others have about as much that is rational and practicable as the legislation of Jack Cade will be found in Whitelock.[1]　These men whom it now suited Cromwell and the Parliament to denominate Levellers had been found extremely useful a year or two earlier ; and a year or two later it will suit Cromwell to bestow very hard names on his good friends Harry Vane and Harry Martyn and others whom he finds useful at present.　It is the old tale so often told of Ambition's march. The friends of yesterday, when their day is done and they are no longer needed, become but " the broken tools that tyrants cast away."

In May, 1649, a mutiny or insurrection was raised in the army by that portion of the officers and soldiers whose discontent at the treatment which the Agreement of the People met with from the body which now called itself the Parliament of England led them to attempt what was far beyond their power, and who have been denominated Levellers. The chief leader of these men was William Thomson, a captain of horse, according to Whitelock and according also to a better authority than Whitelock, the Order-book of the Council of State.

---

[1] Whitelock, p. 384, Feb. 26, 164$\frac{8}{9}$. Lilburne published, a few days after, his address to the Parliament, containing his objections to the Agreement of the People, under the title of " England's New Chains Discovered."

Baxter speaks of Thomson as one of the corporals of that theological troop of Walley's regiment who disputed with him for a whole day in Agmondesham church. But he may have risen from the rank of corporal to that of captain in the interval of three or four years. According to Whitelock Thomson marched up and down with about 200 horse and "declared to join with those of Colonel Scroope's, Colonel Harrison's, and Major General Skippon's regiments in their Declaration and resolution." According to another contemporary writer whose accuracy however is not much to be relied on, the Levellers of the army drew together to a rendezvous about Banbury, in Oxfordshire, to the number of 4000 or 5000, others resorting to them daily from other parts.[1] Thomson published a declaration in print, intituled "England's Standard advanced, or a Declaration from Mr. William Thomson, and the oppressed People of this Nation, now under his Conduct in Oxfordshire, dated at their Rendezvous, May 6, 1649." At the end of this document were these words: "Signed by me William Thomson, at our rendezvous in Oxfordshire near Banbury, in behalf of myself and the rest engaged with me, May 6, 1649, for a new Parliament, by the Agreement of the People."

Now as Lilburne's "Agreement of the People" was dated May 1, 1649 and is specially referred to in Thomson's Declaration, it may be concluded that the "new Parliament by the Agreement of the People," demanded by Thomson and those engaged with him was a new Parliament by Lilburne's and not by Ireton's Agreement of the People. This indeed is expressly stated in the Declaration. There were, as I have said, in Lilburne's Agreement of the People, amid some provisions that were

---

[1] Clement Walker's History of Independency, part ii. p. 179, et seq.

unobjectionable others that savoured somewhat of the legislation of Jack Cade. But as the men called Levellers have been usually condemned by writers who have not given themselves the trouble to obtain any accurate knowledge respecting them, it is but justice that they should be judged by their own words and not by the construction put upon those words by their enemies. Their words and deeds are a part of the drama of this troubled period of English history, without a tolerably accurate knowledge of which, the whole meaning of that drama cannot be known. The Declaration thus commences :—

"Whereas, it is notorious to the whole world, that neither the faith of the Parliament, nor yet the faith of the army formerly made to the people of this nation in behalf of their common right, freedom, and safety, hath been at all observed, or made good, but both absolutely declined and broken, and the people only served with bare words and fair promising papers, and left utterly destitute of all help or delivery: and that this hath principally been by the prevalency and treachery of some eminent persons, now domineering over the people, is most evident. The solemn engagement of the army at Newmarket and Triplo-heath by them destroyed, the Council of Agitators dissolved, the blood of war shed in time of peace, petitions for common freedom suppressed by force of arms, and petitioners abused and terrified, the lawful trial by twelve sworn men of the neighbourhood subverted and denied, bloody and tyrannical courts, called a High Court of Justice and a Council of State, erected, the power of the sword advanced and set in the seat of the magistrates, the civil laws stopped and subverted, and the military introduced, even to the hostile seizure, imprisonment, trial, sentence, and execution of death, upon divers of the free people of this nation, leaving no visible authority, devolving all into a factious Juncto and Council of State, usurping and assuming the name, stamp, and authority of Parliament, to oppress, torment and vex the people, whereby all the lives, liberties and estates, are subdued to the wills of those men, no law, no justice, no right or freedom, no case of grievances, no removal of unjust barbarous taxes, no regard to the cries and groans of the poor to be had, while utter beggary and famine, like a mighty torrent, hath broken in upon us, and already seized upon several parts of the nation." [1]

The Declaration then proceeds to state that they are resolved as one man, " even to the hazard and expence of their lives and fortunes," which would imply that some of them had property to lose as well as life, " to endeavour the redemption of the magistracy of England, from under the force of the sword, to vindicate the Petition of Right, to set the unjustly imprisoned free, to relieve the poor, and settle this commonwealth, upon the grounds of common right, freedom, and safety." They then, " that all the world may know particularly what they intend," declare that they " will endeavour the absolute settlement of this distracted nation, upon that form and method by way of an Agreement of the People, tendered as a peace-offering by Lieut.-Col. John Lilburne, Mr. William Walwyn, Mr. Tho. Prince, and Mr. Richard Overton, bearing date, May 1, 1649."

Now if, the question of abstract right apart, there were certain grave practical difficulties in the way of the Parliament's accepting Ireton's Agreement of the People, there would be practical difficulties far greater, to say nothing of difficulties on the ground of sound principle, in the way of

---

[1] This Declaration has been reprinted at the end of the report of the trial of Lieut.-Col. John Lilburne, in State Trials, vol. iv. pp. 1410–1413.

their accepting Lilburne's Agreement of the People. Besides, if they acceded to the demand of those who offered them Lilburne's Agreement of the People "with their swords in their hands,"[1] the sovereignty passed at once from their hands to the hands of the leaders of this section of their army. And though the immediate consequence might have been the erection for a short time of a goverment partaking considerably more of the nature of a democracy, or a democratic republic, than the commonwealth of the Rump of the Long Parliament, the ulterior consequence would have been such a political chaos as the substitution of the brains of Lilburne, Overton and Thomson, for the governing power, in the place of the brains of Cromwell, Ireton and Vane, would be likely to produce.

Colonel Reynolds first attacked these men, and afterwards Fairfax and Cromwell surprised them in their quarters at Burford, in Oxfordshire, with a very superior force. A small number escaped. Thomson was pursued and slain, making a brave defence singly to the last, near Wellingborough, in Northamptonshire. The rest, the number of whom is variously stated, were taken prisoners at Burford, and, with one or two exceptions, were pardoned. "So that," to borrow the words of Baxter, "the Levellers' war was crusht in the egg."[2]   On the 12th of May, the Council of State made an order, " that a letter of thanks be written to Colonel Reynolds for his good service done in dispersing the rebellious troops under Captain Thomson."[3]

The important part performed by Cromwell in the

---

[1] " Be it therefore known," says the Declaration, "to all the free people of England, and to the whole world, that (choosing rather to die for freedom, than live as slaves), we are gathered and associated together upon the bare account of Englishmen, with our swords in our hands, to redeem ourselves and the land of our nativity from slavery and oppression."

[2] Baxter's Life, by Himself, part i. p. 61.   Whitelock's Memorials, pp. 401, 402.

[3] Order Book of the Council of State, 12th May, 1649.   MS. State Paper Office.

putting down of this dangerous insurrection is beyond a doubt ; though here, as elsewhere, some of his enemies have been bold enough to charge him with want of personal courage. Clement Walker's account of Cromwell's behaviour on the occasion is rather an amusing specimen of the style of that scurrilous and mendacious writer. "Cromwell," says Walker, "not knowing what party to draw out against them, that would be steadfast to him, shunned the danger, and put his property the General upon it to oppose the rendezvous, and, looking as wan as the gills of a sick turkey-cock, marched forth himself westward, to intercept such as drew to the rendezvous." [1]

We have now, taking the testimony of Baxter, a credible witness, who was for two years [2] chaplain to the principal Ironside regiment, the Agreement of the People, drawn up by Ireton, and the proceedings of Lilburne, Overton, Thomson, and others, altogether, the means of analyzing the Parliamentary army ; that is, of decomposing it into its component parts ; and we find that it consisted of two parts—one, the larger and more powerful, headed by Cromwell and his friends or partizans (not including Ireton nor Harrison, except so far as the latter was duped by Cromwell), who were the sort of men described by Baxter as for a settlement of the business similar to that of William the Norman and his officers ; the other, much weaker, who were for a republic in reality, not merely in name, like the "Commonwealth"—a republic such as the instrument called the Agreement of the People, if fully carried into operation, would have created. But the smaller party was rendered much weaker than it would otherwise have been by the mischievous activity of Lilburne and

[1] Clement Walker's History of Independency, part ii. p. 179.

[2] Baxter's Autobiography, part i. p. 57.

one or two others, who, as stated above,[1] proposed
several alterations in Ireton's Agreement of the People.
Without imputing any superfluous dishonesty to Cromwell, it may be supposed that so practical a logician, as he
was, considered this republic according to Ireton's Agreement of the People, much more according to Lilburne's
Agreement of the People, as a visionary and even an
impossible project, which he was justified in crushing and
which he accordingly crushed with his characteristic decision
and promptitude. And as both Ireton and Blake served
under the Government which had destroyed under the
name of Levellers some of those who sought to carry out
by force some at least of the provisions of Ireton's Agreement of the People, it may I think be concluded that
those two brave and able men tacitly at least admitted
that the difficulties in the way of a republic were at that
particular time insurmountable. Still, the question is an
extremely complicated one, and I do not feel by any means
unlimited confidence in this solution of it, but it appears at
least some clearing up of the darkness and confusion in
which this period of English history has to me always
appeared to be enveloped.

During this month of May 1649 the new Government of
England had more than even its ordinary share of dangers
and difficulties to cope with, for, besides the mutiny in the
army, which, but for the rapidity and decision of Fairfax
and Cromwell might have overthrown them, they received

---

[1] In the two subsequent chapters I will
endeavour however to do that justice
which has by no means been done to
Lilburne in regard to his quarrel with
Cromwell and the remnant of the Long
Parliament. His penetration in dis-
covering Cromwell's designs long before
others discovered them and his defence
of himself on his trial, fighting singly
without counsel against the whole
power of the Government and their
law officers, prove that he possessed
abilities of a much higher order than
modern writers attribute to him.

information of the assassination of Dr. Dorislaus, their resident at the Hague.

Dr. Dorislaus, who though a native of Holland had lived long in England, and had acted as judge-advocate in Essex's army and as assistant counsel against the late king, had been sent towards the end of April to the Hague as resident jointly with Walter Strickland for the Parliament in Holland. Soon after his arrival at the Hague, while seated at table in his own lodgings Dr. Dorislaus was assassinated by some Royalists, in revenge, as they said, for their king's murder. On the 10th of May, a Memorial on the murder of Dr. Dorislaus at the Hague was ordered by the Council of State to be drawn up and delivered to the Dutch ambassador.[1] On the following day, the 11th of May, it was ordered by the Council of State "that it be reported to the Parliament that it is the opinion of this Council, in regard Dr. Dorislaus lost his life in the service of the Commonwealth, being murthered in so barbarous a manner, his children being deprived of their father and thereby of the maintenance they had by him, that the Parliament will settle £200 per annum as a pension on his son during his life— and that each of his two daughters may have £500 to be paid to her forthwith—also that there may be £250 appointed for the interment of Dr. Dorislaus in an honourable way at Westminster."[2] On the 10th of May, there is in the Order Book of the Council of State a minute of the committal of one Walter Breame "prisoner to Peterhouse upon suspicion of having a hand in the death of Dr.

---

[1] Order Book of the Council of State, May 10, 1649. MS. State Paper Office.

[2] Order Book of the Council of State, 11th May, 1649. MS. State Paper Office.

H

Dorislaus." The general opinion was, that the assassins of Dorislaus were six Scotchmen in the train of the Marquis of Montrose.

A minute of the Council of State of 12th May directs "That the informations had concerning the death of Dr. Dorislaus be reported to the House, and withall that the Council hath informations that there are designs for assassination of the Lord President and some members of the Parliament and of this Council." [2] On the 14th the Council considered that the mutiny in the army wore so dangerous an appearance as to render it necessary to suspend the preparations for the expedition to Ireland. They ordered " that a letter be written to the generals of the fleet to let them know that by reason of some present disturbance in this nation the soldiers formerly designed for the service of Ireland are not in such readiness as was formerly expected they by this time would have been ; to desire them therefore that the vessels by them prest for transporting forces thither be discharged from further exportation at present." [3]

On the 15th the very day following, the Council of State received the news that the revolt in the army had been put down and they immediately took off the temporary stoppage of the transportation of troops to Ireland.

I may mention in this place an instance of the weight of Vane in the councils of the English Government at that time. A Spanish ship the *Santa Clara* had been taken at sea carrying near 200 Irishmen for the military service

[1] Order Book of the Council of State 10th May, 1649. MS. State Paper Office.

[2] Order Book of the Council of State, 12th May, 1649. MS. State Paper Office.

[3] Order Book of the Council of State, 14th May, 1649, à Meridie. MS. State Paper Office.

of Spain. On the 16th of April 1649, before Vane's arrival in the council-room, there was a considerable number of members of the Council of State present, including Fairfax, Cromwell, Ludlow, Martyn; and a good deal of business had been gone through, chiefly relating to the details of transporting troops to Ireland. The importance of the business dealt with in the order made next after Vane's arrival, an order which might and did lead eventually to war with Spain, manifests in a remarkable degree Vane's weight in the Council. It was probably a matter that had been committed to Vane's particular consideration and immediately on his arrival in the Council, it was propounded, and then the important order made. Cromwell and Vane may certainly be regarded as the two great men—the men of genius—of the Council of State—Cromwell chiefly as a soldier or rather as a statesman-soldier—Vane as a statesman only, not at all as a soldier. As compared with these two, the others must be regarded as mere men of detail. The following is this important order :—" That it be returned in answer to the Spanish ambassador That, upon due consideration of the contents of the paper given in by his secretary, it is the opinion of this Council that it is not contrary to any of the alliances between the two nations of England and Spain to hinder the carrying of Irishmen into the service of Spain, and that it is in their power to dispose of them as they shall conceive best for the Commonwealth, which accordingly they have done."[1]

The " Instructions to Sir Oliver Fleming, Master of the Ceremonies, to be observed in his Address to the Lord Ambassador of Spain " are these, and their import must have convinced even Gondemar, had he then filled the place of Spanish ambassador, that he had now another sort

[1] Order Book of the Council of State, 16th April, 1649. MS. State Paper Office.

of men to deal with than King James and his minions:
—"You are to make your repair to the said Lord Ambassador of Spain and shall signify to his lordship that we
have taken the petition into consideration, and have consulted with the judges and advocates of the Admiralty
about it, and find that the taking of the said ship and
men therein is not against any treaties or articles of
alliance between the Commonwealth of England and any of
the countries of the jurisdiction and obedience of Spain,
which treaties we shall be careful to maintain inviolably.

"You shall also inform his lordship that the Irish nation
are dependents upon the Commonwealth of England, and
therefore neither the nation nor any party or particular
man of them have any power to treat or agree with any
foreign State or their ministers for their levying or transporting of men to their service without special licence first
obtained from the Commonwealth of England, which hath
not in the case of these men been either desired or granted.

"You shall further inform his lordship that the Irish are
declared long since by Act of Parliament to be rebels
against the sovereignty of England and therefore it is
justly in the power of the English to deal with them as
such wherever they shall take them.

"That therefore the Council hath given order for the
disposing of the men, and shall leave the ship and goods to
their just trial in the Court of the Admiralty.

"And lastly you shall signify to his lordship that this
Commonwealth cannot permit these nor the rest of the men
to be transported, it being (besides other important reasons)
a private transaction of a rebel and against the honour
and sovereignty of the Commonwealth of England."[1]

---

[1] Order Book of the Council of State,　　State Paper Office.
Die Martis, 17th April, 1649.　MS.

On the 24th of May it is ordered in pursuance of an order of the House that it be reported to the House " as the opinion of this Council that .those houses and parks hereunder named be kept for the public use of the Commonwealth and not sold viz. Whitehall House, and St. James's Park, St. James's House, Somerset House, Hampton Court and the Home Park, Theobald's and the Park, Windsor and the little park next the house, Green wich House and Park, Hide Park."[1] On the 28th of May the warrant for the clearing of Whitehall was delivered out to the Serjeant-at-Arms to put in execution ; and after that day the Council of State removed from Derby House and held their sittings at Whitehall.[2] On the 31st of May, as if conscious of an increase of dignity by the change from Derby House to Whitehall, they ordered " that there shall be a mace provided for the use of the Council at the charge of the State."[3]

In forming a judgment of men engaged in such a contest as that which was the business of those who now governed England, it is necessary to bear in mind that defence not wealth was their object, while the object of political economists is wealth solely. This distinction is admitted even by Adam Smith himself in his criticisms of their famous Navigation Act, passed about two years after the time of which I am now writing. " It is not impossible," says Adam Smith, " that some of the regulations of this famous Act may have proceeded from national animosity. They are as wise, however, as if they had all been dictated by the most deliberate wisdom. National

---

[1] Order Book of the Council of State, 24th May, 1649. MS. State Paper Office.

[2] Order Book of the Council of State, 28th and 29th May, 1649. MS. State

Paper Office.

[3] Order Book of the Council of State, 31st May, 1649. MS. State Paper Office.

animosity, at that particular time, aimed at the very same object which the most deliberate wisdom would have recommended, the diminution of the naval power of Holland, the only naval power which could endanger the security of England." And after stating some economical disadvantages consequent upon that Act, such as that of buying foreign goods dearer and selling our own cheaper, he adds, "As defence, however, is of much more importance than opulence, the Act of Navigation is, perhaps, the wisest of all the commercial regulations of England." [1]

The Navigation Act carried the animosity between England and Holland into open war. But more than two years before the passing of that Act namely at the point of time to which the present narrative has reference, grave matter of offence had arisen on both sides. On one side the Dutch authorities had taken no effective measures to punish the cowardly and infamous assassination of Dorislaus by the partizans of the Stuarts ; and by such criminal neglect they had offered a mortal affront to a body of men who taught the Dutch and all the world that they were not men who could be insulted with impunity. On the other side it must be admitted that the English Government only a few weeks after the assassination of Dorislaus afforded to the Dutch Government grave cause of offence. The Dutch were at that time, and indeed for more than a century after, the great carriers of Europe. In that capacity it was natural that the Council of State should seek to employ Dutch vessels for the transport of their troops to Ireland. But the matter was urgent, the English Government pressed their own ships, colliers and others, and they resolved to press the Dutch ships, if their masters or owners

---

[1] Adam Smith's Wealth of Nations, book iv. ch. ii.

should refuse to contract with them. On the 6th of June 1649 the Council of State made an Order " That a warrant be issued to the Commissioners of the Navy to contract with 20 Dutch Prams,[1] or other needful vessels for the transportation of forces into Ireland ; and that they have warrant to the sergeant of the Admiralty to make stay of them in case they shall refuse to stay to make a contract with the said commissioners for the aforesaid service." And on the same day a warrant was issued to " make stay by the marshal of the admiralty of 20 Dutch prammes."

At the same time they ordered a letter to be written to their agent in Holland Mr. Strickland " to use his best en- deavours to stop clamour, if any should arise thereupon "[3]— not an easy task for Mr. Strickland, it may be supposed. On the 8th Sir Oliver Fleming was ordered to go to the Dutch ambassador to give him an explanation that the Dutch ships are only stayed for a contract with them for transporting of troops to Ireland and that the State will dismiss as many of them as possibly they may.[4] On the 13th they ordered a letter to be written to Mr. Walley at Chester to desire him to make stay of all Dutch bottoms and other fit ships for the transportation.[5] And on the same day they made an order " That £2500 be paid upon account to the Commissioners of the Navy, out of which the masters of the several colliers' ships who are now pressed for the service of Ireland shall be presently, according to

[1] This word is in the warrant in the Order Book spelt " prammes." John- son in his dictionary gives the word " prame — a flat-bottomed boat. — Bailey."

[2] Order Book of the Council of State, 6th June, 1649. MS. State Paper Office.

[3] Order Book of the Council of State,

6th June, 1649. MS. State Paper Office.

[4] Order Book of the Council of State, 8th June, 1649. MS. State Paper Office.

[5] Order Book of the Council of State, 13th June, 1649. MS. State Paper Office.

contract, paid." [1] On the same day the 13th of June they ordered " That Mr. Scott do report to the House as the opinion of this Council that Commissary General Ireton shall be the person who shall be the next commander-in-chief of the forces in Ireland, under the command of Lieutenant General Cromwell." [2]   On the 15th of June Mr. Scott brought up this report to the House, who confirmed the appointment.

Thursday the 14th of June was the day appointed for the public funeral of Dr. Dorislaus.   The Council of State resolved to show every mark of respect in their power to the remains of the man who had been so basely assassinated in executing the commands of the Parliament of England.[3]   The body of Dorislaus was accompanied to the grave by the members of the Council of State, by the two Lords Chief Justices and the Lord Chief Baron, and by the Lord General and the general officers of the army ; and the Lord General was directed by the Council to give order for a fit guard to prevent any disorder that might happen by so much concourse of people as might be at such a solemnity.[4]

Under the date 20th June the Order Book contains " a list of Bills proposed by the Council to the House to be put

[1] Order Book of the Council of State, 13th June, 1649.

[2] Order Book of the Council of State, 13th June, 1649.

[3] There are many instances in the Order Book of the Council of State as well as in the Commons' Journals of the prompt punishment of all injury or insult offered to or by their public servants, and of their prompt acknowledgment of the claims of the widows and children of those who died in their service. Dr. Dorislaus would appear to have died very poor, to judge from the following minute :—" That £10 be paid unto Mr. Dorislaus, as part of the arrear due unto the Dr. his father, to enable him to pay the taxes charged upon their lodgings."—Order Book of the Council of State, 2nd June, 1649. MS. State Paper Office.   The reason assigned for this payment tells much respecting the weight of taxation at that time.

[4] Order Book of the Council of State, 13th June, 1649.   MS. State Paper Office.

into Acts before the adjourning of the House," and likewise a list of "things to be put in a way during the recess to ripen them for the judgment of the House at their meeting again." Among the former are "An Act for the further and better prevention of the exportation of gold and silver;" "An Act for preventing and punishing the printing and publishing of scandalous pamphlets and regulation of the press;" and "The Act touching restraining and punishing the licentiousness of the pulpits in seditious and derogatory expressions touching the Parliament and their proceedings." The latter are these "1. That a commission be granted to fit persons in the several parts of this nation for the valuing of tithes throughout England in order to the taking of them away and settling in their room an honourable and competent means for the preachers of the gospel. 2. That the business depending before a committee of settling future parliaments may be proceeded in during the recess to be ready for the consideration of the House at their next meeting. 3. That the regulating of the proceedings in law and courts of justice and equity for preventing the tediousness of suits and abuses burthensome to the people may be proceeded in during the recess, and an account thereof be given at the next meeting after the adjournment, and the same committee to consider what unnecessary and inconvenient laws are fit to be repealed, and their opinion to be therein proposed."[1]

It is extremely difficult to strike a balance with such nicety as to do perfect justice to those men who now formed the Parliament and the Council of State of England. While some of their proceedings evince a spirit of the most grinding despotism, others exhibit an anxious care for

[1] Order Book of the Council of State, 20th June, 1649. MS. State Paper Office.

justice and even liberty to the subject. They conscien-
tiously and justly paid for whatever was taken even under
the most urgent pressure of necessity. Thus on the
13th of September of this year the petition of Mr. John
Davis for fish taken by Sir Charles Coote for the use of
the garrison of Derry is referred to the consideration of the
committee for Ireland who are to report to the Council what
is fit to be done for his satisfaction.[1] The title which
they assumed to themselves of *Custodes Libertatis Angliæ*[2]
does indeed forcibly suggest the question " Quis custodiet
ipsos custodes libertatis Angliæ ? " A defence might
indeed be made for them, that at least many—a large
proportion—of their harsh acts were the necessary result
of their very difficult situation. Though this again may
be called the tyrant's plea, necessity. But in troubled
times men must either destroy or be destroyed ; and it is
not fair to style men tyrants absolutely for taking the
means necessary for their deliverance from destruction.
Then again many of their measures were simply the result
of ignorance, which they shared with the wisest men of
their age, of the true laws of political science ; such measures as those already mentioned, their attempts to keep
down by force the price of corn, and the rate of interest
and their great exertions, by searching ships and interrupt-
ing trade by embargoes, to prohibit the exportation of gold
and silver. The English Government at this time was
in fact an anomaly. Though called a Commonwealth
governed by a Parliament, it was not strictly parliamentary

---

[1] Order Book of the Council of State,
13th Sept. 1649.   MS. State Paper
Office.

[2] Commons' Journals, Die Mercurii, 7
Martii, 164⅜. "The form of a writ
for election of a knight for the county

of Berks was this day read ; and upon
the question agreed unto ; and was *in
hæc verba;* viz. 'Custodes Libertatis
Angliæ, Auctoritate Parliamenti, Vicecomiti salutem,' " &c.

government. For it wanted the essentials of true parliamentary government, a second chamber and a parliamentary opposition. It thus wanted the counterpoise absolutely necessary to protect any man or body of men from *themselves* when exposed to the corrupting influence of undivided and unchecked power. In this point of view the history of the proceedings of this Government becomes a most instructive chapter in the history of the great experiments made by man in the art of government.

The Council of State now directed all their energies to the hastening off of the expedition to Ireland. On the 25th of June, they ordered a warrant to be sent to the masters of the twelve ships impressed for the service of Ireland to fall down forthwith into the Downs, and thence with convoy to set sail with the first fair wind to Milford Haven, where they are to receive orders from the new Lord Lieutenant of Ireland. On the same day they sent a letter to the Commissioners of the Navy to impress eight ships more for the service of Ireland.[1] They also on the same day issued warrants to the treasurers at war to pay to each of the four old regiments of foot designed for Ireland £20 to buy chirurgians' chests, viz. the Lord-Lieutenant's regiment, Colonel Hewson's, Colonel Ewer's, and Colonel Cooke's; and to pay to each of the four new regiments £25 for a chirurgian's chest, viz. Colonel Venables', Colonel Phaire's, Commissary General Ireton's, and Colonel Stubber's regiments—" those having never yet had any." They also issued warrants to the eight regiments " for ten colours each at £20 each ;" and warrants

---

[1] From a document in the Order Book intituled "The Agreement with the Six Colliers' Ships " it appears that these six ships varied from 120 to 160 tons—four being 120 tons—one being 150 and one 160 tons — that they carried three, five, six, eight guns, and were all of Yarmouth.— *Order Book of the Council of State*, 27th August, 1649. MS. State Paper Office.

to furnish the said eight regiments each with ten waggon-horses at £8 16s. each horse, payable to the respective colonels. On the same day they ordered letters to be written to Mr. Walley to let him know that Major Elliott's troop is to consist of 80 soldiers besides officers—a fact further illustrative of the strength of their regiments of horse.

On the 26th of June, for the first time Cromwell's name appears in the list of the members of the Council of State present at that sitting, as Lord Lieutenant of Ireland. On the same day the Council issued an order "to the treasurers of deans' and chapters' lands, Goldsmith's-hall, and the Excise, to certify to-morrow to the Council what the present state of their several treasuries is in present money: and that they do twice in every week viz. Mondays and Thursdays give unto Mr. Frost the younger an extract [abstract] of all the moneys that shall come in and be paid out, who shall upon those days repair unto them for that purpose and that he have power to view the books concerning that affair." [1]

On the 28th of June the Council made an order that £1000 be paid by the Treasurer at War to Captain Tomlins, Comptroller of the Train of Artillery for Ireland, for the buying of horses to-morrow in Smithfield; [2] and on the following day a warrant was issued to Captain Edward Tomlins to carry the horses by him bought for the service of the train for Ireland "to Maribone Park and to put them there, and there continue them till Monday come sevennight."

On that same day, Friday the 29th of June, a minute

---

[1] Order Book of the Council of State, 26th June, 1649. MS. State Paper Office.

[2] Order Book of the Council of State, 28th June, 1649. MS. State Paper Office.

was made, "that the next Monday in the afternoon be appointed for the Council to take an account of the state of the affairs of Ireland from the Lord Lieutenant of Ireland before his going out of town;—and that the usher is to give notice to all suitors to forbear their attendance at that time." [1]

On the 30th of June a warrant was issued to the Treasurer at War to pay £700 by way of imprest for the buying one hundred carriage-horses for the service of Ireland.[2] On the 2nd of July an order was made for £2000 by way of imprest for buying of 500 draught horses. And on the same day "Rules and Orders" were made as to the arrears to the troops for Ireland, according to which all were to have one month's pay "to be discounted upon arrears;" and those who were in the Parliament's service in January 1647 and have so continued since without receiving the benefit of the former disbanding were to have a month's pay more of their arrears advanced to them before their shipping.[3] This shows that the Parliament habitually kept the pay of their troops very much in arrear. And that not merely the soldiers but the officers, at least those who were not Parliament-men, suffered from this cause, appears strikingly from the following minute:—"That a warrant be issued to the contractors for Ireland to pay £100 to Lieutenant Valentine Wood and such others as they shall think fit as part of their arrears." The concluding words of the minute are remarkable—"but that they do not suffer it to be public lest it draw upon the State a greater payment than they can make good." [1] This want of money is further shown by such minutes as

[1] Order Book of the Council of State, 29th June, 1649.   MS. State Paper Office.

[2] Order Book of the Council of State, 30th June, 1649.

[3] Order Book of the Council of State, 2nd July, 1649.

the following:—"That a letter be written to Colonel Horton and the rest of the Commissioners in South Wales for the money there, to let them know that information was given to the Council that £10,000 of the composition of South Wales was ready at Bristol, whereupon deputies and a waggon were sent to Bristol to bring it away; to desire them to hasten the payment of it, in regard it is very much wanted here, and the carriage stays there for the bringing the money away." [2]

In this want of money to pay their troops it seems to me viewing the question at this distance of time that it was the duty of the Parliament to have acted upon the advice of Ireton when he refused the £2000 per annum which they settled on him, and to have "paid their just debts before they made such presents." Nevertheless on the very day after that on which the Council of State made those rules as to the soldiers' arrears by which they declared they could or would pay only a small fraction of them, namely, on the 3rd of July, the Parliament settled "lands of inheritance of the clear yearly value of £1000 upon Colonel Henry Marten in consideration of several great sums of money disbursed by him and of the arrears due to him as a colonel." [3]   I do not remember to have met with any record or any notice whatever of any military service performed by Henry Marten. But the rewards of services given by parliaments were somewhat strangely proportioned. On the 27th of March of that year the Parliament ordered "that £300 per annum land of inheritance be settled upon Major General Lambert and his heirs for ever in respect of his many great and eminent

---

[1] Order Book of the Council of State, 10th April, 1649. MS. State Paper Office.

[2] Order Book of the Council of State,

[1] 11th April, 1649.

[3] Commons' Journals, Die Martis, 3 Julii, 1649.

services." [1] There is record enough of the great military services of Lambert, but as they are estimated by the Parliament as bearing to the services of Marten the proportion of three to ten, we may thence form some idea of the parliamentary scale of merit. And this will tend to make us feel little surprise that when certain men saw that their chief portion had been hard blows while the Parliament-men had sat comfortably and voted themselves good estates, it should occur to the men of hard blows to say— " Let us pull those talking fellows out by the ears."

On the 3rd of July the Council of State made an order, " That the Lord Lieutenant of Ireland, Sir William Masham, Sir William Armyn, and Sir Henry Vane, do go forth and confer with the Commissioners of the Excise concerning the advancing of the £150,000, and that they do acquaint them with the necessity of having present money for the public service." [2] On the same day it was ordered " That a warrant be issued to the treasurer for deans' and chapters' lands to pay to the Treasurers at War the sum of £30,000 out of their receipts, saving the third part .appointed for the use of the navy ; " and " that a warrant be issued to the Treasurers at War to send £30,000 unto the head-quarters of the Lord Lieutenant of Ireland." [3]

On the 4th of July the following warrant, the last clause of which directing " that the great shot be first delivered, that it may serve for ballast to the ships," is particularly deserving of attention, was issued by the Council of State to the officers of the Tower :—

" These are to will and require you upon sight hereof

---

[1] Commons' Journals, Die Martis, 27 Martii, 1649.

[2] Order Book of the Council of State, 3rd July, 1649. MS. State

Paper Office.

[3] Order Book of the Council of State, 3rd July, 1649. MS. State Paper Office.

to deliver unto Captain Edward Tomlyns, Comptroller of the Train for Ireland, the arms and ammunition hereunder expressed (which we are informed by certificate from Captain Vernon to be now in the Tower) to be by him presently shipped away for Ireland : and that the great shot be first delivered, that it may serve for ballast to the ships ; of which you are not to fail and for which this shall be your warrant. Given at the Council of State at Whitehall, this 4th of July 1649.

" The particulars are—

" Cannon of 8	200
" 24-lb. bullet	200
" Demi-cannon	79
" Culverin	226
" Demi-culverin	600
" Sacre [Saker]	788
" Match—ton	50
" Matchlock musquets	400
" Powder	40 [1]
" Musquet-shot—ton	30
" Grenado-shells, $14\frac{1}{2}$-inch	111
" Grenado-shells, $12\frac{1}{2}$-inch	187
" Hand Grenado-shells	200." [2]

On the 10th of July the Council made the following minute respecting the raising of certain regiments of volunteers :—" That, to the end the regiments of foot in the several garrisons may be free to take the field when there is occasion, the Council of State do give commissions for raising such regiments of volunteers near the said garrisons as they shall find necessary ; which additional forces are not to expect pay but when they are employed in service,

[1] Qy. barrels.
[2] Order Book of the Council of State, 4th July, 1649. MS. State Paper Office.

and are to be in readiness to join with the marching forces or be put into garrisons as the Lord General shall think fit and shall be ordered from time to time by the Parliament in Council of State."[1]

On the evening of that same day, the 10th of July, 1649, about five o'clock, the Lord Lieutenant of Ireland, after prayers for the success of his expedition by three ministers, and an exposition of the Scriptures by himself, Goff, and Harrison in the presence of a large assemblage at Whitehall, set out on his journey to Ireland by the way of Windsor and Bristol. Seven years had made a transformation like that in an ancient fable or Arabian tale upon the rustic if not clownish Member for the town of Cambridge, the Huntingdon brewer, and St. Ives and Ely gentleman farmer. He now began his journey amid the acclamations of an immense concourse of spectators "in that state and equipage," says a contemporary journal, "as the like hath hardly been seen. Himself in a coach with six gallant Flanders mares, whitish grey, divers coaches accompanying him, and very many great officers of the army; his life-guard, consisting of eighty gallant men, the meanest whereof a commander or esquire; in stately habit, and many of them colonels, with trumpets sounding almost to the shaking of Charing Cross had it been now standing. The Lord Lieutenant's colours are white."[2]

The ordinary strength of a regiment of foot appears to have been 10 companies of 100 each, and of a regiment of horse 10 troops of 80 each. On the 10th of July an order was made "That there be added to the present

---

[1] Order Book of the Council of State, 10th July, 1649. MS. State Paper Office.

[2] Mod. Intel. July 5–12, 1649, in Cromwelliana, p. 62.

establishment of the army, when the Council of State shall see necessary to make up the regiments of foot 1200 the several single companies 120, and the troops of horse 100, and for such time only as the Council of State shall find the safety of the Commonwealth to necessitate the same." [1]

On the 12th of July the Council of State made the following order :—"In pursuance of the order of the House it is this day ordered that the Lord Lieutenant of Ireland shall be allowed from the day of the date of his patent the sum of £10 per diem as General of the forces of Ireland during the time that he shall continue in England ; and that from the time he arrives in Ireland he shall have and receive as General of the said forces of Ireland the sum of £2000 each quarter, which is not understood to be in order to any salary or emolument which he ought by this patent to receive as Lord Lieutanant of Ireland ; and shall have £3000 immediately for transportation and furnishing himself with provisions of stuff and for such like charges." [2]

On the 18th of July the Council ordered a letter to be written to the Lord Lieutenant of Ireland to inform him that for supply of the £100,000 desired by him, £30,000 were to be sent from the Excise in the beginning of the next week ; and that it had been proposed to the Council that the £70,000 may be had out of the deans' and chapters' lands, and that no money shall be paid to the navy till the whole of that £70,000 be paid, " if his

[1] Order Book of the Council of State, 10th July, 1649. MS. State Paper Office.

[2] Order Book of the Council of State, 12th July, 1649. MS. State Paper Office. On the same day was made the following order : "That so many of the horses bought for the train of artillery for the service of Ireland as cannot be grazed in Marrowbone [sic] Park be put into Hide Park, there to be grazed until they be ordered to march to the waterside."

judgment be that that way will be satisfactory, and if he shall signify so much to this Council." [1] These words have very much the appearance of the language of men writing to their master.

Immediately after Cromwell's departure for Ireland the Council of State employed themselves assiduously in giving orders, with a view to the diminution of the military charges, for the reduction of garrisons to citadels, and for the demolition of castles. Thus on the 13th of July they gave orders that the garrisons of Oxford and Yarmouth should be reduced to citadels; and they also took into consideration the same measures with regard to Gloucester, Liverpool, and Shrewsbury. They also ordered that Killingworth Castle and Tamworth Castle should be demolished: and "that the castle of Scarborough shall be demolished and a work built, in the place where the platform now stands for the securing of the harbour." [2] Their order with regard to Killingworth is "That Killingworth Castle be made untenable with as little spoil to the dwelling-house of it as may be." [3] In many cases, if not in all, some compensation is awarded to the owners for the demolition of defensible castles. Thus a report is ordered to be made to the House " that £1.000 be given to the Countess of Kent in

[1] Order Book of the Council of State, 18th July, 1649. MS. State Paper Office.

[2] Order Book of the Council of State 13th July, 1649. MS. State Paper Office. On the 7th of August they ordered "that the castle of Wrezell be demolished." — *Ibid.*, 7th August, 1649.

[3] Order Book of the Council of State, 21st July, 1649. MS. State Paper Office. In regard to the demolition of Lancaster Castle there is this order: "That the gentlemen entrusted for the demolition of Lancaster Castle be written unto to reserve the Portcluse, lead, and tymber belonging unto that castle for the repairing of the castle of Liverpool."—*Ibid.*, 17th August, 1649. Although Johnson under the word portcullis, gives also portcluse, *quasi porta clausa*, yet in the five quotations from English writers which he subjoins there is not one in which portcluse is used for portcullis. This is the only instance I have happened to meet with of its use.

respect of the demolishing of Gootherich Castle and that it
be paid out of the revenue." [1]

On the 28th of July the office of Master of the
Ordnance was formally put into a committee of the
Council of State by the following order:—"That the trust
formerly exercised by the Master of the Ordnance of
England be put into a committee of the Council,
and that &c. [the names are given] or any two of them
shall be the committee, and Mr. Frost is to attend on
this business, and they are to use all possible diligence to
provide arms ammunition and all other necessary provisions
of war at equal and reasonable prices, at convenient days
of payment for the service of this Commonwealth, and
they are to consult with whom they shall think fit for the
better carrying on of their business." [2] The Council of
State therefore performed the work which is now appor-
tioned among many departments. For, besides the business
of the Treasury and of the several secretaries of State, the
Council of State now did the work of the Master of the
Ordnance. It will not be uninstructive to record what
number of secretaries and clerks this Council of State employed, and on what scale it paid them, to do that work which
was done so well. Their whole staff of secretaries and
clerks consisted of Walter Frost, the elder, secretary;
Walter Frost, the younger, his son, assistant secretary;
John Milton, secretary for foreign tongues; and four clerks.
The salary of Milton was, as I have before stated, £300
a year. The salaries of the others are set forth in the
following minute of the Council of State of the 4th of
July 1649. "Ordered that from the time of the constitution of this Council of State there shall be allowed to Mr.

---

[1] Order Book of the Council of State,
6th July, 1649. MS. State Paper
Office.

[2] Order Book of the Council of State,
28th July, 1649. MS. State Paper
Office.

Frost secretary to this Council forty shillings per diem for his salary, and to his eldest son appointed to be his assistant, twenty shillings per diem ; and for 4 clerks 26s. 8d. per diem."[1]

Cromwell proceeded from Bristol by Swansea to Milford Haven, and there embarked for Dublin, which he reached on the 15th of August.[2]

[1] Order Book of the Council of State, 4th July 1649. MS. State Paper Office.

[2] M. Guizot in his Historical Study of Monk says that Cromwell embarked with his army at Bristol, and that Monk met at Bristol Cromwell on the point of embarking. Besides other evidence to the same effect, the following minute in the Order Book of the Council of State proves that Cromwell did not embark at Bristol. "That the letter of the Lord-Lieutenant of Ireland from Swansey of the 30th of July in behalf of Lieut.-Col. Owen O'Connelly be referred to the consideration of the Committee of Ireland."—*Order Book of the Council of State*, 3° Augusti, 1649. MS. State Paper Office. Moreover, besides the positive authority of Whitelock (p. 415) that letters (July 27, 1649) stated that Col. Monk was landed at Chester, there is an order of the Council of State which is totally at variance with M. Guizot's statement that Cromwell, when he met Monk at Bristol, "apprised him of the excitement which the report of his league with O'Neal had produced in London ; that the national anger had burst forth with an energy which was irresistible ; that the Independents, whom Monk had obeyed, very far from avowing these orders, allowed the storm to fall upon him." Now it is proved by the minute set forth above that Cromwell was at Swansea on the 30th of July, and it appears from the following minute of the Council of State of 7th August that down to that date of 7th August the whole busines of Monk's negotiation with O'Neal was kept secret and consequently could have produced neither public excitement nor national anger ; and, besides the affirmation of total disapproval from first to last of Monk's proceeding, there is not a trace in the Order Book of the Council of State of any order or authority given to Monk to treat with O'Neal. The following is the important minute to which I have referred :—" That it be reported to the House that the letter and papers hereunto annexed concerning a cessation made by Col. Monk with Owen Roe M'Art Oneale were sent to the Lord-Lieutenant of Ireland by Col. Monk and were by the Lord-Lieutenant brought and delivered to the Council, and by them taken into consideration ; and the whole business then disapproved by the Council. But upon serious debate it was not then thought fit for divers reasons to return any answer thereupon to Col. Monk ; but enjoyned secrecy upon the whole. That Col. Monk being now come into England and having presented himself to the Council, the Council hath declared unto him that they neither did nor do approve of what he hath done therein : and have ordered that both the foresaid letter and papers and also the reasons now exhibited to the Council by Col. Monk for his making the said cessation should be reported to the House." — *Order Book of the Council of State*, 7° Augusti, 1649,

The minutes of the Council of State lay open the whole system of the machinery by which the government called the Commonwealth of England did its work, in a manner and to an extent of which, as far as I know, no other State papers in existence furnish an example. [1] While those minutes show with what indefatigable diligence, with what rapid promptitude, unremitting vigilance, and courage that work was done ; the results prove by the most infallible test, success, that the statesmanship which predominated in its Council of State was as sure-footed as it was energetic and laborious. I am speaking now merely with reference to its administrative qualities ; its legislative genius, as I have before said, I do not rate so high. And with regard to this administrative question, it may be instructive to compare this Government with one or two other Governments which like it bear the form at least of Councils of State. The Privy Council or Cabinet of the United States at Washington is not recognized by the Constitution and is not a deliberative council where the arguments or opinions of the ablest men shape the result of the deliberations. They may do so sometimes, but the president admits or rejects their arguments and conclusions according to his own convictions or caprice. He is in fact a sort of dictator for four years, the term of his office. It was natural enough that this form of government should suggest itself to the framers of the United States' constitution, having a man of such extraordinary qualities in Washington to select as their first president. But when, instead of a Washington, an

---

MS. State Paper Office. On the 6th of August there is also this minute : "Resolved that the treaty between Col. Moncke and Owen M'Art Oneale was wholly against the judgment of this Council when they first heard of it and that they are still of the same opinion. That Col. Moncke have this sense of the Council made known to him."—*Ibid.*, 6th August, 1649.

[1] Neither the English nor the United States Cabinet Council keeps, I believe, any minutes.

incompetent man is made a dictator for four years, the result is not very different from that of having an incompetent man made the absolute master of the destinies of millions by the accident of birth. The English Cabinet, like the Washington Cabinet, is not recognized by the Constitution; and in it the person called the Prime Minister occupies nearly the same position as the United States' President, except that he does not hold his office for a fixed term of years, but may be turned out any day. But the English Cabinet resembles much more the Washington Cabinet than it resembles the Council of State of the government called the English Commonwealth. If there were two Presidents and two chief ministers, for the same reason that induced the Romans to have two consuls, namely, that neither of them might be subjected to the corrupting influence of undivided power even for a single year; the chances of having the government administered with ability and vigour would be infinitely smaller than if the power were placed, as in the case of the English Council of State, in the hands of a really deliberative Council, consisting of such a number as would give a good chance of there being some men amongst them of ability for government, whose arguments and opinions would determine the deliberations of the whole body.

A council with an incompetent man to control it is worse than no council at all. And as regards its control, even by a man of great ability, it may I believe be shown that the English Government was administered with fully more ability when it was administered by a really deliberative Council of State than when it was administered by Cromwell alone under the title of Protector. I believe it might also be shown that when the Duke of Wellington was Prime Minister, the other ministers com-

posing his Cabinet had about as much weight with him as
Cromwell's Council had with Cromwell.   Those two great
men were not infallible, and they may have erred in thinking that they could best govern a nation as they governed
an army.   Though Cromwell was a great soldier and Vane
no soldier at all, I believe Cromwell found Vane's abilities
as a statesman of the highest value in the deliberations of
the Council of State.   Indeed it is proved by Cromwell's
own letters that in trying emergencies he was desirous to
have the opinion of Vane to aid and guide his own conclusions.   But when "lone Tyranny commanded" he could
never more have the benefit of that aid and that guidance.

It will be seen by those who consider the subject with
the attention it deserves and requires that the history of
this Council of State furnishes a new and most important
fact towards the formation of political science, if that
science be considered as an experimental and therefore a
progressive science.   Lord Macaulay, though he thus considers the science of politics, has altogether omitted this
important experiment supplied by the working of the
Council of State, in his investigation of the question of
executive administration in his essay on Sir William
Temple.   He says "the largest cabinets of modern times
have not, we believe, consisted of more than fifteen members.   Even this number has generally been thought too
large.   The Marquess Wellesley, whose judgment on executive administration is entitled to as much respect as that
of any statesman that England ever produced, expressed,
during the ministerial negociations of the year 1812, his
conviction that even thirteen was an inconveniently large
number.   But in a cabinet of thirty members what chance
could there be of finding unity, secrecy, expedition, any of
the qualities which such a body ought to possess?"

Now whether or no this Council of State can be con-sidered sufficiently analogous to a cabinet to make the same reasoning applicable to both, there can be no question that the Council of State of the Interregnum possessed in the highest degree ever possessed by any administrative council recorded in history, unity, secrecy, expedition, all the quali-ties required in a council formed for executive administra-tion. And this Council consisted not of thirteen pronounced by the Marquess Wellesley an inconveniently large number, but of forty-one members. The difference between the ordinary case of a cabinet in modern times and the case of this Council of State was only this, that from the end of the 17th century the Crown retained the shadow of that authority of which the Tudors had before and the Parliament then held the substance ; and that during the Interregnum the Parliament had both the shadow and the substance. Consequently the Council of State of the Interregnum held very much the same relation to the Sovereign, when the Parliament was both shadow and substance, as the Cabinet Council held afterwards when the Parliament was the substance, though the shadow was elsewhere. In both cases we have a Sovereign and a Council of executive administration to that Sovereign ; and why, when the Council of forty-one members proved itself an executive Council of efficient action rarely if ever equalled in the world's history, the dictum of the Marquess Wellesley that even thirteen was an inconveniently large number for such a council, and the dictum of Lord Macaulay against there being any chance of finding in a cabinet of thirty members unity, secrecy, expedition, any of the qualities which such a body ought to possess, can be accepted as settling the question, it is not easy to see.

If the science of politics be, like all other sciences, except the purely mathematical, the *rationale* of *accurately-*observed facts, surely such a fact as this of the existence and successful action of this Council of State consisting of forty-one members cannot be left out of the problem of determining the number of members of which a council of executive administration may consist.   Even if we apply to the question *à-priori* reasoning, why should the number thirteen be too large for unity, secrecy, and expedition, and the numbers ten, eleven, or nine not too large?   Why indeed should not a council of three be an inconveniently large number if there be any truth in the old proverb that " two may keep counsel, when the third's away " ?   A proverb, the fallacy of which when applied to a council of executive administration consists in the assumption that the members of such council are not men of at least average faith and honour, but a pack of scoundrels tied together only by the common bond of crime.   In truth this dog-matizing on the subject of the numbers of councils of executive administration is only an example of that mode of dealing with the science of politics, which considers it not as an experimental and therefore a progressive science but as a science founded and built-up on short synthetical arguments drawn from truths of the most vulgar notoriety, and which no writer has been more ready to condemn than Lord Macaulay.

I have said " *accurately-*observed facts," and therefore it will be proper to meet a question that may be fairly asked ; did the whole number of forty-one members com-posing the Council of State attend the meetings of the Council ?   Now it appears from a minute of 14th May 1649 that down to that date some members had never attended at all.[1]　 The result at which I have arrived from a minute examination of the Order Book is that the number present varied very much, varied from thirty-four or thirty-five[2] down to nine, which is the lowest number I have met with.　 This low scale, however, belongs to the month of October when many of the members were probably out of town.　 The result abundantly proves that a Council of executive administration actually and not merely nominally consisting of a number exceeding thirty members was found to possess unity, secrecy, expedition, in short all the qualities which such a body ought to possess ; for never did any Government in any age or country evince greater ability for administration than this Council of State did at that time when contending single-handed against nearly all the world.

[1] "That a letter of summons be sent unto such gentlemen appointed to be of this Council as never yet appeared here to come to the Council and attend the service of the Commonwealth."—*Order Book of the Council of State*, 14 May, 1649, à Meridie. MS. State Paper Office.

[2] Order Book of the Council of State, 19 Feb. 164⅞. MS. State Paper Office.—*Ibid.*, 3 Oct. 1649.—*Ibid.*, 5 and 6 Oct. 1649.—*Ibid.*, 11, 14, and 17 January 1652. On the 17th January 1652 the number present was 31. This was the time when the Dutch war engaged their attention, and when the pressure and importance of their business were such that the Council met on Sundays.—*Ibid.*, Sunday 5 Dec. 1652; Sunday 23 May 1652 ; Sunday 30 May 1652.

CHAPTER III.

THE English Parliament had hitherto been obliged, by the pressure of business that absorbed all its resources, in a great measure to neglect Irish affairs, and to leave unpunished the abominable cruelties committed upon the defenceless English in Ireland in 1641, cruelties equalling in atrocity and far exceeding in the number of victims those perpetrated in 1857 by the sepoys in India. For eight years the perpetrators of the Irish massacre might be said to have gone not only unpunished but triumphant; and it might seem that there was to be no reckoning upon earth for that enormous crime. But the spirit of England, though it might seem to have slumbered, was not dead, and the time had come at last when she was to make Ireland feel both her power and her vengeance.

We have seen that throughout the whole of this spring and summer the Parliament and Council of State had been making great exertions to send reinforcements to their three commanders in Ireland Michael Jones, Sir Charles Coote, and Monk. All these were able men and for their services had received repeatedly the thanks of the Parliament and Council of State; and in August we find that Jones was promoted to the rank of Lieut.-General and Monk to that of Major-General. In the beginning of August Michael Jones had defeated the army of Ormond before Dublin ;[1] but the means at his disposal were much too small to bring the war to an end. Indeed his victory had little more effect than to relieve Dublin, which had been for some time besieged by Ormond's army. Ormond retired northward, and placed a body of some three thousand of his best troops as a garrison in Drogheda. Before I proceed to state what occurred after Cromwell's arrival at Dublin, I think it necessary not only for understanding the subsequent proceedings, but in justice to Cromwell, to direct the reader's attention to some events that took place in Ireland eight years before this time.

It was a part of the character of Oliver Cromwell, as it is of the characters of all great men, to understand the spirit and the wants of his time. We who have lived in the year 1857 cannot cease to remember while we remember anything the sepoy massacre of 1857. One effect of the feeling of indignation which that massacre produced in England was to make men, who never before thought of being soldiers, not only willing but eager to fight against the perpetrators of that massacre. In like manner there existed very generally in England in 1642, when Cromwell raised his first troop of horse, and also when he enlarged that troop to a regiment, a strong and

---

[1] " That the letter from Lt.-Gen. Jones of the 6th of this instant August relating the victory which it hath pleased God to give the forces in the city of Dublin against the army of Ormond before that city together with the list of prisoners and ammunition taken and the narrative of the messenger Capt. Otway who was in the action be forthwith printed and published," &c. — *Order Book of the Council of State, Die Saturni*, 11 Augusti 1649. MS. State Paper Office. The news both of this victory by Jones, and of the successful storm of Drogheda by Cromwell reached London on a Saturday; and an order was issued by the Council of State for all the ministers to publish them in their churches and give thanks to God for them, " to-morrow being the Lord's day." " That a letter be written to the Lord Mayor of London to cause the letter of Lieut.-Gen. Jones to be published by the ministers of London in their respective churches." — *Ibid.*, same day.

fierce indignation against the perpetrators of the massacre
of the English Protestants in Ireland in the preceding year
1641.   This spirit of indignant revenge enabled Cromwell
to obtain a better class of men as soldiers than he could
have obtained in ordinary times.   Now, if eight years
after the sepoy massacre of 1857, namely in the year
1865, that massacre were still unpunished, but in 1865
circumstances should give to the English nation the
power before withheld of punishing that massacre, I believe that it would be punished with the severity which
a sense of justice as well as a spirit of indignant revenge
naturally excites against the murderers not merely of men,
but of women and children.   In like manner there still
existed in England in 1649 a strong and deep indignation
against the perpetrators of the massacre of the English
Protestants in Ireland in 1641, and against all their
abettors, indeed against all Papists.   It is as unfair to judge
of the storm of Drogheda without keeping in view the
inhuman massacres of 1641, as it would be to judge of the
storm of Lucknow without remembering the massacre of
Cawnpore.   And it is as unfair to call Cromwell inhuman
because he gave no quarter at Drogheda, as it would be to
call Sir James Outram inhuman for the storm of Lucknow.
If the former did not possess all the chivalrous generosity
of the latter, he was not inferior even to him in generous
compassion for the sufferings of the weak and helpless.
"He was naturally compassionate" says one who knew
him well, "towards objects in distress to an effeminate
measure."[1]   And as his compassion was great towards
sufferers, so was his wrath terrible against the cowardly
cruelty which had taken advantage of their helplessness.

[1] Letter from John Maidstone in the   loe's State Papers, p. 766.
Appendix to the first volume of Thur-

In all this Cromwell only differed in degree not in kind
from any man of common humanity who has courage and
strength enough added to his humanity to entitle him to
be emphatically called a *man*. A very eminent person
with whom I was speaking of Julius Cæsar, who like
Cromwell was naturally compassionate though at times he
might appear to be cruel, described him to me in these
words—" He had a great .deal of human nature in him."
So it may be said of Oliver Cromwell that he had a great
deal of human nature in him ; both for good and evil :
though unhappily what Shakspeare makes Antony say in
his funeral oration on Cæsar, " the evil which men do
lives after them, the good is oft interred with their bones,"
is true of Cromwell as well as of Cæsar. For those whose
nature is prone enough to imitate the evil are incapable of
imitating the good, the intelligence, the magnanimity
and humanity. The same spirit in the early part of
Cromwell's career dictated this order to one of his
officers—" Hang the fellow out-a-hand, and I am your
warrant : for he shot a boy at Stilton-bee by the Spin-
ney, the widow's son, her only support : so God and
man must rejoice at his punishment " ; and it was no fanatical imitation of the Hebrew at Jericho and at Ai, which
directed the avenging slaughters of Drogheda and Wexford, not against unarmed men but men armed to the teeth,
and who even if not themselves the murderers were the
abettors of the murderers of unarmed men, and of women,
and children.

There is one principle, which men of average ability for
empire understand and act upon, that if they conquer a
country and cannot or do not place the conquered upon an
equality in respect to all rights civil and religious with the
conquerors, but keep them in a state of subjection, they

must live among them as in a hostile country, with arms
ever in their hands, and in habitations like fortified camps.
This was thoroughly understood and acted upon by that
brave and astute race of men, the Normans, both in Normandy and England, and at first in Ireland too as the term
" lords of the pale " implies.   In accordance with this
principle, it had been the policy of Queen Elizabeth, probably the ablest ruler except Cromwell that England has
ever had, not only never to employ the Irish as soldiers,
but to deny them liberty to enlist into the service of
foreign states.   Some writers have fallen into the absurdity of praising James the First as a promoter of civilization on the ground of his planting new colonies in
Ulster by sending out great numbers of colonists from
England and Scotland, by which means, according to Hume,
the Irish were taught " husbandry and the arts."   What
" arts " they were taught or had learnt sufficiently appeared
in the massacre of 1641, which raged with peculiar magnitude and atrocity in Ulster, where the feelings of the
Irish were the more exasperated from their having been
more recently stripped of their lands.   The " arts " were
the arts of torture ; to slash and cut so as to inflict wounds
that should not prove immediately mortal, and then to
hang the bleeding victims on tenter-hooks, the boy of
tender years beside his father ; to strip some of their
clothes[1] and leave them to perish of cold ; to delude others
with passes from Sir Phelim O'Neal and with promises of
being safely conveyed to their friends in England under the
escort of men calling themselves soldiers and officers, who had
learnt cruelty in the service of Spain, and who drove them

---

[1] When Montrose stormed Aberdeen
his Irish soldiers made the citizens
take off their clothes before they killed
them, that the clothes might not be
spoiled by the blood.   They thus practised in Scotland what they had before
practised in Ireland and learnt in the
service of Spain. *See Temple*, p. 85.

like cattle till they came to a river and then forced them into the water, men women and children, and knocked on the head such as swam to the shore ; to draw others up and down the water with ropes about their necks ; and to hang up, take down and hang up again others several times, to make them confess their money and then dispatch them ; to persuade some with the promise of life to be the executioners of their nearest kindred, and then butcher them upon their murdered relations ; to tempt others by the same promise to conform to the Romish rites, and then murder them lest they should relapse into heresy; to dash out the brains of infants, or bury them alive with their murdered mothers ; and to do many other deeds of horror which I will not write down. A record of them is preserved in the depositions of eye-witnesses attested upon oath, which are published in Sir John Temple's history of that most disgusting massacre, called the Irish Rebellion of 1641. I will give one or two of these depositions in the words of the witnesses,—words which are well calculated to leave an impression on the mind of any one who reads them not easily effaced.

William Parkinson late of Castle Cumber in the county of Kilkenny deposeth "That he saw Lewes O'Brenan, with his sword drawn, in the said town, pursue an English boy of eight or nine years of age, or thereabouts, by name Richard Bernet, into a house, and saw the said Lewes lead the said boy forth of the house, the blood running about his ears, in a hair-rope ; and he led the boy to his father's tenters and there hanged him with John Banks, another little boy." [1]

A youth of about fifteen years of age meeting with his schoolmaster, the latter drew his skein, and began furiously to slash and cut the boy, who cried to him

[1] Temple, p. 89, ed. Maseres, London, 4to, 1812.

K

"Good master, do not kill me, but whip me as much as you will!" But the merciless wretch murdered him.[1]

"Near Kilfeale in the Queen's county, an Englishman his wife, four or five children and a maid were all hanged and afterwards put all into one hole; the youngest child being not fully dead put out his hand, and cried 'Mammy l mammy!' upon which they buried him alive."[2]

But these proceedings were merciful compared to many others which are too horrible to be transcribed. Their most revolting cruelties were committed on women and children. In a wood near the town of Cutherlagh a woman was hanged and her daughter hanged in the hair of her mother's head.[3] Some had their eyes plucked out, and their hands cut off, and so were turned out to wander up and down.[4] The Irish women and children were as cruel as the men.[5] Master Cunningham deposeth "That the amount of the persons killed by the rebels from the time of the beginning of the Rebellion, Oct. 23, 1641, unto the month of April following was as the priests weekly gave it in, in their several parishes, one hundred and five thousand."[6]

These were "the arts" which the government of small mean incapable tyrants like James and Charles, like Laud and Strafford, is fitted to teach mankind. And of those four men before all others the English nation had a right to demand an account of the blood that was shed and the

[1] Temple, p. 109.
[2] Temple, p. 88.
[3] Temple, p. 95.
[4] Temple, p. 95.
[5] Temple, p. 94.
[6] Temple, p. 99. "Sir Phelim O'Neale and Roger Moore were the actors in the massacres, and by public directions of some in place, and of the titulary bishops, for the sending of an exact account of what persons were murdered throughout all Ulster, a fourth part of the kingdom of Ireland, to the parish-priests in every parish, a particular account was sent in; and the account was 104,700 in one province, in the first 3 months of the rebellion."—Sir Charles Coote's testimony concerning the generality of the Rebellion, in the Trial of Lord Macguire, 20 Charles I., 1645. State Trials, vol. iv. p. 679.

suffering that was endured in this detestable massacre. For let us look at their doings. James departed from the wise policy of Elizabeth, and permitted and encouraged Irish regiments under Irish officers to enter the Spanish service. These regiments were therefore ready to return to their native country with all the advantages of military discipline and with all the arts of Spanish cruelty superadded to their own, whenever it suited the interest of the house of Austria to disturb the English Government, or whenever it suited the interest of the house of Stuart to employ them for the destruction of the English Constitution and the establishment of a pure despotism in its place. Charles in his presumptuous folly, which in many cases exceeded even that of James, went much farther. He not only permitted such levies but actually granted a commission to the Earl of Antrim to raise an army of native Irish to be employed against Scotland, from the wildest portion of the nation, "as many O's and Macs" wrote Strafford who had sense enough at least to remonstrate against this, "as would startle a whole council board on this side to hear of."[1] Antrim's propositions, which are nineteen in number,[2] conclude with "names of my friends." Among these will be found some of those who were very active in the subsequent massacre—Macgennis, Macguire, Phelim O'Neale and his brother, and Hugh McMahon. So that the ringleaders of this massacre were literally the same persons to whom Charles had granted a commission to make war in Scotland—and how they made war was shown afterwards in the butcheries they committed in Ireland in 1641, and in Scotland under Montrose.

---

[1] The Lord Deputy (Strafford) to Mr. Secretary Windebank, March 20, 163⅝. Strafford's Letters and Dispatches, vol. ii. p. 300.

[2] They will be found in Strafford's Letters and Dispatches, vol. ii. pp. 305, 306.

There is reason to believe that the queen of Charles, Henrietta Maria, had nearly as much to do with the Irish massacre as her relative Catherine de' Medici had with that of St. Bartholomew. There is a letter from her to Strafford in 1638 which shows that she was in confidential communication with the Earl of Antrim two or three years before the massacre.[1] And the English House of Commons, in one of their Declarations concerning Ireland, charge the king with delaying to proclaim the perpetrators of the Irish massacre rebels and traitors to the Crown of England till almost three months after the breaking out of the rebellion, and then commanding that but forty copies of the proclamation should be printed, nor they published till further directions should be given by his Majesty, although the rebels had styled themselves the Queen's army and professed that the cause of their rising was "to maintain the King's prerogative and the Queen's religion against the Puritan Parliament of England."[2] Mrs. Hutchinson says, speaking of Nottinghamshire :—" All the popish gentry were wholly for the king, whereof one Mr. Golding, next neighbour to Mr. Hutchinson, had been a private collector of the Catholics' contributions to the Irish rebellion, and for that was, by the queen's procurement, made a knight and baronet."[3]

Although Strafford remonstrated against the commission to Antrim granted probably, like Mr. Golding's knighthood and baronetcy, "by the queen's procurement," the army which he himself had raised for the same service, amounting to 8000 foot and 1000 horse, consisted entirely of papists. And while this was done to put arms into the

---

[1] See Strafford's Letters and Dispatches, vol. ii. p. 321.

[2] May's Hist. of the Parliament,

book ii. ch. ii. sub. fin.

[3] Memoirs of Col. Hutchinson, p. 117, Bohn's ed., London, 1854.

hands of the Pope's adherents, the severe restrictions upon saltpetre and gunpowder disarmed the Protestants. At the same time Strafford's government had excited general discontent and disgust in both parties. The ecclesiastical innovations introduced by him, in compliance with the urgent demands of Laud, disgusted the Protestants by their approach to Romanism, without gaining the Romish party whom an English Pope did not satisfy, and whose clergy perceived themselves still hopelessly excluded from participatiou in church livings.

Modern writers appear to have come to the conclusion from a general statement of Ludlow that the army did not land in Ireland till September. Ludlow's expression may be so far correct that the landing of the whole of the troops, stores, artillery, ammunition and provisions was not completed till the beginning of September. But the minutes of the Council of State clearly show that regiment after regiment, as it could be got ready at the waterside, was transported during the summer. There are many orders during the month of April for engaging ships for transporting troops and provisions to Ireland.

Where, as frequently happens, the statements of Whitelock do not coincide with those of the Order Book of the Council of State in military matters, there can be no doubt that the Order Book is the more trustworthy authority. Whitelock has misled many modern writers by his statements as to the amount of the forces sent to Ireland. It would be idle to attempt to reconcile Whitelock with the Order Book, inasmuch as a loose and inaccurate statement cannot be reconciled with an exact and accurate one. While Whitelock has made the whole number of regiments sent to Ireland very much less than it was, he has in some instances made a regiment more numerous than the Order

Book. I have shown from the Order Book that Colonel Tothill's regiment consisted of 1000 men, from the fact of there being orders for 400 pikes and 600 muskets. Under date April 30, 1649, Whitelock says "Letters from Ireland that Colonel Tothill's regiment of 1250 was not landed but beaten back by tempest to Anglesey. That Londonderry could not hold out the siege ; that Colonel Monk stood off, and did nothing, being (as he said) not in a capacity." [1] Now on the 11th of May there is an order of the Council of State "That a letter be written to Col. Moncke to let him understand this Council is very sensible of his services to this commonwealth and of his integrity in the carrying of it on in those parts." [2]

Cromwell on reaching Dublin on the 15th of August, set himself immediately to work on his business and he appears to have very soon come to the conclusion that the forces already voted for the service on which he was engaged were insufficient. On the 23rd of August, he wrote a letter to the Council of State asking for reinforcements. This letter seems to have travelled with great rapidity for that time, taking only seven days to go from Dublin to London. It was written at Dublin on the 23rd and was read in the Council of State at Whitehall on the 30th of August. There is a minute in the Order Book of the Council of State under date 30th August 1649 : "That the letter of the Lord-Lieutenant of Ireland of the 23rd instant be reported to the House : that for the reasons expressed in the same the Council is of opinion that his desire for recruits of men should be complied with." [3] On the same day there is a minute that the

[1] Whitelock, p. 399, April 30, 1649.
[2] Order Book of the Council of State, 11th May, 1649.   MS. State Paper Office.

[3] Order Book of the Council of State, 30th August, 1649.   MS. State Paper Office.

Lord General be written to, to hasten the departure of Col. Hacker's regiment of horse for Ireland.[1]

Cromwell however had no intention of waiting for those reinforcements before he began his campaign. Having remained at Dublin about a fortnight, he marched to Drogheda, or Tredagh as it was then usually called. On his march to Drogheda Cromwell set forth a declaration to assure the country "that none of them should be injured behaving themselves peaceably and bringing in their provisions."[2] He also issued a proclamation against the soldiers plundering the country upon pain of death; and three men were condemned to die for plundering and for straggling from their colours of whom two were hanged.[3]

Drogheda was garrisoned with near three thousand foot and two hundred horse,[4] and was considered by the governor, Sir Arthur Ashton, to be almost impregnable. Ormond, expecting that Drogheda, being not far distant from Dublin, would be first attempted by Cromwell, had thrown into it a strong garrison of his best troops under an officer of reputation, with the view of occupying the enemy sometime in the siege of it, while he repaired his forces broken by the defeat they had received from Michael Jones before Dublin. But Cromwell was not a man to lose in a siege time of which he well knew the value. Having completed his batteries on the 10th of September, he summoned the governor to deliver the town to the use of the Parliament of England. Not receiving a satisfactory answer, Cromwell then effected " two reasonable good breaches "

---

[1] Order Book of the Council of State, 30th August, 1649. MS. State Paper Office.

[2] Whitelock, p. 426.

[3] Letter dated Dublin, Sept. 13, 1649, in Cromwelliana, p. 64.

[4] Cromwell to the Speaker, Dublin, 17th Sept. 1649.

in the east and south wall; and upon Tuesday the 11th
of September about 5 o'clock in the evening proceeded
to storm the town. "Through the advantages of the
place," he says in his dispatch, "our men were forced to
retreat quite out of the breach, not without some
considerable loss, Colonel Castle, whose regiment commenced the attack, being shot in the head whereof he
presently died." Cromwell's troops led by himself in
person then made another attempt, "wherein" he says,
"God was pleased so to animate them that they got
ground of the enemy, and by the goodness of God
forced him to quit his intrenchments; and after a very
hot dispute, the enemy having both horse and foot,
and we foot only within the walls, the enemy gave
ground, and our men became masters." Then, a passage
having been effected for his cavalry into the town,
"divers of the enemy" he continues, "retreated into the
Mill Mount, a place very strong, and of difficult access,
being exceeding high, having a good graft, and strongly
pallisadoed. The governor, Sir Arthur Ashton, and
divers considerable officers being there, our men getting up
to them, were ordered by me to put them all to the
sword; and indeed, being in the heat of action, I
forbade them to spare any that were in arms in the town,
and I think that night they put to the sword about two
thousand men. Divers of the officers and soldiers being
fled over the bridge into the other part of the town,
where about one hundred of them possessed St. Peter's
church steeple, some the west gate, and others a strong
round tower next the gate, called St. Sunday,—these
being summoned to yield to mercy refused; whereupon I
ordered the steeple of St. Peter's church to be fired.
The next day the other two towers were summoned, in

one of which were about six or seven score, but they refused to yield themselves; and we, knowing that hunger must compel them, set only good guards to secure them from running away, until their stomachs were come down. From one of the said towers, notwithstanding their condition, they killed and wounded some of our men. When they submitted, their officers were knocked on the head; and every tenth man of the soldiers killed; and the rest shipped for the Barbadoes. .   .   .   . I believe all the friars were knocked on the head promiscuously but two; the one of which was Father Peter Taaff, brother to the Lord Taaff, whom the soldiers took the next day and made an end of. The other was taken in the round tower, under the repute of a lieutenant, and when he understood that the officers in that tower had no quarter, he confessed he was a friar; but that did not save him." Of Cromwell's men not one hundred were killed, though many were wounded; and, besides Colonel Castle, he lost several officers: while, according to the list subjoined to Cromwell's dispatch to the Speaker, the enemy lost all their officers, 220 reformadoes and troopers, and 2500 foot soldiers [1]—a hint to the Medici, Valois, Bourbon, and Stuart school of politicians that a massacre of *English* Protestants might turn out rather an expensive sort of speculation. In a letter to Bradshaw, president of the Council of State, Cromwell says " I do not believe, neither do I hear, that any officer escaped with his life save only one lieutenant, who, I hear, going to the enemy said that he was the only man that escaped of all the garrison. The enemy upon this were filled with much terror. And truly I believe this bitterness will save much effusion of blood

[1] Cromwell to the Speaker, Dublin, 17th Sept. 1649.

through the goodness of God."[1]   In the minute of the
Council of State of Saturday 29th of September 1649,
ordering a public thanksgiving on the following day in
all the churches of London and the neighbouring districts,
it is stated that "there were about three thousand of
the enemy slain and of our men only sixty-five private
soldiers and two officers."[2]

The reasons which Cromwell in his dispatch to the
Speaker assigns for this severity are precisely the same
as a British commander might in 1857–8 have assigned
for ordering no quarter to be given to sepoys taken in
arms, and will be better appreciated now than they
were some years ago. "I was persuaded" he says
"that there is a righteous judgment of God upon these
barbarous wretches who have imbrued their hands in so
much innocent blood, and that it will tend to prevent the
effusion of blood for the future ; which are the satisfactory
grounds to such actions which otherwise cannot but
work remorse and regret."   If on the other hand it be
asserted that the garrison of Drogheda were not chiefly
Irish, since according to Ludlow the royalists had "put

[1] Cromwell to Bradshaw, 16th Sept.
1649.

[2] Order Book of the Council of
State, Die Saturni, 29 Sept. 1649.
MS. State Paper Office. The following
is the minute :—"Whereas it hath
pleased God to bless the endeavours of
the forces of the Commonwealth
against the Irish rebels and their adherents in the town of Drogheda which
was taken in by storm there being in
it a strong garrison of the choice of
Ormond's army put into it. There
were about three thousand of the
enemy slain and of our men only sixty-
five private soldiers and two officers.
It is therefore this day ordered that all
the ministers in London &c. do publish

the same to the people to-morrow
being the Lord's day the 30th of this
instant September in their several
churches and chapels and stir up the
people to give thanks to God for his
goodness in still crowning and blessing
the endeavours of this Commonwealth,
for the settling of peace against the
enemies thereof."   On the 17th of
October the Council of State made an
order "That a warrant do issue out to
Mr. Jackson to pay unto Capt. Porter
who brought the good news out of Ireland of the taking of Drogheda the
sum of £100 according to an order of
Parliament made to that purpose."—
Ibid., 17th October, 1649.

most of their army into their garrisons, having placed three or four thousand of the best of their men, being mostly English, in the town of Tredagh (Drogheda), and made Sir Arthur Ashton governor thereof," the answer is that if Englishmen will join with Nana Sahib, they must take the fate of Nana Sahib. In regard to the assertion that women and children were slaughtered in the storm of Drogheda, it is an assertion unproved and most probably altogether false.[1]

The garrison of Wexford having offered resistance shared the fate of the garrison of Drogheda. Cromwell in his dispatch reckoned that there were lost of the enemy not many less than 2000, while of the besiegers not twenty were killed.[2] Most of the other places of strength yielded at his approach, and the Protestant troops under Inchiquin revolted to the Parliament. The season was so far advanced (24th of November) before he attempted Waterford that he was obliged to raise the siege, and soon after retire into winter quarters. He first however reduced Dungarvan, at which place he had the misfortune to lose by a rapid fever his lieutenant-

---

[1] Mr. Carlyle (Cromwell's Letters, vol. ii. p. 205, note) says the old Parliamentary History, vol. xix. pp. 207–9, has added after the concluding "Surgeons, &c.," in Cromwell's list of the slain, "and many inhabitants," of which there is no trace in the old pamphlets. And yet M. Guizot in his Histoire de la République d'Angleterre et de Cromwell (Paris, 1854), tom. i. p. 94, in quoting the list in question has concluded thus—"les chirurgiens et beaucoup d'habitans," and has actually cited Carlyle's Cromwell's Letters as the first of his authorities, adding Parl. Hist. vol. xix. pp. 201–210, &c., without noticing Mr. Carlyle's note on the most important, and as it would appear altogether unwarrantable addition of "many inhabitants," made by the royalist compilers of the Parliamentary History. In regard to the question, Had children or women also imbrued their hands in innocent blood ? the depositions on oath printed in Sir John Temple's History of the Irish Rebellion or Massacre show that they had—not that even this might be a valid ground for retaliating upon *them*, and I do not believe that Cromwell's soldiers did so.

[2] Cromwell to the Speaker, Wexford, 14th October, 1649.

general, Michael Jones, to whom Ireton, with that zeal for the public service and freedom from selfish ends and personal aggrandizement that marked his character, had given way on observing his greater knowledge of the country and of the service. The character which his commander-in-chief, Cromwell, gives him in the dispatch which announces his death, will remain a greater honour to his memory than a monument among the sepulchres of kings. "The noble lieutenant-general," says Cromwell, "whose finger, to our knowledge, never ached in all these expeditions, fell sick, upon a cold taken in our late wet march, and ill accommodation, and went to Dungarvan, where, struggling some four or five days with a fever, he died, having run his course with so much honour, courage, and fidelity, as his actions better speak, than my pen. What England lost hereby is above me to speak ; I am sure I lost a noble friend and companion in labours. You see how God mingles out the cup to us."

Owen O'Neal, having quarrelled with Ormond, endeavoured to make his peace with the English Parliament ; but his offers were sternly rejected, and he again united with Ormond.

It would appear, from a minute, and a copy of another document in the Order Book of the Council of State, that the number of the troops of the Parliament at that time in Ireland was greater than has been commonly supposed. There is a minute of 12th October 1649 "that the proposition made by Mr. Downes for the furnishing of sixteen thousand suits of foot soldiers cloaths [*sic*] at 17*s*. per suit and to find packing be accepted of."[1] The Order Book

[1] Order Book of the Council of   Paper Office.
State, 12th October, 1649. MS. State

also contains a copy of the "Articles of Agreement between the Council of State and Robert Downes for the furnishing of 16,000 coats and breeches for the soldiers in Ireland." The Irish committee also contracted for 16,000 shirts, 16,000 pairs of stockings, and 16,000 pairs of shoes.[1] This seems to show that there was only *one* shirt allowed for each man, the number of shirts ordered being the same with the number of suits of clothes.

John Lilburne had, as has been before mentioned, been committed to the Tower on the 28th of March by an order of the Council of State, "upon suspicion of high treason, for being the author of a scandalous and seditious book intituled England's New Chains Discovered."[2] On the 17th of July Lilburne had addressed a letter to Lord Grey of Groby, Henry Marten, and two other members of Parliament, stating that his son had died of the small-pox the day before, and that his wife and two other children were ill, and desiring to be allowed a few days' liberty to visit them. On the following day, the 18th of July, Henry Marten moved the House that he should be liberated on security. This motion was granted, and Lilburne was liberated. But again, on the 19th of September, an order of the Council of State[3] was made for his imprisonment in the Tower, in order to his trial on the charge of new attempts to raise up mutiny in the army, and overturn the Government.

Great preparations were now made for the trial of John

[1] Order Book of the Council of State, 30th October, 1649. MS. State Paper Office.

[2] Order Book of the Council of State, 28th March, 1649. MS. State Paper Office.

[3] "That Mr. John Lilburne shall be committed prisoner in the Tower of London, in order to his trial, Mr. At-torney-General having given the Council satisfaction that he hath evidence sufficient against him to witness him guilty of offending the late Act of Parliament declaring treasons." — Order Book of the Council of State, à Meridie, 19 Sept. 1649. MS. State Paper Office.

Lilburne on these charges. Forty-one persons of station, including one of the Lords Commissioners of the great seal, eight of the judges, three serjeants-at-law, the Lord Mayor of London, and nine aldermen, were appointed the commissioners of this extraordinary commission of Oyer and Terminer.[1] Four counsel were appointed assistants to Prideaux the Attorney General.[2] The following minutes of the Order Book of the Council of State further show the extraordinary anxiety of the Government to rid themselves of this active and troublesome, if not formidable, assailant.

" That letters be sent to the several judges who are out of town to repair to this town to attend the service of the commonwealth for the trying of some grand offenders according to the late Act. And they are to be here within 14 days after the date hereof." [3]

"That Mr. Ambrose and Andrew Broughton be sent unto to repair unto this town to attend upon the Attorney General and receive directions from him for the carrying on of a charge against Mr. John Lilburne, who is to be tried according to a late act for treasons, and that Mr. Nutley shall be solicitor for this cause." [4]

" That letters be written to the militia of London and Westminster to cause sufficient guards to be in a readiness on Wednesday next to prevent any trouble that may arise upon the occasion of the trial of John Lilburne." [5]

" To write to the Sheriffs of London to prepare a fit

---

[1] See the names of the 41 Commissioners in State Trials, vol. iv. pp. 1269, 1270.

[2] Order Book of the Council of State, à Meridie, 19 Sept. 1649. MS. State Paper Office.

[3] Order Book of the Council of State, à Meridie, 19th Sept. 1649.

MS. State Paper Office.

[4] Order Book of the Council of State, à Meridie, 19th Sept. 1649. MS. State Paper Office.

[5] Order Book of the Council of State, Die Saturni, 20 Octobris, 1649. MS. State Paper Office.

place in Guildhall, for the trial of Lt.-Col. John Lilburne, and for the accommodation of the Council of the Commonwealth." [1]

" That the letter now presented to the Council to be sent to Major-General Skippon for keeping the peace and preventing danger at Guildhall upon the trial of John Lilburne be signed and sent." [2]

The " late act for treasons," referred to in the minutes above recited, was "An Act of the 14th of May 1649 declaring what offences shall be adjudged treason." There was another Act of 17th July, 1649 which was the same as the former, with the addition of a clause respecting coining.   Now, while the old English law of treasons required that there should be an attempt to subvert the Government, manifested by an overt act, this new law of treasons of the Government, which styled itself the Commonwealth, enacted that words affirming by writing or otherwise that the government settled in the form of a Commonwealth is tyrannical, usurped, or unlawful, or that the commons assembled in Parliament are not the supreme authority, shall be treason— thereby creating a change in the old constitutional laws of England, which was considered generally a tyrannical innovation.   It is evident that the Parliament and Council of State committed a great blunder in the whole of this proceeding, both in the change of the law of treason, and in the extraordinary constitution of the tribunal, which they created for the trial of an obnoxious individual, whom they thereby raised to an eminence and importance which probably his own abilities, though far greater than modern

---

[1] Order Book of the Council of State, Die Lunæ, 22 Octobris, 1649. MS. State Paper Office.

[2] Order Book of the Council of State, Die Martis, 23 Octobris, 1649. MS. State Paper Office.

writers have supposed, could never have obtained for him. And yet, whatever judgment may be formed of his abilities, a man who was a more popular pamphleteer than Milton, who could thwart and irritate such statesmen as Vane and Cromwell, and baffle all their efforts for his destruction, naturally excites some curiosity respecting his character and history. It is also important towards a clear understanding of the nature of the government then existing in England to enter into some of the details of this trial, from which it will appear that the law-officers of the government called the Commonwealth, both counsel and judges, did not exhibit much, if any, greater fairness towards the prisoner than was exhibited by the counsel and judges of the most despotic times of the Tudors and the Stuarts.

Lilburne was by birth a gentleman, though Clarendon in his account of him, which contains more misstatements than it does sentences, says of him " this man before the troubles was a poor bookbinder." [1] So far is this statement from the truth, that John Lilburne was descended of an ancient family, (quite as ancient and as good as Hyde's), that possessed estates in the county of Durham. He was the second son, (his elder brother Robert being a colonel, as he was a lieutenant-colonel in the army of the Parliament), of Richard Lilburne of Thickney Puncharden in the county of Durham, where John Lilburne was born in 1618. His father Richard Lilburne, besides the estate of Thickney Puncharden, was possessed of lands to a considerable value in the county of Durham. John Lilburne, according to a custom at that time very prevalent with regard to the younger sons of good families, for whom the colonies and the Indian Empire did not then afford a provision, had

[1] Clar. Hist. vol. vii. p. 44, Oxford, 1826.

been put apprentice at twelve years of age to an eminent wholesale clothier near Londonstone ;[1] which may account for what he said on his trial that he did not know Latin or any other language but English.

John Lilburne was fully aware, and even rather more than reasonably proud, of the importance in that age of being of a good family.   For he is reported to have assigned as one reason for refusing to submit to the domination of Cromwell that he was "as good a gentleman, and of as good a family."   And though such men as Cromwell and Bonaparte could well afford to laugh at such reasons for refusing allegiance to them, and content themselves with the reflection that their nobility began at Naseby and Monte Notte ; this reverence for family antiquity is one cause of the stability of hereditary kingship in an old country.   Great would have been John Lilburne's wrath could he have returned from the grave and seen the contemptuous terms in which Hyde presumed to speak of him ; of him whose courage or whose folly, unlike the wisdom and discretion of Hyde, always made him defy a living enemy to his face ; and not wait for the time when he could safely blacken his memory.   For Lilburne knew so little of fear, that he was ready on all occasions to fight against any odds.   Lilburne said in the course of this trial, " I bless God I have learnt to die, having always carried my life in my hand, ready to lay it down for above this twelve

---

[1] Biog. Brit., art. Lilburne, John.— " When John Lilburne's cause was pleaded at the bar of the House of Lords in 1640, among other aggravations of the cruelty of the sentence passed upon him by the Judges of the Star Chamber in 1637, it was urged by the managers in his behalf that he was descended from an ancient family in the north, a town in Northumberland still bearing the name of Lilburne, or rather Leisle-bourne, by reason of the water called the Bourne that was about it ; and that the arms belonging to the family are three water-budgets, which is an ancient bearing of arms." —Ibid., note (A).

years together." This was true to the letter, for he had begun his struggle against tyranny in 1637, when, though only nineteen years of age, for his undaunted defence of the constitutional rights of Englishmen, he was fined £500, and further ordered to be whipt through the streets, and set in the pillory. The punishment was inflicted with the utmost severity. But nothing could subdue the spirit of John Lilburne. While in the pillory he inveighed bitterly against the tyranny of the bishops, and the government of Charles, and scattered pamphlets among the people, which the Star Chamber then, like the Council of State now, pronounced to be seditious. The Star Chamber also, having heard of his speaking in the pillory, ordered him to be gagged The joker of the Long Parliament, Henry Marten, is reported to have said of John Lilburne, that "if there was none living but himself, John would be against Lilburne, and Lilburne against John."[1]

On Monday, the 22nd of October, 1649, there is a minute in the Order Book of the Council of State, "That Colonel Robert Lilburne be called in to hear what he hath to propound to the Council."[2] Though no further information is afforded by the Order Book as to what Colonel Robert Lilburne had to propound to the Council of State, there is no doubt that his business with the Council related to a proposition made by his brother, John Lilburne. On that same day a petition from Colonel Robert Lilburne, and Elizabeth Lilburne, the wife of Lieut.-Col. John Lilburne, was presented " to the right honourable the supreme authority of this nation, the Commons of England in Parliament assembled, in the behalf of Lieut.-Col. John Lilburne, prisoner in the Tower of London." It is

[1] Rushworth, vol. ii. p. 468.
[2] Order Book of the Council of

State, Die Lunæ, 22 Octobris, 1649. MS. State Paper Office.

good evidence in favour of the private character of John Lilburne, that both his wife and his brother Robert were most devotedly attached to him.   In this petition the petitioners say "considering his principles are a burthen to this State, they do most humbly present their assurance and confidence of his purpose to withdraw himself into some foreign country, desiring he may have his money, which is necessary to his and his family's subsistence in their transplantation, and convenient time to prepare himself to go." [1]   This petition was however altogether fruitless.   The proposition which Colonel Robert Lilburne had to make to the Council of State on the 22nd of October, referred to in the minute of that date, was a proposition of John Lilburne entituled " The Innocent Man's Second [2] Proffer : made unto his present adversaries, Oct. 22, 1649, and communicated unto them by his loving Brother, Col. Robert Lilburne." This proposition is in the form of a letter to his brother, dated "Tower Oct. 22 1649," and thus commences, " Brother ; In answer to your late letter, I can make no other proposition, besides what is in my letter to Mr. Hevenningham of the 20th present, than this. That seeing myself, and the principles I profess, are a burthen to the

---

[1] State Trials, vol. iv. pp. 1424, 1425.

[2] "The Innocent Man's First Proffer" was a proposition of Lt.-Col. John Lilburne in the form of a letter dated Tower of London Oct. 20, 1649 to William Hevenningham, Esq. of Hevenningham, in Suffolk, a member of the Council of State, to submit the judgment of his cause to a tribunal composed of one of the twelve judges chosen by himself and such of the other eleven as his adversaries shall choose, provided the hearing be public, and the judges give their judgment in writing with their reasons for it, and provided he may choose two friends to take notes of all the proceedings without danger to their persons, liberties or estates.   The letter thus commences : "Honoured Sir ; Having sometimes the opportunity to discourse with you, there appeared that in you unto me, that gives me encouragement to pick you out above all men that now remain sitting in your House, to write a few lines unto, in as moderate a way as my condition and provocations will permit me."—State Trials, vol. iv. pp. 1421-1423.

men in present power, therefore (for peace and quietness' sake only), I will engage, (enjoying my money and my immediate liberty), that I will within six months' time transport myself into some part of the West Indies." He then adds a proviso that all those that are free and willing to go with him, of what quality soever, may have free liberty to go, and may have their arrears or money lent to the public paid to them. He concludes by saying that seeing he knows no plantation already planted, he would sooner choose to be cut to pieces in England than engage singly to go alone. [1] This proposition was as fruitless as the petitions of his wife and brother.

On the 23rd a remarkable petition, entituled "The humble petition of the well-affected, in and about the city of London, Westminster, and parts adjacent," was offered to the House, with most earnest and importunate solicitation to have it received, but neither the serjeant-at-arms, nor any member would so much as touch it, the former telling the petitioners that the House would not receive any petition in Lieut.-Col. Lilburne's behalf; although they had themselves declared that it is the right of the people of England to petition, and their duty to receive petitions, even though against law established. Some passages of this petition set some of the proceedings of the existing Government in a very striking light.

"Every one believed," say the petitioners, "that after the expulsion of the greater number of the members of this honourable House (as betrayers of their trust) a new representation should immediately have been ordered, according to that model of an Agreement of the People, tendered by the Council of the Army, or in

[1] State Trials, vol. iv. p. 1426.

some other way.   And that because that honourable Council in their declaration of December last, declared 'That they should not look on the remaining part as a former standing power to be continued; but in order unto and until the introducing of a more full and formal power in a just representative to be speedily endeavoured by an Agreement of the People.'

"And we were the more confident hereof, because they had formerly declared also, 'That where the supreme authority was fixed in the same persons during their own pleasure, it rendered that Government no better than a tyranny, and the people subject thereunto, no better than vassals: That by frequent elections men come to taste of subjection as well as of rule,' (and are thereby obliged for their own sakes to be tender of the good of the people), so that considering those expressions, and those extraordinary things done (declaredly) for a speedy new elected Parliament; how it should come not only to be wholly deferred, but to be matter of blame for us, or any of our friends, earnestly to desire what is so evidently just and necessary in itself, and so essential to the liberties of the nation perplexeth us above measure; and we intreat some satisfaction therein.

"And truly, when you had voted the people under God to be the original of all just power, and the chosen representatives of the people the supreme authority, we conceived that you did it to convey those righteous principles (which we and our friends long laboured for) to the next full and formal representative, and not that you intended to have exercised the supreme law-making power.   Much less that such ensnaring laws should ever have issued from a House of Commons, so often and so exceedingly purged (intentionally by the army) for the freedom of the Commonwealth, as is your Act against treason, wherein, contrary to the course of former Parliaments and to Magna Charta, so many things are made treason, that it is almost impossible for any to discourse with any affection for performance of promises and engagements, or for the liberties of the nation, but he is in danger of his life,[1] if judges and juries should take it for good law, which God forbid.

"Also your Act for continuance and receipt of excise, (which everyone hoped upon the prevailing of the army would have had a final end), to trade more oppressive than all the patents, projects, and ship-money put together.

"Also your Act for continuance and strict receipt of customs was exceeding cross to exportation, that and the other for excise being esteemed most destructive to all kinds of commerce, shipping, and navigation, and are so chargeable in the receipt, as that if what is disbursed to officers and collectors were raised in an ordinary way of

---

[1] The Order Book of the Council of State furnishes full confirmation of this statement in the frequent orders for proceedings against persons on the charge of speaking against or using menacing words against the Parliament and Council of State, and on suspicion of treason. There are also many minutes relating to the taking down obnoxious placards that have been fixed on churches and public places. Thus on the 22nd of November 1649 we find the following orders : "That George Wharton be committed to Newgate for suspicion of treason and that a warrant be issued for that purpose." "That a warrant do issue for the apprehending of John Wingfield for speaking menacing words against the Parliament and Council of State."—*Order Book of the Council of State*, Die Jovis, 22 Novembris 1649. MS. State Paper Office. On the following day a warrant is issued for the apprehension of Francis Leyton of the Charterhouse "for speaking of words dangerous to the Commonwealth."—*Ibid.*, Die Veneris, 23 Nov. 1649. Warrant for apprehending one John Hinde for speaking opprobrious language against the Parliament.—*Ibid.*, 30 Octobris 1642. "That the printed paper that was taken down from the church door in Covent Garden and brought to this Council be reported to the House by Col. Wauton." "That the marshalls be directed to pull down all scandalous papers that they shall find posted up and to apprehend all such as shall countenance the same."—*Ibid.*, Die Saturni, 17 Novembris 1649. A man like their Attorney-General Prideaux would perhaps have sought to make out reading or even looking at these posters to be " countenancing the same."

subsidies, it would go very far towards the public charge, which it was hoped you would have seriously laid to heart, and have prepared a way to have eased the nation of both, and to have raised all public moneys by way of subsidies.[1]

" It was also expected upon the prevailing of the army, and the reducement of this honourable House, that the printing presses should have been fully opened and set at free liberty, for the clear information of the people, the stopping of them having been complained of as a great oppression in the bishops' times, and in the times of the late unpurged Parliament, rather than such an Act against all unlicensed printing, writing, or publishing, as for strictness and severity was never before seen in England, and is extremely dissatisfactory to most people.

" What a sad thing, we beseech you, is it, that it should be thus in this nation, in the first year of England's liberty, (as you would have it esteemed), which in our apprehension exceeds in misery and thraldom the worst of England's bondage.   For, besides what hath been mentioned, what is more frequent than to examine men against themselves, to imprison men by votes of committees, to seize upon men's persons by pursuivants and messengers, to swear men against themselves ; taxes and impositions never so high, and soldiers [2] (not civil officers) set to gather them, to the terror of the people ; and, upon the least denial, either violence or an imprisonment certainly ensueth : lawyers in effect are said to rule all, the laws are trod under foot by

---

[1] The celebrated Marquis of Halifax in a tract intituled " An Essay upon Taxes calculated for the present Juncture of Affairs, 1693," endeavours to show the mischievous as well as unjust nature of the excise, in place of which method of raising money he proposes "that of the antient way of subsidy, upon a true pound rate, according to the wisdom and constant practice of our ancestors, as the most equal, most reasonable, and most suitable to our condition."

[2] I have given some instances of this from the minutes of the Order Book of the Council of State.

them, and wrested to what sense they please,[1] and law-
suits extended beyond all reason, in respect of time and
charge; then (as is verily supposed) having evaded the
clear intentions of this House, and perverted the just intentions of the army, poor impotent prisoners for debt and
small offences abound, and starve in prisons, through
poverty and the cruelty of lawyers and gaolers, and the
poor abroad even perish for want of employment, and
through the excessive price of food,[2] and few or none lay
these things to heart : and if any do, and become pas-
sionately affected therewith, and but speak their minds
freely thereof, or (as hath been usual and commendable)
endeavour to get people together in meetings, and propose
petitions for redress, the Puritans were never more
reproached in the bishops' times, nor the Independents and
Anabaptists in the late defection of Parliament than now
all such are, with more odious titles (or the same in
a more odious form) as Atheists, Levellers, Libertines, in-
troducers of monarchy, anarchy, and confusion; which
are poisoned arrows shot principally at us and our
friends, though most unjustly, none hating or abhorring
either the principles or the practice more than we or
our relations.

" To our understandings this is truly our miserable
condition, and the sad condition of the Commonwealth,
and which is the more grievous, because in a time when
upon promise in the presence of God and with appeals to
His most righteous judgments, we justly expected the
clearest and largest freedoms, with even a total redress of
all grievances, and which is no small addition to our

---

[1] Some remarkable examples of this
will be seen in the trial of Lilburne
which follows.

[2] These statements are confirmed
by the evidence of various minutes in
the Order Book of the Council of
State.

sorrow, that we are wounded thus sorely, by the hands whence we expected our most perfect cure.

"So that what to say or do, we are exceedingly to seek, and therefore we most humbly and ardently beseech the divine goodness to vouchsafe you a true Christian-like spirit of condescension, whereby you may be inclined to appoint some impartial persons to inform our understandings aright of many things here complained of, that if we be, we may appear to have been mistaken, professing from our consciences, that as yet we are confirmed in these our apprehensions of things, not only from our own reasons, but from the declarations, promises, and engagements of parliaments; and we trust, this way of reasoning out of differences will appear more like unto the ways of God, than by force or threats to stop our mouths, or suppress our understandings.

"Also that God will soften your hearts, that you may instantly look back from whence you are fallen, to the just ends for which the army reserved you together, and then we would beseech you to render up unto the people their long withheld right of new elections, and a new elected parliament; and to fulfil your promises concerning Magna Charta, and the Petition of Right." [1]

On the same day, the 23rd of October, Colonel Robert Lilburne presented another petition from himself, in which, after alluding to the failure of the petition presented the day before in his own and his sister's name in behalf of his dear brother, and adding, "yet so strong are my affections towards him, not only as a brother, but as confident of his integrity, and that he hath been very serviceable formerly in his generation, though possibly accompanied with human frailties, but also exceedingly

[1] State Trials, vol. iv. pp. 1427-1430.

afflicted with the long-continued sufferings of his faithful, dear, and now almost distracted wife," and further stating his belief that if the proceedings against his brother should be suspended for some reasonable time he should be able to prevail with him to give no further disturbance to the Government, he says: "And therefore as an humble servant and faithful soldier of yours, for whose safety and preservation I have often readily adventured my life, I have taken the boldness again to presume upon your serious affairs, and most humbly and earnestly to entreat, as the only favour that ever you intend towards me, that you would be pleased to vouchsafe upon this my humble suit, that my dear brother's trial may for some reasonable time yet be suspended." [1]

Upon the delivery of this, Mrs. Lilburne, perceiving that nothing would satisfy them but her husband's life, and having been extremely shocked by the revilings and threats of the members, but especially, says the contemporary report, "old Mr. Valentine that used her most unworthily and basely," went home to the Tower to her husband in a half-distracted condition, and with much importunity, in the bitterness of her spirit, besought her husband to stoop as low as possibly he could for the safety of his life, in the preservation of which hers was locked up. "Her bitter mourning and crying" says the report, "and the beholding the anguish of spirit of her that had been so faithful and hazardous a yoke-fellow to him in his above seven years' sorrow, wrung from him, with much a-do," a letter to the Speaker which is dated from the Tower 24th Oct. 1649, and in which he says, "Honoured Sir ; As a man being somewhat at present confounded in myself, through a strong confidence in my own innocency

[1] State Trials, vol. iv. pp. 1431, 1432.

(having suffered above measure, but intentionally done
injury to none) and pressed under with the importunity of
friends, especially with the heart-breaking sighs of my
dear, but even half-distracted wife; as when my late
children lay in a most disconsolate condition (which ended
their lives) your House did me the favour to grant me my
liberty to visit them, which I think was the saving of her
life : So now greater importunities lying upon me from
divers, and her that is dearer to me than many lives, I as
earnestly entreat you to move your House, in the most
effectual manner you can, that my trial (so suddenly intended) may for some reasonable time be suspended, that
so I may have time to hear and consider what many of
them say they have to offer by way of reason and argument to persuade me to what at present my conscience is
not convinced of.   .   .   .   .
Upon the knowledge of the acceptance of which, during
all that time of suspension of trial, I do hereby faithfully
promise not in the least to disturb those that shall grant
me this favour." [1] This letter however was of no avail,
and only added to his wife's sorrow. So that Lilburne
got his friends to prevail on her to go into the city and
there to keep her till his trial was over.

I have repeatedly had occasion to notice the sensitiveness
of the Government on the subject of the expression of any
opinions except such as were favourable to themselves. In
regard to the liberty of the press they had all along been
as arbitrary and tyrannical as Henry the Eighth or Archbishop Laud; but, in the atrocious act which has been
cited, and which adjudged what by the English law was
merely liable to the punishment of libel to be high treason,
they not only went beyond any former English tyrant, but

---

[1] State Trials, vol. iv. pp. 1432, 1433.

beyond themselves. What the Star Chamber, directed by the savage intolerance of Laud, had punished with the pillory, and mutilation, they punished with death; at least they sought to punish with death, for they found that an English jury would not carry out their law, and this very fact proves that the people were disposed so far to take Lilburne's advice as "not to side with or fight for the chimeras, fooleries, and pride of the present men in power." And chimeras they were, the imaginations that those men or any of them entertained that the government they had established was a republic, and that it would last. I do not say that an actual republic—a democracy—such as Lilburne and his friends denominated the Levellers aimed at —would have secured the end of good government—but it would at least have had the merit of being what it called itself. It might have been a tyranny no less, or it might have fallen to pieces at once; but it would not have been an oligarchical tyranny under the name of a republic. Moreover there is one thing that seems a little strange. Even the panegyrists of Vane and Marten do not claim more for them than that, after the battle of Worcester, towards the close of the third year of their Commonwealth, they began to have doubts respecting Cromwell's designs. Now long before that time, more than two years before, Lilburne had declared, in several of his publications that the "false Saint Oliver," as he calls him, was aiming at the supreme power. His very words read against him at this trial in October 1649 actually came to pass to the very letter, three or four years after they were written and published. "The present contest of the present dissembling interest of Independents for the people's liberties in general" he says "is merely no more but self in the highest, and to set up the false saint, and most desperate apostate, mur-

derer,[1] and traitor, Oliver Cromwell, by a pretended election of his mercenary soldiers, under the false name of the
godly interest, to be King of England, (that being now too
apparently all the intended liberties of the people that ever
he sought for in his life) ; that so he might rule and govern
them by his will and pleasure, and so destroy and evassalize
their lives and properties to his lusts : which is the highest
treason that ever was committed or acted in this nation in
any sense or kind ; either, 1. in the eye of the law : or,
2. in the eye of the ancient (but yet too much arbitrary)
proceedings of Parliament : or, 3. in the eye of their own
late declared principles of reason (by pretence of which,
and by no rules of law in the least, they took away the
late king's head)." [2]

Now Lilburne published this in the summer of 1649,
and the very men, who now in October 1649 sought to
destroy him for promulgating such opinions, such men as
Bradshaw, Vane, Marten, Scot, when at last the proceedings of the memorable 20th of April 1653 opened their

---

[1] In his "Legal Fundamental Liberties of England," p. 1, Lilburne says,
"I positively accuse Mr. Oliver Cromwell for a wilful murderer for murdering Mr. Richard Arnold near Ware."
To which the Attorney-General's answer
was, "Which man, my lord, was condemned for a mutineer by a council of
war, where the Lord-Lieutenant of Ireland was but one member ; and the
Parliament gave him and the rest of
the Council thanks for shooting that
mutinous soldier to death ; and yet
Mr. Lilburne calls him murderer therefore ; and this is laid to my Lord-
Lieutenant's charge for his part." In
answer to the Attorney-General Lilburne talked of the Petition of Right,
and cited the case of the Earl of Strafford, which in fact is not a parallel
case.—State Trials, vol. iv. pp. 1367,
1368. This charge of murder against
Cromwell is one of the weakest points
of Lilburne's case.

[2] From "An Impeachment of High
Treason against Oliver Cromwell, and
his son-in-law Henry Ireton, esquires,
members of the late forcibly-dissolved
House of Commons ; presented to public view, by Lieutenant-Colonel John
Lilburne, close prisoner in the Tower
of London, for his real, true and
zealous affections to the liberties of
his native country," page 5, cited in
State Trials, vol. iv. pp. 1359, 1360.

eyes, must have been forced to admit that Lilburne's opinion of Cromwell was right and that theirs was wrong. Marten, when he saw his beloved oligarchy, which he called a republic, destroyed, precisely as Lilburne had predicted four years before, might feel when too late that, when making jokes on John Lilburne for the amusement of Cromwell, he somewhat resembled the fowl comfortably at roost on the boa constrictor, though destined for part of that animal's supper. The cause of Lilburne's seeing the truth so much sooner may have been this. Lilburne, who was unquestionably an acute, observing, clear-sighted man, had occasion to see Cromwell under circumstances more calculated to bring out his whole character than those under which the parliamentary men who were not soldiers saw him. To the latter he could wear a mask, or even a mask within a mask. Now it would happen at times that all his masks would drop off or be thrown aside in the tumult of those stormy debates that sometimes occurred in the councils of the officers of the army.

Lilburne has himself described one of those stormy scenes in a passage which has an instructive significance, and which like that already quoted is one of those produced against him at his trial by the Attorney-General. "But alas, poor fools!" he says, "we were merely cheated and cozened, it being the principal unhappiness to some of us, as to the flesh, to have our eyes wide open, to see things long before most honest men came to have their eyes open. And this is that which turns to our smart and reproach, and that which we commissioners feared at the first, viz. That no tie, promises, nor engagements were strong enough to the grand jugglers and leaders of the army, was now made clearly manifest;

for when it came to the Council, there came the general, Cromwell, and the whole gang of creature-colonels, and other officers, and spent many days in taking it all to pieces, and there Ireton showed himself an absolute king, if not an emperor ; against whose will no man must dispute. And then Shuttlecock, Roe their scout, Okey, and Major Barton (where Sir Hardress Waller sat president) began in their open council to quarrel with us, by giving some of us base and unworthy language ; which procured them from me a sharp retortment of their own baseness and unworthiness unto their teeth, and a challenge from myself into the field. Besides, seeing they were like to fight with us in the room in their own garrison, which when Sir Hardress Waller in my ear reproved me for it, I justified it, and gave it him again, for suffering us to be so affronted. And within a little time after, I took my leave of them for a pack of dissembling, juggling knaves, amongst whom in consultation ever thereafter I should scorn to come (as I told some of them) ; for there was neither faith, truth, nor common honesty among them. And so away I went to those that chose and entrusted me, and gave publicly and effectually (at a set meeting appointed on purpose) to divers of them, an exact account how they had dealt with us, and cozened and deceived us ; and so absolutely discharged myself from meddling or making any more with so perfidious a generation of men, as the Great Ones of the army were ; but especially the cunningest of Machiavelians, commissary Henry Ireton." [1]

If Lilburne's view of the character of Ireton be accepted as the true one, Ireton's ulterior designs must be considered as not less fatal to constitutional liberty than those of

---

[1] From Lilburne's "Legal Fundamental Liberties of England asserted and vindicated," page 35, cited in State Trials, vol. iv. pp. 1368, 1369.

Cromwell. But I am still of the opinion expressed in a former page that Ireton was sincere in his profession of political faith, and that though a fanatic in his way, " self in the highest," to use Lilburne's happy expression, was not his god as it was that of Cromwell. In regard to Cromwell " the grand juggler," and his " gang of creature-colonels," there is, as I have said, an instructive significance in the passage I have quoted above. Cromwell's whole nature was so thoroughly imbued with craft, that when we consider that his unsleeping vigilance in the contrivance of snares was assisted by great natural sagacity and astute-ness, by promptitude of decision and unbounded daring, we see that he gradually must have enveloped the men who sat and talked at Westminster in net within net, like so many flies in the wide-spread and powerful web of a huge and active spider. The fact is, that even with much less employment of spider machinery Cromwell might have accomplished his end. The victorious general of an army which has rendered itself all-powerful can always make himself supreme if he be so minded. Washington might have done so, if " self in the highest " had been his god. In 1782, Washington refused, " with great and sorrowful surprise " (these were his words) the supreme power and the crown, which certain discontented officers offered him. A far greater soldier than either Washington or Cromwell, Hannibal, might have had, according to the worshippers of successful crime, a more glorious end, if, after the battle of Cannæ, he had turned his victorious army to the destruction of his own country's constitution, such as it was. But Hannibal, though making no pretensions, like Cromwell, to saintship, was content to employ his unequalled strategic genius in overreaching and destroying enemies who were on their guard against him, not in overreaching and destroying friends and colleagues who trusted him. And in strange contrast to the English Christian, the Carthaginian heathen, to borrow the eloquent words of Arnold, "from his childhood to his latest hour, in war and in peace, through glory and through obloquy, amid victories and amid disappointments, ever remembered to what purpose his father had devoted him, and withdrew no thought or desire or deed from their pledged service to his country."[1]

There is an English word, treachery, which means perfidy, that is, breach of faith, or breach of trust. There is another English word, treason, which means a breach of faith or of trust against the State, in other words treachery, not against a private individual, but against the public individual, or body of individuals, as representing all the individuals composing the State or nation. But there is a particular kind of this treachery, perfidy, or breach of trust against the State, for which the English language happily has no name, but which in the French language has received the name of *coup d'état*. The particular act which has received this fine name is an act of perfidy, treachery, or breach of trust against the State, performed by some individual placed in a position of special trust, and therefore of extraordinary power ; which position often enables him to make his treachery or treason successful. Charles I. attempted some acts of this kind, but his brains were far from equal to the successful performance of them. Now, although to overreach and destroy friends who trust you and are off their guard is a far easier business, and requires far smaller abilities, than to overreach and destroy armed enemies, who are watching all your slightest movements, it still requires a certain portion of ability, chiefly of that kind which can simulate friendliness, frankness, and truthfulness towards

[1] Arnold's History of Rome, vol. iii. p. 387.

men whom you intend to destroy. Of this faculty there are many degrees. The man, who possesses it in the highest degree, will not use any more falsehood than is absolutely necessary for the attainment of his ends. He will not, like Jonathan Wild in Fielding's story, put his hands into his friend's pockets, even when he knows there is nothing in them, or, like the Count, pack the cards, when he knows his adversary has no money. He will not be a habitual liar, quack, or renegade, whom no man of common-sense would trust. On the contrary, he will be a man with qualities that, besides making him loved by his wife and children, will make him liked, honoured, and trusted by many political and military comrades, with whom he will live for many years on terms of confidence and friendship, and then, when his time comes, will some day suddenly turn round upon them and, with the name of the God of Truth on his lips, ruin them and their cause. Such a man was Oliver Cromwell.

It will be more convenient to give the narrative of the trial of John Lilburne in a separate chapter. But in connection with that trial I will observe here that, although I have compared the Council of State in some points to the Star Chamber, I should be doing an act of gross injustice if I did not also carefully mark the essential points of difference. The Star Chamber took what may be called a mean as well as cruel revenge on those who opposed its tyranny. The Council of State was tyrannical too and vindictive against what appeared to it the audacity with which Lilburne disowned and defied its authority. But the members of the Council of State were honourably distinguished from all the other tyrants whom history has recorded. The Star Chamber scourged, mutilated, imprisoned in distant fortresses, and dared not submit their cause to a jury of Englishmen. The tyrants of other countries and other times rid themselves of troublesome opponents by secret assassination, as well as judicial murder. The men of the Council of State of 1649 in England pursued their revenge in a different fashion. They had high, brave, English hearts; and what they did, whether for good or evil, they did like men, not like ignoble wild beasts or assassins. Even in England before their time, the captivity of a king or of a king's son was but a step distant from his assassination. But though with them too the king's captivity was the path to his grave, and though his trial was not an act of justice, his execution was the act of brave men, not of cowardly assassins, like the murders of Edward II., of Richard II., and of the sons of Edward IV. Those men erred, and in some points grievously; and grievously did some of them answer for their errors; nevertheless Englishmen will never forget that they raised England from what the Stuarts had made it, a name of scorn among the nations, to be a name to call up very different emotions, a name that, humanly speaking, connoted invincibility, a name "famous and terrible over the world." [1]

Besides their exertions against open enemies, such as the Royalists in arms, and political adversaries, such as John Lilburne, the Council of State had abundance of other work on their hands. There are minutes from time to time about the "scavengery" of the streets, and "the nuisance —the common sewer." The streets being undrained as well as unpaved, the rain descending in small torrents from the waterspouts and mingling with the filth and offal from the houses, converted them into a quagmire. The projecting upper stories of the houses in the lanes, and in many

---

[1] These are the words applied by Clarendon to the Parliamentary army.

parts even of the main streets, almost meeting overhead shut out both light and air. The consequences were stench, disease, and death, the plague being then never altogether out of London.

But the Council of State had other nuisances to contend with. Amid the fogs and darkness of the month of November, 1649, which succeeded Lilburne's trial, "robbers and thieves" appear to have given them much trouble. After nine o'clock even in ordinary times during the early part of the seventeenth century it was unsafe to walk the streets of London. Passengers were insulted, robbed, wounded, and sometimes killed. A sheriff's officer, in making a civil arrest, had often to be backed by a band of well-armed followers ; and the night-watchmen and constables had an office proportionately dangerous. Such being the case in ordinary times, the evil was necessarily much increased by the long civil war, which had taken many persons from their usual occupations, and thrown them loose to swell the numbers of those who lived upon beggary or plunder. The disorders of times long past, handed down upon doubtful or imperfect evidence, and exaggerated or coloured by writers who, like certain rhetoricians, are content to draw upon their imaginations for their facts, are apt to be sometimes discredited altogether, or considered as belonging only to the romance of history. However, of the condition of London and the surrounding districts in this month of November, 1649,[1] the minutes of the Order Book of the Council of State furnish a picture which, that I may not be tempted in the smallest

---

[1] "That an order be drawn up against to-morrow in the afternoon for the prohibiting of the walking in the streets after [blank in orig.] of the night."—*Order Book of the Council of* *State,* Die Jovis, 22 November, 1649. MS. State Paper Office. The hour after which the streets were unsafe specified in Somers' Tracts and other authorities was 9 o'clock.

degree to colour or exaggerate it, I will give in the words of the original.

A minute of the 14th November 1649 sets forth the following facts and provisions [1] respecting those facts.

"Whereas there are daily great robberies and outrages committed not only in the highways on passengers travelling on their lawful occasions, but also many houses broken open and murders committed, whereby the very trade and commerce of this commonwealth is in danger to be ruined : for prevention therefore of such mischiefs in the future it is ordered that the directions following be put in due execution.

"1. That of the two regiments upon the guards for London and Westminster the officers take care to send out ten men out of every troop daily eight miles to scour the roads about London, viz. Rumford, Epping, Waltham, Barnet, Uxbridge, Brentford, Shooter's Hill, Kingston, and Croydon roads.

"2. That twenty horse [2] be upon the guard upon every road in two several guards which are to correspond one with another by scouts.

"That every constable provide an able guide well acquainted with the several roads and ways and an able horse

---

[1] By a former minute of 24th October 1649 it is ordered "that it be referred to the committee that consults with the officers of the army, to whom are to be added for this purpose only the Lords Commissioners of the Great Seal, the Chief Justices of both benches, and the Lord Chief Baron, to consider how the soldiers may be assistant to the civil power for preventing of the robberies murthers and outrages committed upon the highways and in houses, and to consider of some reward and encouragement to be given them for that purpose, and that they also draw up an Act to be offered to the Council to be from them presented to the House." — Order Book of the Council of State, Die Mercurii, 24 October, 1649. MS. State Paper Office.

[2] In describing in a former page the arms of the "horse," I ought to have added that they sometimes at least were armed with musquetoons as well as pistols, as appears from the following passage of Ludlowe's Memoirs — " The committee of Irish affairs raised also a troop consisting of a hundred horse to accompany me, and armed them with back, breast, head-pieces, pistols, and musquetoons." — Ludlowe's Memoirs, p. 128, folio. London, 1751.

to the end the said guide so accommodated may (upon any robbery) give speedy notice to the next guards and so conduct them in pursuit of the robbers as occasion may require, and that upon notice the justices of peace respectively give order to the constables for the doing thereof, the charge of the same to be borne by the respective towns.

" 3. That no soldier pass above five miles from his quarter but by a pass from the field officer or chief officer present with the regiment.

" 4. That the officer of every troop and party that shall have the charge of any guard for this service give order every night to all innkeepers alehouse-keepers or victuallers that shall lodge travellers to give an account to the officer of the guard in writing of the number of all guests that lodge in every such inn and alehouse or victualling-house with a description of their wearing clothes, with the marks and colour of the horse of every person to be set down in writing.

" 5. That the captain of every guard give order to all innkeepers that lodge guests before they depart such place that they show themselves to the captain of the guard to be examined by the said captain ; and the said captain is to secure all suspicious persons to be further examined by the next justice of the peace.

" 6. That the quartering of the rest of the regiments of horse upon the several roads in this commonwealth for the purpose aforesaid be referred to the special and speedy care of his Excellency and the Council of War.

" 7. That his Excellency and Council of War be desired to appoint such and so many troops as by them shall be thought requisite for securing the highways &c. within fifty miles of London more or less as they shall see cause, and the places of their abode with such particular directions and orders as to them shall seem fit. No trooper or foot soldier stirring from the place he shall be quartered in above one mile, or to the next market town, upon pain to be punished by a Council of War, unless he have a pass from his field officer or the chief officer then present with the regiment; and the said officers every week are to give an account in writing to his Excellency and Council of War of their proceedings therein." [1]

While a portion of the land forces was thus employed against robbers, a portion of the fleet was employed against pirates. Thus on the 24th of August 1649 Col. Popham is informed by the Council of State of the depredations committed on the eastern coast upon merchant ships, which are carried into Dunkirk and Ostend contrary to treaty; and he is desired "to go over to that coast, making use of the countenance of those great ships which are now going out, and to expostulate the business with the governors of those places." And again on the 3rd of Sept. 1649 it is ordered "That a letter be written to the generals of the fleet with information of some pirates preparing to come out of Dunkirk to spoil the fishermen." It further appears from the Order Book that the Court of Admiralty was a good deal occupied with the business of trying pirates, who abounded considerably in those days. [2]

The officers of the Council were often wounded and sometimes killed in the execution of their duty. The fol-

---

[1] Order Book of the Council of State, 14 Nov. 1649. MS. State Paper Office. As a further illustration of the spirit with which the Council of State acted I am tempted to give here the minute that immediately follows in the Order Book. "That the forms of the medals which are now brought in to be given to the several mariners who have done good service this last sum-

mer be approved of—viz. the arms of the Commonwealth on one side with Meruisti written above it and the picture of the House of Commons on the other."—*Order Book of the Council of State*, 15 Nov. 1649. MS. State Paper Office.

[2] Order Book of the Council of State, 24th August, and 3rd and 11th Sept. 1649. MS. State Paper Office.

lowing minute describes a case of this kind. "That it be reported to the Parliament that there hath been two of the officers of this Council slain while they were about the execution of a warrant of this Council for the apprehension of a malefactor, and one other wounded, and all these by a dagger, and that the Council making inquiry thereinto do find that use of daggers and pocket-pistols do grow very common and the danger thereby be great :—to desire the House to consider of a way to prevent that mischief by forbidding the making or the use of daggers, stilettos, or pocket-pistols." [1]

There are various other minutes throwing light on the condition of London at that time, and showing that though this government of a Council of State held its power and place by virtue of a victorious army, its position was by no means one that indicated a settled and tranquil state of society. The following minutes and orders of 30th August 1649 may be given as evidence.

"That it be reported to the House that Sir Kenelm Digby is now in England without licence for aught that is known to the Council and that they conceive him a dangerous man, and to desire the House to declare their pleasure concerning him."

"That the same report be made concerning Mr. Walter Montague." [2]

---

[1] Order Book of the Council of State, Die Mercurii, 13th Feb. 16$\frac{49}{50}$. By the time Oldham wrote his imitation of the third satire of Juvenal, 1682, pocket pistols had become the ordinary weapon of the robber. When the shops are closed, he says

" Hither in flocks from Shooter's Hill
    they come,
  To seek their prize and booty nearer
    home :

'Your purse !' they cry ; 'tis madness to resist,
Or strive, with a cocked pistol at
  your breast.
And these each day so strong and
  numerous grow,
The town can scarce afford them jail-
  room now."

[2] Order Book of the Council of State, 30th August, 1649. MS. State Paper Office.

" That a warrant be issued for the seizing of a cabinet in the custody of Mrs. Shepheard [wife of a tailor] in Whyte Fryars belonging to some of Sir Robert Heath's sons." [1]

" That all the keys of all the gates and doors of St. James's Park and of all back doors into the same be delivered unto Colonel Pride ; and that all the doors belonging to private houses that come into the park be also railed up ; and that a warrant be also issued to Colonel Pride for that purpose." [2]

" That a letter be written to the Earl of Pembroke to let him know of what course is taken about the doors of St. James's Park ; and that it is done for the safety of the Council that there may be no attempt upon the garrison." [3]

On the following day there was an order that the late king's plate be melted down and converted into coin ; and that the gilt plate be improved to the best advantage.   The hangings, carpets, chairs, stools, and beds were ordered to be reserved for furnishing the lodgings of the Council of State. It was also ordered at the same time " That rooms at Hampton Court be reserved furnished for the use of the Commonwealth " ; [4] i. e. for the use of some score or two of individuals who called themselves the Commonwealth.

On the 20th of September a sort of Committee of Safety was appointed for six months with extraordinary powers for apprehending suspected persons.   This committee consisted of the Lord General (Fairfax), the Lord President of the Council of State (Bradshaw), Mr. Scott, and Sir William Armyne." [5]

---

[1] Order Book of the Council of State, 30th August, 1649.   MS. State Paper Office.

[2] Order Book of the Council of State, 30th August, 1649.   MS. State Paper Office.

[3] Order Book of the Council of State, 30th August, 1649.

[4] Order Book of the Council of State, 31st August, 1649.

[5] Order Book of the Council of State, 20th Sept. 1649.   MS. State Paper Office.

This government of England in the year 1649, which year they were pleased to denominate " the first year of England's liberty," determined, like other despotisms, whether of one or of a few or of many, to be its own news writer. On the 21st of September it was ordered. by the Council of State " That Mr. Frost (their secretary) shall be the person whom the Council doth authorize to publish intelligence every week upon Thursday according to an Act of Parliament to that purpose."[1] Only two days before they had issued a warrant to apprehend Charles Collins " for publishing a treasonable and seditious libel intituled *The Outcry of the Apprentices.*"[2] It may be superfluous to say that Milton's noble defence of the freedom of the press, of the liberty of unlicensed printing, had no influence on the Parliament to whom it was addressed. It was treated by them pretty much as John Knox's arguments for a suitable provision for the Church of Scotland were treated by the nobility of Scotland. In such times the arguments of men, who do not wield the sword as well as the pen, avail nothing. Indeed it may be contended on the part of those statesmen who then governed England, that at such a time they had no choice, and that, if they had not done all that was in their power to hinder the press from being employed in the service of their adversaries, they would have shown themselves to be pedants and dreamers and not statesmen. But however this may be, there can be no question that they committed a blundering as well as a tyrannical act, when they attempted to make bare words treasonable and punishable with death.

If, what with political adversaries, with pirates, robbers,

[1] Order Book of the Council of State, 21st Sept. 1649. MS. State Paper Office.

[2] Order Book of the Council of State, 19th Sept. 1649.

and thieves, and with unscavengered streets, the members of the Council of State did not live at home altogether at ease, while Cromwell, Ireton, Michael Jones, and others roughed it in Ireland, they evidently took thought how to make themselves as comfortable as circumstances permitted. I do not think Mrs. Hutchinson has thought fit to make any mention of such matters as the following : "That all the members of the Council of State that have lodgings in Whitehall shall have hangings and accommodations for those lodgings out of the £10,000 worth of goods (the late king's) reserved for the use of the State."[1] "That the Earl of Pembroke be added to the committee for providing accommodation in Whitehall for the members of this Council."[2] "That several warrants be issued to Mr. Kinnersley to furnish the lodgings of Col. Wauton and Col. Hutchinson in Whitehall out of the £10,000 worth of goods reserved for the State."[3] "That the door into the gallery out of St. James's Park be made up and a lock set upon the door."[4] "That all the members of the Council shall have keys of the garden at Whitehall. That the secretary shall also have a key to the said garden. That Mrs. Hamden (*sic*) shall have a passage into St. James's Park and that she be desired to have a care who passes through by means of that key."[5] John Milton appears to have been in especial favour with his masters, the Council of State. On the 19th of November 1649 it is ordered "That Mr. Milton shall have the

[1] Order Book of the Council of State, 8th Nov. 1649. MS. State Paper Office.

[2] Order Book of the Council of State, 8th Nov. 1649. MS. State Paper Office.

[3] Order Book of the Council of State, 8th Nov. 1649. MS. State

Paper Office.

[4] Order Book of the Council of State, Die Mercurii, 24 Octob. 1649. This I suppose was the raised gallery that crossed the street.

[5] Order Book of the Council of State, 15th Sept. 1649. MS. State Paper Office.

lodgings that were in the hands of Sir John Hippesley in Whitehall for his accommodation, as being secretary to the Council for foreign languages."[1] The following minute corroborates what appears from other minutes, and shows that Milton's duties as secretary were not confined to foreign languages. "That a warrant be issued to Mr. Milton and to Mr. Sergeant Dendy to view the books and papers of Mr. Clement Walker that are seized at Kensington and such others as he hath here in Westminster or elsewhere and to report what they find therein to the Council."[2]

This Clement Walker, who, as one of the secluded Presbyterian members, was violently exasperated against the Independents, that is, the sitting part of the Parliament, is the writer upon whose authority Hume states[3] that the Parliament from the commencement of the war had levied in five years above forty millions. Hume does indeed add that these computations are probably much exaggerated. But whilst he gives this absurd and incredible statement on the authority of a writer whose authority he says is very considerable from his "being a zealous parliamentarian," and omits to mention that when Walker wrote he had been secluded and had become most bitterly exasperated against the Parliament, his remark is none the less just that the taxes and impositions were far

---

[1] Order Book of the Council of State, Die Lunæ, 19th November, 1649. On the same day it is ordered "That a commission be drawn up for Charles Vane, Esq. brother to Sir Henry Vane to be his deputy as he is treasurer to the navy and that it be brought in this afternoon." It is stated by Sikes the friend and biographer of Sir Henry Vane that having been appointed sole treasurer of the navy and considering the fees, amounting in time of war to little less than £20,000 a-year, as too much for a private subject, he gave up his patent which he had for life from King Charles to the Parliament desiring only that £1000 a year should go to his deputy and the remainder be applied to the use of the State.

[2] Order Book of the Council of State, Die Mercurii, 24 Octob. 1649.

[3] Chap. 59.

higher than in any former state of the English government. One of the worst consequences of this war was
the imposition of the excise, a grievous and oppressive
mode of taxation unknown to and contrary to the
principles of the English constitution. In a report to
the Parliament, contained in the Order Book of the
Council of State "concerning the moneys arising out of
the receipt of the grand excise," it appears by an abstract
of the accounts delivered to the Council of State by the
Commissioners of the Excise "that there hath been made
of the excise (salaries and other charges not deducted)
the three years last passed, beginning 29th Sept. 1646
unto 29th Sept. 1649 as follows :—

> " From Sept. 29, 1646 to Sept. 29, 1647 . . . £357,423 11 8
> Do.   1647 to   do.   1648 . . . 266,094 4 10
> Do.   1648 to   do.   1649 . . . 277,917 6 6" [1]

In the same report the amount of "custom and
subsidy" from 26th March 1649 to 8th October 1649
is £138,463 5s. $0\frac{1}{2}d$. Although it may be impossible
to obtain a completely accurate account of the money
raised by the Government about this time, it is evident
that the abstract given by Sir John Sinclair in his
history of the public revenue, who considers Walker's
account to be a great exaggeration, is much above the
truth, since, to take one item, the excise, which may
be considered as correctly stated above for three years,
he estimates the excise at £500,000 per annum [2] which
is almost double the amount set forth in the above
quoted official abstract. The Council of State appear
from various minutes in their Order Book to have been
themselves sufficiently aware of the extraordinary charges

[1] Order Book of the Council of
State, Die Martis, 23 Octob. 1649.
MS. State Paper Office.

[2] Sinclair's History of the Public
Revenue of the British Empire, vol. i.
p. 284.

of their government, charges which were in a great measure unavoidable by reason of the wars in which they were constantly engaged. In the afternoon of the same day in which the above abstract of the receipts of the excise was laid before them they made the following minute : " That an effectual letter be written by the Council to the Lord-Lieutenant of Ireland to let him know what charge we have been at, what preparation we have made for Ireland, and how our treasury is drawn : and to desire his special care and diligence to improve the revenue of Ireland for the carrying on of that service." [1] It was probably in reference to the letter written in accordance with this minute that Cromwell says, in one of his despatches from Ireland :—" Sir, I desire the charge of England as to this war may be abated as much as may be, and as we know you do desire out of your care to the commonwealth ; but if you expect your work to be done, indeed it will not be for the thrift of England, as far as England is concerned in the speedy reduction of Ireland, if the marching army be not constantly paid. The money we raise upon the counties maintains the garrison forces, and hardly that ; if the active force be not maintained, and all contingencies defrayed, how can we expect but to have a lingering business of it? Surely we desire not to spend a shilling of your treasury wherein our consciences do not prompt us. We serve you, we are willing to be out of our trade of war, and shall hasten (by God's assistance and grace) to the end of our work, as the labourer doth to be at his rest. This makes us bold to be earnest with you for necessary supplies, that of money is one ; and there be some other things which indeed I do not think for your

[1] Order Book of the Council of   MS. State Paper Office.
State, 23 Octob. 1649, à Meridie.

service to speak of publicly, which I shall humbly represent
to the Council of State, wherewith I desire we may be
accommodated." Cromwell then winds up after his fashion
with an exhortation "to fear the Lord, to fear unbelief and
self-seeking." Was this hypocrisy? Or did Cromwell
really believe that there was no self-seeking in him? Or,
being a clear-sighted man and knowing that it abounded in
him, did he sincerely pray to God to be delivered from it?
If he did, it would appear that his prayers as regarded that
particular were unheard or unheeded.

In the beginning of the month of January $16\frac{49}{50}$ an
estimate was brought in of the charge of fitting and setting
out a fleet of 44 men-of-war and 28 merchant ships,
manned with 8082 men,[1] to serve for eight months on the
narrow seas, as a summer's guard for the year 1650. The
House approved of this estimate, amounting to £886,220,
and ordered the commissions of their three admirals, Popham, Blake, and Deane, to be renewed for the whole year.
The names of all the ships intended for this summer's guard
are entered on the journals. Three of these ships being
styled the *Prince*, the *Charles*, and the *Mary*, the House
ordered that it be referred to the Council of State to give
other fit names to those ships.[2] If their care for constitutional liberty was open to many doubts, they were determined to extinguish all traces of the monarchy which they
had abolished.

The Parliament having received letters from General
Cromwell, lord-lieutenant of Ireland, from Major-General

---

[1] Some estimate may be formed of
the number of men in each of the
larger ships from a minute of the
Council of State which specifies "4 of
the great ships appointed by this Council to be set to sea manned with the
number of 1000 men."—*Order Book
of the Council of State*, 22 March,
164⅞. MS. State Paper Office. I
suppose this means 1000 men for the
4 great ships—250 men for each ship.

[2] Parl. Hist. vol. iii. p. 1344.

Ireton, and from Lord Broghill, dated at Cork, the 18th and 19th of December, passed a resolution on the 8th of January, that the said Lord-Lieutenant be desired to come over, and give his attendance in Parliament: and that the Council of State do prepare a letter to be read to him for that purpose, to be signed by the Speaker; and at the same time to render him the thanks of the House for his great service and faithfulness to the Commonwealth. On the same day a Bill, which had been some time depending, for settling certain lands upon Cromwell and his heirs, was reported to the House and ordered to be read a second time.[1] Cromwell's services may certainly be said to have been far greater than either Ireton's or Vane's. Nevertheless the contrast between his conduct and theirs in regard to the acceptance of Parliamentary grants cannot be overlooked. While Cromwell readily accepted votes of £6500[2] per annum in land, a handsome residence at Whitehall, the use of the palace at Hampton Court, and other provisions from the Parliament, Ireton absolutely refused the grant of £2000 per annum in land, and Vane voluntarily gave up in consideration of his country's necessities his very lucrative appointment of treasurer of the navy, and even refunded £2500, being the moiety of what he had received from the time the Parliament had made him sole treasurer.[3] Such

---

[1] Parl. Hist. vol. iii. p. 1345.

[2] This would make at that time one of the largest rentals in the possession of a subject. The Duke of Buckingham's rental, which was reckoned exorbitant, is stated by Pepys in 1669 to have been £19,600 a year. Pepys says "The Duke of Buckingham's condition is shortly this: that he hath about £19,600 a-year of which he pays away about £7000 a year in interest, about £2000 in fee farm-rents to the King, about £6000 in wages and

pensions, and the rest to live upon and pay taxes for the whole."—*Pepys' Diary*, Feb. 14, 1668-9. It may be mentioned as an example of the gross inaccuracy of satirists that Pope in a note on his lines on this Duke of Buckingham, erroneously describing him as dying "in the worst inn's worst room," describes him as "having been possessed of about £50,000 a year."

[3] Sikes, after saying that at the beginning of the war with Holland

is the effect always when "self in the highest" predominates. We see it in many forms. But it presents itself very prominently in the spectacle of what a politician, a lawyer, and sometimes but far more rarely a soldier will do that they may have money enough to support the dignity of a peerage.

On the 10th of January the House ordered their Attorney-General to prepare a patent to be passed under the great seal of England, appointing Major-General Ireton to be President of the province of Munster, he observing such instructions as should be given him by the Parliament, Council of State, or the Lord-Lieutenant of Ireland for the time being.[1]

On the 30th of January, upon the Lord Grey's report from the Council of State, that they had agreed that the style to be used in all transactions with foreign Powers should run thus, " Reipublicæ Anglicanæ Ordines," unless the Parliament thought fit to appoint any other; after debate it was resolved, " That in all negotiations and transactions with foreign States, the style or title to be used should be, ' Parliamentum Reipublicæ Angliæ : ' that the Lords Commissioners of the great seal be required to pass, under the great seal of England, several commissions in common form, *mutatis mutandis*, to the two agents ap-

---

Vane resigned his treasureship of the navy which during that Dutch war, would have amounted to near £20,000 a year, adds—"He had also long before this, upon the self-denying ordinance (little observed by others) refunded five and twenty hundred pounds, for public uses, being the moiety of his receptions in the said office, from such time as the Parliament had made him sole treasurer, who, before the war, was joined with another person."— *Life and Death of Sir Henry Vane,*

Knight, 1662. Ludlowe says he was very much blamed by his good friend Sir Henry Vane for preventing the sale of Hampton Court. Vane said "that such places might justly be accounted amongst those things that proved temptations to ambitious men, and exceedingly tend to sharpen their appetite to ascend the throne."—*Ludlowe's Memoirs,* p. 258, folio. London, 1751.

[1] Parl. Hist. vol. iii. p. 1345.

N

pointed by the Council of State, to be employed to Spain and Portugal: and that the style and title of every address to the Parliament from foreign princes and States shall be, 'The Parliament of the Commonwealth of England,' and no other style or title whatsoever." [1]

On the 31st of January the House received letters from the Lord-Lieutenant of Ireland, at Cork, advising that several garrisons in Munster had surrendered to the Parliament's forces without blood, or striking a strike; and that the army was in so good health that regiments which lately marched only 400 men, now marched 800 or 900; and that the horse were disposed of into garrisons. [2]

The time appointed for the continuance of the present Council of State expiring about the middle of February, $16\frac{49}{50}$, the House proceeded to the election of a new Council of State for the ensuing year. They first agreed that the number, as before, should not exceed 41. They next read over a list of the names of the present Council, and proceeded to put the question upon every single person; when they were all re-elected except the Earl of Mulgrave, the Lord Grey of Warke, and Sir John Danvers. Besides these three vacancies, however, there were two more caused by the deaths of the Earl of Pembroke and Alderman Rowland Wilson. There were thus five vacancies to be filled up. The filling up of these vacancies in the Council of State gave occasion to much debate and many divisions of the House. On such occasions the contest for place and power caused the number of members present to amount to more than double the number which met for the dispatch of ordinary business. On this occasion the number present was 98; and the following five persons were nominated of the Council of State for the year

---

[1] Parl. Hist. vol. iii. p. 1345. [2] Parl. Hist. vol. iii. p. 1345.

ensuing, Mr. Thomas Challoner, Mr. John Gurdon, Col. Herbert Morley, Sir Peter Wentworth, the Lord Howard. "The question being propounded that Sir Henry Vane, senior, be one of the Council of State for the year ensuing; and the question being put, ("the previous question"), that that question be now put;

"The House was divided.

"The Noes went forth.

"Colonel Ludlow ⎰Tellers for the Noes:⎱
"Colonel Martin ⎱With the Noes,⎰ 54

"Sir William Armyn, ⎰Tellers for the Yeas:⎱
"Sir John Trevor, ⎱With the Yeas, ⎰ 44

"So it passed with the negative." Philip the new Earl of Pembroke was rejected without a division.[1]

The Parliament, as before mentioned, having desired Cromwell to come over into England, made an order on the 25th of February, "That His Excellency have the use of the lodgings called the Cockpit, the Spring Garden, St. James's House, and the command of St. James's Park."

During the months of April and May the Parliament signalised themselves by legislation on which it will be necessary to make some observations. In April they passed an Act "For inflicting certain Penalties for breach of the Lord's Day and other Solemn Days." By this Act no person was to use or travel with boat, horse, coach, or sedan, except to church, upon pain of 10s. The like penalty was inflicted for being in a tavern, alehouse, &c. Where distress could not be found sufficient to satisfy the respective penalties, the offender was to sit in the stocks

[1] Commons' Journals, Die Mercurii, 20° Februarii, 16⁴⁹⁄₅₀. This division is given here partly to show to the general reader the meaning of what is called "THE PREVIOUS QUESTION," which is often misunderstood.

six hours.   In May an Act was passed for suppressing the detestable sins of incest, adultery, and fornication.   Of this Act the most material provisions were these : That all persons guilty of incest shall suffer death, without benefit of clergy ; that incestuous marriages shall be void, and the children illegitimate : that adultery shall also be deemed felony, and punished with death ; but this shall not extend to every man who, at the time of committing such offence, did not know the woman to be married ; nor to any woman whose husband shall be three years absent from her, so as she did not know him to be living.   In case of fornication, both parties, for the first offence, were to suffer three months' imprisonment without bail, and also give security for their good behaviour for one whole year after. Every common bawd, for the first offence, was to be openly whipped, set in the pillory, and there marked with a hot iron in the forehead ; also to be committed to the house of correction for three years without bail, and until sufficient security be given for good behaviour during life : and the persons a second time found guilty of the last recited offences were to suffer death. [1]

In addition to this, the Long Parliament put down all public amusements whatever.   There might undoubtedly be much that was objectionable in bear-baiting as well as in stage-plays ; but they did not consider sufficiently the necessary consequences of their purblind fanatical tyranny. And yet they might have reflected, from what they had themselves seen only some ten years before in the fate of Archbishop Laud's attempt to enforce conformity to his notions of religious doctrine and discipline, what was likely to be the ultimate fate of a similar attempt on their part.   In some points too their attempt was even more

[1] Scobell, 121.

dangerous than his. For if amusements are prohibited, vices are apt to take their place. Where the theatre is closed and all public amusements are put down, the tavern takes the place of the theatre, and cards and dice are substituted for stage-plays and farces.[1] I have no doubt that such consequences followed the legislation of the Long Parliament — I mean among the people during the period before the Restoration—for with regard to the irruption of profligacy that made its appearance at the Restoration in the Court circle, that I think had a remoter origin than the Puritan legislation of the Long Parliament; though that legislation may have undoubtedly had its effect in giving to it an added impulse.

Every one with the least experience of life must have known cases of some of the greatest reprobates having been those who were subjected in their youth to such discipline as formed the Puritan code. There is one case of this kind belonging to this time which has a curiously melancholy interest, and furnishes another illustration of the remark that truth is stranger than fiction.

There was a certain Presbyterian divine, by name Stephen Marshall, who was held in high repute among the leading men of the Long Parliament, and bore a prominent part in those long prayers, and still longer preachings, with which that Parliament diversified their secular business. When John Pym lay on his deathbed, Stephen Marshall attended him, and also preached the sermon at Pym's funeral, in which he gave a narrative of some of the

---

[1] When Prynne wrote his Histrio-mastix and condemned utterly the theatre as an amusement, he should have recollected that every man had not like himself an amusement that never failed in writing a sheet for every day of his life. Between the tyranny of the Stuarts and the tyranny of the Puritans it was rather a hard choice.

particulars of the great parliamentary leader's last moments, telling his audience, which included all the members of Parliament in London, with what "clear evidence of God's love in Jesus Christ and subjection to God's will" Pym met death ; and how he declared to him (Marshall) "that if he died he should go to that God whom he had served, and who would carry on his work by some others."[1]   Some twenty years after this time, when a strange change had come over the aspect of England since that day, we find some facts recorded by Pepys respecting two daughters of Stephen Marshall which were enough to make their father's bones move with horror in their grave. Pepys in his Diary frequently mentions as celebrated actresses of that evil time, when actress and courtesan were convertible terms, Anne Marshall and her younger sister Becke.[2]   Their career was probably the effect, so often observed, as to be called the natural effect, of religious exercises carried to an immoderate excess to the total exclusion of all even innocent amusements.   The result of such a course of discipline is intense disgust for the discipline itself, and a violent desire, amounting to a sort of insane passion, to rush into the very worst of all the long and sternly-forbidden pleasures.   This is an extreme, at least a remarkable case : since the daughters were as celebrated as actresses at a time when as Lord Macaulay has said, "the comic poet was the mouthpiece of the most deeply-corrupted part of a corrupted society," as the father had been as a

---

[1] Stephen Marshall's sermon preached before the Parliament at the funeral of Mr. Pym, 4to, 1644. This Stephen Marshall is the first of the five ministers (Stephen Marshall, Edmund Calamy, Thomas Young, Matthew Newcomen, William Spinstow) of whose names the first letters made the word *Smectymnuus,* celebrated in the controversies of those times.

[2] Under date Oct. 26th, 1667, Pepys says, "Mrs. Pierce tells me that the two Marshalls at the King's house are Stephen Marshall's the great Presbyterian's daughters."

Puritan divine and preacher.   But even the average result would be that the bending the bow so forcibly in the direction of the conventicle would be its rebounding as forcibly in the opposite direction.

It seems to be a law of human nature that all governments, unless when under strong pressure from without, should make a job of appointments, that is, should appoint persons to offices for other reasons than their fitness for such offices.   There is reason to think that even Oliver Cromwell, who knew better than most men the value of the right man in the right place, when the brunt of the war was over, in the disposal of any considerable officer's place, looked not so much at the man's valour as at his opinions.[1]   And the two greatest rulers that England ever had, Queen Elizabeth and Oliver Cromwell, in the selection of a successor, showed no more discrimination and foresight than the feeblest and most short-sighted of the sons or daughters of Adam. Elizabeth had an intelligent agent at the Court of James in Scotland who kept her well informed, as his despatches prove, of what passed there, and she must have known what manner of man she was imposing as a king upon England.   Yet such was her prejudice in favour of kings that she considered all men not born kings as "rascals" in her phraseology, and declared that "no rascal" but the thing which at that time in Scotland " the semblance of a kingly crown had on " should be her successor on the throne of England.   And Oliver Cromwell, although he knew that he with all his capacity and valour could hardly keep his seat, so far forgot, we may say, all his former self as to imagine that his son Richard could succeed him.   It took a struggle of near a hundred years' duration to repair the mistake of Elizabeth, for it was supported by a gigantic

---

[1] Richard Baxter's Life by Himself.   Part I. p. 57, folio.   London, 1696.

array of blind and barbarous prejudices that carried with them the force of an old religion. Oliver's mistake as far as it regarded the choice of his son Richard was repaired in almost as many hours, but as it regarded wider interests than those of the family of Cromwell, it left consequences lasting and disastrous, and will remain to all time one of the most remarkable "follies of the wise."

Though the stringent legislation of the Long Parliament against immorality and against stage-plays and other amusements had undoubtedly the effect which attends all such legislation, the deeply-corrupted state of society which prevailed after the Restoration in England cannot be justly viewed as altogether due to that legislation, but must be considered not as an innovation, as has been usually supposed, but only as a restoration. The great puritan rebellion had a twofold character. It was an insurrection against tyranny and it was also an insurrection against vice—vice in the revolting and infamous shape it had assumed at the Court of James the First. It was this latter feature of the insurrection which gave to it so much of the character of interfering with matters beyond its reach, of attempting to make men saints by Act of Parliament, instead of being content to confine its authority to the legitimate object of protecting religion and public morals from insult. As it was, when the Royalists returned to power, a Court more resembling that of James the First than that of Charles the First returned with them. Although the personal character of Charles II. differed very much from the personal character of James I., contemporary writers describe the character of the Court of Charles in language very similar to that applied by contemporaries to the Court of James. In one place Pepys writes " Mr.

Povey says 'of all places, if there be hell, it is here, [at Court].' " [1] And again under date July 27th, 1667. "He [Fenn] tells me that the king and Court were never in the world so bad as they are now for gaming, swearing, women, and drinking, and the most abominable vices that ever were in the world." [2] This was not a new deluge of vice, the creation of the Puritan legislation. It was the fiend returned to his abode with all his evil passions and appetites only strengthened by his temporary expulsion, during which he had wandered through dry places seeking rest and finding none.

During the winter Cromwell received considerable reinforcements from England. On the 19th of October, the "report of the recruits of foot for Ireland" having been brought in to the Council of State, it was ordered "That the 5000 recruits be divided into 5 regiments. That for the raising and conducting of each of the said regiments to the waterside and so into Ireland there be appointed by the Lord-General out of the several regiments of the army 1 major, 4 captains, 5 lieutenants, 20 sergeants, 10 drums. That as soon as the said men are landed in Ireland, they are to be taken into the several regiments there, and receive pay as other the soldiers there. That the ports where they are to ship the said men be Appledore and Minehead for the west, Milford Haven for South Wales and counties adjacent; Liverpool and Chester for those that shall march from London and so northward, and Anglesey for North Wales. That the Council give order that moneys be sent down to the several ports, to be there delivered to the several treasurers for the payment of quarters and providing of

---

[1] Pepys's Diary, vol. i. p. 436. 1st 4to edition, 1825.

[1] Pepys's Diary, vol. ii. p. 99.

shipping and victuals for transportation as aforesaid, viz. To

" Appledore " Minehead	. . . .	£1330
" Milford	. . . .	£570
" Chester " Liverpool " Anglesey	. . . .	£2850
Total		£4750 " [1]

It appears from the minutes cited below that the Council of State granted blank commissions for the officers who were to conduct the recruits over to Ireland, and that the Lord-General had the power of filling up the names of the blank commissions granted by the Council of State.[2] The following minute further shows the care of the Council of State formerly noted to guard against oppression in the way of soldiers' quarters. " In respect of the season of the year and the former sufferings of the country by soldiers, that there be an allowance of 8d. per diem [instead of 6d. per diem] to pay their quarters." [3] Colonel Pride was appointed to command the recruits in chief. [4] On the

[1] Order Book of the Council of State, 19 and 25 October, 1649. MS. State Paper Office.

[2] " That the charge of transportation of the 5000 recruits for Ireland shall be borne out of the deans and chapters' lands—and that my Lord General be desired to give out commissions."— Ibid. 19 October, 1649. — " That blank commissions for the officers that are to conduct the recruits now to be sent over to Ireland be granted by the Council of State." — Ibid. 20 October, 1649. Another minute of the same date shows the principle of paying officers adopted by the Council —" That the Scout - Master - General shall have £4 per diem when there is any action in the field as he hath had hitherto. But for that there is no action at present [i. e. in England] that he shall have 20s. a day during the time there is no action in the field." Ibid. 20 October, 1649.

[3] Order Book of the Council of State, 23 October, 1649, à Meridie.

[4] Order Book of the Council of State, 23 October, 1649. Further by a minute of the 25th of the same month it was ordered " That £200 be im-

3rd of November a warrant was issued to Charles Walley, Esq., treasurer for the paying of quarters at Chester, to impress all ships belonging to or coming into any of the ports of Lancashire, Cheshire and North Wales for this service.[1]

Besides the 5000 foot, a reinforcement of horse was also sent to Ireland. On the 15th of November it was ordered " That the Report brought in by the committee for the affairs of Ireland be approved of, viz.

"That it be reported to the Council in order to the sending of recruits of horse into Ireland out of every troop of the several regiments following, viz.

" The Lord General's regiment of horse.

" Major-General Lambert's regiment of horse

" Col. Whalley's	do.	do.
" Col. Fleetwood's	do.	do.
" Col. Rich's	do.	do.
" Col. Tomlinson's	do.	do.
" Col. Twisleton's	do.	do.
" Col. Robert Lilburne's	do.	do.
" Col. Desbrow's	do.	do.
" Col. Sanders'	do.	do.

prested to Colonel Pride toward the conduct of the soldiers to the water-side. That sergeants shall have 12d. per diem in place of 9d. and that drums shall have 9d. in place of 6d." On the same day it was ordered " That Mr. Frost do write unto Mr. Parker secretary to the army in Ireland to take care that a constant knowledge may be given to the Council of State of all matter of fact which passeth in Ireland."—*Order Book of the Council of State*, 25° Octobris, 1649. On the following day there is an order " To write to Mr. Walley to dispatch away the foot of Colonel Moore and Colonel Fenwicke with all expedition to Belfast if he can and with them so many musquets as he can in regard there are no arms there—but if it cannot be done thither or that you cannot arm them, then let them be sent to Carling-ford, to which place if they go, there will be no need of the said arms. We leave it to you there to do it in such manner as you conceive may be best for the service, but to send them away with all expedition."—*Order Book of the Council of State*, 26° Octob. 1640.

[1] Order Book of the Council of State, 3° Novemb. 1649. MS. State Paper Office.

" 1. That there be 20 troopers reduced out of every troop of the said several regiments.

" 2. That the said horsemen so to be reduced be taken on for recruits to go into Ireland, or so many of them as are willing to go.

" 3. That, instead of such of the said recruits of horse as shall refuse to go recruits as aforesaid, the officer or officers to be appointed to take the charge of marching them to the waterside and so into Ireland may have power to entertain any other well-affected person or persons that shall, well furnished with horse and arms, be willing to go until the number be completed.

" 4. That a captain, lieutenant, quartermaster, three corporals, and two trumpets be chosen by the colonel of every regiment to take the charge." [1]

Further directions are added that the colonels take especial care that the men save their pay to discharge their quarters till they be shipt. Wexford is appointed as the port where they are to land in Ireland. Letters are also ordered to be written to Colonel Blake and Colonel Deane to provide convoys at the several ports and to assist the treasurer for paying quarters at those ports to press and provide shipping.

On the 16th of November there is a minute " That the committee for the affairs of Ireland do take care to advance £20 to a messenger who is to be sent over into Ireland express to the Lord-Lieutenant according to what Mr. Scot hath moved in that behalf." [2] Mr. Scot, whom John Lilburne called their Secretary of State, was a very active member of the Council of State, and among other business committed to him had the charge of the secret service.

[1] Order Book of the Council of State, 15° Novemb. 1649. MS. State Paper Office.

[2] Order Book of the Council of State, 16° Novemb. 1649. MS. State Paper Office.

Cromwell having allowed his troops to remain in winter quarters about two months, again took the field early in February.   He made himself master of Kilkenny and Clonmel, and many other places of less importance.   At Clonmel he met with a vigorous resistance.   "We found in Clonmel," says one of his officers, "the stoutest enemy that our army has encountered in Ireland."   Thus Cromwell had reduced the greater part of Ireland to sub-jection in the space of about ten months, from the middle of August 1649 till May 1650, "a time inconsiderable" says a contemporary writer,[1] "respect had to the work done therein, which was more than ever could be done in ten years before by any king or queen of England.   Queen Elizabeth, indeed, after a long and tedious war there, at last drove out the Spaniards that came in to the assistance of the rebellious natives, but could never utterly extin-guish the sparks of that rebellion."   When Cromwell was recalled from Ireland, there remained only Limerick, Water-ford, and some few inconsiderable garrisons to be reduced. This business was left to the charge of Ireton, who was appointed Cromwell's successor in Ireland with the title of Lord Deputy, and performed the work assigned to him with great ability and success.

There is an anecdote preserved by tradition respecting a certain bridge in a remote part of Ireland which gives a very vivid idea of the impression which Cromwell left behind him in Ireland—an impression not dissimilar to that he made on the boy Bill Spitfire in Woodstock, who described his face as "a face one would not like to say No to."   Cromwell seeing the importance of a bridge at the particular point to which the story refers, and knowing something of the habits of the people of the neighbour-

[1] Perfect Politician.

knew," says the story, " that the ould villain
of his word, and so they took care to have
built by the time he came back."

CHAPTER IV.

ON Thursday the 25th of October 1649, John Lilburne was brought to trial at Guildhall before the extraordinary tribunal specially appointed for his destruction. The trial lasted two days. But the first day was entirely consumed in preliminary discussion between the prisoner and the judges, and the jury were not sworn till the second day. At the opening of the Court on the first day the Lieutenant of the Tower of London brought up the prisoner, who was guarded by a special guard of soldiers. When he was brought to the bar, the sheriffs of London were directed to take him into custody. Lilburne being ordered to hold up his hand, turned to Keble, one of the commissioners of the Great Seal, and President of the Court, and made a long speech, in the course of which he introduced some passages of his life that have a public interest.

" I have several times," he said " been arraigned for my life already. I was once arraigned before the House of Peers for sticking close to the liberties and privileges of the nation, and those that stood for them, being one of those two or three men, that first drew their swords in Westminster Hall against Col. Lunsford and some scores of his associates. At that time it was supposed they intended to cut the throats of the chiefest men then sitting in the House of Commons." On that occasion, he said, when arraigned before the House of Peers he had free liberty of speech.

Again, he said, with reference to the affair at Brentford when he as yet only served as a volunteer, "we were but about 700 men at Brentford, that withstood the king's whole army in the field above five hours together, and fought it out to the very sword's point, and to the butt-end of the musket; and thereby hindered the king from then possessing the Parliament's train of artillery, and by consequence the City of London, in which very act I was taken a prisoner, without articles or capitulation, and was by the king and his party then looked upon as one of the activest men against them in the whole company, yet, said Lord Chief Justice Heath" (at his trial at Oxford for levying war against the king) "we will not take advantage of that to try you by the rules of arbitrary martial laws, or any other arbitrary ways; but we will try you by the rules of the good old laws of England : and whatsoever privilege in your trial the laws of England will afford you, claim it as your birthright and inheritance, and you shall enjoy it with as much freedom and willingness, as if you were in Westminster Hall, to be tried amongst your own party. . . . . And accordingly he gave me liberty to plead to the errors of my indictment, before I ever pleaded Not Guilty ; yea and also became willing to assign me what counsel I pleased to nominate, freely to come to prison to me, and to consult and advise with me, and help me in point of law. This last he did immediately upon my pleading to the indictment before any fact was proved : all which is consonant to the declared judgment of Sir Edward Coke, that great oracle of the laws of England, whose books are published for good law by special orders of Parliament, dated May 12, 1641, and June 3, 1642."[1]

[1] State Trials, vol. iv. pp. 1271, 1272, 1273.

Lilburne then went on to say—"By the laws of this land all courts of justice always ought to be free and open for all sorts of peaceable people to see and hear and have free access unto; and no man whatsoever ought to be tried in holes or corners, or in any place, where the gates are shut and barred, and guarded with armed men: and yet, sir, as I came in, I found the gates shut and guarded, which is contrary both to law and justice."

"Judge *Keble*.   Mr. Lilburne, look behind you, and see whether the door stands open or no."

"Lt.-Col. *Lilburne*.   Well then, sir, I am satisfied as to that."

The prisoner then entered into a long argument against the legality of a special commission of Oyer and Terminer, and also of the constitution of the Court before which he was now brought for trial.   He also attempted to show the inconsistency of the present proceedings of some members of the present Government with their former proceedings, thus.   "I say and aver, 1 ought to have had the process of the law of England, due process of law according to the fore-mentioned statutes and precedents; for I never forcibly resisted or contended with the Parliament; and therefore ought to have had my warrant served upon me by a constable, or the like civil officer; and upon no pretence whatsoever, ought I to have been forced out of my bed and house by mercenary armed officers and soldiers. But, sir, coming to Whitehall, I was there also kept by armed men, contrary to all law and justice; and by armed men against law, I was by force carried before a company of gentlemen sitting at Derby House, that looked upon themselves as authorized by the Parliament to be a committee or Council of State, (who by the law I am sure in any kind had nothing at all to do with me in cases of pretended treasons) where I was brought before Mr. John Bradshaw, sometime a counsellor for myself before the House of Lords, against my unjust Star-Chamber judges; who there in my behalf, Feb. 1645, did urge against the lords of the Star-Chamber, as the highest crimes against the liberties of the people that could be, as being illegal, arbitrary and tyrannical, that the lords in Star-Chamber should censure me to be whipped, pilloryed, &c., for no other cause but for refusing to answer their interrogatories against myself. And when I was brought before the said Council of State I saw no accuser, no prosecutor, no accusation, no charge nor indictment; but all the crime that there was laid unto my charge was Mr. Bradshaw's very seriously examining me to questions against myself: although I am confident he could not forget, that himself and Mr. John Cook were my counsellors in February 1645, at the bar of the House of Lords, where he did most vehemently aggravate, and with detestations condemn the lords of the Star-Chamber's unjust and wicked dealing with English freemen, in censuring them for their refusing to answer to questions concerning themselves; and yet notwithstanding walked with his dealing with me in the very steps that formerly he had bitterly condemned in the Star-Chamber lords." [1]

Here Judge Jermin interrupted him, saying—"Mr. Lilburne, you very well know Mr. Bradshaw is now denominated by another name, namely, Lord President to the Council of State of England; and it would well become you in your condition so to have styled him." But Lilburne without taking any notice of this went on to say —"By their power and will I had my pockets and

<hr>

[1] State Trials, vol. iv. pp. 1279, 1280.

chamber[1] searched to find out advantages against me; and was also locked up close prisoner, with centinels night and day set at my door, and denied the access and sight of my wife and children for some certain time; and for about twenty weeks together in the heat of summer kept close prisoner, and denied the liberty of the prison, and my estate with a strong hand taken away from me, without any pretence, or due process of law, to the value of almost £3000, that was legally and justly vested in me, and in my possession. But being I will avoid (at this time especially) provocations as much as I can, I will name no person by whose power and will it hath been done, although he be notoriously known;[2] but the gentleman that took it away by his pleasure, without all rules of law or justice, told my father to this purpose, That I was a traitor, and under the Parliament's displeasure: and therefore he would secure it from me, although I were not in the least convicted of any crime, neither in law then, or for many months after had I the least pretence of crime laid unto

[1] "That a warrant be issued to the serjeant at arms to search Lt.-Col. Lilburne, Mr. Walwin, Mr. Overton, and Mr. Prince, their chambers, closets, trunks, boxes, and other places to them belonging, for all treasonable, seditious, and scandalous books, papers, and other writings and seal them up and bring them to this Council."—*Order Book of the Council of State*, 4th July, 1649. MS. State Paper Office. This is exactly what when done by Charles I. led to the civil war.

[2] The individual here alluded to was Sir Arthur Haselrig. The statement in "The Mystery of the Good Old Cause" charges Haselrig with great rapacity in the neighbourhood of Newcastle, of which town he was governor under the Rump; and this lends a colour to the charge made against him by Lilburne, whose property was in that part of England. Keble the president of the Court in reference to this charge, said "If there be anything that hath been done by others in the north, there is no man here that will justify them in their evil."—*State Trials*, vol. iv. p. 1285. Now if Lilburne's charge against Haselrig had been notoriously the creature of his own busy brain, the judge would not have referred to it in such terms. M. Guizot in his Essay on Monk describes Haselrig as "a rapacious, headstrong, and conceited agitator." He had more, however, of the wisdom of the serpent than poor John Lilburne, whose unresting agitation was productive of much notoriety but little profit to himself.

my charge.   And although my own estate by force, against law, was taken from me, yet was I also denied in my close imprisonment that legal allowance that should have kept me alive ; for in all this miserable condition I never yet received a penny of my legal allowance." [1]

By way of answer to Lilburne's objections to the commission, Judge Jermin said : " For the commission itself, it is in general for the trial of all treasons whatsoever.   But the grand inquest have found out no other traitor, that they may accuse, but Master John Lilburne, who is now here at the bar.   But it is not a bare accusation, but it is the solemn verdict of almost a double jury that hath appeared upon the roll ; and upon their oaths do conceive those crimes of treason that are laid against you, to be of so dangerous consequence against the State and Commonwealth, that they do call for justice against you as a traitor already found guilty.   And therefore I do require you, as you are an Englishman, and a rational man, that you do conform yourself and tell us plainly what you will do, as in reference to your putting yourself upon your trial by the law, and hear with patience those offences of treason that are laid to your charge." [2]

But Lilburne fought every point.   He had desired to hear the commission by which the court was instituted read.   " But," he said, " you have positively denied me that.   And therefore I desire all my friends, and all the people that hear me this day, to bear witness, and take notice, that you, contrary to reason and common equity, denied me to let me hear read your commission, by virtue of which you go about to take away my life ; which I cannot choose but desire them to take notice, I declare to

[1] State Trials, vol. iv. pp. 1280,   [2] State Trials, vol. iv. p. 1287.
1281.

be very hard measure.—But, sir, to save myself from your forelaid snares and desired advantage against me, I will come a little closer to the business. You demand I should hold up my hand at the bar ; and I know not what it means, neither what in law it signifies. It is true, I have read the most part of the laws that are in English, which I take to be the foundation of all our legal English privileges ; and in them I cannot find anything that doth clearly declare unto me the full signification or meaning of a man's holding up his hand at the bar. . . . . .
In which regard, for me to hold up my hand at the bar before I understand the true signification of it in law, (which tells me it is in itself a ticklish thing), were for me to throw away my own life upon a punctilio or nicety that I am ignorant of ; and therefore truly I think I should be a very fool, in my own ignorance, to run that danger. And therefore, sir, I humbly desire the clear explanation of the meaning of it in law, and after that I shall give you a fair and rational answer.

"Lord *Keble*. Mr. Lilburne, you shall see we will deal very rationally with you, and not ensnare you in the least manner, if that be all. The holding up of your hand, we will tell you what it means and signifies [1] in law. The calling the party to hold up his hand at the bar is no more but for the special notice that the party is the man enquired for, or called on ; and therefore if you be Mr. John Lilburne, and be the man that we charge, do but say that you are the man, and that you are there, and it shall suffice.

"*Lilburne*. Well then, sir, according to your own

---

[1] The Judge and Lilburne both use two words of equivalent meaning—"means and signifies"—which, like "love and affection," so much used in English deeds, may perhaps be ascribed to the same cause, the notion that it was proper, if not necessary, to have a word of Saxon and a word of Latin origin to express the same idea.

explanation, I say my name is John Lilburne, son to Mr. Richard Lilburne of the county of Durham, a freeman of the city of London, and sometime lieutenant-colonel in the Parliament's army : and if you will not believe that I am the man, my guardian the Lieutenant of the Tower there (pointing to him) will aver that I am.

" Lord *Keble.*   So then you are the man.

" Judge *Jermin.*   Ask him again : Hearken, Mr. Lilburne, hearken what he says, and use that moderation, and temper, and discretion that you have promised.

"*Lilburne.*   One word more, and I shall have done ; and that is by the law of England—" [But being interrupted he cried out] " With your favour, sir, I will come to the main thing ; I hope you do not go about to circumvent me, therefore hear me, I beseech you.

" Lord *Keble.*   Hear the Court, Mr. Lilburne, there shall be nothing of circumvention or interruption : but as you have professed to be a rational and understanding man in words, let your deeds so declare you.

" *Lilburne.*   Sir, I beseech you, do not surprise me with punctilios or niceties, which are hard things for me to lose my life upon.   I tell you again, my name is John Lilburne, son to Mr. Richard Lilburne.

" Lord *Keble.*   Talk not of punctilios with us, nor talk not of judges made by the laws ; you shall not want law : but if you talk of punctilios here in this room, we will stop that language.

" *Lilburne.*   Truly, sir, I am upon my life, and shall my ignorance of the formalities of the law, in the practic[1] part thereof, destroy me ? God forbid !   Therefore give me but leave to speak for my life, or else knock me on the head, and murder me where I stand ; which is more

[1] Practic or practick, the old word for practical.

righteous and just than to do it by pretence of justice. Sir, I know that Mr. Bradshaw himself, President of the, High Court of Justice, as it was called, gave Duke Hamilton (a hostile enemy) leave to speak to the punctilios of the law ; yea, and to my knowledge, again and again made an engagement unto him, and the rest tried with him, that the Court nor he would not, by virtue of their ignorance of the niceties or formalities of the law, take advantage against them, to destroy them ; but did declare, again and again, that all advantages of formalities should be totally laid aside, and not in the least made use of against them to their prejudice. And I hope you will grant me, that have often been in arms for you, but never against you, as much favour and privilege as was granted to Duke Hamilton, never of your party, but a general of a numerous army against you.

"Lord *Keble*. Take it as you will, we have had patience with you, and you must and shall have patience with us. We will pass over all that is by-past, but take heed, by your surly crossness, you give not advantage in the face of the Court, to pass sentence against you, without any further proceedings, or proof of your actions, but what our own eyes see. The ceremony is for your advantage more than you are aware of; but if you confess yourself to be Mr. John Lilburne, we have done as to that." [1]

The President then ordered the Indictment to be read. Mr. Broughton the clerk of the Court who had been one of the two clerks of the Court at the trial of King Charles, and had, as we have seen, been specially appointed for this trial of Lilburne by an order of the Council of State, having read the indictment, put the question : " What say'st thou, John Lilburne, art thou guilty of this

---

[1] State Trials, vol. iv. pp. 1288–1292.

treason whereof thou standest indicted, or not guilty? Here a new struggle ensued between the Court and the unconquerable Lilburne, who instead of answering " Guilty " or " Not Guilty," as the Court required, asked to be allowed counsel, a copy of the indictment, or so much of it as he might ground his plea upon, and reasonable time to consult with his counsel, although it were but eight or nine days.[1]

---

[1] It is remarkable how often in the course of this trial Lilburne showed a more accurate knowledge of the law than the Court and the law officers. The following is one example of this.

" Judge *Thorp*. Mr. Lilburne, I desire to correct a mistake of yours in the law : You are pleased to condemn it as unjust, for the Attorney-General's speaking with me when your indictment was a reading ; you are to know, he is the prosecutor for the State here against you, and he must confer with us upon several occasions, and we with him, and this is law.

" *Lilburne*. Not upon the bench, sir, by your favour, unless it be openly, audibly, and avowedly, and not in any clandestine or whispering way : And by your favour, for all you are a judge, this is law, or else Sir Edward Coke in his 3rd Institute, cap. High Treason, hath published falsehoods, and the Parliament hath licensed them ; for their stamp in a special manner is to that book.

" Judge *Thorp*. Sir Edward Coke is law, and he says, the Attorney-General, or any other prosecutor may speak with us in open Court, to inform us about the business before us in open Court.

" *Lilburne*. Not in hugger-mugger, privately or whisperingly.

" Judge *Thorp*. I tell you, sir, the Attorney-General may talk with any in the Court, by law, as he did with me.

" *Lilburne*. I tell you, sir, it is unjust, and not warrantable by law, for him to talk with the Court, or any of the judges thereof, in my absence, or in hugger-mugger, or by private whisperings.

" Lord *Keble*. No, sir ; it is no hugger-mugger for him to do as he did ; spare your words, and burst not out into passion ; for thereby you will declare yourself to be within the compass of your indictment without any proof."—*State Trials*, vol. iv. p. 1301. The reader may easily judge whether the Court or the prisoner declared the law accurately by reading the few words that follow. Coke, 3rd Inst. fol. 30, says :—" Hereupon it followeth that if the peers of the realm, who are intended to be indifferent, can have no conference with the judges or with the high steward in open Court in the absence of the prisoner : *à fortiori* the king's learned counsel should not in the absence of the party accused, upon any case put, or matter showed by them, privately preoccupate the opinion of the judges." Any doubt as to the meaning of the words " in the absence of the party accused " is removed by the words used by Coke in another place (2nd Instit. fol. 49)— " After the lords be gone together to consider of the evidence, they cannot send to the high steward or ask the judges any question of law, but in the hearing of the prisoner."

" *Lilburne.* Under favour thus, for you to come to ensnare and entrap me with unknown niceties and formalities that are locked up in the French and Latin tongue, and cannot be read in English books, they being not expressed in any law of the kingdom, published in our own English tongue ; it is not fair play according to the law of England, plainly in English expressed in the Petition of Right, and other the good old statute laws of the land. Therefore I again humbly desire to have counsel assigned to me, to consult with, what these formalities in law signify ; so that I may not throw away my life ignorantly upon forms.

" Lord *Keble.* You shall have that which is according to the law; therefore, Mr. Lilburne, I advise you to plead, and you shall have fair play, and no advantage taken against you by your ignorance of the formality of the law.

" *Lilburne.* Well then, sir, upon that engagement, and because I see you are so positive in the thing— this is my answer : That I am not guilty of any of the treasons in manner and form, as they are there laid down in that Indictment " (pointing to it). " And therefore now, sir, having pleaded, I crave the liberty of England, that you will assign me counsel.

" Mr. *Broughton.* By whom wilt thou be tried ?

" *Lilburne.* By the known laws of England, and a legal jury of my equals, constituted according to law.

" Mr. *Broughton.* 'By whom wilt thou be tried ?

" *Lilburne.* By the known laws of England, I mean, by the liberties and privileges of the laws of England, and a jury of my equals legally chosen. And now, sir, I again desire counsel to be assigned me, to consult with in point of law, that so I may not destroy myself through my ig-

norance.   This is but the same privilege that was granted
at Oxford unto me, and the rest of my fellow-prisoners
arraigned with me.

"*One of the Clerks.*   You must say, by God and your
country ; that's the form of the law.

"*Lilburne.*   Why must I say so ?

Judge Jermin then explained to him the meaning of the
form of words—"by God and your country "—by God as
God is everywhere present ; by your country, that is by
your country or neighbourhood, by a jury of the neighbourhood.

"*Lilburne.*   Sir, under your favour thus ; then in the
negative I say God is not locally or corporally here present
to try me, or pass upon me ; but affirmative, I return this
answer, That I desire to be tried in the presence of that
God, that by his omnipotent power is present everywhere,
and beholds all the actions that are done upon the earth,
and sees and knows whether any of your hearts be possessed with a premeditated malice against me, or whether
any of you come with so much forethought of malice
against me, as that in your hearts you intend to do the
utmost you can, right or wrong, to destroy me : and before
this all-seeing God I desire to be tried, and by my
country, that is to say, by a jury of my equals, according
to the good old laws of the land.

"Justice *Thorp.*   You have spoken very well.

"Lord *Keble.*   You have done like an Englishman so
far as you have gone ; and I do assure you, that in any
formalities (as you express or call them) there shall be no
advantage against you, if you mistake in them.   Now
what you have the next to think upon, is your jury of
your countrymen or neighbours of your equals ; and

I promise you, we will take care of that, that they shall
be good and lawful men of England."[1]

But here Lilburne entered into another contest with the
Court as to the matter of counsel.   There is great force in
some of his remarks, a force which proves that modern
writers have underrated his abilities, which are very conspicuous on this trial, where he fought singly and without
a legal education against so many professional lawyers and
judges.   He showed the glaring inconsistency of a body of
men who pretended to be the instruments of introducing a
new era of liberty and happiness and of abolishing the old
servitude and misery, and nevertheless not only maintained
when it suited them the most unjust of the old laws of
treason, but created new treasons before unheard of.   " I
know very well," said he, "and I read it in your own
law-books, such a prerogative, as that in cases of treason
no counsel shall plead against the king, hath been sometimes challenged to be the king's right by law ; but, let
me tell you, it was an usurped prerogative of the late
king,[2] with all other arbitrary prerogatives and unjust
usurpations upon the people's rights and freedoms, which
has been pretended to be taken away with him.   And, sir,
can it be just to allow me counsel to help me to plead for

---

[1] State Trials, pp. 1292–1295.

[2] It was not correct to say that this
particular prerogative was an innovation of the late king, since it was a
rule at common law that no counsel
should be allowed a prisoner on his
trial for any capital crime, unless
some point of law should arise—" a
rule " says Blackstone, " which seems
to be not at all of a piece with the
rest of the humane treatment of prisoners by the English law."—4 *Com.*
355. But Lilburne's conclusion was
quite correct for, whether this par-

ticular tyranny originated with Charles
the First or not, it was a strange spectacle to see it exercised by those who
styled themselves " custodes libertatis
Angliæ " and who ordered the king's
statues to be taken down and the
words " Exit Tyrannus Regum ultimus,
Anno Libertatis Angliæ restitutæ
primo—Anno Domini 1648 (9). Jan.
30 " to be inscribed on the places
where they stood.   The " last of the
kings," however, was evidently not the
last of the tyrants.

my estate, the lesser ; and to deny me the help of counsel to enable me to plead for my life, the greater ?[1] Nay, sir, can it be just in you judges, to take up seven years' time in ending some suits of law for a little money or land, and deny me a few days to consider what to plead for my life ? Sir, all these pretences of yours were but all the prerogatives of the king's will, to destroy the poor ignorant and harmless people by, which undoubtedly died with him ; or else only the name or title is gone with him, but not the power or hurtful tyranny or prerogative in the least. Therefore seeing all such pretended and hurtful prerogatives are pretended to be taken away with the king, by those that took away his life, I earnestly desire I may be assigned counsel to consult with, knowing more especially no pretence why I should be denied that benefit and privilege of the law, of the just and equitable law of England, having put myself upon a trial according to the privileges thereof."[2]

Lilburne further insisted on the fact that when he appeared at the bar at Oxford and pleaded " Not Guilty " to his indictment and made exceptions against his indictment, he and the two other gentlemen arraigned with him had counsel assigned them and a week's time to consider with their counsel what to plead for their lives. But the Court would not admit that what was done at Oxford was a precedent for them, declaring that they knew at Oxford that it was no treason and also knew that whatsoever was done to any of those fighting for Parliament, the like would be

[1] No one who reads this trial carefully can speak slightingly of Lilburne's capacity. About a century later Blackstone uses in his Commentaries an argument precisely analogous to Lilburne's. Blackstone says— " For upon what face of reason can that assistance be denied to save the life of a man, which yet is allowed him in prosecutions for every petty trespass ?" —4 *Com.* 355.

[2] State Trials, vol. iv. pp. 1301, 1302.

done to those fighting for the king and therefore gave them
more privileges than were their right by law. This opinion
of the Court is partly supported by Lilburne's own account
of the use he made of the week's time allowed him to consult with counsel. " In which time," he said " being freed
of my irons, and of my close imprisonment, and enjoying
pen, ink, and paper at my pleasure, by special order from the
other two gentlemen, I writ a letter to my wife, and in it
inclosed another to your Speaker, and another to young Sir
Henry Vane, then my familiar acquaintance ; all which I sent
in post-haste away to my wife by the hands of Captain
Primrose's wife, which Captain Primrose was prisoner there ;
and his wife, who brought up the letter to my wife, is now
in London. Which letter my wife delivered to the Speaker,
&c. and by her importunate solicitation procured the declaration of Lex Talionis ; the substance of which, in a letter
from Mr. Speaker, my wife brought down to Oxford, and
delivered to the Lord Heath's own hands upon the Sunday after the first day of our arraignment. And the
third day before we were to appear again, my wife arrived
at Oxford with the Speaker's letter, which she delivered to
Judge Heath himself ; which letter taking notice of our
trial, threatened them with Lex Talionis, to do the like to
their prisoners that they did to us, or any of us. And
they having many of their great eminent men prisoners in
the Tower and in Warwick Castle, and other places, did
induce them to stop all further prosecution of Colonel
Vivers, Captain Catesby, and myself. And if it had not
been for this threatening letter, in all likelihood we had
all three been condemned by a commission of Oyer and
Terminer, and executed : for my wife did hear Judge
Heath say to some of his associates, at the reading of the
letter, that as for all the threatening part of it, as to his

particular self, 'I value it not ; but' said he, 'we must be
tender of the lives of the lords and gentlemen that serve
the king, and are in the custody of those at Westminster.'
And that clause of Lex Talionis put a stop to our proceedings, and further trials at law."[1]

Lilburne then desired that his solicitor might speak
two or three words for him.   But Mr. Sprat, his solicitor,
beginning to speak, was stopped by the Court, Judge Jermin exclaiming " What impudent fellow is that, that dare
be so bold as to speak in the Court without being called ? "
and proceeded to say that the Court would allow him
counsel, " if matter of law, upon the proof of the fact,
do arise : but for any other counsel to be assigned you
before that appear, is not by law warranted : we shall
tread the rules of justice."

" Lord *Keble.*   And this, Mr. Lilburne, I will promise
you, that when there comes matter in law, let it be a
lawyer, or yourself, he shall speak in your behalf; but
before he cannot.

" *Lilburne.*   Sir, the whole indictment, under favour, is
matter of law ; and the great question that will arise
(admit the fact should be true, and admit it should be
granted) is, Whether the words be treason in law, yea or
no ?   And also it is matter of law in the indictment,
whether the matter in the indictment be rightly alledged
as to matter, time, and place.   And it is matter of law in
the indictment, where there are divers several pretended
treasons committed in divers and several counties, put into
one and the same indictment, whether that be legal, yea or
no ?

" Lord *Keble.* Upon proof of the matter of fact, you shall
hear and know whether matter of law will arise ; and till

[1] State Trials, vol. iv. p. 1304.

the words be proved, we cannot say whether that be the law that you suppose.

"*Lilburne.* Truly, sir, you promised me a fair trial, and that you would not take advantages of my ignorance in the law's formalities; but the Lord deliver me, and all true-hearted Englishmen, from such unjust and unrighteous proceedings as I find at your hands, who go about, I now clearly see, to destroy me by my ignorance, in holding me to a single and naked plea, which is purely as bad, if not worse, than all the prerogatives, in a more rigorous manner than they were used in his lifetime, to be thus pressed upon me at this day, after he hath lost his life for pretended tyranny and injustice; liberty and freedom in public declarations declared to the kingdom: I say, if there be justice and equity in this, I have lost my understanding; and the good Lord God of Heaven deliver me from all such justiciaries!" [1]

Then came some of the stereotyped eulogies by the Court on the excellence of the laws of England—that " the law of God is the law of England "—that " the laws of God, the laws of reason, and the laws of the land are all joined in the laws that you shall be tried by;" [2]—the truth of which may be judged of by the fact that this very law of which Lilburne justly complained and which the judges extolled was, after this country had been finally delivered from the tyranny of the Stuarts ·as well as that of those who destroyed the Stuarts but retained their instruments of tyranny, altered by a statute [3] of William the Third, and that measure of justice was granted to persons indicted for high treason for which Lilburne had pleaded so well and so bravely in vain. When Lilburne found that he pleaded to

---

[1] State Trials, vol. iv. pp. 1305, 1306.

[2] State Trials, vol. iv. p. 1307.

[3] 7 W. 3, c. 3.

no purpose for counsel, for a little time to consult with them and to produce his witnesses, and for a copy of his indictment, he said : " Sir, I have no more to say. It is but a vain thing to spend any more words. Sir, I have cast up my account, and I know what it can cost me: I bless God I have learned to die, having always carried my life in my hand, ready to lay it down for above this twelve years together, having lived in the favour and bosom of God ; and I bless his name, I can as freely die as live."[1]

In answer to Lilburne's further request for time to bring in his witnesses, some of whom he said lived eighty or a hundred miles off, and others were parliament men, and others officers of the army who would not come in without subpœnas, Keble replied, " For your witnesses, you should have brought them with you ; we will give you leave to send for them ; we will give you time to do this, and to consider with yourself what to say for yourself; you shall have till seven o'clock to-morrow morning." Accordingly the Court adjourned till the next morning, and the prisoner, after humbly thanking the Court for what favour he had already received, was remanded to the Tower.[2]

In order to render intelligible what follows it will be necessary to state here that general orders had been issued to the army Feb. 22, $164\frac{8}{9}$ forbidding any private meetings of officers and soldiers, such as had been found useful to their commanders in 1647, to be held without previous permission from the Council of War. And a committee was appointed to consider of a way in which those might be punished who should endeavour to breed any discontent in the army, not being themselves members of the army.[3] This last provision was expressly pointed against Lil-

[1] State Trials, vol. iv. pp. 1308, 1309.

[2] State Trials, pp. 1312—1314.

[3] Whitelock, Feb. 22.

burne, who was not then a member of the army, though
he had been formerly, and had risen by his own merit as
one of its best soldiers to the rank of lieutenant-colonel.
And by the acts of the 14th of May 1649, and 17th July
1649, declaring what offences shall be adjudged treason,
it was enacted "that if any person shall maliciously publish, by writing, printing, or openly declaring, that the present Government is tyrannical, usurped, or unlawful ; or that
the Commons in Parliament assembled are not the supreme
authority of this nation ; " and further, "if any person,
not being an officer, soldier, or member of the army, shall
plot, contrive, or endeavour to stir up any mutiny in the
said army, or withdraw any soldiers or officers from their
obedience to their superior officers, or from the present
Government : that every such offence shall be adjudged
by the authority of this present Parliament to be High
Treason."

On the second day of the trial, Friday the 26th of
October, the prisoner was again brought to the bar, and
his brother, Col. Robert Lilburne, his solicitor Mr. Sprat,
and others of his friends standing beside him, the Court
objected to this.

"Lord *Keble.* Mr. Lilburne, I will have nobody
stand there, let all come out but one man.

"*Lilburne.* Here's none but my brother and my
solicitor.

"Lord *Keble.* Sir, your brother shall not stand by
you there ; I will only have one hold your papers and
books, and the rest not to trouble you : wherefore the rest
are to come out." [1]

The jury having been sworn, after Lilburne had
challenged several who were set aside, Mr. Broughton

[1] State Trials, vol. iv. p. 1315.

read the indictment which was very long, enumerating various of Lilburne's alleged publications and also containing passages from several of those publications. Lilburne then declared that on the previous day he had pleaded conditionally and that he was much wronged in their saying that he pleaded Not Guilty : "and now," he said, "I make my absolute plea to the indictment, which is this : That I except against the matter and form of it, matter, time, and place, and humbly crave counsel to assign and plead to the errors thereof." To this request the Court returned answer "that we have done we must maintain." [1]

The Attorney-General first proceeded to call the witnesses against the prisoner, then ordered the clerk to read the Acts of the 14th of May, 1649 and of the 17th of July, 1649, declaring what offences shall be adjudged treason, and also to read certain passages from the publications alleged by him to be Lilburne's. The passages read were numerous and some of them long. As it is absolutely necessary for the comprehension of this critical period of English History to have a clear view of this trial, I will give a few of the passages read by order of the Attorney-General.

"Mr. *Attorney.* I shall produce his book, entitled 'The Legal and Fundamental Liberties of England revived, &c.' Read the title-page.

"*Clerk.* 'The Legal Fundamental Liberties of the People of England revived, asserted and vindicated : or an epistle written the 8th of June, 1649, by Lieut.-Col. John Lilburne (arbitrary and aristocratical [2] prisoner in the

---

[1] State Trials, vol. iv. pp. 1329, 1330.

[2] He means by this word that he is imprisoned by the arbitrary and un-

constitutional power of the oligarchy or aristocracy, calling itself a commonwealth that then ruled in England by the power of the sword.

Tower of London) to Mr. William Lenthall, Speaker to the remainder of those few knights, citizens and burgesses, that Col. Thomas Pride at his late purge thought convenient to leave sitting at Westminster, (as most fit for his and his masters' designs, to serve their ambitious and tyrannical ends, to destroy the good old laws, liberties, and customs of England, and by force of arms to rob the people of their lives, estates and properties, and subject them to perfect vassalage and slavery, as he clearly evinceth in his present case, &c., they have done) and who (in truth no otherwise than pretendedly) stile themselves the Parliament of England.'

"Mr. *Attorney.*   Read page 2.

"*Clerk.*   'Sir, for distinction-sake, I will yet stile you Mr. Speaker, although it be but to Col. Pride's juncto, or Parliament sitting at Westminster (not the nation's, for they never gave him authority to issue out writs to elect or constitute a Parliament for them).'

"Mr. *Attorney.*   Read page 28.

"*Clerk.*   'The like of which tyranny the king never did in his reign ; and yet by St. Oliver's means lost his head for a tyrant.'

"Mr. *Attorney.*   Read page 37.

"*Clerk.*   'For if ever they had intended an Agreement, why do they let their own be dormant in the pretended Parliament ever since they presented it ? seeing it is obvious to every knowing eye, that from the day they presented it, to this hour, they have had as much power over their own Parliament now sitting, as any school-master in England had over his boys.'[1]

It will be seen that this passage opens a most momentous question.   The "Agreement of the People" to which he

---

[1] State Trials, vol. iv. pp. 1355, 1356.

refers and which he calls "their own" meaning that of
the chiefs of the army, is the Agreement of which I have
given an account in a preceding chapter and which is
commonly stated to have been chiefly drawn by Ireton.
Now Lilburne's opinion evidently was that neither Cromwell nor Fairfax nor even Ireton himself wished this
Agreement to be acted upon, that if it lay dormant in
the pretended Parliament, it lay dormant with their
consent, since they ruled the army which ruled the
Parliament.   It is manifest also that a much better and
really more effective answer to those they called Levellers
than putting some of them to death by the sword or the
provost-martial,[1] and attempting to put to death others
such as Lilburne by new and unconstitutional laws of
treason, would have been to have put that "Agreement" in
force and to have called a new Parliament in accordance
with its provisions.   The measure might have failed after
all, but then those who, as it is, have left their names a
doubt to some, an object of execration to others, might at
least have been entitled to the verdict of having acted
consistently.   In regard to the question how far Ireton
acquiesced in the putting aside or postponement *sine die*
of the "Agreement of the People," which he had drawn
up, I think the more probable explanation is that Ireton

---

[1] Provost-*marshal* is an error—the
word having no relation to *mareschal*
but meaning a provost to execute
martial law.   The word is thus spelt
in the Order Book of the Council of
State :—as appears by the following
minute—"That Col. Pride shall be
allowed for the recruits to be raised
for Ireland—a Martiall at 3s. 4d. per
diem, a Quarter Master at 3s. 4d. per
diem.   And for two carriage-horses to
carry the money that is to pay the
soldier's quarters 6s. 8d. per diem; and
the arms following, viz. 50 drums at
20s. a piece, 100 halberts at 5s. a
piece."—*Order Book of the Council
of State*, 24 Oct. 1649.   MS. State
Paper Office.   On the same day it was
ordered that two apothecaries more
be sent to Ireland at 5s. per diem
each, in consequence of letters from
the Lord-Lieutenant of Ireland signify-
ing the want of them.

prevailed on Cromwell to acquiesce in the drawing up and presenting to Parliament the "Agreement of the People," but could prevail no farther with him. As to Ireton's opposing Lilburne, assuming both to have had honest intentions, and both to have been in their ways men of ability, Ireton would see soon enough that, whatever might be Lilburne's ability and courage, and honest and disinterested views, neither his peculiar character nor his rank and power in the army gave him the least chance of contending successfully with Cromwell. As I have said before, in every such case it must always depend on the victorious general whether a military despotism or a constitutional government be the result; and such men as Ireton and Blake might be honest as well as able and brave men, though they submitted to a fate which their practical good sense told them no resistance of theirs could have averted.

" Mr. *Attorney.*   Read page 58.

" *Clerk.*   'And let the present generation of swaying men, that under pretence of good, kindness, and friendship, have destroyed and trod underfoot all the liberties of the nation, and *will not let us have a new Parliament*, but set up by the sword their own insufferable tyranny.'

" Mr. *Attorney.*   Read page 68.

" *Clerk.*   ' That the High Court of Justice was altogether unlawful, in case those that had set it up had been an unquestionable representative of the people, or a legal Parliament : neither of which they are in the least ; but, as they have managed their business in opposing all their primitive declared ends, are a pack of traitorous, self-seeking, tyrannical men, usurpers of the name and power of Parliament.'

" Mr. *Attorney.*   My lord, that which we shall offer you next is the ' Salva Libertate,' which the lieutenant of the Tower had from Mr. Lilburne himself. Read at the mark.

" *Clerk.* 'A Salva Libertate:' 'although I then told you I judged a paper warrant (although in words never so formal) coming from any pretended power or authority in England, now visible, to be altogether illegal ; because the intruding General Fairfax and his forces had broke and annihilated all the formal and legal magistracy of England, yea the very Parliament itself; and by his will and sword (absolute conqueror like) had most tyrannically erected and imposed upon the free people of this nation a Juncto or mock-power, sitting at Westminster, whom he and his associates call a Parliament; who, like so many armed thieves and robbers upon the highway, assume a power, by their own wills, most traitorously to do what they like, yea, and to fill the land with their mock and pretended magistrates, amongst the number of which is the pretended Attorney-General ; in perfect opposition of whom, to the utmost of my might, power, and strength, I am resolved by God's gracious assistance, to spend my blood, and all that in this world is dear unto me, supposing him not really and substantially worthy the name of an English freeman, that in some measure, in this particular, is not of my mind." [1]

The Attorney-General then said " My lords, I hope you and the gentlemen of the jury will take notice of it, as to be very clear proof that Mr. Lilburne hath thus published, and thus said. And besides this, you see what he does go to. He denies magistracy. So that now we are all alike, a class, a confusion." Upon this in the original edition of the report of the trial there is this note : " He doth no such thing ; but at most saith, the army hath destroyed

[1] State Trials, vol. iv. p. 1357.

all the legal magistracy of the nation ; and they are the men that thereby are the real Levellers and Rooters." The Attorney-General had said a short time before " Mr. Lilburne is a very great rooter, not a leveller, but a rooter to root out the laws of England by the roots."

The Attorney-General thus proceeded : " My lords, I shall not aggravate ; and if I did say no more, it were enough. But I come to the second general head of the charge ; which is, that he hath plotted and contrived to levy or raise forces to subvert and overthrow the present established Government, in the way of a free state or commonwealth. My lords, if I should say nothing more to the jury, this that hath been already read is evident proof of that : For certainly those that shall say that the governors be tyrants, that the Parliament is tyrannical, that they are men of blood, destroyers of laws and liberties ; this cannot be of any other use but to raise force against them, for subverting and destroying of them, as he himself saith, as so many weasels or polecats ; especially if you consider to whom these words were declared, to the army in general, especially to the general's regiment of horse, that helped to plunder and destroy Mr. Lilburne's true friends, defeated at Burford ; and some of which were most justly, as traitors, executed." [1]

Upon this there is the following note in the original edition of the report : " In calling tyrants weasels and polecats, he hath said no more but what he hath learned out of St. John's Argument of Law against the Earl of Strafford : at which you have no cause to be angry, because they are the words of one of your own brother lawyers."

The Attorney-General after quoting some passages from

[1] State Trials, vol. iv. pp. 1358, 1359.

Lilburne's "Impeachment of High Treason against Oliver Cromwell," proceeded to cite passages from his "Agreement of the People," to show that it amounted to High Treason, inasmuch as it set forth how many the Parliament should consist of, the time when the present Parliament should dissolve, and the time when the new Parliament should meet. And yet this was no more than Ireton's "Agreement of the People" had done, the only difference in one respect being that Ireton had fixed the last day of April, 1649, as the day upon or before which the present Parliament should end and dissolve, and Lilburne, finding that the men who sat and talked at Westminster let the last day of April, 1649, pass without taking any notice of Ireton's Agreement of the People, put forth his Agreement of the People on the 1st day of May, 1649, and had fixed the first Wednesday in August, 1649, as the day on which the said Parliament should end. And if the Parliament had not neglected Ireton's Agreement of the People, there would have been no need to set forth Lilburne's or any other Agreement of the People. It is also a very significant fact that the outbreak of that part of the army called the Levellers did not take place till the Parliament, by letting the month of April expire without acting in the least on Ireton's Agreement of the People, showed that they considered themselves as ruling by a sort of right divine almost as much as the Stuarts whom they had deposed. They were, as I have said, most able and energetic administrators; but if they had possessed that higher statesmanship which can employ a comprehensive survey of the past in a wise divination of the future, they might have seen clearly enough what the end of such a course would be. Perhaps the only man that could, if he had been so minded, have saved them from such a disastrous as well as disgraceful end was Cromwell. And yet one can only say "perhaps," for more than two years after they had thus neglected Ireton's Agreement and prosecuted Lilburne for his, we find the following entry in their Journals:—"Friday, the 14th of November, 1651—The question being propounded That it is now a convenient time to declare a certain time for the continuance of this Parliament, beyond which it shall not sit, and the question being put (which is now termed " the previous question "),[1] " That this question be now put," was carried by a majority of 50 to 46, the Lord General Cromwell being one of the Tellers for the Yeas. It was then resolved " That this business be resumed again on Tuesday evening next."[2] Accordingly on Tuesday the 18th of November it was resolved "That the time for the continuance of this Parliament, beyond which they resolve not to sit, shall be the Third day of November, 1654 ;"[3] a day which they did not live to see.

The Attorney-General then thus proceeded : " My lord, we shall go on with more yet, and that is with his Outcry. My lord, if you please to see the title, and see to whom it is directed, what was intended to be done with it : it is intitled, ' An Outcry of the Young Men and Apprentices of London, directed August 29, 1649, in an epistle to the private soldiery of the army, especially all those that signed the 'Solemn Engagement' at Newmarket-heath, the 5th of June, 1647, but more especially to the private soldiers of the general's regiment of horse, that helped to

---

[1] I have before (page 179) given an example of this.

[2] Commons' Journals, Friday the 14th of November, 1651. It is curious that on the first division, namely on the previous question " That this question be now put," the majority of the Yeas was 50 to 46, when on the main question being put, the majority became only 49 while the minority became 47.

[3] Commons' Journals, Tuesday, the 18th of November, 1651.

plunder and destroy the honest and true-hearted English-men, traitorously defeated at Burford, the 15th of May, 1649.' A good encouragement! they were traitorously defeated at Burford; but we are rebels and traitors, and our army murderers and butchers, for giving some of those declared traitors their due deserts. But that you may see his tendency by this Book, read page 11.

" *Clerk.* 'You, our fellow-countrymen, the private soldiers of the army, alone being the instrumental authors of your own slavery and ours; therefore, as there is any bowels of men in you, any love to your native country, kindred, friends or relations, any spark of conscience in you, any hopes of glory or immortality in you, or any pity, mercy, or compassion, to an enslaved, undone, perishing, and dying people! O help! help! save and re-deem us from total vassalage and slavery, and be no more like brute-beasts, to fight against us or our friends, your loving and dear brethren after the flesh, to your own vas-salage as well as ours! And as an assured pledge of your future cordialness to us, (and the true and real liberties of the land of your nativity) we beseech and beg of you (but especially those amongst you that subscribed the Solemn Engagement at Newmarket-heath, the 5th of June, 1647,) speedily to chuse out amongst yourselves two of the ablest and constantest faithful men amongst you in each troop and company, now at last, by corresponding each with other, and with your honest friends in the nation, to con-sider of some effectual course, beyond all pretences and cheats, to accomplish the real end of all your engagements and fightings, viz. the settling of the liberties and freedom of the people; which can never permanently be done, but upon the sure foundation of a popular agreement, for the people in justice, gratitude, and common equity, cannot chuse but voluntarily and largely make better provision for your future subsistence, by the payment of your arrears, than ever your officers or this pretended Parliament intends, or you can rationally expect from them : witness their cutting off three parts of your arrears in four for free-quarter ; and then necessitating abundance of your fellow-soldiers (now cashiered, &c.) to sell their debentures at 2s. 6d., 3s., and at most 4s. for the pound.' " [1]

" Mr. *Attorney*. See, my lord, here we are styled tyrants, usurpers, introducing government oppressions of the people ; and Mr. Lilburne is resolved with his friends to join together, and to lay down their very lives for this. This, I think, is a trumpet blown aloud for all the discontented people in the nation to flock together, to root up and destroy this Parliament, and so the present Government. But read also the same book, page 9.

" *Clerk*. ' For the effectual promotion of which said Agreement, we are compelled to resolve in close union to join ourselves, or our commissioners, with our foresaid Burford friends or their commissioners ; and to run all hazards to methodize all our honest fellow-prentices, in all the wards of London, and the out-parishes, to chuse out their agents to join with us or ours, to write exhortative epistles to all the honest-hearted freemen of England, in all the counties thereof, to erect several councils among themselves ; out of which we shall desire and exhort them to chuse agents or commissioners, empowered and entrusted by them, speedily to meet us and the agents of all our (and the Agreement of the People) adherents at London, resolvedly to consider of a speedy and effectual method and way how to promote the elevation of a new and equal representative, or Parliament, by the agreement of the

---

[1] State Trials, vol. iv. pp. 1363-1365.

free people : Seeing those men that now sit at Westminster, and pretendedly stile themselves the Parliament of England, and who are as they say (although most falsely) in the Declaration for a free state, dated March 17, 164$\frac{8}{9}$, page 27, intrusted and authorized by the consent of all the people of England, whose representatives they are ; make it their chiefest and principallest work continually to part and share amongst themselves all the great, rich, and profitable places of the nation ; as also the nation's public treasure and lands ; and will not ease our intolerable oppressions, no not so much as of late receive our popular petitions." [1] The truth of the words of the last passage of this extract sent the sting of the libel home.

The language [2] of many passages produced from Lilburne's

---

[1] State Trials, vol. iv. p. 1365.

[2] In addition to the specimens already given of the language used by Lilburne, I will add here a few more examples. From "The Apprentices' Out-cry" the Attorney-General ordered the clerk to read the following passages : "But even our Parliament, the very marrow and soul of all the people's native rights put down, and the name and power thereof transmitted to a picked party of your forcible selecting, and such as your officers, our lords and riders, have often stiled no better than a mock parliament, a shadow of a parliament, a seeming authority, or the like, pretending the continuance thereof, but till a new and equal representative by mutual agreement of the free people of England, could be elected ; although now for subserviency to their exaltation and kingship, they prorogue and perpetuate the same, in the name, and under colour thereof, introducing a Privy Council, or, as they call it, a Council of State, of superintendency and suppression to all future parliaments for ever, erecting a martial government, by blood and violence impulsed upon us," page 2.—"Trade is decayed and fled ; misery, poverty, calamity, confusion, yea, and beggary grown so sore and so extreme upon the people, as the like never was in England, under the most tyrannical of all our kings that were before these in present power, since the days of the Conqueror himself : no captivity, no bondage, no oppression like unto this ; no sorrow and misery like unto ours, of being enslaved, undone, and destroyed by our large pretended friends, page 3. "And yet nothing but the groundless wills and humours of those aforementioned men of blood rageth and ruleth over us," page 4.

"We are compelled to do the utmost we can for our own preservation and the preservation of the land of our nativity, and never by popular petitions, &c., address ourselves to the men sitting at Westminster any more, or to take any more notice of them, than as

publications was clearly enough treason according to the new laws of treason of May and July last, which new laws going beyond the law of treasons of Edward the Third made bare words treason. The charge of stirring up mutiny in the army was not established farther than that written words such as I have quoted, addressed to the soldiers specially, have a tendency to stir up mutiny. Moreover the Attorney-General and the Court appear not to have considered the case against the prisoner strong on this point, and to have felt the force of Lilburne's observation in his defence: " the testimony doth not reach to accuse me of any evil or malicious counsel given them [three soldiers whom he met accidentally] or any aggravations of spirit, as though I did incense them against their officers, thereby to stir them up to mutiny and rebellion. For truly I have made it my work, to be as sparing of my discourse as I could be, in the company of any belonging to the army ; yea, and to shun coming nigh the place, if I can avoid it, where they are." [1]

When Colonel Purefoy was sworn as a witness against the prisoner, Lilburne said :—" Under favour but one word, I crave but one word, I have an exception. First, Colonel Purefoy is one of those that call themselves the keepers of the liberties of England ; and for committing crimes against them I am indicted, and he is one of them and therefore a party, and in that respect in law he can be no witness against me. ' It would have been very hard for the king to have been a witness against that man that was indicted for committing crimes against him, such a thing in

of so many tyrants and usurpers," page 11, in State Trials, vol. iv. pp. 1353, 1354. From " The Preparative to a Hue-and-Cry after Sir Arthur Haselrig "—" That those men that now sit at Westminster are no parliament either upon the principles of law or reason." Page 2, in the margin.—*State Trials*, vol. iv. p. 1354.

[1] State Trials, vol. iv. p. 1384.

all his reign was never known." [1]   To this the Attorney-
General's answer was :—" Mr. Lilburne, you are mistaken ;
Colonel Purefoy is a Member of Parliament, he is none of
the keepers of the liberties of England." This is a strange
assertion on the part of the Attorney-General, when the
writ of the Parliament ran thus—" Custodes Libertatis
Angliæ, auctoritate Parliamenti Vicecomiti salutem." [2]
Does not this prove that the members of the Parliament in
the aggregate and the Custodes Libertatis Angliæ in the
aggregate were identical? and that each member of Parliament was a member of this body constituting the
sovereign in England at that time.   Lilburne also showed
that one of the publications specified in the indictment,
namely his " Agreement of the People," which, as has been
shown, was very different in some things (though similar
in many others) from Ireton's " Agreement of the People,"
bore a date anterior to the date of any of those new acts
under which he was indicted, and therefore was not
within the compass of it. [3]

When the Attorney-General had ended his address to
the jury, the foreman said, " We desire the Act of Treasons
to make use of."

" *Lilburne.*   I beseech you hear me a few words : they
desire to have it along with them.   Sir, with your favour,
I shall humbly crave liberty to speak a few words : I shall
keep me close to that which is my right and my duty, and
that is to the matter of law in my indictment.   There are
many things put into the indictment by the testimonies of
witnesses now sworn, that are pretended to be acted in
several counties.   Whether that be according to law, or
no, I do not know whether you will judge it so or no ; but

[1] State Trials, vol. iv. p. 1342.   7 Martii, 164⅚.
[2] Commons' Journal, Die Mercurii,   [3] State Trials, vol. iv. p. 1388.

sure I am, if either those express statutes that I have
already cited to the jury, or the third part of Coke's Institutes, be law, I ought not to be tried for treason but by a
jury of the next neighbourhood, in the self-same county
the fact is pretended to be committed in.   And therefore it
is very questionable to me, whether my indictment be legal,
for that it chargeth me with facts of treason committed in
three several counties; and that being matter of law, I
desire counsel to argue that point, in the first place.
There are also a great many things arise out of the matter
of fact that will be points of law likewise.   There were
never two clear and positive witnesses to one fact sworn
against me; but to most of the particular [alleged] treasons
there is but one a-piece; and I cannot yield that to be
legal, but questionable in law, which I desire counsel to
dispute.   I know not of any of all the books fixed upon
me, but the "Outcry," that hath two plain witnesses to it;
and yet it is not sworn that I am the author of it.   The
state of the fact is this: that I was at the printer's before
the copy was taken away; and that I gave one of those
books to a soldier.   To sum up the notes of the matter of
fact that thereon hath been endeavoured to be proved, is
too hard a task to be done by me immediately; and therefore I conceive it but just for you to assign me counsel, to
agree with the counsel against me what are the points of
fact upon the proof, from which the points of law are to be
deducted.   This, with a larger privilege, was granted by
one of your own brother judges to Major Rolfe last year,
as his right by law; and I do again appeal to Mr. Justice
Nichols, then one of Rolfe's counsel, for the truth of this.
I pray speak, sir; is it not true?"   [But the judge sitting
" as if " says the contemporary report, " he had neither life
nor soul," Lilburne went on :]—" I hope, sir, it doth not

enter into your thoughts presently to put me to an un-digested extemporary answer to so large an indictment as that is that hath been read against me, that it is impossible for any man, if his brain were as big as the biggest magazine in London, to carry it in his head. I hope you do not lie upon the catch, to weary and tire me out, by putting more upon me than a horse is able to endure; and then go about to hang me, because I, through tiredness, want bodily strength and abilities to make and pronounce my defence." [1]

To this the answer of the Court was—" Free yourself from the matter of fact, if you can, and then make it appear that from the matter of fact law arises. But if you do not first make out this, which is the issue upon the point, to answer the matter of fact, we cannot allow you any counsel."

"*Lilburne.* There is Judge Nichols, that I understand was one of Major Rolfe's counsel : and I understand from Mr. Maynard's own mouth, that he and Mr. Maynard were by Baron Wyld assigned of Rolfe's counsel, in case of the highest treason that the law of England ever knew, and that before the grand inquest found the indictment ; and that Mr. Maynard, &c. had liberty as Major Rolfe's counsel, by Baron Wyld's order, to stand in the Court, not only to hear the witnesses sworn, but also to hear the words of their testimony, then caused by the judge to be given in open Court. And there being but two witnesses to two facts contained in the indictment, Mr. Maynard, upon the allegation of the two statutes of Edward the 6th, that requires two witnesses to the proof of every fact of treason, and that to be plain and clear, overthrew Rolfe's indict-ment in law, that it was never found ; and so saved the

[1] State Trials, vol. iv. pp. 1373–1375.

poor man's life.   And all this Mr. Justice Nichols knows is very true, and that I have told you nothing about it but what is just." [1]

" Lord *Keble*.   Mr. Lilburne, you at this time have here such a Court, which never any of your condition ever had in England, so many grave judges of the law.

"*Lilburne*.   Truly I had rather have had an ordinary one ; sir, I mean a legal and ordinary assize or sessions.

" Lord *Keble*.   But this you have, and this is to take off, or prevent that which you would do now, if there had been one judge, and no more ; and if you had not had this great presence of the Court, you would have been malapert, and have out-talked them ; but you cannot do so here.

"*Lilburne*.   Truly, sir, I am not daunted at the multitude of my judges, neither at the glittering of your scarlet robes, nor the majesty of your presence, and harsh austere deportment towards me ; I bless my good God for it, who gives me courage and boldness." [2]

The Court then called on the prisoner to make his defence.

"*Lilburne*.   I have been a great while yesterday pleading my right by law for counsel, and now I have stood many hours to hear your proofs to the indictment. I hope you will not be so cruel to put me to a present answer, when my bodily strength is spent.

" Lord *Keble*.   Dispute no more, we must go on.

"*Lilburne*.   I desire but a week's time to return you an answer to your large indictment ; and if not so long, then give me leave but till to-morrow morning to consider of my answer.   I am upon my life.

" Lord *Keble*.   No, you must dispatch it now.

[1] State Trials, pp.-1375, 1376.   [2] State Trials, vol. iv. p. 1377.

Q

"*Lilburne.*   Then give me leave but to withdraw into any private room for an hour to recollect my thoughts, peruse my notes, and refresh my spirits."

Here Judge Jermin whispered the President of the Court, Keble, in the ear; and presently Judge Jermin said "It is against the law to allow you any more time; the jury stand here charged, the evidence is given, you must immediately go on, or yield that for truth which hath been proved against you.

"*Lilburne.*   Well, then, if it must be so, that you will have my blood, right or wrong; and if I shall not have one hour's time to refresh me, after my strength is spent, and to consider that which hath been alleged against me, then I appeal " ["which" says the contemporary report, "he uttered with a mighty voice"] " to the righteous God of heaven and earth against you, where I am sure I shall be heard and find access; and the Lord God Omnipotent, and a mighty Judge betwixt you and me, require and requite my blood upon the heads of you and your posterity, to the third and fourth generation!"

Immediately after the uttering of these words the scaffold on the left hand fell down, which occasioned a great noise and some confusion, by reason of the people's tumbling down.   Silence being made, the prisoner was busy at his papers and books, having been invited by Sheriff Pack to come out of the bar, for fear he should have fallen with the rest, and so the sheriff might have lost his prisoner.

"Lord *Keble.*   How came the prisoner there?

"*Lilburne.*   I went not thither of my own accord, but by Mr. Sheriff's invitation; and if I am in a place where I ought not to be, blame Mr. Sheriff, and not me.

" Lord *Keble*. Dispatch, sir.

" *Lilburne*. Sir, if you will be so cruel as not to give me leave to withdraw to ease and refresh my body, I pray you let me do it in the Court. Officer, I entreat you ———" Here there was a short pause till the prisoner had obtained what he asked for.

" Lord *Keble*. Proceed, Mr. Lilburne."

But the prisoner pressed for a little respite, which was granted him with much ado, as also a chair to sit down upon. But within a very little space the Lord President Keble said

" The Court cannot stay for you, proceed on to answer.

" *Lilburne*. Good sir, would you have me to answer to impossibilities? Will you not give me breath? If you thirst after my blood, and nothing else will satisfy you, take it presently without any more to-do.

" Lord *Keble*. The Court can stay no longer; take away his chair, for I cannot see the bar, and plead what you have to say, for it grows very late.

" *Lilburne*. Well, seeing I must do it, the will of God be done !"

But his brother Col. Robert Lilburne being next to him was heard to press him to pause a little more. " No, brother," said he, " my work is done; I will warrant you, by the help of God, I will knock the nail upon the head." And so he went into the bar, and set the chair before him, and laid his law books open upon it in the order in which he intended to use them. He then before commencing his defence entered into a contest with the Court for the establishment of the position that by the law of England the jury are not only judges of fact but of law also, in the course of which he said " You that call yourselves judges of the law are no more but Norman intruders ; and indeed and in truth, if the jury please, are no more but cyphers to pronounce their verdict." [1]

" Judge *Jermin.*   Was there ever such a damnable blasphemous heresy as this is, to call the judges of the law cyphers ?

" *Lilburne.*   Sir, I entreat you give me leave to read the words of the law, then ; for to the jury I apply, as my judges, both in the law and fact.

" Lord *Keble.*   We will not deny a tittle of the law.

" Judge *Jermin.*   Let all the hearers know, the jury ought to take notice of it, that the judges that are sworn, that are twelve in number, they have ever been the judges of the law, from the first time that ever we can read or hear that the law was truly expressed in England ; and the jury are only judges, whether such a thing were done or no ; they are only judges of matter of fact.

" *Lilburne.*   I deny it ; here's your own law to disprove you ; and therefore let me but read it.   It is a hard case where a man is upon the trial of his life, that you will not suffer him to read the law to the jury, for his own defence ; I am sure you have caused to be read at large those laws that make against me.

" Lord *Keble.*   But I shall pronounce to clear the righteousness of that law, whatsoever others will pretend against it that know it not.

" *Lilburne.*   Sir, under favour, I shall not trouble myself with anything, but what is pertinent to my present purpose.   Here is the first part of Coke's Institutes ; it is owned by all the lawyers that I know, or ever heard of in England for good law.

" Lord *Keble.*   If you can convince us, that matter of law does concern the jury, you say something.

[1] State Trials, vol. iv. p. 1379.

"*Lilburne.*   Sir, I have been shuffled too much out of my liberties already, give me leave to read but the law to the jury."

And here it is to be noted, as a confirmation of a remark I have made in a previous note how often in the course of this trial Lilburne showed a more accurate know-ledge of the law than either the Court or the law officers, that the almost only advantage they obtained over him was on this occasion when, by a slip of the tongue very natural to a man who had not been bred a lawyer, he said "Coke's Commentaries upon Plowden" instead of "Coke's Commentaries upon Littleton." Upon this the President interrupted him.

"Lord *Keble.*   Have we dealt so fairly with you all this while?   Pray be confident, those that are quotations there, are not for your purpose; but I thought how good a lawyer you were to set Coke's Commentaries upon Plow-den, when there is no such book or commentary. Go to your matter of fact, which is clear; but for this, let it fall down, and spare yourself, and trouble yourself no more with Coke; he has no commentary upon Plowden."

Here Lilburne pressed to speak.

"Judge *Jermin.*   Hold, sir.

"*Lilburne.*   What, will you not allow me liberty to read your law?   O unrighteous and bloody judges!

"Judge *Jermin.*   By the fancy of your own mind, you would puzzle the jury; we know the book a little better than you do: there is no such book as Coke's Commentary upon Plowden.

"Lord *Keble.*   Sir, you shall not read it.

"Judge *Jermin.*   You cannot be suffered to read the law; you have broached an erroneous opinion, that the jury are the judges of the law, which is enough to destroy

all the law in the land; there was never such damnable
heresy broached in this nation before."

The Crier cried out, " Hear the Court."

" *Lilburne.* Do your pleasure, then here I'll die : Jury,
take notice of their injustice ; but seeing they will not
hear me, I will appeal to you, and say, It is an easy matter
for an abler man than I am, in so many interruptions as I
meet with, to mistake Plowden for Littleton.   I am sure,
here are Coke's Commentaries upon Littleton (366) and
these be his [Littleton's] words : ' In this case the recog-
nitors may say and render to the justices their verdict at
large upon the whole matter.'   Which I am sure is good
law, for as much as we see it continually done in all actions
of trespass or assault, where the jury doth not only judge
of the validity of the proof of the fact, but also of the
law, by assigning what damages they think is just.   And
in section 368, Littleton hath these words : ' If the inquest
[jury] will take upon them the knowledge of the law upon
the matter, they may give their verdict generally.'   Coke's
commentary upon this is—' Although the jury, if they will
take upon them (as Littleton here saith), the knowledge
of the law, may give a general verdict.'   I am sure this is
pertinent to my purpose, and now I have done, sir." [1]

Although Lilburne stopt his quotation from Coke's Commentary in the middle of a sentence, his statement of the
law generally as then in operation appears to have been
correct.   The sentence in Coke's Commentary concludes
thus : " Yet it is dangerous for them [the jury] so to do,
for, if they do mistake the law, they run into the danger
of an attaint ; therefore to find the special matter " (*i. e.*
the fact without applying the law to it) " is the safest way
where the case is doubtful." [2]   Originally the consequences,

---

[1] State Trials, vol. iv. pp. 1379–1381.   [2] Co. Litt. 228, a.

implied in the word " attaint," of the jury's mistaking the
law consisted of penalties so heavy that they must have
deterred the jury in most cases from giving a verdict involving the law of the case. But the severity of the old
law was mitigated by various statutes and the practice
established by this time, as indicated by a case in Moore's
Reports, appears to have been that the jury had a right
to give a verdict involving both the law and the fact,
subject however to revision and correction as to law
where they had mistaken the law.[1] But long after the
right of the jury to return a verdict involving the law as
well as the fact was admitted in other cases ; their right
to do so in the special case of libel, particularly political
libel, was questioned and more than questioned by judicial
authority, as will appear from the following scene that
occurred in 1784, in a case of trial for libel where the Dean
of St. Asaph was indicted for publishing the " Dialogue
between a Gentleman and a Farmer," written by Sir
William Jones—a case remarkable for the eloquent speech
of Erskine which Charles James Fox repeatedly declared
he thought the finest argument in the English language, and
which is considered to have prepared the way for the introduction of Mr. Fox's Libel Bill.

"Mr. *Erskine*.   Is the word *only* to stand as part of
your verdict ?

"*A Juror*.   Certainly.

" Mr. *Erskine*.   Then I insist it shall be recorded.

" Mr. *Justice Buller*.   Then the verdict must be misunderstood.   Let me understand the jury.

---

[1] Lee v. Lee, Moore, 268. " Et les justices diont que lou les jurors trove matter encounter ley, les justices ne pûderont notice de ceo, mes adjudg-eront comme le ley voit." " And the justices said that, when the jurors find matter contrary to law, the jus-tices will not take notice of that, but will give judgment according to law." See also 15 Vin. Abr. 523.

" Mr. *Erskine.*   The jury do understand their verdict.

" Mr. *Justice Buller.*   Sir, I will not be interrupted.

" Mr. *Erskine.*   I stand here as an advocate for a brother-citizen, and I desire that the word *only* may be recorded.

" Mr. *Justice Buller.*   Sit down, sir ; remember your duty, or I shall be obliged to proceed in another manner.

" Mr. *Erskine.*   Your lordship may proceed in what manner you think fit.   I know my duty as well as your lordship knows yours.   I shall not alter my conduct." [1]

By the word " only," the jury meant to find, as Mr. Erskine observed, that there was no sedition.   In the course of his speech Mr. Erskine cited the case of Penn and Mead, two Quakers, who in the year 1670 being indicted for *seditiously* preaching to a multitude *tumultuously* assembled in Gracechurch Street, were tried before the Recorder of London, who told the jury that they had nothing to do but to find whether the defendants had preached or not ; for that whether the matter or the intention of their preaching were seditious were questions of law, and not of fact, which they were to keep to at their peril.   The jury found Penn guilty of speaking to people in Gracechurch Street ; and on the Recorder's telling them that they meant, no doubt, that he was speaking to a tumult of people there, he was informed by the foreman that they allowed of no such words in their finding, but adhered to their former verdict.   The Recorder refused to receive it, and desired them to withdraw, on which they again retired, and brought a general verdict of acquittal, which the Court considering as a contempt, set a fine of forty marks upon each of them, and condemned them to lie in prison till it was paid.   Edward Bushel, one of the jurors, refused to pay his fine, and, being imprisoned in

---

[1] State Trials, vol. xxi. pp. 950, 951.

consequence of his refusal, sued out his writ of *habeas corpus*, which, with the cause of his commitment, viz. his refusing to find according to the direction of the Court in matter of law, was returned by the Sheriffs of London to the Court of Common Pleas, when Lord Chief Justice Vaughan delivered his opinion as follows:—"We must take off this veil and colour of words, which make a show of being something, but are in fact nothing. If the meaning of these words, finding against the direction of the Court in matter of law, be, that the judge, having heard the evidence given in Court (for he knows no other), shall tell the jury, upon this evidence, that the law is for the Crown, and they, under the pain of fine and imprisonment, are to find accordingly, every man sees that the jury is but a troublesome delay, great charge, and of no use in determining right and wrong, and therefore the trials by them may be better abolished than continued; which were a strange and new-found conclusion, after a trial so celebrated for many hundreds of years in this country." He then applied the doctrine with double force to criminal cases, and discharged the juror from his commitment.[1] However Lord Mansfield in delivering the judgment of the Court in the Dean of St. Asaph's case made some observations to the effect that from the Revolution down to that time, nearly a hundred years, the direction of every judge, as far as it could be traced, had been consonant to the doctrine of Mr. Justice Buller, viz. that the matter for the jury to decide was, whether the Defendant was guilty of the fact or not.[2] It will appear however that in the case

[1] Penn and Mead. State Trials, vol. vi. p. 999.

[2] In 1791 Mr. Fox brought in a bill, which was finally passed in 1792, and became the statute 32 Geo. 3, c. 60, that on trial for libel the jury may give a general verdict upon the whole matter put in issue, and shall not be required by the Court to find a verdict merely on the matter of fact.

of Lilburne, though the presiding judge in his charge to
the jury told them that they were the proper judges of the
" matter of fact," and though notwithstanding this, the jury
brought in a verdict of " Not Guilty of Treason," the
Court took no exceptions to their verdict.

Lilburne now proceeded to make his answer to the proof
of the indictment in the same order in which the several
witnesses had given their evidence.   The principal points
on which he insisted were, that there were not two witnesses, as required by law, to any one fact sworn against
him ; and that his " Agreement of the People " was before
the new law of treason of May and July of that year,
1649.

The circumstances attending the conclusion of Lilburne's
defence are very characteristic both of the man and of the
time.   The Lord Commissioner Keble having interrupted
him, saying " do not tell us a story, but go on to finish the
matter of fact," and again " what is material, you shall not
be debarred in it," Lilburne thus went on and concluded
his long defence.   " O Lord, sir ! what strange judges are
you, that you will neither allow me counsel to help me to
plead, nor suffer me myself to speak for my own life !   Is
this your law and justice, sir ?   I have no more to say but
this, seeing you straiten me ; although you said you would
hear me till midnight.   I hope I have made it evident to
all rational men, that all or any part of the testimony
given in against me does not in the exact eye of the law
in the least touch me, although I have been most unjustly
imprisoned, and most barbarously used, and tyrannized
over ; yea, and my estates by will and power taken from
me ; that should have kept me and mine alive, and the
legal and customary allowance of the Tower denied me to
this day.   And although I have used all Christian and fair

means to compose my differences with my adversaries, yet
nothing would serve their turns, but I must have oppression upon oppression laid upon me, enough to break the
back of a horse ; and then if I cry out of my oppressions
in any kind, I must have new treason-snares made to catch
me, many months after their oppressions were first laid
upon me, that if I so much as whimper or speak in the
least of their unjust dealing with me, I must die therefore
as a traitor.　　O miserable servitude ! and miserable bondage, in the first year of England's freedom ! I have now
no more to say unto you, but only this.　　Your own law
tells me, Sir Edward Coke speaks it three or four times over
in his third part of Institutes, That it is the law of England,
that any by-stander may speak in the prisoner's behalf, if
he see anything urged against him contrary to law, or do
apprehend he falls short of urging any material thing that
may serve for his defence and preservation.　　Here is your
own law for it, sir ; Coke is full and pregnant to this purpose in his third part of Institutes, fol. 29, 34, 37.　　But
this hath several times been denied me in the case of Mr.
Sprat, my solicitor ; and now I demand it again, as my
right by law, that he may speak a few words for me,
according to his often desire both to me and the Court.　　I
have almost done, sir ; only once again I claim that as my
right which you have promised, that I should have counsel
to matter of law.　　And if you give me but your own
promise, which is my undoubted right by your own law,
I fear not my life.　　But if you again shall deny both these
legal privileges, I shall desire my jury to take notice, that I
aver you rob me of the benefit of the law, and go about to
murder me, without and against law : and therefore as a
freeborn Englishman, and as a true Christian that now
stands in the sight and presence of God, with an upright

heart and conscience, and with a cheerful countenance, I cast my life, and the lives of all the honest freemen of England, into the hands of God, and his gracious protection, and into the care and conscience of my honest jury and fellow-citizens ; who, I again declare, by the law of England are the conservators and sole judges of my life, having inherent in them alone the judicial power of the law, as well as fact : you judges that sit there being no more, if they please, but cyphers to pronounce the sentence, or their clerks to say Amen to them : being at the best in your original but the Norman Conqueror's intruders. And therefore you, gentlemen of the jury, are my sole judges, the keepers of my life, at whose hands the Lord will require my blood, in case you leave any part of my indictment to the cruel and bloody men. And therefore I desire you to know your power, and consider your duty both to God, to me, to your own selves, and to your country : And the gracious assisting spirit and presence of the Lord God Omnipotent, the governor of heaven and earth, and all things therein contained, go along with you, give counsel and direct you, to do that which is just, and for His glory ! " [1]

When Lilburne had ended, the people with a loud voice cried, *Amen, Amen,* and gave an " extraordinary great hum ; " which made the judges look "something untowardly " about them, and caused Major-General Skippon to send for three more companies of foot-soldiers.[2]

Mr. Attorney-General Prideaux in his reply exhibited an instructive lesson to all after-ages ; for he showed that the " servile subtlety of crown lawyers " could be exercised as shamelessly for this remnant of a Parliament, which boasted that it had put down tyrants and tyranny in England for ever, as it had been exercised to gratify the lust

[1] State Trials, vol. iv. pp. 1394, 1395.   [2] State Trials, vol. iv. p. 1395.

of unjust dominion of any single tyrant bearing the name of Tudor or of Stuart.   He also exhibited in a remarkable degree, if not the "ingenium velox," the insensibility to shame, the "audacia perdita" which has characterized too many advocates, and has also most unhappily raised too many of them to an eminence at the bar from which they have "rotted into peers."   Many, many have been the Attorney-Generals who have lied as audaciously as Prideaux, and few the prisoners who have dared to tell them what Lilburne told Prideaux when he said "I wonder, Mr. Prideaux, you are not ashamed to aver such notorious falsehoods, as you do, in the open face of the Court, before thousands of witnesses."

"The prisoner" said Prideaux, "began to cite you two Acts of Parliament; the one in the 1st of Edward VI., and the other 5th and 6th of Edward VI.; and by these two Acts he would signify to you, that you should have two plain and evident witnesses to every particular fact : yet he did forget to cite another statute made in the first and second years of Philip and Mary, that overthrows and annihilates those two statutes that would have two plain witnesses to every fact of treason."   Prideaux then went on to say with regard to the evidence of one of the witnesses Newcombe : — "The prisoner did not repeat fully what he said ; for I remember he said this, That Mr. Lilburne and Captain Jones came together, and brought the copy of the last sheet that was to be printed.   They came again the same day at night ; and when the first sheet was printed, to be sure it was true and right Mr. Lilburne did take the pains to take one of the copies in his hand, and corrected it."

Here Lilburne interrupted the Attorney-General with these words : — "By your favour, sir, he urged no such thing : by your favour, sir, they are the express words of the testimony to the quite contrary ; and I wonder, Mr. Prideaux, you are not ashamed to aver such notorious falsehoods, as you do, in the open face of the Court, before thousands of witnesses ; for Newcombe said no such thing as you falsely affirm ; neither is there any such statute in Queen Mary's time that doth abolish those two statutes of Edward VI., that I insist upon for two witnesses : name your statute if you can ; here is the statute-book, let the jury hear it read ; do not abuse them with your impudent falsehoods."

All the answer Mr. Attorney-General made was this : " Well, sir, I leave it to the judgment of the jury, sir." [1]

Now it is important to see how far the Attorney-General's assertion was true, as he himself would declare, or false, as Lilburne declared. The Attorney-General asserted as we have seen that Mr. Lilburne " took one of the copies in his hand, and corrected it." On the other hand Thomas Newcombe the printer when sworn had said : " My lord, I shall tell you the manner of our trade in this particular. The manner is, that after we have set a form of the letter, we make a proof of it, which proof we have a corrector does read : my corrector he had one, being he corrected it, and Captain Jones looked upon the manuscript. And Lieutenant-Colonel Lilburne had a copy of the same sheet uncorrected ; but he did not correct it, nor read to the corrector." [2] Again as regards Mr. Attorney-General Prideaux's assertion that a statute of Philip and Mary repealed the statutes of Edward VI. which required two witnesses in all cases of high treason, it is true that the statute 1 Mary sess. 1, cap. 1, is an Act repealing and taking away all treasons but such as are declared by the statute of

---

[1] State Trials, vol. iv. p. 1396.   [2] State Trials, p. 1334.

treasons of Edward III. But this statute did not repeal
the statutes of Edward VI. requiring two witnesses, those
statutes of Edward VI. being still unrepealed. And the
statute 1 & 2 Ph. & Mar. c. 10, so far from repealing, as
the Attorney-General asserts, the statutes of Edward VI.
which required two witnesses in all cases of treasons, is as
follows (sect. 11) :—" That upon the arraignment of any
person which hereafter shall fortune to be arraigned for
any treason mentioned in this Act, all and every person
and persons (*or two of them at the least*) who shall hereafter write declare, confess or depose any thing or things
against the person to be arraigned shall, if living and
within the realm, be brought in person before the party
arraigned if he require the same, and object and say openly
in his hearing what they or any of them can against him,
for or concerning any the treasons contained in the indictment whereupon the party shall be so arraigned, unless the
party arraigned for any such treason shall willingly confess
the same at the time of his or their arraignment." And
the 12th section of the same statute is—" That in all cases
of high treason concerning coin current within this realm,
or for counterfeiting the king or queen's signet, privy seal,
great seal, or sign manual, such manner of trial and none
other be observed and kept as heretofore hath been used
by the common laws of this realm." Blackstone's statement is this : " In all cases of high treason, petit treason,
and misprision of treason, by statutes 1 Edw. VI. c. 12, and
5 & 6 Edw. VI. c. 11, *two* [1] lawful witnesses are required
to convict a prisoner ; unless he shall willingly and without
violence confess the same. By statute 1 & 2 Ph. & Mar.
c. 10, a farther exception is made as to treason in counterfeiting the king's seals or signatures, and treasons concerning

---

[1] The italics are Blackstone's.

coin current within this realm."[1] So far indeed is this statute of Philip and Mary from repealing that of Edward VI. as to the necessity of two witnesses, that it expressly confirms it on that point, requiring, as before stated, *two witnesses at the least,* with the exceptions above specified. Such a proceeding therefore as this, which has been exhibited on the part of Prideaux the Attorney-General, was discreditable not only to that law officer, but to the Government which employed and countenanced him in this audacious and shameless mendacity.

Prideaux having again asserted that one witness was " sufficient enough by the forementioned Act of Queen Mary," Lilburne again interrupted him, and it will be seen in what follows that both judge and Attorney-General make but a sorry figure.

"*Lilburne.* Sir, I beseech you produce your Act of Parliament in Queen Mary's time, to prove, in cases of treason, there ought to be but a single witness.

" Mr. *Attorney.* Do not interrupt me, Mr. Lilburne.

" *Lilburne.* I pray you then do not urge that which is not right nor true, but notoriously false ; for, if you persevere in it, I will interrupt you, and tell you of it to the purpose.

" Justic *Jermin.* Though you do recite many things, yet I must tell you, the law of the land saith, the Counsel for the Commonwealth must be heard.

" *Lilburne.* I beseech you, then, let there be no more added to the testimony than right and truth ; for my life lies upon it, and I must and will declare the baseness and falseness of it.

" Mr. *Attorney.* I would not do the tenth part of the hair of your head wrong ; but being entrusted I shall do

---

[1] 4 Blackst. Com. 356, 357.

my duty, and discharge my conscience in my place, which is fully and plainly to open that unto them which in my conscience I think is right and just.

"*Lilburne.* I do repeat it thus, as in my conscience, that he did say, when the copy was first brought, Captain Jones gave him the copy, and Captain Jones did agree with him for the printing of it; and Captain Jones did read the original to his corrector, which corrector amended the printer's faults, and that I had an uncorrected sheet away; and that his forms were taken before he had perfected that.

"Mr. *Attorney.* And Mr. Lilburne came the second time.

"*Lilburne.* Will you spend all day in vain repetitions? You would not give one leave to breathe, nor freely to speak truth, without interruption, although you were laying load upon me for five hours together: I pray, sir, do not now go about to tire the jury with tedious repetitions, nor to sophisticate or adulterate their understandings with your falsehoods and untruths.

"Justice *Jermin.* Mr. Lilburne, the law of the land is, that the counsel for the State must speak last.

"*Lilburne.* Sir, your law is according to the law of God, you said; and that law, I am sure, will have no man to bear false witness: why doth Mr. Prideaux tell the jury such falsehoods as he doth, and take up six times more time to take away my life, than you or he will allow me to defend it." [1]

It will be observed that this Justice Jermin did not put in his word to admonish the Attorney-General with respect to his false statements, both of law and fact. Yet one should think that this was the principal, the first and

[1] State Trials, vol. iv. pp. 1396, 1397.

R

paramount duty of a judge. Why this sacred and paramount duty was left unperformed in 1649, and why it is still left unperformed after the lapse of two centuries of boasted civilization; is a question which may seem easier to answer to those who know only the theory of law than to those who know how much the practice of law is complicated by causes that lie deep in the darkest recesses of human nature. But one remark is obvious enough, that in the present state of society where what passes at a trial in a court of justice is immediately circulated by the press to an extent unknown and unimagined in the 17th century, a very few cases of such bold exposure of mendacity in a counsel as Lilburne's exposure of the mendacity of Prideaux would go far to keep the "licence of counsel" within some bounds of decency.

The Attorney-General admitted that Lilburne's "Agreement of the People" was dated the 1st of May, 1649, and was therefore before the new law of treason of May and July, 1649. But he asserted that when Lilburne "came to bring in those books in August last, then he does now publish that 'Agreement of the People.'"[1] And he afterwards made use of some words which, besides containing a clear admission that, by the old constitutional laws of England, they had no case of treason against Lilburne, evinced an injudicious and even indecent eagerness on the part of the Government for his destruction. Indeed, whatever might be the want of respect evinced by Lilburne towards the Court, the defects both of the Attorney-General and of the judges as regards tact, acuteness, constitutional knowledge, and regard for constitutional rights are very apparent throughout this whole proceeding. The words are these: "Mr. Lilburne

---

[1] State Trials, vol. iv. pp. 1397, 1398.

had been tried for his life sooner, upon my knowledge; I say, Mr. Lilburne had been sooner tried, and sooner condemned and executed, if the law had been sooner made and published. But, as he saith right well, 'where there is no law, there is no transgression;' and therefore there being a law against which he hath offended, he must smart for it." [1]

"*Lilburne.* I am sure I was imprisoned most unjustly, without any the least shadow or colour in law, many months before your acts were made, and extremely oppressed; and now you go about to hang me as a traitor, for at most but crying out of your oppression. O unrighteous men! The Lord in mercy look upon me, and deliver me and every honest man from you, the vilest of men!

"Mr. *Attorney.* And that law was published and proclaimed in this city, by means of which, Mr. Lilburne and others had timely notice that they should not do such things as are there forbidden; it is also told them the penalties of it, which are those that are due for the highest high treason: and yet notwithstanding you see with what boldness, with what conscience, in despite of all law and authority, these books have been made and published by Mr. Lilburne. And whereas he is pleased to say many times, that many men have petitioned for him to the Parliament, he will not affirm to you that ever he petitioned himself; but in all his discourses here, he calls them 'the present men in power, the gentlemen at Westminster;' nay, my lord, he hath not so much as owned the power of the Court, since he came before you, but hath often called you cyphers, and the like.

"*Lilburne.* That is no treason, sir, they entitled them-

[1] State Trials, vol. iv. p. 1400.

selves 'the present power;' and would you hang me for not giving them a better style, than they themselves give to themselves? I think the style of 'present power or present government,' is a very fit style for them.

"Mr. *Attorney*.   My lord, I have told you long, it is the jury that are judges upon the fact; and to you I must appeal for law, if you do believe the evidence is plain and full against him, for which he stands indicted; and so God direct all your judgments! I have done.

"*Lilburne*.   Sir, by your favour, I shall desire to address myself in one word to you; which is, to desire that the jury may read the first chapter of Queen Mary, in the statute-book, and the last clause of the chapter of the 13th of Elizabeth; where they shall clearly see, especially in the statute of Queen Mary, that they abhorred and detested the making of words or writing to be treason; which is such a bondage and snare, that no man knows how to say or do, or behave himself, as is excellently declared by the statutes of Hen. 4, c. 2.[1]   I have done, sir."[2]

The presiding judge, Keble, now commenced his charge to the jury. He began by informing or at least reminding the jury that they are men of conscience, gravity, and understanding; by telling them of the sacredness of an oath " which a man must not transgress in the least, not to save the world;" and then at once proceeded to deal with the matter of two witnesses upon which the Attorney-General had already tried his forensic powers. The judicial attempt to remove the difficulty is a little different from that of the advocate but not more successful. "Mr. Lilburne," said the judge, " hath cited two statutes of Edward VI. to prove there must be two witnesses;

---

[1] By the statute 4 Hen. 4, c. 2, words *insidiatores viarum* and *depopulatores agrorum* are not to be used in an indictment.

[2] State Trials, vol. iv. pp. 1400, 1401.

but I must tell him, were there but one to each fact, it were enough in law; for as for that which was cited of King Edward VI., you have had it fully amended by a latter law of Queen Mary, which doth over-rule that, and also enacts that the common law of England shall be the rule by which all treasons shall be tried; which reacheth to this case too, that there need no more but one witness, and this is law." [1]

It will be seen from this that, whereas the Attorney-General had cited the statute of Philip and Mary which

[1] State Trials, vol. iv. p. 1401. It is worthy of notice that in an edition of the "Statutes at Large, with the titles of those expired and repealed," folio, London, 1676, by Joseph Keble of Gray's Inn, Esquire, a son of this Judge Keble, both these statutes of Edward VI. requiring two witnesses are printed in full. Lord Campbell in his Lives of the Chancellors confounds this Joseph Keble, the reporter, with his father, Richard Keble, serjeant-at-law, and one of the commissioners of the Great Seal under the Commonwealth. Lord Campbell says (vol. iii. p. 351, 4th edition), "A drowsy serjeant of the name of Keble, known only for some bad law reports, was added to the number [of Commissioners of the Great Seal], and joyfully accepted the appointment." Now Joseph Keble the reporter was born in 1632 (Biog. Brit. Keble, Joseph), and was called to the bar in 1658, consequently according to Lord Campbell he must have been appointed a commissioner of the Great Seal before he was called to the bar and at the age of 17. Neither was Keble the reporter ever a serjeant. The account of the even tenour of life of this Joseph Keble gives an idea of the life at the Inns of Court in those days. "Rising before six in the morning he employed himself in his study till eleven; then met company in the walks; from thence to dinner: thence back to his study, and at six to the walks again." That is, when he was not in the Court of King's Bench, which he attended constantly for near 50 years, from 1661 to 1710. In the vacation time he usually walked to Hampstead, having purchased a small copyhold estate at North-end. The writer of his life in the Biographica Britannica says he is informed by Mr. Samuel Keble, Bookseller in Fleet Street, that his relation generally performed the walk in the same number of steps, which were often counted by him. "He continually laboured with his pen, not only to report the law at the King's Bench Westminster, but all the sermons at Gray's Inn Chapel, both forenoon and afternoon, amounting to about 4000. This was the mode in those times when he was young."—*Biog. Brit. Keble, Joseph*, note [B]. Wood (Ath. Oxon. Joseph Keble) says Joseph Keble was made fellow of All Souls' College (from that of Jesus where he first studied) by the visitors appointed by Parliament in 1648; and afterwards settling in Gray's Inn, became a barrister and at length a bencher. But there is no evidence whatever that Keble the reporter was ever a serjeant; or that Keble the serjeant, the father of the other, was ever a reporter.

went directly against him in expressly requiring two witnesses " at the least," the judge suppressed all allusion to that statute of Philip and Mary, and grounded his argument on the repealing statute of the first year of Queen Mary, which was made for the purpose of removing from the statute book the new treasons introduced by the tyranny of Henry VIII. The argument of the judge was so far less blundering than that of the Attorney-General, inasmuch as it relied more on a suppression of the truth, whereas the argument of the Attorney-General was grounded on not a mere suggestion but on a positive assertion of a falsehood. This jury however who tried Lilburne proved themselves on this occasion better keepers of the liberties of England than those who had conferred that title upon themselves, for when the judge's charge to them was ended, the foreman of the jury desired to have the act for treason.[1] At the same time one of the jury desired to drink a cup of sack, assigning as a reason for his request, that they had sat long, and how much longer the debate of the business might last he knew not ; he therefore desired that they might have amongst them a quart of sack to refresh them. But a quart of sack was, it seems, too strong a dose for the conscience of Mr. Justice Jermin, who said, " Gentlemen of the jury, I know for my part in ordinary juries that they have been permitted to drink before they went from the bar ; but in case of felony or treason, I never so much as heard it so, or so much as asked for ; and therefore you cannot have it." One of the judges moved they might have it. But Justice Jermin was firm in the matter of sack, saying,—" I may not give leave to have my conscience to err ; I dare not. And thus if the rest of the judges

---

[1] State Trials, vol. iv. p. 1404.

be of opinion, you shall have a light if you please, the fellow that keeps you shall help you to it; but for sack, you can have none, and therefore withdraw about your work."

The Jury went forth about five o'clock. The Court adjourned till six o'clock, commanding the Lieutenant of the Tower and the Sheriffs to carry the prisoner into the Irish Chamber; which they did. The prisoner staid there about three quarters of an hour; at the end of which time the Jury being come into the Court again, the prisoner was sent for; and after the Crier had caused silence, the Jury's names were called. The Clerk then asked "Are you agreed of your verdict?

"*Jury*. Yes.

"*Clerk*. Who shall speak for you?

"*Jury*. Our Foreman.

"*Cryer*. John Lilburne, hold up thy hand. What say you, look upon the prisoner, is he guilty of the treasons charged upon him, or any of them, or Not Guilty?

"*Foreman*. Not guilty of all of them.

"*Clerk*. Not of all the treasons, nor of any of them that are laid to his charge?

"*Foreman*. Not of all, nor of any one of them.

"*Clerk*. Did he fly for the same?

"*Foreman*. No."

Which "No" being pronounced with a loud voice, immediately the whole multitude of people in the Hall, for joy of the prisoner's acquittal, gave, says the contemporary report, "such a loud and unanimous shout, as is believed was never heard in Guildhall, which lasted for about half an hour without intermission;" a shout "which made the judges for fear turn pale, and hang down their heads;"[1] a shout

---

[1] State Trials, vol. iv. p. 1405.

which Milton had most probably heard and remembered
when he more than ten years after described that scene

> " At which the universal host up sent
> A shout that tore hell's concave."

Meanwhile the prisoner stood silent at the bar, rather more
sad in his countenance than he was before. Silence being
at last made, the Clerk said: "Then hearken to your verdict, the Court hath heard it: You say, that John Lilburne
is Not Guilty of all the treasons laid unto his charge, nor
of any one of them; and so you say all, and that he did
not fly for it?

"*Jury.* Yes, we do so.

"*Clerk.* Gentlemen of the Grand Inquest, the Court
doth discharge you. And you gentlemen of life and
death, the Court doth discharge you also. Lieutenant of
the Tower, you are to carry your prisoner to the Tower
again, and Major General Skippon is to guard you: and
all whom you desire are to assist you." [1]

The prisoner was then removed, and the Court adjourned
till Wednesday following.

Extraordinary were the acclamations for the prisoner's
deliverance, "as the like" says the contemporary narrative
"hath not been seen in England." These acclamations
" and loud rejoicing expressions " went quite through the
streets with him to the very gates of the Tower, and for
joy the people caused that night abundance of bonfires to
be made all up and down the streets. And yet notwithstanding his acquittal by the law, his adversaries kept him
afterwards so long in prison, that the people wondered, and
began to grumble that he was not discharged; and several
of his friends went to the judges, the Parliament, and
Council of State, by whose importunities, and by the

---

[1] State Trials, vol. iv. p. 1405.

seasonable help of the Lord Grey of Groby, Colonel Ludlow, Mr. Robinson, and Colonel Martin, his discharge was
procured, for which a warrant was issued bearing date the
8th of November, 1649.[1]

It is observable that the conduct of the Attorney-General
and of the judges, though discreditably marked by palpably
dishonest dealing with evidence and misstatement of law,
was not disgraced by the brutality and insolence which,
superadded to the cruelty and violation of law, have stamped
with imperishable infamy the political trials of the Stuarts.
Their demeanour towards the prisoner at the bar compared
with that of Scroggs and Jefferies in similar circumstances
was humane and courteous. If the Parliament and Council
of State had been men of greater wisdom and foresight, and
greater knowledge of the English constitution, they would
have taken warning from the very unequivocal demonstra-
tion of public opinion at Lilburne's trial and acquittal.
The assertion of one of their advocates that the greater
part of those who rejoiced at Lilburne's acquittal consisted
of "women, boys, mechanics, and the most sordid sediment
of our plebeians," with "some few Royalists, or turbulent
Levellers," amounting to "some ten or twenty thousand

---

[1] State Trials, vol. iv. p. 1405.
"Whereas Lieut. Colonel John Lilburne hath been committed prisoner to
the Tower, upon suspicion of High
Treason, in order to his trial at law ;
which trial he hath received and is
thereby acquitted : These are therefore
to will and require you, upon sight
hereof, to discharge and set at liberty
the said Lieutenant Colonel John Lilburne from his imprisonment ; for
which this shall be your sufficient
warrant.   Given at the Council of
State at Whitehall this 8th day of
November, 1649.—Signed in the name

and by the order of the Council of
State, appointed by authority of Parliament.   John Bradshaw, President."
"To the Lieutenant of the Tower
of London, or to his Deputy."
On the same day a warrant was
issued for the discharge of Mr. William Walwyn, Mr. Thomas Prince, and
Mr. Richard Overton from their imprisonment in the Tower ; and Orders
in their case as well as in that of Lt.-
Col. John Lilburne were made by the
Council of State accordingly.—*Order
Book of the Council of State*, 8 Nov.
1649.   MS. State Paper Office.

heads in all," [1] besides coming badly from those who called
themselves the rulers or guardians of the commonwealth of
England, refutes itself when amid much weak and irre-
levant verbiage its author, in reference to Lilburne's argument that the law required two witnesses, can do no more
than reiterate the misstatements of the Attorney-General
and the Judges. [2]   But with all their talk about liberty
this rump of the Long Parliament and their Council of
State appear to have become as great enemies to constitutional liberty as the Stuart whose tyranny they had overthrown.   So difficult has it always been, as I have before
said, to get rid of one tyrant without the substitution of
another in his place.   For there seems to be considerable
truth in the saying that the most violent "liberty boys"
are often the greatest tyrants when they have the power.
But this being an imperfection incident to human nature
can only be guarded against or remedied by those safeguards which good constitutional laws interpose between
the subject and the will of any man or any body of men.
The Long Parliament may in this way furnish a warning
to their successors.   And fortunately they were neither
the first nor the last who fought for English constitutional
liberty.   The great barons had fought before them, and had
left to England the germs at least of much of what distinguished her from all the nations of the earth.   It is
worthy of observation that such an acquittal as this of
Lilburne could not have taken place in Scotland, in France,
or anywhere else but in England.   It proved that some
spark of the old constitutional liberty still lived under the
iron heel of the parliamentary armies, though they had
marched from victory to victory till their masters had

<hr>

[1] Answer to the Account of Lil-   p. 1469.
burne's Trial.   State Trials, vol. iv.   [2] State Trials, vol. iv. p. 1449.

almost forgot that an English Court of Justice was a field where even they might sustain a defeat that would be equal to the loss of a battle.

Lieutenant-Colonel John Lilburne, soon after his acquittal on the charge of high treason, having been elected a common-council-man of London, a petition was presented to the House on the 26th of December, 1649, from several aldermen and the sheriffs of London against him; on which the Parliament resolved, "That Lieut.-Col. Lilburne was, by the late Act 'For disabling the election of divers persons to any office or place of trust within the city of London,' disabled to be chosen a common-council-man; and his election was void." [1]

[1] Parl. Hist. vol. iii. p. 1344.

CHAPTER V.

WE must now direct our attention to the state of affairs in Scotland, where the Presbyterian oligarchy was preparing to give effect to the indignation and hatred entertained by them against that party which now ruled England, and which they designated by the contemptuous appellation of the "English Sectaries."

The state of parties had undergone a great change since the times when the predecessor of the "Council of State" had been the "Committee of both Kingdoms," in which together with several members of the present Council of State had sat as the representatives of Scotland, the Earl of Loudon, the Lord Maitland, the Lord Wariston, Sir Charles Erskine, Mr. Robert Barclay, Mr. Kennedy.[1] In the earlier part of the struggle between King Charles and his Parliament the English and the Scottish Parliaments had a common interest, namely the interest of securing themselves against the King's attempt to make himself absolute. In this earlier period the Presbyterians were the

---

[1] Journal of the resolutions and proceedings of the Committee of both kingdoms, commencing February 164¾. MS. State Paper Office. "Orders for the manner of proceeding. 1. A chairman to be chosen to continue a fortnight. 2. The Earl of Northumberland the first fortnight. 3. That the chairman be instructed to provide some minister of the Assembly to pray daily at the meeting and rising of the Committee." The Committee met first at Essex House; then Feb. 19, 164¾, at Yorke House; Feb. 20, at Warwick House; Feb. 21, at Arundell House; Feb. 22, at Worcester House; Feb. 23, at Derby House; and there they continued to meet. Journal, *ibid.*

dominant party in the English Parliament, and during this period the English Parliament and Scottish Parliament agreed in the main; inasmuch as they both held and acted upon the principle that all the higher offices and commands belonged of right, that is by right of birth, to the nobility. But when the Independents, who held on the other hand and acted on the principle that at least military and naval commands were to be conferred, not on men of large rent-rolls or long pedigrees, but on men who knew how to win battles, turned the Presbyterians out of the English Parliament, the Scottish Parliament prepared for war against them. This was the real point on which they were at issue. The question however was complicated by many other considerations that entered into it, some of which I will endeavour to explain. Some of these considerations, particularly the Scottish Parliament's professions of zeal to avenge the King's blood, were introduced to attempt to wash out some portion of the infamy of selling their king to the English Parliament.

There is perhaps no part of modern history where the truth has been more systematically kept out of sight than the history of Scotland. The explanation of the transaction of the sale of King Charles the First to the English Parliament for a sum of money under the name of arrears of pay, given by Sir Walter Scott, is one among a hundred examples of this. Sir Walter Scott says that "this sordid and base transaction, though the work exclusively of a mercenary army, stamped the whole nation of Scotland with infamy." [1] Now I believe the army and the people of Scotland had no more voice or part in the transaction than the people of Germany have or had in the sale of their bodies and blood by their princes and

---

[1] History of Scotland, contained in Tales of a Grandfather, vol. i. p. 464.

potentates. The Scottish army was not an army of mercenaries at all, but an army levied partly on the feudal, partly on the Celtic clan principle carried into operation with an unrelenting severity. Such men did not serve for pay, but their service was the condition on which they held, some their estates, some their farms, some their kail-yards of their feudal superiors. Arrears of pay were claimed and paid. Paid to whom? To the covenanted oligarchy for the time being, who paid perhaps some part of the money to the colonels of regiments. Now who were at that time the colonels of regiments in the army of the Covenanted Oligarchy and Kirk of Scotland? This is a subject somewhat dark; but after much digging in the rubbish heaps and fossil remains of Scotch records and Scotch peerages and baronages, we obtain some glimpses of light.

Thus in 1644 we find a certain individual styled the Laird of Lawers petitioning the Scotch Parliament that his troop of horse may be mustered and paid.[1] Again, we find that the body of horse under Strahan that defeated and captured Montrose in Ross-shire was partly composed of 36 musquetaires of Lawers' regiment.[2] Again, we are told that, at the battle of Dunbar, Lawers' regiment of Highlanders "stood to the push of pike and were all cut in pieces."[3] Now the first impression naturally is that this Laird of Lawers must have been some long tried and very distinguished officer; probably some hardy old veteran of Gustavus Adolphus. Some small misgiving is indeed con-

---

[1] Balfour, vol. iii. p. 176.

[2] Balfour, vol. iv. p. 9. It is observable that the word "musquetaires" is here used in the sense of the French "mousquetaires" who corresponded to the English or Scottish regiments of Life or Horse Guards.

At the same time, as the infantry regiments were then composed partly of musketeers, partly of pikemen, when the word "musketeers" is used with reference to English regiments, it must be understood to mean infantry.

[3] Gumble's Life of Monk, p. 38.

veyed by two or three words of Monk's old chaplain——
"the colonel was absent of the name of the Campbells."
But then though Monk, as he led on his brigade of foot
himself pike in hand, could not fail to know what regiment
offered most resistance to his charge, he was not likely to
know or care very much about the family names of the
Scotch lairdships.   And the question still remained who
was this Laird of Lawers who had such distinguished
regiments of horse and foot?   Now we find on the
authority of "Douglas's Peerage of Scotland," title Campbell Earl of Loudoun, that Sir John Campbell of Lawers
was created Earl of Loudoun[1] by a patent dated at
Theobald's, 12th May, 1633.   This Earl of Loudoun was
also, at the time he was receiving pay for these troops of
horse and this regiment of Highlanders, the Scotch Chancellor, and seems to have been a sort of orator and fond of
hearing himself talk.   Some years before this time, when
Whitelock and Maynard as two eminent English lawyers
were sent for late one evening to Essex House, where the
debates of the Presbyterian chiefs, namely the Scottish
Commissioners and such English Presbyterians as the Earl
of Essex and Holles, were held, to give their opinion as to
the meaning of the word incendiary in English law,
Whitelock describes the Lord Chancellor of Scotland as
making a speech, the burthen of which was " You ken vary
weel that General Lieutenant Cromwell is no friend of ours
—and you ken vary weel the accord 'twixt the twa
kingdoms, and the union by the Solemn League and Covenant, and, if Lt.-Gen. Cromwell be an incendiary between
the twa nations, how is he to be proceeded against ?"   We
shall see this chancellor inflicting on Montrose, when poor

---

[1] The estate of Loudon belonged by   John Campbell of Lawers.
inheritance to the wife of this Sir

man he could not escape from it, a large dose of his
rhetorical invective. And he is represented as on one
occasion "haranguing to the army the sense of the Kirk
and the Committee." [1] His Lordship probably considered
this both a safer and easier way of earning his pay as a
colonel of horse and foot, than leading his regiments into
action. But the Roman military commanders who were
most successful were those members of their oligarchical
body who cultivated the art of war as well as the art of
public speaking, and also exposed their own persons where
there was most danger.

We are also informed that the Lord Lorne, the Marquis
of Argyle's eldest son, had a regiment ; [2] but of his sharing
the dangers and hardships of his regiment we are not
informed any more than of Lord Loudoun's sharing the
dangers of the troops of horse and the regiment of foot
whose pay he found it convenient to receive under the
name of the Laird of Lawers. [3] Such were some of the
men among whom the money paid by the English Parliament for the person of the king under the name of arrears
of pay was divided. I do not mean by these words that
there was not some agreement between the English and
Scottish Parliaments for allowing pay to the army of the
Scots. But is it true that the Scottish Parliament or
Convention of Estates first taxed the people of Scotland to
defray the expense of their army and then claimed pay-

---

[1] Sir Edward Walker, p. 169.

[2] Sir Edward Walker, p. 165. In
the Order Book of the Council of
State—under date 5 March, 164$\frac{3}{8}$ (MS.
State Paper Office), there is a pass for
Mr. Archd. Campbell and his two
servants to go to France and return
with "the lord of Lorne, eldest son of
the Marquis of Argyle, and his retinue

consisting of ten persons."

[3] There is some confusion in this
matter which is not easy to clear up.
Spalding says that Campbell of Lawers
was killed at Aulderne, with his regiment. He also mentions Loudon's
(the chancellor's) regiment as being
there. Lawers' regiment was probably
led by a relation of the chancellor.

ment of the English Parliament? If so, did they return the money they had taken from the poor people's pockets? Wishart, who is not indeed a conclusive authority on such a point, says that to defray this expense they imposed much higher taxes and subsidies upon the people than had been ever before known.[1] It is not in the least surprising that a Government composed of such men should be annihilated by a Government the colonels of whose regiments were such men as Cromwell, Ireton, Lambert, and Monk, who, whatever their faults might be, did not receive the pay of regiments which other men led into action.

There was some years ago, and may be still, a sword kept at Douglas Castle, bearing two hands pointing to a heart placed between them, and the date 1329, being the year in which Robert Bruce charged Sir James Douglas, commonly known as the Good Lord James, to carry his heart to the Holy Land. The sword resembles a Highland claymore of the usual size, is of an excellent temper, and admirably poised. Could its original owner, whose knightly truth and honour were as undoubted as his valour and military genius, have looked up from his grave after the lapse of three hundred years, and beheld the stain which a few sordid hypocrites or fanatics had brought upon the country for which he had fought so well, he might have said in answer to the taunts of Clarendon,[2] Sidney,[3] and Mrs. Hutchinson,[4] in the sorrowful words of Othello—

> —— " I am not valiant neither,
> But every puny whipster gets my sword :——
> But why should honour outlive honesty ?
> Let it go all " ——

[1] Mem. of Montrose, p. 37, Edin. 1819.

[2] Clarendon in his History generally, and particularly in his account of the battles of Dunbar and Worcester.

[3] Algernon Sidney in his Discourses concerning Government, chap. ii. sect. 28, p. 222, folio, London, 1698.

[4] Memoirs of Colonel Hutchinson generally, and particularly in her account of the death of Colonel Thornbagh.

When a man has committed such an act, probably the least thing he can do next is to go and hang himself like Judas Iscariot. A portion of these Scottish Iscariots composed of what was called the more moderate part of the Presbyterians, led by the Duke of Hamilton, his brother the Earl of Lanark, the Lord Chancellor Loudoun, and the Earl of Lauderdale, when they saw all the consequences of their act of treachery, repented themselves ; and, though they did not follow the example of their Hebrew prototype, and bring again to the English Parliament the pieces of gold which were the price of blood, they entered into an Engagement to restore the King by force of arms—whence they were called Engagers. The attempt failed and Hamilton was taken and beheaded ; the English Parliament regarding their repentance pretty much as the chief priests and elders of the Jews regarded that of Iscariot, when they said " What is that to us ? See thou to that." But Loudoun and Lauderdale lived and flourished to commit new treacheries, cruelties, and crimes.

The base transaction to which I have referred had indeed the sanction of what was called the Scottish Parliament. But it is to be borne in mind that the body of persons so called no more represented the Scottish nation than the Thirty Tyrants represented the Athenian people, or the Decemviri represented the Roman people. The Scottish people were no more responsible for the acts of that oligarchical assembly than the Roman people were responsible for the crimes of the Decemviri, or the Athenian people for the crimes of the Thirty Tyrants, or the French peasants for the crimes of the French nobility.[1] The Scottish Par-

---

[1] Barrington quotes an old French and an old Scotch proverb to show that the peasants or villeins were regarded in the same light in France and in Scotland :—

" Oignez vilain, il vous poindra;
   Poignez vilain, il vous oindra
—" which we apply to spaniels at pre-

liament was an assembly in which there was no freedom of debate and no freedom of vote. The representatives of the counties and of the boroughs sat in the same house [1] or chamber with the peers and "ran in a string," to use the words of Baillie,[2] now "after the vote" of Hamilton, now after that of Argyle, according as the faction of one or other of these "great men" might happen to be uppermost: and on the heads of the members of that wretched oligarchy rest the guilt and the shame of the treachery, rapacity, hypocrisy, of the misgovernment, disaster, and defeat, which have long stamped with infamy a whole nation of brave, high-spirited, and honourable men.

Between the fall of the old nobility and the rise of the new to political power in England there was a long interval, extending from the accession of the Tudors to the expulsion of the Stuarts, during which the new nobility constituted neither an aristocracy nor an oligarchy in the proper sense of those terms, but were the mere creatures and satellites of the Court. In Scotland the old feudal or military aristocracy may be considered to have existed for about a century longer than in England. The successful armed opposition of the nobility to the misgovernment of Queen Mary is a proof of this. And, though on the accession of James to the throne of England, such of the nobility as were adherents of the Court became thoroughly servile, and ready to follow the king to whatever extent he pleased in all

sent. Thus likewise the Scotch proverb :

" Kiss a carle, and clap a carle, and
    that's the way to tine a carle,
  Knock a carle, and ding a carle,
    and that's the way to win a carle."

Barrington on the Statutes, p. 310, note, 5th ed. 4to, London 1796. The French nobility reaped the fruit of this at the French Revolution. The Scotch nobility escaped reaping similar fruit by the union of Scotland with England.

[1] House anciently meant room or chamber.

[2] Letters and Journals, vol. iii. p. 35, Edinburgh 1842.

matters, either of Church or State ;[1] during a great part of the 17th century, the power which the Scottish nobility still retained over their vassals, the strength of their fastnesses, and their distance from the seat of Government, gave them when banded together so much power of a not ineffectual armed resistance, that they might still be considered as retaining some of the features of a military aristocracy. But the Parliament of England and its General Cromwell showed them that neither their feudal power, nor the military habits of their vassals, nor the rugged and mountainous nature of their country could resist a military aristocracy, compared to the valour, skill, and resources of which their pretensions to military aristocracy were but a shadow and an empty name. For this, among other reasons, I will in these pages generally designate them as an oligarchy rather than an aristocracy.

The Reformation or religious revolution in England and Scotland in the sixteenth century, and the political revolution in the seventeenth century stand to each other in the relation not only of antecedent and consequent, but of cause and effect. May,[2] as it appears to me, makes a great mistake in saying that mixing up religion in the dispute about laws and liberties rather injured the cause of the Parliament. On the contrary the forces of the Parliament had the worst of it till Cromwell beat up his drum for the ardent and energetic souls lodged in strong bodies, who had long been groaning under a most grievous spiritual thraldom, and were burning to do battle against the Powers of Darkness, which in their vocabulary meant the Powers

---

[1] Lord Fleming in a letter to King James expresses his zealous desire to follow his master in all matters, either of Church or State, declaring that different conduct was inexcusable in a subject.—*Lord Hailes's Letters of the Time of James I.* Letter 2nd.

[2] History of the Parliament, lib. i. p. 115.

Spiritual and Temporal that then ruled in England. M. Guizot[1] endeavours to account for the important part which the religious revolution played in the political revolution by saying that in England the religious revolution had been brought about by the king and nobility, not, as in Germany, by the people ; that consequently, while royalty, nobility and episcopacy divided among them the rich spoils of the papal church, the religious revolution left many of the popular wants unsatisfied. The case of Scotland might appear at first sight to bear more resemblance to the case of Germany than to that of England, inasmuch as in Scotland the religious revolution presented some popular features which it did not in England, and the form of church government which the Reformation established in Scotland was democratical. But I much doubt whether the popular will had more to do with the Reformation in Scotland than it had in England. There were moreover many amusements and not a few things of a more substantial kind, (when the church lands passed into the hands of laymen), which the people lost by the change, and the loss of which was grievous to them at the time. For instance, the exhibition of Robin Hood and his band was a favourite amusement in Scotland as well as in England. And though in 1555 it was ordered by a statute of the Parliament of Scotland that "na manner of person be chosen Robert Hude, nor Little John, Abbot of Unreason, Queen of May, nor otherwise," we find six years after, in 1561, John Knox complaining that "the rascal multitude were stirred up to make a Robin Hude, whilk enormity was of many years left and damned by statute and Act of Parliament ; yet would they not be forbidden." They raised a

[1] Histoire de la Civilization en Europe, Leçon 13.

serious tumult, and made prisoners the magistrates who
endeavoured to suppress it. They continued these festivities
down to 1592. It is evident that the furious presbyterian
zeal of the Jenny Geddeses and Manse Headriggs was the
growth of a later period—was the product in fact of the
teaching of a church rendered democratical (at least as far
as democratical implied poverty) by the aristocracy or oligarchy who brought about the reformation in Scotland.
For, though it may appear somewhat paradoxical, the popular or democratical form which the Church government
assumed in Scotland was really owing to the intensely aristocratical nature of the religious revolution in that country.[1]
And the aristocratical nature of that religious revolution
was owing to the power of the aristocracy in Scotland.
This power, though it was in part, in great part no doubt,
a consequence of the low state of manufactures and commerce, of the comparatively small power of the Crown, and
of the physical character of the country itself, was also
connected with moral causes which had exercised for many
ages a deep and strong influence on the minds of the people
of Scotland, an influence which it required many ages of
misgovernment, of injustice, of oppression, and cruelty to
destroy.[2] The reformed clergy complain that those who

[1] The Scottish nobility and gentry
are directly charged by the Scottish
historians with preferring the Presbyterian form of church government
from the hope of plunder. Johnston, *Hist. Rer. Brit.* Lib. I. p. 16,
1655, says two classes of men approved the Presbyterian form "unum
genus laicorum, qui ad proprietatem
ac directum dominium bonorum Ec-
clesiæ munitam hanc viam putarunt,
alterum cleri, qui ambitione lapsi, et
gloriæ cupidi, in licentiam turbarum

effrenatam ac indomitam eruperunt ;
disputationibus ac tribunitiis con-
cionibus populum paratam incitarunt."
See also *Spottiswood*, pp. 86, 164,
folio, London, 1677.

[2] That this influence still continued
in great force in the middle of the
17th century appears from abundant
evidence. Captain Hodgson, when he
first entered Scotland with Cromwell
in Septr. 1648, was struck with it.
" The gentry of the nation " he says,
Memoirs, p. 124, " have such influence

had got possession of the Church lands, and tithes, and who had before made a great outcry against the exactions of the Romish Church, " are now more rigorous in exacting tithes and other duties paid before to the Church, than ever the papists were, and so the tyranny of priests is turned into the tyranny of lords and lairds.   For this we require that the gentlemen, barons, lords, earls, and others be content to live upon their own rents, and suffer the Church to be restored to her right and liberty, that by her restitution the poor that heretofore have been oppressed may now receive some comfort and relaxation." [1]   But the lairds, lords, and earls turned, as might have been expected, a deaf ear to the requisition of John Knox and his clerical bre-thren.

There was an essential difference between the English and Scottish feudal aristocracies.   The English feudal aris-tocracy consisted of the leaders of a conquering caste ; and, though they might inspire fear and perhaps admiration not unmixed with hatred, could call up none of that other class of emotions which were associated in the mind of a Greek with Miltiades, Leonidas, Themistocles, in that of a Roman with Camillus and the Scipios, in that of a Scotchman with Wallace, Bruce, and Douglas.   There are, or at least were, no names that an English poet could invoke with such effect as a Greek poet or orator could invoke the names of those who fought at Marathon, at Salamis, at Platæa, or as

over the commonalty that they can lead them what way they please." his is however an exaggerated state-ment, since, as we shall see, they often could not lead them to serve in these wars.   They were obliged to use force, to drive not lead.

[1] Spottiswood, p. 164.   The extract in the text is from a form of Church policy framed by John Knox, partly in imitation of the reformed churches of Germany, partly of that which he had seen in Geneva, and presented in the Convention held at Edinburgh in January 1559-60.

Scott invoked the to a Scotchman talismanic names in these
lines—

> " What vails the vain knight-errant's brand ?
> O Douglas, for thy leading wand !
> Fierce Randolph for thy speed !
> O for one hour of Wallace wight,
> Or well-skill'd Bruce to rule the fight !"

While the English feudal aristocracy owed their lands to
their conquest of those who tilled those lands, the Scottish
feudal aristocracy, or the best portion of them, held or were
understood to hold lands which had been granted to their
ancestors for services done with their swords in the defence
of Scotland against foreign invaders, Danish or English.
This at least was the theory.   But this theory did not
apply to that large extent of lands which had belonged to
the Roman Catholic Church and were seized by the nobility
at the Reformation.   The root of the title to the other
lands remained however undisturbed, and entwined with
many heroic memories.   The names of those who had once
held those lands are linked indissolubly with many an old
but well-remembered battle-field, with many a mountain,
with many a grey rock, with many a wild glen and moun-
tain-stream, which, though there now only the solitary
angler throws his fly, and the as solitary water-ouzel seeks
its food, rolls on haunted for ever by the spirits of those
who in times long gone by fought and bled and died for
religion and liberty.   It is this historic renown that gives
a tenfold charm to scenes wild and rugged indeed but of
great natural beauty.   The stream clear as crystal pursues
its course at the bottom of a deep glen, the sides of which
are crags of stupendous height and fantastic shape, hoary
with the storms of innumerable ages, and rugged and bare,
save where some solitary birch-tree, or oak, or wych-elm, or

mountain-ash has twined its roots amid the rocky crevices. But the wild ravine is associated with memories not its own. Rock, cave, tree, torrent speak still of the deeds and sufferings of those who bled and died for the independence of Scotland, who " fell devoted, but undying." And though those men have been dead near 600 years, the eye of the dullest peasant in Scotland will still brighten at the very sound of their names. The heaths, the mountains, the crumbling ruins of the rock-built castles are all consecrated by the same memories : and form the imperishable monument of those who have no other sepulchre, to whom the barbarous policy of the English invader refused even a grave ; affording a striking illustration of the truth of the words in the funeral oration of Pericles, in Thucydides, that " of illustrious men all their native land is the sepulchre." [1]

In Scotland, the whole of the property which had belonged to the Roman Catholic Church, and which has been estimated as amounting at the time of the Reformation to " little less than one-half of the property in the nation," [2] was seized by the nobility and gentry. This seizure, in all cases an act of public robbery, was in some instances attended with the most savage cruelty. Nor was it likely that those, who had thus gotten possession of all this property, would give up their prey at the solicitation of the reformed clergy. When the latter proposed a plan for the

---

[1] ἀνδρῶν ἐπιφανῶν πᾶσα γῆ τάφος— Thucyd. II. 43. Hobbes translates these words " to famous men all the earth is a sepulchre," which, though the word γῆ is ambiguous, was not what was here meant ; the meaning, as is apparent from the context, being not the whole earth absolutely, but only the whole earth or territory of Attica.

[2] " The Scottish Clergy paid one-half of every tax imposed on land ; and as there is no reason to think that, in that age, they would be loaded with any unequal share of the burden, we may conclude that, by the time of the Reformation, little less than one-half of the property in the nation had fallen into the hands of a society which is always acquiring and can never lose."—*Robertson's Hist. of Scotland*, vol. i. pp. 141, 142, 4th edn., London, 1761.

maintenance of a national Church out of this national property, and also of hospitals, schools, and universities,
though they did not go farther than Henry the Eighth so
liberal in promises had done, the lords who had seized the
Church property said the plan of John Knox was a
"devout imagination," but visionary and impracticable;
and they retained by force the whole of the church property for their own use.   Hence not only the poverty
of the church, but of the universities in Scotland, and the
consequent discouragement and decay of sound learning,
together with many consequences of this, tending to a
slavish subjugation on one side and an exorbitant insolence
on the other.   And hence those revenues of a few individuals in Scotland; revenues which at the present day by
the enormous increase of rent within the last century, if
devoted to their legitimate purpose, would not only edu-
cate the great bulk of the people well, and give to those
who evinced superior abilities a superior education, but
would relieve all classes nearly altogether from taxation.

The passage which I have quoted in a note a page or
two back from a contemporary historian [1] describes the
Presbyterian form of Church government as supported by
two classes of men, the one consisting of the powerful laymen who looked to the plunder of the old Church, the
other of the clergy who hoped to attain power and popularity by popular eloquence.   Besides these two classes,
there was a third class consisting of the great body of the
people who, having been kept in a state of very dense
ignorance by the Romish priesthood, were in a condition to
receive any impressions which their new teachers and
preachers sought to stamp on their dark and uncultured
minds.   For convenience these two last classes, the clergy

[1] Johnston, Rer. Brit. Hist. Lib. I. p. 16, 1655.

and the people, may be treated as one, as they both partook, largely of the popular or democratical element. We have thus two classes of Scottish Presbyterians, the one oligarchical, the other democratical.

It is a remarkable feature in the history of the Scottish Presbyterian Church that, though in the scramble at the overthrow of the power of the Church of Rome in Scotland, the nobility contrived to appropriate to themselves even more of the wealth of that church than the nobility in England had done, leaving in fact nothing at all to the Reformed Church, while in England a good deal had been left to the church and universities, yet in Scotland the reformed clergy, unlike the reformed clergy in England, arrogated to themselves all, if not more than all, the power which the pope of Rome had formerly claimed. In the second declinature of Black, of the King and Council, God, it is said, has given the keys of the kingdom of heaven to the church ; and the clergy—(the clergy being " they whom Christ hath called—Christ's servants "[1]—) " are empowered to admonish, rebuke, convince, exhort, and threaten, to deliver unto Satan, to lock out and debar from the kingdom of heaven." [2] And Mr. Black further says, " the discharge and form of delivery of my commission should not nor cannot be lawfully judged by them to whom I am sent, they being as both judge and party, sheep and not pastors : to be judged by this word, and not to be judges thereof." [3]

The Scottish Presbyterians being composed of several distinct parts, we must be careful to assign to each part what belonged to it. Such care is the more needed inasmuch as the clerical part has come in for a larger share of blame than belongs to it. Nevertheless with all the care we can

---

[1] Calderwood, pp. 329, 330.   [2] Calderwood, p. 347.   [3] Calderwood, p. 348.

bestow on the subject, though some modern writers have
written about the clergy's treatment of Charles II. and
their interference with military affairs with as much confidence as if they had been present, it is extremely difficult
if not absolutely impossible to give an account which shall
be more than an approximation to the truth.

We have nothing approaching to a good contemporary
picture of the Scottish Presbyterian clergy of that time.
The representations of them drawn by two literary artists
more than a century after, Hume and Scott, are rather
caricatures than pictures.   There can be no question of
one thing, namely, that they and their successors for some
two or three generations, whatever may have been their
merits and their virtues, contrived to render themselves
extremely disagreeable to many persons, some of whom
could repay the intolerance and the long prayers and longer
preachings with which they had been exercised or assailed
with, the shafts of ridicule, others with even sharper
weapons.   The Scottish Presbyterian clergy were moreover so far true to what they announced as their mission
that they were by no means disposed to look upon the
sins of Charles the Second and the Duke of Buckingham
with the lenient eye with which Archbishop Laud had
regarded the sins of Charles's grandfather and Buckingham's
father.   Besides the exaggerated picture of the interference
of the Presbyterian clergy in political and military affairs,
(and it can be shown that the interference with the
military commanders that led to so many disasters—at
Kelsyth, at Preston, at Dunbar, was not by the clergy but
by the nobility of the Committee of Estates), I am inclined
to think that, though the clergy no doubt interfered much,
though not very much more than the Independent zealots,
in matters of religion and morality, their interference was

not regarded with any great degree of observance far less of terror by the more powerful classes in Scotland. Lord Dartmouth tells a story, told him by Duke Hamilton, of the old Earl of Eglinton, which seems to show that men of that rank took the censures of the church very easily. The Earl of Eglinton was on the stool of repentance for fornication, and on the 4th Sunday the Minister called to him to come down, for his penance was over. "It may be so," said the Earl, "but I shall always sit here for the future, because it is the best seat in the kirk, and I do not see a better man to take it from me."[1]   This Earl of Eglinton, who belonged to the party of Argyle and the rigid Presbyterians, evidently found the censures of his kirk as well as her prayers and sermons bearable, if not even pleasant, provided he had a comfortable seat in the kirk, even though that seat was the stool of repentance.

The truth is, the stool of repentance had in that age been made too common and general to be so much of a distinction any way as it was in the last generation when an eccentric old Scotch peer, being told that a moderate pecuniary fine paid to the kirk session would answer all the purposes of the stool of repentance, replied—"No, he should very much prefer sitting on the stool of repentance." Whitelock says under date Feb. 5, 164$\frac{8}{9}$ "Letters from Scotland that they bring all to the stool of repentance that were in the last invasion of England." Loudon the Chancellor, whose wife had in her own right the estate of Loudon, and threatened to divorce him for his manifold adulteries, unless he submitted to the penance enjoined by the clergy, sat on the stool of repentance in his own parish church, received a rebuke in the face of the whole

---

[1] Burnet's History of his Own Times, vol. i. p. 281, note D, Oxford, 1833.

congregation. The scene as described was very characteristic of the time. The Chancellor with many tears
deplored his temporary departure from the covenant, when
he joined the party of the Engagement, that is, the party
of the Duke of Hamilton which engaged to restore the
king by force of arms, and solicited in his behalf the
prayers of the congregation, who at such a refreshing spectacle were dissolved in tears of joy. Mr. Brodie says
that in a MS. of Wodrow's which he had seen it is said
that Archbishop Sharpe was at first for the Engagement;
but, finding that it was not a politic game, he brought
to the stool of repentance all his parishioners who had in
the least inclined that way.[1]

Hume and Scott, while they indulge their powers of
ridicule in speaking of Puritanical or Presbyterian intolerance, see or appear to see nothing ridiculous and nothing
hateful in the absurd yet savage intolerance of Laud. Now
while we object equally to the intolerance of both, we are
prepared to show (not indeed that either party abounded
in wisdom, but) that the Presbyterians of that time had
among them on the whole more wisdom than the Prelatists.
Laud and the churchmen of his school, among whom I of
course do not include any of those great thinkers and
excellent writers, who, "by the strength of their philo-
sophical genius or by their large and tolerant spirit have
given imperishable lustre to the Church of England,"[2]
might have more of what is called learning than Baillie
and his Presbyterian beethren ; but Queen Elizabeth, no
mean authority, had said long before to the Bishop of St.
David's " I find the most learned clerks are not always the

[1] Brodie's History of the British
Empire, vol. iv. p. 137, note.

[2] Austin's Province of Jurisprudenc
determined, p. 81.

wisest men ; " and we have looked in vain among Laud's letters, diaries, and other writings for any such proof of wisdom as is found in the following sentence of Baillie :— " I am more and more in the mind that it were for the good of the world that churchmen did meddle with ecclesiastical affairs only ; that, were they never so able otherwise, they are unhappy statesmen." [1]

There are no collections of papers relating to those times from which so much true knowledge of them may be obtained as the Earl of Strafford's Letters and Dispatches and Principal Baillie's Letters and Journals. In the letters between Laud and Strafford are stamped, as no hands but their own could stamp them, the characters of the prelate and the peer who licked the dust before the Stuart kings, and were as domineering and insolent to their fellow-subjects as if the Stuarts were already as absolute as the Cæsars or the Bourbons, and they wielded the power of Sejanus or Richelieu. It has been truly said " tell me when a man laughs and I will tell you what he is." The very jokes that pass between Laud and Strafford, the grim, cruel, insolent, tyrannical, and withal base and pusillanimous jokes, tell more of the two men's nature than volumes of grave history could tell. Now turn from those volumes, which contain the correspondence of Laud and Strafford, to the Letters and Journals of Robert Baillie the Covenanter and Presbyterian minister. Here also indeed you find narrowness enough of intellectual vision, and intolerance enough too. But as regards Baillie and his brethren, the Presbyterian clergy—apart from the Scottish oligarchy and a few of the more furious fanatics and firebrands among the clergy by nature tyrants like Laud and Strafford—you find yourself at least among human beings

---

[1] Baillie's Letters and Journals, vol. iii. p. 38. Edinburgh, 1842.

—like their countryman Baillie Macwheeble, men of earthly mould after all—men indeed with many human infirmities, but likewise with human hearts in which the fountains of honesty, simplicity, and pity have not been dried up by that pride and ambition which had transformed Laud and Strafford into such ruthless tyrants. This balance of humanity in favour of the Presbyterian clergy was partly the effect of the absence of the objects of worldly ambition, which the constitution of the English hierarchy set before the eyes of such men as Laud. Yet the Presbyterian church did not really possess that absolute independence of the State which it professed. For the Scottish oligarchy required for their purposes a poor church as the English kings required for their purposes a rich church; and Argyle and his oligarchical committee made use of the Scottish kirk precisely as King James and King Charles made use of the English church.[1] And Oliver Cromwell made a similar use of the religious element among the Independents or sectaries, as the Presbyterians contemptuously called them, a use which leads me to call attention to a main cause of the Independents' strength as it was of the Presbyterians' weakness.

It is important to remark that the troops of Cromwell, whose religious enthusiasm combined with discipline and valour proved more than a match for the high spirit and impetuous onset of the Cavaliers, appear to have enlisted of their own free will, and not to have been forced to serve as the poor oppressed Scottish peasantry were by their lords and lairds. Beside this, every man, however humble his original rank in life, who entered the parliamentary army, might rise by his own merit to the highest military rank;

[1] Sir Edward Walker's Historical Discourses—Journal of Affairs in Scotland in 1650, p. 194. London, folio, 1705.

and moreover if he felt or fancied he had a call from Heaven to preach or teach the peculiar conclusions which he had come to from reading the Bible, he was as much entitled, in the opinion of his comrades and officers, to act as a preacher, as if he had studied at a university and taken orders from a bishop or a presbytery. Yet their toleration admitted the preaching of men who made religion a profession. Thus we are informed that "on Sunday the 27th Oct. 1650 there preached in the cathedral at Carlisle in the forenoon the Governor's chaplain, in the afternoon an officer of our army."[1] Cromwell would indeed take care with his wary eye "ne quid detrimenti respublica caperet," that no harm might come of any preacher unusually violent or mad in his notions; and he would for the most part be able to do that by first listening with an air of edification and then praying and preaching himself. It is clear that by this process such evils as are alleged to have befallen the Presbyterians could not have happened in Cromwell's army. Cromwell did his work by being really supreme in his army, by being at once king, priest, and prophet among his soldiers. He was not the man to permit any holy Mr. Blattergowl or gifted Gilfillan to stop his march or prevent him from fighting on a Sunday on the ground of saving the nation from the sin of Sabbath-breaking; or, under pretence of revelations obtained from Heaven by much wrestling with the Lord in prayer, to force him to fight against his own better judgment. Oliver could wrestle with the Lord in prayer himself, and he had his own revelations and his own signs and visions from on high, of which he knew the interpretation better than any

---

[1] Letters from the Head-Quarters of our Army in Scotland, p. 323 — published in Sir H. Slingsby's and Captain Hodgson's Memoirs, with notes by Sir Walter Scott. Edinburgh, 1806.

ordained interpreter of them all.   And as Cromwell thus
suffered himself to be controlled by no theocracy in the
shape of a Kirk Commission, established at his head-
quarters, neither would he have marched as he did to unin-
terrupted victory, if he had submitted as Baillie did at
Kilsyth,[1] and Preston, and David Leslie at Dunbar,[2] to be
dictated to by the oligarchical members of the Committee
of Estates.

The Independents were also in their own opinion of
themselves a peculiar and chosen people.   For they too
claimed a monopoly of God, and declared, like the Presbyterians, that their enemies were God's enemies.   A favourite expression of Cromwell's was "to have the execution
of," or "to be the executioners of the Lord's enemies."
Nevertheless they were undoubtedly more tolerant towards
other forms of Protestantism than the Presbyterians : and
in some matters connected with toleration they evinced on
several occasions a spirit very different from the Presbyterian.   Thus Mr. Howard, the Sheriff of Cumberland,
having applied to the Council of State for special assistance on the subject of witchcraft, is curtly informed that
the Council can give him no directions concerning the discovery or punishment of witches, but refer him to the
usual course of law.[3]

In estimating the character of fanatics an error, I apprehend, of some magnitude slips into the calculation by
assuming that honest fanatics are necessarily honest men.
Whereas, without professing to state the proportions with
epigrammatic point at the cost of accuracy by saying that
a man is half fanatic and half knave, we may say truly

---

[1] See Lieut.-Gen. Baillie's "Vindication for his own part of Kilsyth, and
Preston" in Principal Baillie's Letters
and Journals, vol. ii. p. 420†.

[2] See Baillie's Letters and Journals,
vol. iii. p. 111.   Edinburgh 1842.

[3] Order Book of the Council of State,
May 13, 1650. MS. State Paper Office.

enough of some men that all of them that is not knave is fanatic, or that all of them that is not fanatic is knave. The keeping this in view will assist somewhat in furnishing a key to the character of such men as Cromwell, where the addition of other ingredients to the composition of the character will of course alter the above-stated proportions, but where the existence of pure or true fanaticism will be no guarantee for the existence of pure or true honesty. An honest man however, if he be a fanatic, will be an honest fanatic and not the less an honest man. But in the case of a knave, in consequence of the falsehood which is a part of his character, if he profess himself a fanatic, it will be always difficult to say how much of his fanaticism is real and how much pretended, for of course a knave is capable of being a fanatic, as he is capable of being a maniac; and in both cases he may pretend to be more than he is: for a man who trades in falsehood may feign fanaticism as he may feign madness or anything else.

Among the Independents as among the Presbyterians of that time there were undoubtedly many honest men, who were likewise honest fanatics. Those men were peculiarly liable to be deluded by men of their respective parties who, though they might be more or less honest in their fanaticism, were as regarded the other part of their nature actuated by motives of self-aggrandizement and worldly ambition. It was thus that Cromwell was able to deceive so long his old friends among the leaders of the Independents, and that the Covenanted Oligarchy of Scotland were able to delude still longer so many of the Scottish Presbyterians. To Cromwell and his parasites the " Good Old Cause " became a thing to sneer at. To Vane, to Scott, to Harrison, and to many more, it was " a cause not to be repented of," though such adherence was the inevitable path to the scaffold and the grave. So, while to the Covenanted Oligarchy (for it were an abuse of language to call that knot of paltry tyrants an aristocracy) the "Covenant" was an instrument, drawn in legal form by that wretched Chancellor, not only to perpetuate their possession of the plunder they had already obtained, but to add to their spoil large slices of the fat lands of the English arch-bishops, bishops, deans and chapters, archdeacons and all other ecclesiastical officers, depending on that hierarchy,[1] who had anything worth taking; and to reduce those noble foundations for the encouragement of sound learning, the English Universities, to the miserable starved condition of the Scotch Universities; to many of the poor people of Scotland the "Covenant" was a cause for which they were ready to suffer persecution, imprisonment, torture, and death.

The Scottish Presbyterians being thus composed of two principal distinct parts or parties, we must be careful, as I have said, to assign to each party what belonged to it. On the side of the popular or democratical party there was in the laymen much sincerity and much ignorance; and in the clergy such pretensions as we have quoted, combined with much vehemence, a little learning, and mental faculties in such a state that, while their credulity was boundless in the matter of witches and hobgoblins,[2]

See the 1st and 2nd clauses of the "Solemn League and Covenant." These clauses were evidently drawn with care by lawyers, while most of the others savour strongly of the Presbyterian pulpit of that day. The words in the first clauses of the Instrument as agreed to by the English Parliament, "according to the word of God" were inserted by Vane, and enabled the English Parliament to deny that they had sworn to adopt the Presbyterian form of Church government.

[2] A remarkable example of this is afforded in the trial, in 1688, of Philip Standsfield for the murder of his father, Sir James Standsfield, of New Mills, in Scotland. One of the witnesses was Mr. John Bell, minister of

they would have rejected Galileo's doctrine about the motion of the earth; and to them, as to the Pope and the Jesuits, "the starry Galileo, with his woes," would have appeared but an impious and blasphemous impostor. On the side of the oligarchical party there were pride, ferocity, rapacity, cruelty and fraud. It was the oligarchical party that roasted men alive to get possession of Church lands; that sold their king to his deadly enemies, and then turned round when it suited their purpose and in the name of that king's son tortured with iron boots and thumbscrews their old Presbyterian friends and allies.

But though this oligarchy may have looked upon humanity, justice, and honesty as plebeian virtues, unworthy of their regard, there was one virtue which it was important to them that they should possess under the circumstances of those troubled times. I mean that quality to which the Romans principally applied the word virtue, and which may be called military virtue. And military virtue, which has been considered to belong especially to an

the gospel, aged forty years. In his written declaration this clergyman, who was a guest in Sir James Standsfield's house on the night of the murder, says:—"I declare that having slept but little, I was awakened in fear by a cry (as I supposed) and being waking I heard for a time a great din, and confused noise of several voices, and persons sometimes walking, which affrighted me (*supposing them to be evil wicked spirits*); and I apprehended the voices to be near the chamberdoor sometimes, or in the transe [passage], or stairs, and sometimes below, which put me to arise in the night and bolt the chamber door further, and to recommend myself by prayer, for protection and preservation, to the majesty of God: and having gone again to bed,

I heard these voices continue. . . . I could testify that Sir James was in his right reason at ten o'clock; wherefore *I inclined to think it was a violent murder committed by wicked spirits.*" —Hargrave's State Trials, vol. iv. p. 283; and Howell's State Trials, vol. xi. p. 1403. The Presbyterian clergy also arrogated to themselves some of the powers of the Hebrew prophets. According to Wodrow, Mr. John Welsh had predicted that this Philip Standsfield would come to a public death by the hands of the hangman. "This was accomplished," says Wodrow, "and Mr. Standsfield acknowledged this in prison after he was condemned, and that God was about to accomplish what he had been warned of."

aristocracy, did certainly once belong to them—when they were an aristocracy and not an oligarchy. They were now fallen upon times that looked lowering enough to suggest a prayer for the aid of some of those heroes of their race, who in days long gone by had, fighting against the most fearful odds, secured by their valour and conduct the independence of their country ; whose very names sounded still to their countrymen like a spell of invincibility. For the time had been when the Scottish aristocracy had abounded in virtues not merely military but even heroic. In one family, in particular, that of Douglas, the most powerful and heroic in the annals of Scotland, there had never been wanting, for more than ten generations, men capable both of managing state affairs and of commanding armies. But that well-spring of military qualities had for ages ceased to flow. And this oligarchy throughout these wars employed soldiers of fortune to lead their armies— men who had made war a profession or trade, but were not the more on that account masters of the art. Yet even at that time that Scottish oligarchy possessed one member whose military talents, if they had known how to employ them to advantage, might have given a different issue to this contest from that which it had.

The history of James Graham, Earl and afterwards Marquis of Montrose, is a remarkable instance of that particular weakness of an oligarchy which Thucydides, who had opportunities of observing the practical working both of oligarchies and democracies which we do not possess, pointed out more than two thousand years ago. Thucydides indeed confines his observation to the case of an oligarchy made out of a democracy, as exemplified in the events which he was narrating as having then taken place at Athens—and when Thucydides's leanings against democracies and demagogues are taken into account, his opinion in this case, being contrary to his general bias or his party or class prejudices, is entitled to the more weight. The substance of what he says is that an oligarchy made out of a democracy is chiefly destroyed by every one, that is, every member of the oligarchy, claiming not to be equal, but to be far the first—but in a democracy, election being made, a man bears the result better, as not being defeated by his equals.[1]   It is certainly true of oligarchies generally, whether made out of a democracy or not, that their internal feuds or quarrels arising out of jealousy or rivalry have produced great mismanagement of affairs both in war and peace, and in consequence great disasters to themselves and the country which had the misfortune to be misgoverned by them.   Dr. Arnold excepts the Roman Senate as being, with respect to the conduct of a war, no fair specimen of oligarchies in general.   But Venice, he says, " shows that no democracy, no tyranny, can be so vile as the dregs of an aristocracy suffered to run out its full course ; the affairs of Athens and of Carthage were never conducted so ably as when the popular party was most predominant ; nor have any governments ever shown in war greater feebleness and vacillation and igno-rance than those of Sparta, and, but too often, of England."[2]   The history of Scotland affords a vast body of facts corroborative of these views ; for it is the history of a country in which, though the Government had always been monarchical in form, the king had gene-rally been so weak and the nobility so powerful, that the Government might be truly said to be in substance more oligarchical than monarchical.   Even in this war, accord-ing to one who possessed a very minute as well as accurate

---

[1] Thucyd. viii. 89.   [2] History of Rome, vol. ii. p. 558.

knowledge of such parts of Scottish history as did not involve a very laborious sifting and weighing of evidence, " the cause of Prelacy or Presbytery, King or Parliament, was often what was least in the thoughts of the Scottish barons, who made such phrases indeed the pretext for the war, but in fact looked forward to indulging, at the expense of some rival family, the treasured vengeance of a hundred years."[1]

The case of Montrose was a notable instance of this. Montrose began his career as a Covenanter, but found himself supplanted by Argyle,[2] a man of considerable political craft, but of no military talent. Now, as the experience of all history from the earliest to the most recent times proves, military talent in any high degree is rare and extremely difficult to discover ; for indeed it can only be discovered by practical experiments of the most costly kind. To the rivalry, which as we have seen is inherent in the nature of oligarchies, there was added on this occasion a deadly ancient feud between the families of Montrose and Argyle. Moreover, while the dark crafty character of Argyle had to ordinary observers the show of prudence and wisdom, Montrose appeared to them, though a bold and to some extent able, a vain and rash young man, whose fiery character and great ambition might

---

[1] Sir Walter Scott. History of Scotland continued in Tales of a Grandfather, vol. i. p. 455. Edinburgh, 1846.

[2] Argyle did not nominally command the army, but the soldiers of fortune, Alexander Leslie, David Leslie, and Baillie, appointed by his influence, were controlled completely and with most disastrous consequences, as appeared at Kilsyth, Preston, and Dunbar, by Argyle and other noblemen of the Committee of Estates. See Lieut.-Ge- neral Baillie's " Vindication for his own part of Kilsyth and Preston," Baillie's Letters and Journals, vol. ii. p. 420.† Edinburgh, 1841. Robert Baillie says of Montrose's desertion of the Covenanters, " His first voyage to Aberdeen made him swallow the certain hopes of a Gene- rallat over all our armies ; when that honour was put on Leslie, he incon- tinent began to deal with the king." Vol. ii. p. 261.

render him perhaps rather a dangerous friend than a formidable enemy. The covenanted oligarchy of Scotland accordingly committed the great political blunder of throwing him aside for Argyle, whose abilities were worse than useless at such a time, and they soon learned to their cost that Montrose, whatever he might have been as a friend, was a very formidable enemy. I am no admirer of Montrose's character, though his great abilities are beyond a question; for, if he was a poet and a scholar, these accomplishments do not appear to have been able to make him a man either of principle or humanity; yet during these wars his must on the whole be considered as coming nearest to the highest standard of military genius. It is true that he was surprised by David Leslie at Philiphaugh. But with such resources as Leslie possessed, Montrose was not likely to have committed the blunders committed by Leslie at Dunbar, even though the first and greatest blunder, that of moving his troops from Down Hill, was not Leslie's but that of the Committee of Estates. And neither Leslie nor Cromwell ever showed military genius approaching to that displayed by Montrose in the battle of Aulderne, which only wanted numbers and slaughter on a greater scale to place it on a level with some of the most wonderful achievements of the genius of Hannibal and Frederic. With such an incapable king as Charles insisting on giving orders and on being obeyed, the ablest general could hardly have achieved final success; but if Montrose had taken the strong instead of the weak side, or rather if the strong side had taken him (for his taking the weak side was not matter of choice, but of necessity), I think it extremely probable that Cromwell would neither have won the battle of Dunbar, nor of Worcester, would not have conquered Scotland, and would not have been Protector.

We should then have had two very able men opposed to each other, the one with the greater military, genius ; the other with the greater political sagacity ; Hannibal to the Roman consul ; but Hannibal with more resources and more vantage ground than the Carthaginian had in Italy. Who shall say what might have been the issue of the contest ?

There were at this time three parties in Scotland, the rigid Presbyterians, the moderate Presbyterians, and the Royalists. The first, headed by Argyle, was made up of a few of the nobility, Eglinton, Cassilis, Lothian, and others, of the greater part of the clergy, and of the people of the middle and lower ranks, chiefly in the western counties. But though many persons of the middle and lower classes might be said to belong to this party, the influence of such persons on its counsels was extremely small. The aristocratical portion of the party, which though small in number, preponderated in influence, was in favour of a republic, so far as a republic might transfer the power of the king to themselves, while they held fast to the appearance of monarchy as necessary to the preservation of their exclusive privileges. This party was determined not to restore monarchy except on certain conditions, which should limit the power of the king and extend their own.

The second party was chiefly composed of the nobility and gentry and the representatives of the larger towns, and was headed by the Hamiltons, Lauderdale, Dunfermline, and others. This party, like the first-mentioned, professed to adhere to the Covenant ; and perhaps the principal distinction between these two parties may be stated to be that the leaders of the moderate Presbyterians more manifestly made use of the Covenant as an instrument for their own worldly aggrandizement. If Lauderdale may be in any degree taken as a type or even as a specimen of this party, the figure which he subsequently made as not only a renegade, but a cruel and tyrannical persecutor of those stern enthusiasts who acted up to what they understood to be the meaning of that Covenant which he had professed as well as they, would lead us to form a very unfavourable opinion of its honesty.

The third party consisted of the absolute Loyalists, friends and followers of Montrose, such as the Marquis of Huntly, Lord Ogilvy, a few other noblemen and gentlemen, and some Highland chiefs. And if Montrose may be taken as a specimen of this party, as Lauderdale of the last-mentioned, the absolute Loyalists, though they committed many savage and unjustifiable acts, may nevertheless, when their crimes are placed beside the hundred villanies and cruelties of Lauderdale, be pronounced brave and honourable men.[1]

After the death of King Charles, the rigid Presbyterians in accordance with their doctrine of monarchy in the State and republicanism in the Church, and likewise in accordance with their doctrine of forcing their opinions upon all other men,—a doctrine expressed in the words of their Covenant, in which they swear that they shall not "give themselves to a detestable indifferency or neutrality in that cause," were bound to call to the throne Charles, the eldest son of their late king, provided he would consent to take the Solemn League and Covenant, for the support of Presbytery, and the putting down of all other forms of religion. Accordingly, in the beginning of February 164$\frac{8}{9}$ Prince Charles was at Edinburgh solemnly proclaimed King of Scotland by consent of the Scottish

[1] Baillie's Letters and Journals, vol. iii. p. 35, et. seq. ed. Edinburgh, 1842. Burnet's Mem. of the Hamiltons, p. 336. Thurloe's State Papers, vol. i. pp. 73, 74.

Parliament; and it was agreed that commissioners with certain instructions should be sent to invite him to Scotland.[1] The instructions given to the Scotch commissioners were : 1. That he take the covenant. 2. That he put from him all who have assisted his father in the war, particularly Montrose—else not to treat with him. 3. That he bring but one hundred with him into Scotland, and none who have assisted his father in arms. 4. That he bring no forces into Scotland from other nations without their consent.[2] And he was not to be admitted to the actual power as king, until he should bind himself to ratify all acts of Parliament by which Presbyterian Government, the Directory of Worship, the Confession of Faith, and the Catechism were established; and in civil affairs to conform himself entirely to the direction of Parliament, and in ecclesiastical to that of the Assembly. Commissioners were sent to Charles at Breda to offer him the throne of Scotland on these terms.

On the 26th of February the Speaker of the English Parliament acquainted the House with a letter the Scots Commissioners had sent him, at their going away, which was without leave. The letter was full of bitterness against the Parliament and their late proceedings against the king, the House of Lords, and the secluded members. The House ordered guards to be sent to Gravesend after the Scots Commissioners to apprehend them, and at the same time passed the following declaration. " The Parliament having received a paper dated Feb. 24th subscribed by the Earl of Lothian, Sir John Chiesley, and Mr. Glendinning, in the name of the Kingdom of Scotland, and taking the same into their serious consideration, they do declare, that the said paper doth contain

---

[1] Whitelock, p. 381. Feb. 12, 164⅞.   [2] Whitelock, p. 392. Mar. 27, 1649.

much scandalous and reproachful matter against the just proceedings of this Parliament; and an assuming, on the behalf of that kingdom, to have a power over the laws and government of this nation to the high dishonour thereof; and lastly, a design in the contrivers and subscribers of it, to raise sedition and lay the grounds of a new and bloody war in this land; that, under the specious pretences in that paper contained, they may gain advantages to second their late perfidious invasion." It was ordered that a message with a duplicate of this declaration be sent to the Parliament and kingdom of Scotland, to know whether they do or will own and justify what hath been presented to this Parliament in their names. On the 28th of February the House was informed that according to the above order the Scots Commissioners had been apprehended at Gravesend, as they were embarking on their return home, and were now under a guard: and the question being put, whether to send them back to Scotland by land so guarded, it passed in the affirmative.[1]

On the 27th of February the Council of State ordered that fifty pounds shall be imprested to Mr. Rowe, who held the post of Scout Master General in the army, for his journey into Scotland to ride post to carry a letter and message to the kingdom of Scotland, and that a post warrant be granted unto him for the more quick dispatch of his journey:[2] and in his instructions he is directed not to stay above a certain number of days for an answer.[3]

---

[1] Whitelock, p. 384, Feb. 26, 1648/9. Commons' Journals, 26 and 28 Feb. 1648/9.

[2] Order Book of the Council of State, à Meridie, Die Martis, 27 Feb. 1648/9. MS. State Paper Office.

[3] *Ibid.* same day—"Instructions to William Rowe Esquire, Envoyé from the Council of State to the Parliament of Scotland: and *ibid.* 28 Feb. 1648/9, "An additional Instruction for Mr. Rowe."

On the same day the Council also ordered "that it be returned in answer to Mr. Sexby that this Council takes notice of his care and diligence used in the execution of the order of the House concerning the staying of the Scotts [sic] Commissioners ; that they do approve of the civilities offered by him unto them in tendring unto them the use of the best Inn in Gravesend for their accomodation."[1] On the 1st of March the Council ordered "that the whole business of the sending of the Scotts Commissioners with a guard into Scotland be referred to the consideration of the Lord General (Fairfax), Lieut.-General (Cromwell), and Sir William Constable, who are to report back their opinion concerning it to this Council." [2] In the afternoon of the same day the Council ordered "that the necessary charges of the Commissioners of Scotland shall be defrayed by the State in their journey home ; and that two hundred pounds be advanced out of the public revenue upon account to the captain of the guard who shall be commanded to the service of conveighging [sic] the Scotts [sic] Commissioners to Scotland." [3]

On the following day, the 2nd of March, it was ordered "that a letter be written to the Earl of Lothian, Sir John Chiesly, and Mr. Glendinning,[4] to let them know that the House did order that they should be sent to Scotland by land, and that we have appointed Captain Richard Dolphyn to command the guard, and that he hath money to provide them diet, horses, coaches, and other necessary accomodations by the way ; that this notice is given that they may put themselves into a posture for their journey." On the

[1] Order Book of the Council of State, 27 Feb. 164⅞.   MS.   State Paper Office.

[2] Order Book of the Council of State, 1 March, 164⅞. MS. State Paper Office.

[3] Order Book of the Council of State, à Meridie ; 1 March, 164⅞.

[4] In the Order Book this name is written " Lendonyng."

same day there are the following minutes : "That there
be also an instruction to Captain Richard Dolphin to keep
a journal of all remarkable passages by his way, and that
he take witnesses of any special matter that shall fall out
so as oath may hereafter be made of it:" "That an
order be sent to Commissary General Ireton to send a
convoy of horse to Tilbury side to go with the Earl of
Lothian and the rest to Scotland, and to be relieved at
Ferry Briggs." [1]   Instructions are likewise given to
Captain Dolphin :—1. As to safe conduct, to protect from
all violence and incivilities on the journey.   2 "You are
to take care that none be suffered to speak with them
upon the way in England but in your presence, that
nothing may be done by them to the prejudice of the
Commonwealth."   3. " When you shall be come to
Berwick you are to dispatch away a messenger with the
letter to the Parliament or Committee of Estates of Scotland.   And if they shall desire that they [the Scots Com-
missioners] may come to Edinburgh or any other place
in Scotland you are to suffer them to go accordingly."
4. " Out of the £200 in your custody upon account you
are to provide coach horses, diet, and other necessary
accomodations." [2]   On the 5th of March a "Private
Instruction " was added, which savours of the military
caution and foresight of Cromwell, who was, as we have
seen, one of the committee of three to whom this business
was referred.   "When your messenger that carries your
letter to Edinburgh shall be returned, if you find by him
that Mr. Rowe [the English envoy before mentioned] be
deteyned [sic] there or elsewhere in Scotland, you are then
only to dismiss the Earl of Lothian and Mr. Lendoning and

[1] Order Book of the Council of State,   [2] Ibid.
2 March, 164⅞. MS. State Paper Office.

deteyn Sir John Chieslie until Mr. Rowe be returned to you or that you have other order from the Parliament or this Council." On the 5th of March it was also ordered "that it be delivered to Captain Dolphin as a verbal in- struction that if the Earl of Lothian, Sir John Chieslie, and Mr. Lendonyng will bear their own charges by land, that he is to let them do it, notwithstanding anything in his Instructions." [1]

On the 7th of March the following "Additional In- struction for Captain Dolphin" was entered in the minutes. "Whereas the Earl of Lothian, Sir John Chieslie, and Mr. Lendonyng have signified that they will bear their own charges in their journey and not accept the defraying of their charge by this State ; you have therefore herewith imprested to you upon account £100 in lieu of the £200 formerly appointed for that service, which is for supply of such extraordinary occasions which may fall out in your journey." And on the same day a post warrant is ordered to be granted to Captain Dolphin for the taking up of twenty horses upon the way for the use of the Scots Commissioners and their retinue, they paying for them the rates usual upon the road. The warrant, after reciting that the Scots Commissioners had resolved to make use of horses from stage to stage for themselves and their retinue, requires all justices of the peace, &c. "upon sight hereof to furnish twenty good and sufficient horses with two sufficient guides from stage to stage and place to place from Blackwall to Berwick for the said service, they the said Earl of Lothian, &c. paying for the same the ordinary and usual rates." [2] At the same time the discharge of the "ship John of Kircaldie" is notified in the minutes.

[1] Order Book of the Council of State, Die Lunæ, 5 March, 164⅘. MS. State Paper Office.

[2] Order Book of the Council of State, 7 March, 164⅘. MS. State Paper Office.

All this appeared a proceeding of a very high nature on the part of a government the leading members of which were designated by Mr. Denzil Holles as "mean tradesmen," and who certainly were men who did not trouble themselves to go for their pedigrees beyond the battle of Naseby, towards an oligarchy of which the principal members valued themselves on the imagination of pedigrees going back to or beyond the Flood.

It appears from the Order Book of the Council of State that the English rulers were fully aware that they would have a war with Scotland upon their hands soon. The following orders evince their unrelaxing vigilance. "That all the guns which were at Pontefract Castle (except only the two guns and mortar-piece belonging to the garrison of Hull) be delivered to such as Sir Arthur Haselrig shall appoint for the better defence of the garrison at Berwick."[1] "That a letter be written to Sir Arthur Haselrig [governor of Newcastle] to have special care that Berwick and Carlisle be carefully garrisoned."[2] "That it be reported to the House that the letter sent to the Parliament of England by that of Scotland is of such a nature as it lays an incapacity of prosecuting the former demands by way of treaty. And Sir H. Vane is to make the report."[3] "That a letter be written to the commander of the two troops of horse of Col. Hacker's regiment that lately were about Carlisle to continue in those parts till they receive further order and in the meantime that they do what they can to repress the mischiefs that are daily done to the country by the moss-troopers."[4] "That a letter be written to the

---

[1] Order Book of the Council of State, à Meridie, 26 March, 1649. MS. State Paper Office.

[2] Order Book of the Council of State, Die Lunæ, 2 July, 1649. MS. State Paper Office.

[3] *Ibid.* same day.

[4] *Ibid.* 23 Octob. 1649, à Meridie.

Commissioners for the Customs to give order unto the several ports of England, That no goods whatsoever which may be made use of for the furnishing of arms or raising of war be permitted to go out of this nation into Scotland upon any pretence whatsoever."[1]

We have seen that one of the instructions given to the Scottish commissioners who were sent to treat with Prince Charles was to insist on his putting from him all who had assisted his father in the war, particularly Montrose. On the other hand Montrose advised Charles to reject the terms of the Presbyterians, and offered his services to place him on the throne by force of arms. Charles was willing to treat with both of these parties at the same time; and he granted a commission to Montrose to attempt a descent on Scotland, while he kept on foot a negotiation with the Presbyterian commissioners.

Montrose, who was somewhat more than suspected of having headed or directed[2] the royalist ruffians who murdered Dorislaus, the resident of the English Commonwealth in Holland, and who is reported by Clarendon and proved[3] by other evidence to have offered to assassinate the Hamiltons and Argyle, but who must be admitted to have been, as Scott has said of Dundee, careless of facing death him-

---

[1] Order Book of the Council of State, Die Veneris, 23 Nov. 1649. MS. State Paper Office.

[2] Even Hume says that the royalists who murdered Dorislaus were "chiefly retainers of Montrose." Chap. 60. Burnet says "Whitford, son to one of their [Scotch] bishops before the wars —the person that had killed Dorislaus in Holland—had committed many barbarous murders with his own hands in Piedmont of women and children." Hist. of His Own Times, vol. iii. p.

115. 8vo. Oxford, 1833; and see Whitelock, p. 460.

[3] Hume endeavours to prove that Clarendon must have been mistaken in ascribing such an offer to Montrose; since, during the time when he was reported to have undertaken the assassination, Montrose was in prison. But see the evidence taken before a secret committee of the Parliament, and published by Mr. Laing, in his History of Scotland.

self, if he was ruthless in inflicting it upon others, accordingly set out on this his last expedition. The events of this expedition showed that in his former enterprises what might at first sight have looked like rashness partook not a little of a daring yet wise and far-sighted policy. But in the present enterprise there appeared far more of rashness than of wisdom of any kind. If it be true, as has been alleged, that he was misled by a pretended prophecy or prediction that to him alone it was reserved to restore the king's authority in all his dominions, we must bear in mind that in that age the giving credence to such predictions did not by any means warrant such inferences respecting the minds of those who gave such credence as it would do now. To say nothing of minor instances, Wallenstein was a believer in astrology, a man who in the excesses committed by his brutal soldiery and perhaps in some other points, bore some resemblance to Montrose, though with far greater forces at his disposal than Montrose ever had, Wallenstein never showed either Montrose's military genius, or his personal hardihood and endurance of fatigue and privation.

In the spring of 1650 Montrose sailed from Hamburgh for the Orkney Islands with some arms and money and about six hundred German mercenaries, officered chiefly by Scottish exiles. The fishermen who inhabited those remote islands were unprepared for resistance, and about eight hundred of them were forced into his service, though unaccustomed to the use of arms. He then crossed to the main land, where he hoped amid the northern clans to be able to raise a large army. But as he marched through Caithness and Sutherland, the natives fled at his approach, remembering his former cruelties. Strachan, an officer under David Leslie, was dispatched against him with about two hundred and thirty horse,[1] while Leslie followed with four thousand more. Montrose had no horse to bring him intelligence, and his cause must have been as unpopular in that part of the country as it was formerly in the neighbourhood of Philiphaugh, where none of the country people gave him any information of the nearness of the enemy. But he probably thought that his affairs were in that condition that he must advance at any risk. However that might be, here as at Philiphaugh, Montrose, whom his enemies on other occasions had never found unprepared, was surprised. As he advanced beyond the pass of Invercharron, on the confines of Ross-shire, Strachan issued from an ambuscade in three divisions and attacked him. The first division was repulsed; but the second, headed by Strachan himself, routed the whole of Montrose's troops. The Orkney men threw down their arms, the Germans retreated to a wood and surrendered; the few Scottish companions of Montrose made a brave but vain resistance. Montrose's own horse had been shot under him. His friend Lord Frendraught gave him his, and the marquis throwing off his cloak bearing the star, fled from this his last fight. He afterwards changed clothes with an ordinary Highland kern, and swam across the river Kyle. Exhausted with fatigue and hunger, he was at length taken by a Ross-shire chief who was out with a party of his men in arms. Montrose discovered himself to this man, who had once been one of his own followers, as to a friend. But, tempted by a reward of four hundred bolls of meal, this chief delivered his old commander into the hands of David Leslie.

The career and fate of Montrose furnish an instructive example of the evils of civil war; and the accounts given

[1] Balfour, vol. iv. p. 9. He adds: "Capt. William Rosse and Capt. John Rosse came up to the execution with 80 foot out of the country forces."

by various writers of that career and that fate afford a not less instructive illustration of the effects of faction in perverting truth, and in turning into poison what should be wholesome food.   Some men have sought power and what is called glory by deeds of the most detestable cruelty, not merely shedding blood in battle, but shedding the blood of unarmed men, nay of women and children.   And other men have sought to make the evil spirit that prompted such men to seek glory through such deeds assume the semblance of an angel of light.   If a time shall ever come when men shall be seen as they are or were, and not darkly through the coloured clouds which poets and historians have thrown around them, and their deeds; and if those men in whose deeds the evil greatly preponderated over the good shall be judged according to their deeds; a corresponding judgment will be pronounced on those who have held up such men as fit objects for the unqualified approval of mankind.

It is undoubtedly the part of a mean spirit to celebrate its victory over an honourable enemy by dragging him in triumph from town to town in a mean garb.   But they who thus treated Montrose would no doubt deny that a man who carried on war as Montrose carried it on was an honourable enemy.   Sir Walter Scott says that his "unworthy victors now triumphed over a heroic enemy in the same manner as they would have done over a detected felon."[1] Yet what account does Sir Walter Scott himself give of Montrose's treatment of the town of Aberdeen?   "Many were killed in the street; and the cruelty of the Irish in particular was so great, that they compelled the wretched citizens to strip themselves of their clothes before they

[1] History of Scotland contained in   chap. 46, p. 479.
"Tales of a Grandfather," vol. i.,

killed them, to prevent their being soiled with blood. The women durst not lament their husbands or their fathers slaughtered in their presence, nor inter the dead which remained unburied in the streets until the Irish departed." [1] There were other frightful outrages committed by those barbarians on the women and children which Sir Walter Scott does not mention. The defence made by Sir Walter Scott for Montrose is that he "necessarily gave way to acts of pillage and cruelty, which he could not prevent, because he was unprovided with money to pay his half-barbarous soldiery." [2] But if Montrose wanted the citizens' money, might he not have taken it without permitting his soldiers to murder them and their children? Such cruelties were not only a crime but a blunder and proved that Montrose, while he undoubtedly possessed military genius of no common order, altogether wanted political genius. Cromwell's severity in Ireland was partly dictated by policy, partly meant as punishment not merely to ordinary rebels, but to mutineers and murderers who had committed crimes with circumstances of almost unexampled cruelty. Montrose's cruelty at Aberdeen (for it cannot be called mere severity), as regarded policy, only served to make about three-fourths of the population of Scotland the mortal enemies of him and his cause, and, as regarded punishment, so far was the town of Aberdeen from deserving punishment for rebellion against Charles, that Montrose himself had actually on a former occasion punished it for its loyalty. Altogether then Montrose's treatment of Aberdeen seems the conduct of a man in whom the logical errors of the head were not corrected by the instincts of the heart, which saves many men from the errors of the head.

[1] History of Scotland, contained in   42, p. 437.
"Tales of a Grandfather," vol. i. chap.   [2] *Ibid.*

It is not easy to analyse the heart of that man who in his dying hour could look without remorse or even regret on those four days of September, 1644, including that Sunday, the 15th of September, when there was neither preaching nor praying in Aberdeen and nothing but the death-groans of men and the shrieks and wail of women through all the streets, and when the king's lieutenant, who had in the name of "King Charles the Good" caused all these things, could not enter or leave his quarters in Skipper Anderson's[1] house without walking upon or over the bloody corpses of those not slain in battle and over streets slippery with innocent blood. Montrose's chaplain and panegyrical biographer Bishop Wishart has prudently thought fit to pass over the proceedings of his hero in Aberdeen altogether in silence. Montrose himself declared that he had never shed blood except in battle. But the facts are proved by Spalding, a townsman of Aberdeen, present on the occasion, who was firmly attached to episcopacy and the king's cause, and a well-wisher to the general success of Montrose, who must consequently in this case have been an unwilling witness, and whose testimony may therefore be considered as conclusive. We therefore have before us the strange phenomenon of a man, who cannot be considered as a pure barbarian by blood, birth, and education, performing deeds that place him on a moral level with Nana Sahib, and for what? to enable King Charles the First to do with impunity whatever had been done by King James, who had murdered by divine right two of Montrose's uncles.

The explanation may be found partly perhaps in two qualities which entered largely into the character of Mon-

---

[1] Spalding, vol. ii. p. 266.

trose, unbounded pride [1] and strong fanaticism. The pride
of a Scottish oligarch was then, as it is now, boundless. To such a man the body of the people of Scotland
were, if they are not still, a mere mass of base gutter-
bloods; whose ignoble blood was, to borrow the words
which Sir Walter Scott has put into the mouth of Montrose's antitype Graham of Claverhouse, but "the red
puddle that stagnated in the veins of psalm-singing mechanics, crack-brained demagogues, and silly boors." To
murder such human beings in the most cruel and cowardly
manner in cold blood was, it seems, to judge from what we
know of Montrose and Dundee, an act of which there was
no need to be ashamed. Their fanaticism, for those men
were fanatics too and worshipped an idol as loathsome and
as cruel as the superstition which they imputed to their
enemies, altogether silenced within them the voice of conscience. There is no mild remedy to cure such fanaticism
as this. In those days the charge of Cromwell's cuirassiers
and the shock of his pikemen did something; in later times
the crash of the guillotine and the thunder of Bonaparte's
cannon have done something more towards giving to the
class of Montrose and Dundee in Scotland and elsewhere a
rather dim perception that they had made some slight errors
in their reckoning concerning the canaille or gutter-bloods.

Is it surprising that Montrose as he was led a prisoner
through the country and the towns where his troops had
committed so many deeds of rapine and cruelty should
have been assailed with curses? Is it not rather surprising

---

[1] Montrose's inordinate pride is particularly recorded by his contemporaries; and it was united with great
power of dissimulation, by no means so
unusual a combination as Baillie seems
to imagine. "The man" says Baillie,
"is said to be very double, which in
so proud a spirit is strange. . . .
He, Antrim, Huntly, Airlie, Nithsdale,
and more are ruined in their estates;
public commotions are their private
subsistence."—*Baillie's Letters and
Journals*, vol. ii. p. 74. Edinburgh,
1841.

that he should not have been torn in pieces? Let any one place himself in the situation, not of a man who had lost his male relatives in battle against Montrose—that would have been a thing in the ordinary course of events—but of a man whose fields had been laid waste, whose houses had been burned, whose father, mother, wife, daughters, sisters had been butchered by this hero after the model of one of the heroes of Plutarch, (many of whose heroes were in truth but sorry scoundrels), and then let such a one say whether he would have considered Montrose entitled to the treatment of an honourable and generous enemy? Nay more—if there was a man wearing the "semblance of a kingly crown," who commissioned this Montrose and who avowed and sought to profit by his atrocities, will any man say there was no good done by "garring such a king ken that he too had a lithe in his neck?"

The route by which Montrose was conducted to Edinburgh crossed the river South Esk not far from his own house of Old Montrose. The beautiful valley through which the South Esk flows from the Grampians to the sea is rich in historical associations. Towards the upper part of it stand Glammis, the ancient castle of Macbeth, and the ruins of Finhaven, the castle of that Earl of Crawford, known as "the Tiger Earl." Farther down on a rock overhanging the river is the castle of Brechin, which Sir Thomas Maule bravely defended against Edward I. and his army, till he was killed upon the ramparts, with his last breath commanding his men not to surrender. But the greatest name associated with that valley and that river is that of the Marquis of Montrose, who was born in the town of Montrose where the South Esk joins the sea, and passed much of his boyhood and youth at his house of Old Montrose about four miles up the river. The aspect of that quiet valley more rich and wooded than is usual in Scotland, the gentle sloping green hills near, the huge chain of the blue Grampians in the distance, the clear and rapid stream rushing over its pebbled bed—all, while they reminded Montrose of those other days before ambition and revenge had done their work upon a character by nature brave and chivalrous, formed a strange contrast with that stormy and adventurous life which was soon to have a violent and terrible end.

Montrose's guards stopped with him for a short time at Kinnaird, the house of his father-in-law, the Earl of Southesk. Kinnaird is only about two miles distant from Montrose's own house at Old Montrose, situated like Kinnaird on the banks of the river South Esk. Between Montrose's mansion-house of Old Montrose and the town of Montrose is a basin or sort of estuary about four miles in length and two in breadth, dry at low water and filled by every returning tide, through which the South Esk rushes to meet the German Ocean. At Kinnaird Montrose procured liberty from his guards to see two of his children. But neither the sight of them nor of the scenes of his early and tranquil days appears to have occasioned in him the display of any outward sign of emotion. " Neither at meeting nor parting," says Wishart, " could any change of his former countenance be discovered, or the least expression heard which was not suitable to the greatness of his spirit. During the whole journey his countenance was serene and cheerful as of one who was superior to all reproach."[1]

But the captive conqueror, though his pride and force of character enabled him to bear with no outward sign of emotion that terrible reverse of fortune, and to smile at

[1] Wishart, p. 380.

the insults of his enemies with a sedate and unshrinking eye, was a poet as well as a great soldier, and those scenes of his youth beheld under such circumstances must have awakened a host of recollections. The electric power of thought would bring back, though but for a moment, the memory of early friends—some of them dead—others friends no longer—the memory too of those dreams of early youth when the bound of his ambition was but to make one loved name "famous by his pen and glorious by his sword," and accomplish for it more than Brian de Bois Guilbert did for the name of Adelaide de Montemare. And though Montrose's early life may have been as unprosperous as that of the haughty Templar, it may have left, in a soul still haughtier and more daring than Bois Guilbert's, the traces of a life-long sorrow.[1] But it is but for a fleeting hour he can look on those scenes now with all their sweet and bitter memories. Though there had passed his childhood ; though there his youth had felt the spell of beauty and dreamt the dream of love ; though there the clear and rapid stream, the dark pine wood, the broomy haugh, the furze and the very ragwort had for him a charm denied to the luxuriance of a more southern clime ; his age shall not repose there : and strangers shall dwell in the ancient abode of his fathers. Some of the walls of his house and some of the trees he planted may still stand. So fleeting is man ! The feeblest work of his hands is more enduring. The houses' he builds, the trees he plants, outlast him by centuries. The trees which Bacon planted in Gray's Inn Gardens, the trees under which Cromwell,

[1] In his "Legend of Montrose," Sir Walter Scott, who was deeply versed in Scottish family history, makes Montrose say to Lord Menteith in reference to the latter's love for Annot Lyle—"I am sorry for you—I too have known—but what avails it to awake sorrows which have long slumbered !"

and Milton and Newton walked at Cambridge, still stand
and are conscious of the presence of summer and winter,
of spring-time and autumn, but the hands that planted
them are dust, and the hearts that throbbed under their
shade shall be gladdened by spring no more. Strange ! that
to this intellectual being, with faculties to comprehend the
Universe, with " thoughts that wander through Eternity,"
there should have been assigned an earthly existence of
such brief duration, as to make it hardly a poetical
licence to say that " Earth is but a tombstone."   To-day the
eye is lightened with electric thought, and the brain is busy
with work not unworthy of angels.   Yet a little while—it
may be a few years, a few months, or only a few days, and
the eye is darkened, and the brain motionless for ever.

An act of attainder had been passed by the Scottish
Parliament against Montrose while he was laying waste
the country of Argyle in the winter of 1644.   Under this
act he was condemned before he reached Edinburgh to the
death of a traitor. He was, according to the special order
of Parliament, met at the gates of Edinburgh by the magistrates attended by the common hangman.   With his arms
pinioned and bareheaded he was placed on a high bench
fixed on a cart, and conducted through the streets, his
principal officers coupled together preceding him.   When he
was brought before the Parliament to hear his sentence,
Loudon the Chancellor, formerly Sir John Campbell of
Lawers, a kinsman of Argyle, upbraided him in a long
and violent declamatory harangue with his breach of the
Covenant, with his cruel wars, and the murders, treasons,
and conflagrations which they had occasioned.   Montrose
was sentenced to be hanged on a gibbet thirty feet high,
and to hang for three hours ; his head to be fixed on the
tolbooth or prison of Edinburgh, his body to be quartered,

and a limb to be placed over the gates of each of the other four principal towns of Scotland, Glasgow, Stirling, Perth, and Aberdeen.

It was not to be expected that Montrose, whose courage and fortitude had been proved not only on so many fields of battle, but in marches in the midst of winter over trackless mountains covered with snow, where the pangs of hunger had been added to an amount of fatigue and cold, which alone would have destroyed men of softer frames and weaker nerves—should have shrunk to meet the death which Strafford and Laud, which Vane and Argyle faced courageously. So far from feeling any uneasiness about the consequences of his acts Montrose spent part of the night before his execution in the composition of some verses, which he wrote with the point of a diamond upon the window of his prison, and in which he expresses his confidence[1] that the God, whose attributes the Christian faith certainly does not reconcile with Montrose's butcheries of the unarmed and defenceless, " will raise him with the just." A man, who could believe that the God whose attributes are wisdom and justice would " raise him with the just " for committing deeds of rapine and murder for the avowed purpose of making us and our children and our children's children to all generations the slaves of the Stuarts, must be pronounced hardly less a fanatic than the fifth-monarchy man who believed that at the great battle of Armageddon he was destined to ride as one of the captains of Him on the White Horse, conquering and to conquer, when the voice of the angel shall call all fowls that fly in the midst of heaven

---

[1] The two concluding lines of these verses,—which consist of only eight lines altogether and are not a fair specimen of Montrose's poetical genius for he has left some verses which are above mediocrity while these are rather below it—are :—

" I'm hopeful thou'lt recover once my dust,
And confident thou'lt raise me with the just."

to feed on the flesh of kings, and the flesh of captains, and the flesh of mighty men.   Fanaticism under many aspects is always the same at heart ; and that heart being possessed by a fire unquenchable may be said to carry about with it its own hell.   That fire burns with the same fury in Mahomet, in Mary Tudor, in Beaton, in Calvin, in the murderers of George Wishart, in the murderers of Thomas Aikenhead.   When human selfishness, fierce and ravenous as the brute instinct of the most ferocious beast of prey, regards its own gratification as a duty and a virtue, the result is that degree of unrelenting cruelty which knows neither forgiveness, nor pity, nor remorse.   Montrose's enemies were God's enemies.   Cromwell's enemies were God's enemies.   The Presbyterians again held that both Montrose and Cromwell were to be hewed in pieces as Samuel hewed in pieces Agag, when he rebuked Saul for sparing the king of the Amalekites, and for having saved some part of the flocks and herds of that people although he had strictly complied with the command of the prophet in "slaying both man and woman, infant and suckling."   Here were three distinct parties who hated each other with the most deadly hatred, all and each laying claim to be special favourites of the Almighty, and to have a special commission from the Most High to do unto each other as the Jews did to the heathen, that is, to the nations whose country they seized.   If it be not blasphemy to turn the name of God to such uses, what is blasphemy ?

On the 21st of May, 1650, Montrose walked from his prison to the Grassmarket, the common place of execution for felons, where a gibbet of extraordinary height was erected.   Here the clergy again pressed him to own his guilt, and refused him absolution, unless he manifested repentance.   Montrose's pride and courage did not and were not likely to bend to any of their threats of damnation, grounded as they were on the audacious assumption that, like their old and hated enemy the Bishop of Rome, they were the vicegerents on earth of the Omnipotent. A book containing the printed history of his exploits was hung around Montrose's neck by the hangman. He smiled and said he was prouder of the history than he had ever been of the Garter. Having finished his prayers and asked if any further insult remained to be put upon him, he calmly submitted to his fate. He was in the 38th year of his age. Sir Walter Scott in the Legend of Montrose, speaks of Montrose's long brown hair, grey eye, and sanguine complexion. An original miniature exhibited in the Loan Court of the South Kensington Museum in 1862 represents him with yellowish hair, high cheek bones, and a rather pale complexion. It is probable when we compare the impression made on us by his portraits with the impression his living self made on so good a judge of men as De Retz who knew him personally and mentions him in his memoirs as one of those heroes of whom there are no longer any remains in the world, and who are only to be met with in Plutarch, that his features when lighted up by the soul within produced an impression more favourable than that which his portraits convey. According to the sentence the head of the Marquis of Montrose was fixed upon the tolbooth of Edinburgh, (over against that of his unfortunate uncle the young Earl of of Gowrie murdered by King James in August, 1600), with an iron cross over it lest any of his friends should take it down.[1] After the battle of Dunbar, Montrose's head was

[1] Wishart's Memoirs of the Marquis of Montrose, p. 405. Edin. 1819. The head of the Earl of Gowrie being there in 1650 when Montrose's head was set up must have remained there 50 years; not blown away by the wind as Birrell intimates it might be. "The 19 Nov. (1600) the Earl of Gowrie and his brother haulit to the gibbit and hangit and quarterit. And thairefter

taken down by Cromwell's orders; and it may be hoped that the Earl of Gowrie's was taken down at the same time and decently buried.

Although Montrose's military genius rose far above that of the other men of that time who united qualities that are not now found together, he was only one of many who in Britain during the sixteenth and seventeenth centuries, as in Spain during the sixteenth century, were eminent at once as soldiers and as men of letters.　Cervantes greatly distinguished himself at the battle of Lepanto, where he received three arquebuse wounds, two in the breast, and one in the left hand, which maimed him for life.　Lope. de Vega sailed in the Armada.　Boscan served with distinction as a soldier.　His friend Garcilaso de la Vega fell at the head of a storming party, being the first to mount the breach of a tower, which he was ordered to carry by assault.　The Earl of Surrey, to whom as a poet both Spenser and Milton are indebted, and whose works went through four editions in two months, and through seven more in the thirty years after their first appearance in 1557, besides their circulation in garlands, broadsheets, and miscellanies, served two campaigns in France.　Sir Philip Sidney was a poet as well as a soldier.　Sir Walter Raleigh was at once a soldier, sailor, poet, and historian.　Richard Lovelace fought for the king all through the civil war; and afterwards raised a regiment in the French service, commanded it, and was wounded at Dunkirk.　George Withers served as a captain of horse in the expedition of Charles I. against the Scotch Covenanters in 1639, (which was also the first campaign of Lovelace); and three years after he

thair twa headis set upoun the haid of the prisone-hous, thair to stand quhill the wind blaw thame away."—*Robert Birrell's Diary,* Nov. 19, 1600, cited in "Pitcairn's Criminal Trials," vol. ii. pp. 45–247, from Original MS. Adv. Lib. Edinburgh.

sold his estate and raised a troop of horse for the Parliament. John Bunyan served as a private soldier in the Parliamentary army. But of all these, if some have surpassed Montrose in literary, none have come near him in military achievements; and I am not aware that there is any other man on record who has united in an equal degree poetical and military genius. Montrose was certainly a most accomplished man ; and I regret, for the honour of human nature, that he should have tarnished his name by cruelty. There are indeed well-authenticated facts in his history that seem to show that he was not by nature cruel or ungenerous, and that he was not an exception to the rule that brave men are not cruel. Nevertheless the plea put forward for him that he necessarily gave way to acts of pillage and cruelty from inability to pay his half-barbarous soldiery will not avail him much ; and history, painting him as he was, will paint him as a great man with dark spots on his fame.

The royalist writers represent the people, and many even of Montrose's bitterest enemies as weeping on the occasion of his execution. That age was much addicted to tears, as is manifested when we find such a man as Cromwell, and even the whole House of Commons, occasionally dissolving into floods of tears. It may therefore, though it certainly seems strange, be true that the people of Scotland should weep even for a man who had treated them as Montrose had done, as people naturally weep at any great reverse of fortune. In regard to the mean spite imputed to the ruling party in Scotland at the time, as exhibited in the various studied insults offered to Montrose, the whole matter may be summed up in a very few words. If Montrose in his wars adhered to the recognized course of warfare of civilised men as the term was then understood, all insult offered to him as a prisoner was undoubtedly a mean revenge, and an ignominy recoiling upon those who offered it. But if, on the other hand, it be true that Montrose carried on war like a cruel and reckless savage, it would be drawing rather too largely on human forbearance in Scotland two hundred years ago to expect that he should receive the treatment which men of honour and humanity are anxious to give to a conquered enemy who has done nothing to forfeit his right to honourable treatment.

Some writers have asserted, but without producing authority for the assertion, that Montrose at the beginning of his career joined the Covenanters from disgust at neglect from the Court. But when we call to mind that Montrose's mother was the sister of the Earl of Gowrie and of Alexander Ruthven, so basely murdered by James the First, and that his aunt Beatrix Ruthven had received through the Queen and Sir Thomas Erskine a very different version of that dark transaction called by King James the Gowrie Conspiracy, from that which King James put forth, we do not need to have recourse to any supposition of neglect from the Court to account for the fact of a young man, so intelligent and so well-educated as the Earl of Montrose, thinking it necessary to devise means to diminish rather than to increase the power to do evil, both to the nobility and people, of the royal family of Stuart. Wishart's work is so much a mere panegyric that it is no authority on disputed points. But the testimony of Principal Baillie, the best authority and beyond all suspicion, is, before Montrose's desertion of the Covenanters, very favourable to his general character, and throws no doubt on his sincerity. It is remarkable too that, so far from affording the least hint of cruelty in Montrose's character, Baillie objects to his too great lenity. " The discretion," he says, "of that generous and noble youth was but too great. A great sum was named as a fine to that unnatural city [Aberdeen] but all was forgiven."[1] And again : " Our forces likewise disbanded, it was thought, on some malcontentment either at *Montrose's too great lenitie in sparing the enemies' houses*, or somewhat else."[2] This was in March 1639 when Montrose then only twenty-six or twenty-seven years of age went against Aberdeen as Lord General, with the Earl Marischall, the Lord Erskine, the Lord Carnegie, the Lord Elcho, "his Excellencie Felt Marshal Leslie," and an army of 9000 men.[3] Now, as one of the charges brought against Montrose by the Parliament of Scotland in their declaration of the 24th January 1650 was, that "being a man of a mean and desperate fortune, and not meeting with that esteem and reward which he in his vanity proposed to himself, at the first pacification he began to hearken to the promises of the Court," how came it that, "being a man of a mean and desperate fortune," and so young, he was appointed to this important command ? The inference is that the oligarchy which then governed Scotland must, notwithstanding their habitual blindness to such qualities, have perceived in Montrose, young as he was, the qualities fit for command ; and that Argyle possessing great craft, (though no talent for war), and the power arising from a much greater estate or at least a much greater "following," than Montrose, which in an oligarchy confers the highest offices without regard to fitness, had influence in the Council to have Montrose superseded and Alexander

---

[1] Baillie's Letters and Journals, vol. i. p. 197. Edinburgh 1841. Bannatyne Club edition. Baillie calls Aberdeen "that unnatural city" on account of its leaning to prelacy.

[2] Baillie's Letters and Journals, vol. i. p. 205.

[3] Spalding, vol. i. p. 107. Edinburgh, 1829. 2 vols. 4to. Bannatyne Club edition.

Leslie, an old soldier of fortune and military pedant, put in his place. Montrose's vindictive feelings on this occasion were also probably much exasperated by the fact of the existence of an old feud between his family and that of Argyle. Seeing therefore no hope for the exercise of those great military talents, which with the instinct of genius he felt that he possessed, in the service of the Covenanters, he determined to offer his services to the Royal cause. And however much reason he may have had to dislike the supremacy of the Stuarts, he would probably have very much preferred it to the supremacy of Argyle and Loudon, which would have been in other words the supremacy of the Campbells. If this was the alternative, it is idle to say that it was Montrose's duty as a man of principle to bow to the order which superseded him and placed another in his command. Moreover, where the Government is little else but a scramble for power among a few families, the modern standard of political morality cannot be applied. It is proper to add that some of Montrose's greatest enemies have allowed that, though he could not bear an equal, and was always ready to destroy an adversary, whether by heroism in the field or less honourable means, he was always generous to those who testified their sense of his superiority. There can be little doubt that, if Montrose with his military genius had held the command of the armies of the Scottish Covenanters, the struggle would have assumed an aspect different in many respects—but that the result would have been more favourable to the ultimate establishment of good government and of civil and religious liberty is very far from probable, for to look for such a result from that corrupt and tyrannical oligarchy which then and long after misgoverned Scotland, was quite out of the question. In such a case it is absolutely necessary to destroy before there can be any hope to reform.

Montrose, when brought before the Scottish Parliament to hear his sentence, had said in reply to the Chancellor Loudon's violent harangue against him, that "although it was impossible in the course of hostilities absolutely to prevent acts of military violence, he had always disowned and punished such irregularities. He had never," he said, "spilt the blood of a prisoner, even in retaliation of the cold-blooded murder of his officers and friends, nay he had spared the lives of thousands in the very shock of battle." He might also have told that Chancellor and the rest of his judges that all the crimes imputed to him, if proved on the clearest evidence, would not leave behind them a stain so indelible as the fingering of a certain sum of English gold, which was not unknown to that Chancellor and his accomplices or brother judges, and which was the price of blood. Though those men died in their beds and Montrose died by the hands of the hangman, had they all come before Dante's infernal tribunal, the prisoner would not have been condemned to so deep a part of the abyss as some of his judges. For if to Montrose would have been assigned a place with Ezzelino in the lake of boiling blood of Bulicame, the traitors who sold the king who trusted them would have had their portion with Judas Iscariot in the eternal ice of Giudecca.

Urry, who had changed sides several times during the civil war, and had been sometimes the enemy, sometimes the follower of Montrose, was executed with others of the marquis's followers, among whom was Whitford,[1] one of the assassins of Dr. Dorislaus. Lord Frendraught, who when

---

[1] Whitelock, p. 460.

Montrose's horse was killed under him had generously given him his own to enable him to escape, having been taken prisoner, to avoid the ignominy of a public execution, starved himself to death. The Marquis of Huntly, after having been sixteen months in prison, had been beheaded at Edinburgh more than a year before.[1]

Meanwhile the commissioners of the Scottish Parliament continued to carry on the treaty with Charles. That prince had little inclination to agree to the terms the covenanted oligarchy offered him, and no hesitation about the morality of accomplishing his ends by any other means, even by the means proposed by Montrose, namely butchering one half of his subjects that he might reign absolutely over the other half. But when Montrose's defeat and execution were reported to him, he agreed, seeing no other resource for the present, to accept the crown of Scotland on the terms offered, which were taking upon him the obligations of the Solemn League and Covenant, and absolute compliance with the will of the Scottish Parliament in civil, and with that of the General Assembly of the Kirk in ecclesiastical affairs. The treaty having been concluded on these conditions,—conditions which to a man of Charles's tastes and habits made his life as a king in Scotland considerably less pleasant than life in a garret in some continental town where he might at least enjoy, unmolested by the howl of Presbyterian sermons and imprecations, some scantling of the luxuries he loved—Charles sailed from Holland about the middle of June, landed on the coast of Scotland near the mouth of the river Spey, and advanced to Stirling.

About the middle of June in this year Mr. Ascham,

---

[1] Whitelock, p. 392. March 27, 1649. "The Marquis of Huntly was beheaded at the cross in Edinburgh."

whom the English Parliament had sent as their agent into
Spain, was assassinated at an inn in Madrid, together with
his interpreter, by six Englishmen ; who inquiring for Mr.
Ascham were admitted to his chamber.   As Mr. Ascham,
who was at dinner with his interpreter, rose from the table
to salute them, the foremost laid hold on him by the hair
and stabbed him.   The interpreter endeavoured to escape,
but he was stabbed by another ; and they both fell down
dead.   The murderers fled for refuge to the Venetian
ambassador's house, but he refused them entrance, and they
then took sanctuary in the next church.   When the Parliament were informed of this affair by their late agent's
secretary, they first ordered that a letter should be written
to the King of Spain, and signed by their Speaker, to
demand justice on the murderers of Mr. Ascham.   Next,
Sir H. Mildmay reported from the Council of State, that,
in regard of this horrible assassination and murder and
also of several late advertisements they had received of
divers persons being come into England with intention of
like murder and assassination ; and because some faithful
persons to the State are particularly designed to be attempted
upon, it was the Council's opinion the House should be
moved to take into consideration what they published, in
the Declaration of the 18th of May, 1649, on occasion of
the murder of Dr. Dorislaus, and give order that something might be done effectually in pursuance thereof, to
discourage and deter such bloody and desperate men, and
their accomplices, from the like wicked attempts for the
future. Thereupon the House resolved that six of those
persons who had been in arms against the Parliament,
and who, not being admitted to composition, were then in
their power and at their mercy, should be speedily proceeded
against to trial for their lives, before the High Court of

horrid and execrable assassination of Mr. Ascham and his interpreter.[1] It was not however till the 17th of February 165$\frac{1}{2}$, when they probably felt themselves ready for a war with Spain, that the Council of State ordered a paper to be delivered to the Spanish ambassador, demanding justice on the murderers of Mr. Ascham.[2]

[1] Parl. Hist. vol. iii., pp. 1351, 1352.

[2] Order Book of the Council of State, 17 Feb. 165$\frac{1}{2}$. MS. State Paper Office.

CHAPTER VI.

As soon as the English Parliament heard that the eldest son of the late king of England had arrived in Scotland, they prepared for war with that country. Cromwell, who had been summoned home from Ireland by the Parliament some months before, had taken his seat in the House on the 4th of June.[1] His entry into London almost resembled a Roman triumph. Many members of the Parliament and Council of State, among whom was Fairfax the Lord General, guarded by a troop of horse and a regiment of foot, and attended by a large concourse of citizens, went out two miles to meet him. When Cromwell came to Tyburn, the place of public execution, where a great crowd of spectators was assembled, a certain flatterer pointing with his finger to the multitude exclaimed: "Good God, sir, what a number of people come to welcome you home!" Cromwell smiling replied— "But how many more, do you think, would flock together to see me hanged, if that should happen?" The contemporary writer who relates this incident adds, "there was nothing more unlikely at that time, and yet there was a presage in these words, which he often repeated and used in discourse."[2]

[1] Parl. Hist. vol. iii. pp. 1345, 1347.
[2] Bates—Rise and Progress of the late Troubles in England—(Translation of the Elenchus Motuum)—Part ii. p. 97.

Fairfax, though not himself a presbyterian, being as has been commonly supposed persuaded by his wife and her presbyterian chaplains, declined the command of the English army and threw up his commission. The Council of State sent a deputation consisting of St. John, Whitelock, Cromwell, Harrison and Lambert, to Fairfax to endeavour to prevail on him to take the command of the army destined to march into Scotland. The main argument of Fairfax for resigning his command was that the invasion of Scotland could not be justified, as the Scots had proclaimed no war with England, and it was contrary to the Solemn League and Covenant for the one country to commence war against the other. To this the answer was that the Scots had already broken the Covenant by the Engagement; and that, though the Engagement had been disavowed by a subsequent Parliament or party, yet their whole conduct latterly had manifested a determination to support the cause of Charles Stuart against the people of England; that therefore war was inevitable, and the only question was whether Scotland should be the seat of war, or the Scots should be allowed to organize their forces, to march into England, and be joined by a party there. Fairfax declared his willingness to march against the Scots if they entered England, but he was against hostilities till that event occurred. It being however resolved to carry the war into Scotland, he resigned his command.[1]

An act was passed on the 26th of June repealing the act whereby Thomas Lord Fairfax had been appointed captain general and commander-in-chief of all the forces of the English Parliament; and another act was passed the same day, nemine contradicente, constituting and

[1] Whitelock, p. 460.   Ludlow, vol. i. p. 314.

appointing Oliver Cromwell, Esquire, to be captain general
and commander-in-chief of all the forces raised and to be
raised by authority of Parliament within the Commonwealth of England.   By the 29th of June Cromwell had
left London and was on his march to Scotland.[1]   He was
desired by the Council of State to assume the title of
" General of the forces of the Parliament of England," and
to receive no letters from Scotland without such address.[2]

Mrs. Hutchinson affirms that what many said that
Cromwell undermined Fairfax, was false ; for in Colonel
Hutchinson's presence he most earnestly importuned
Fairfax to keep his commission, lest his resignation should
discourage the army and the people in that juncture of
time, but by no means prevail, although he laboured almost
all the night with most earnest endeavours.[3]   Ludlow
says " he acted his part so to the life that I thought him
sincere."   The opinion that Cromwell was sincere was
entertained at the time by all those who formed the
deputation sent by the Council of State to Fairfax.
Subsequent events however induced them to alter their
opinion, and to think that Cromwell did not wish to
succeed in persuading Fairfax to retain his commission,
but already regarded his appointmeut to Fairfax's place as
a step to the absolute power he aimed at.   But in all
these persons this opinion as to Cromwell's sincerity in
trying to persuade Fairfax to retain his commission was an
afterthought ; and I think it not improbable that their
first opinion was correct, and that Cromwell was sincere.
Neither would his sincerity on this point affect the
question of any ulterior designs he might then have

[1] Whitelock, p. 460. Parl. Hist.
vol. iii. pp. 1350, 1351, 1352.
[2] Order Book of the Council of State,
29 June, 1650.   MS. State Paper
Office.
[3] Mrs. Hutchinson's Memoirs of
Colonel Hutchinson, p. 344. Bohn's
edition. London, 1854.

formed, for he had found by long experience that Fairfax's being commander-in-chief did not prevent him, the
lieutenant-general, from doing nearly what he liked in and
with the army. Besides, independently of the question
of his sincerity or insincerity on this occasion, there are
several contemporary witnesses who affirm that by that
time he had begun his operation of moulding the army to
his mind by weeding out of it the godly and upright-
hearted men, both officers and soldiers, and filling their
places partly with cavaliers, partly with personal friends
and relatives and others who would "make no question
for conscience' sake." These last words are Mrs. Hutchinson's,[1] who joins them with some others which, being rather
more than "almost scolding,"[2] do not mend her argument. Her testimony however is supported by that of
Richard Baxter, and by that of Ludlow. But then their
memoirs like hers were written after the event ; and we
may be permitted to doubt whether the event did not,
perhaps involuntarily, colour their recollections of the past.
In fact Ludlow, like Harrison and many others, discovered
Cromwell's designs somewhat of the latest—that is, after
they were executed. Moreover Cromwell was a man who
rather watched and took advantage of opportunities than
sought to make them. It is therefore improbable that he
had any designs of a definite character at this time or
indeed long after. And though Mrs. Hutchinson takes
credit afterwards for penetration in seeing what Cromwell
was about when she says that his mode of proceeding
"was unperceived by all that were not of very penetrating
eyes,"[3] anyone who takes a comprehensive view of the

---

[1] Memoirs of Col. Hutchinson, p.
342. Bohn's edn. London, 1854.

[2] Whitelock's description of the

terms of the women's petition to the
parliament in behalf of John Lilburne.

[3] Memoirs, p. 342.

whole business must see that the deeper designs of a man of the capacity of Cromwell were not likely to be so laid as to be discovered by so common-place a man as Colonel Hutchinson, or by a woman, who however praiseworthy in her character of a wife, evinced so little penetration as to mistake her husband for a hero. Honest Ludlow was almost as little likely to penetrate and countermine such a man as Cromwell as Colonel Hutchinson. Ludlow indeed in after days, when in poverty and in exile he wrote his memoirs, sad and disenchanted though still unsubdued, having indeed if any man ever had a " soul invincible," noted that at a certain time the grand moral distinction between the parliamentary and all other armies began to be destroyed—" and then the troops of the Parliament," he says " who were not raised out of the meanest of the people and without distinction, as other armies had been, but consisted of such as had engaged themselves from a spirit of liberty in the defence of their rights and religion, were corrupted by him, kept as a standing force against the people, taught to forget their first engagements and rendered as mercenary as other troops are accustomed to be." [1]

Whether or not those who mention what they call Cromwell's designs of usurpation in their subsequently written memoirs penetrated Cromwell's designs at the time, there is sufficient evidence that he was not only suspected but publicly charged with such designs at an early period by John Lilburne and other discontented officers of the army. But then the very fact of such charges being made by such men, whatever degree of penetration the making of them might show, rather tended to strengthen Cromwell's power than to shake it. For even assuming that Lilburne's charges were proved, and Cromwell dis-

---

[1] Ludlow's Memoirs, vol. iii. p. 21.

missed from his command, and Lilburne or some one
recommended by Lilburne's party put in his place, what
result could have been expected but the bringing in the
royalists upon the nation pell-mell? For the whole of poor
Lilburne's short, busy, restless life shows that, with some
talent as a pamphleteer and even more talent as a speaker,
he had no talent whatever as a man of effective action,
none of that talent of which both Cromwell and Monk
had so much.

At the head of an army of sixteen thousand [1] men
Cromwell now invaded Scotland. If we compare the
number of this army with the numbers of the armies with
which the first and second Edwards invaded Scotland,
taking into account also the considerable increase of population between the fourteenth and seventeenth centuries,
though the increase cannot be ascertained with any degree
of exactness, we are struck with the smallness of the
amount of this army of the seventeenth century. But
sixteen thousand men, well-treated, well-fed, well-armed,
animated by a religious enthusiasm that made them look
on death not merely without fear but as a passage to
eternal happiness and honour, accustomed to discipline and
to victory, and led by Oliver Cromwell, were really more
formidable than a hundred thousand men led by King
Edward the Second, when moreover in the one case the
army opposed to them was led by the Committee of
Estates, in the other case by Robert Bruce.

About the time of Charles's landing, the Scottish Parliament having received certain intelligence of Cromwell's

---

[1] "Mordington, 24 July, 1650. A
list of the regiments of horse and
foot rendezvoused and marched with
the Lord General Cromwell into Scotland. The whole thus, the train 690,
the horse 5415, the foot 10,249 ; in
toto 16,354."—*Sev. Proc. in Parl.*
July 25 to August 1, in Cromwelliana,
p. 85.

advance, were under a necessity of reinforcing their army then consisting of 2500 horse and 3000 foot.[1] After much debate an act of levies passed for raising above 30,000 horse and foot throughout the kingdom. Very different from the mode pursued in England was the mode of recruiting the army for the Kirk, as it was called, though it was in fact an army raised for the purpose of establishing in Scotland under the name of Charles II., as a phantom king, a sort of heptarchy composed of a body of petty kings, whose tyranny was likely to be as galling as that of the worst of the Stuarts.[2] Those who have not examined the matter are apt to imagine that the Scottish peasantry flocked to the so-called standard of the Kirk in 1650 as some thirty years later when, goaded into madness by the cruelty of Claverhouse and Lauderdale, they opposed successfully their undisciplined valour to the onset of veteran troops at Drumclog. This is very far from being the case. The same great writer, who has given a picture of the skirmish at Drumclog that will live as long as the language in which it is written, has also on another occasion given a description of the state of mind in which a Scottish peasant followed his lord to the battle of Bothwell Bridge, which represents to the life the feelings with which, according to abundance of the best evidence, the bulk of the Scottish peasantry left their homes under the conduct of their lairds and lords to be slaughtered at Dunbar, or as prisoners either to die of famine and pestilence or be transported to the English settlements in America. Such was the fate for which thousands of poor men were dragged from their homes by their native oppressors, by those who neither knew how to

---

[1] Sir Edward Walker, p. 160.   [2] *Ibid.* p. 194.

lead armies themselves nor would leave them to the leading
of those who did know.   Duke Hamilton pressed every
fourth man in certain districts for his miserable expedition
into England.[1]   Many yeomen in Clydesdale " upon fear
to be levied by force " fled from their houses to Loudoun
Hill.[2]   The English army in their march through Berwickshire saw not any Scotchman, but the streets of the small
towns and villages were full of Scotch women, very many
of whom bemoaned their husbands, who, they said, " were
enforced by the lairds to gang to the muster." [3]   The
Highlanders, notwithstanding their vaunted attachment to
their chiefs, were, latterly at least, as little disposed to go to
war at the command of their tyrants as the Lowlanders.
Obedience to his chief was indeed the creed in which the
Highlander was brought up.   But how far that obedience
was hearty and willing appears from the fact that in 1745
nothing but force could draw the men from their houses.[4]
And in 1715 the methods adopted by those feudal or
patriarchal tyrants to force their vassals into a rebellion
against the established government appear from a letter
written by the Earl of Mar to the baillie of his lordship of
Kildrummie and dated September 9, 1715, in which he
says, " I have used gentle means too long.   .   .   .   Let
my own tenants in Kildrummie know that if they come
not forth with their best arms, I will send a party immediately to burn what they shall miss taking from them.
And they may believe this only as a threat, but, by all
that's sacred, I'll put it in execution, let my loss be what

---

[1] Captain Hodgson's Memoirs, p.
124.

[2] Baillie's Letters and Journals,
vol. iii. p. 48.   Edinburgh, 1842.

[3] Relation of the Fight at Leith, p.
270, published with Slingsby's and

Hodgson's Memoirs, and other original
documents, namely dispatches and
letters relating to this campaign.

[4] Jacobite Correspondence, quoted
in Mr. Hill Burton's Life of Simon
Lord Lovat, pp. 151, 152.

it will, that it may be an example to others.   You are to
tell the gentlemen that I expect them in their best accoutre-
ments on horseback, and no excuse to be accepted of." [1]
Add to this that the men were miserably paid, if paid at
all, and very scantily fed on food of the coarsest description, and that they could never rise to the rank of officers,
and you have a strong contrast to the well-fed, well-clothed,
and, though punished for breach of discipline with unrelenting severity, well-treated freemen who filled the ranks
of the English Parliamentary armies. The officers appointed
to command the Scottish levies thus raised were, at least
according to the authority of a royalist who did not regard
them with a favourable eye, " for the most part ministers'
sons, clerks, and such other sanctified creatures, who hardly
ever saw or heard of any sword but that of the spirit." [2]
Good officers must have discovered by this time that it was
better to seek service where it was more likely to lead to
promotion and reward than under a Government whose

---

[1] The letter is printed in full in Sir
Walter Scott's History of Scotland, contained in "Tales of a Grandfather,"
vol. ii. pp. 271, 272, Edinburgh,
1846. We now see that the description given by the old sexton of Her-
mitage to the Master of Ravenswood
is hardly over-coloured:—" There was
auld Ravenswood brandishing his Andrew Ferrara at the head, and crying
to us to come and buckle to, as if we
had been gaun to a fair,—there was
Caleb Balderston, that is living yet,
flourishing in the rear, and swearing
Gog and Magog he would put steel
through the guts of ony man that
turned bridle,—there was young Allan
Ravenswood, that was then Master, wi'
a bended pistol in his hand,—it was a
mercy it gaed na aff,—crying to me,

that had scarce as much wind left as
serve the necessary purpose of my ain
lungs, ' Sound, you poltroon ! sound,
you damned cowardly villain, or I will
blow your brains out !' and, to be
sure, I blew sic points of war, that
the scraugh of a clockin-hen was
music to them." The inducement applied to their soldiers by the Prussian
tyrants was of a similar nature to this.
In action a line of sergeants, each
armed with a heavy cane, stood behind
each rank, one for every three soldiers,
so that they had the enemy in front,
and these terrible tyrants behind, who
rendered running away a matter of
difficulty and danger. The cuirassiers
and pikemen of Cromwell had no need
of such stimulants.

[2] Sir Edward Walker, p. 162.

chancellor was a colonel of regiments of horse and foot, of which he took the pay, leaving others to do the duty.

It is indeed true that men treated as the Scottish peasants and even the Scottish gentlemen (as appears from what has been said) were treated by their feudal superiors have fought successfully. But there was when, as in the great Scottish war of independence, whether better treated or not, they fought under great and popular leaders, Wallace, Bruce, and Douglas, for a popular and worthy object ; or, it might be, under one of those great and terrible tyrants, such as Frederic of Prussia, a tyrant of invincible energy, untiring industry, and extraordinary capacity, but not under an oligarchy or knot of small imbecile tyrants, which for three centuries among all its members had not mustered brains enough to govern a hen-roost or to drive a flock of geese across a common.

It has sometimes been supposed that the Scottish armies during these wars were in part at least composed of the veteran Scottish troops of Gustavus Adolphus, on whom that great.king relied the most not only for their invincible steadiness but for their unbounded daring ; who at the battle of Leipsic almost annihilated the terrible veterans of Tilly ; and who in the storm of the castle of Marienberg performed a feat of arms more wonderful even than Bonaparte's famous passage of the Bridge of Lodi. But this was not the case. In 1650 application was made to the French Court for permission for Douglas's (formerly Hepburn's) and the other Scots regiments, which since the death of Gustavus Adolphus had passed into the service of France, to return to Scotland with Charles II. But Lewis XIV. declined to accede to the request, and promised to give them their pay with greater regularity in future.[1] It is undoubtedly true that there were several officers in the service of the Scots Parliament (the two Leslies and others) who had served under Gustavus Adolphus. But though in common and inaccurate language they may be said to have learnt the art of war under a great master, the art of war is an art which cannot be learnt under any teacher but nature. And events proved but too well that neither Alexander nor David Leslie was ever a master of it. One fact tells volumes against both. I have already mentioned the introduction of the use of the cartridge by Gustavus Adolphus as well as the fact that it was not generally used till near a century after.[2] The deadly effect of the fire of the Scots brigades in the wars of Gustavus Adolphus in consequence of the advantage of the cartridge was often proved. And the first thing that a commander of any superior intelligence would have done would have been to introduce it wherever he commanded. That it was not introduced among the Scots troops sufficiently appears from one of the articles of the surrender of Edinburgh Castle to Cromwell, by which it is stipulated that the soldiers may depart "with their arms and baggage, with drums beating and colours flying, matches lighted at both ends, and ball in their mouths as they are usually wont to march." This clearly shows that the cartridges were not used, and that the ball was put loose or separately into the gun.

It is a strange spectacle to observe the language which these two bodies of fanatics, each of which believed them-

[1] Records of the British Army— Printed by Authority—Historical Record of the First or Royal Regiment of Foot. Compiled by Richard Cannon, Esq., Adjutant-General's Office, Horse Guards. London, 1847. P. 44.

[2] Historical Record of the First Regiment of Foot.

selves the special and exclusive favourites and confidants
of Heaven, held to each other.   The Presbyterians declared the army commanded by Cromwell to be a union of
the most perverse heretical sectaries of every different
persuasion, agreeing in nothing but their desire to effect
the ruin of the Christian Church, and the destruction of
the Covenant, to which most of their leaders had sworn
fidelity.   Cromwell was Antichrist, over whose head the
curse of God hung for murdering the king, and breaking
the Covenant.[1]   He was Agag, and revelations had been
made to them that he, with his army of sectaries and
heretics, was delivered into their hands to be dealt with as
Samuel had dealt with Agag and the Amalekites.   The
Independents were by no means behind-hand in this war
of words, though after their success at Dunbar they could
afford to exhibit a little more profession than their adversaries of Christian charity, which was rather a scarce com-
modity everywhere in those days.   They called Heaven
and Earth to witness whether they had not cause to defend
themselves by coming into Scotland with an army to
hinder the Scots from taking their time and advantage to
impose on them their grand enemy, whom the Scots had
engaged to restore to the possession of England and Ireland.[2]   They declared that they valued the Christian
Church ten thousand times more than their own lives ; and
that they were not only a rod of iron to dash asunder the
common enemies, but a hedge (though unworthy) about
the divine vineyard.   As for the Covenant, were it not for
making it an object of idolatry, they would be content to

---

[1] Relation of the Fight at Leith,
p. 220, in Original Memoirs written
during the Civil War.   Edinburgh,
1806.

[2] Declaration of the English Army,
in Cromwelliana, p. 84.

place it on the point of their pikes, and let God judge whether they or their opponents had best observed its obligations. Those, they said, that were acquainted with the secrets of God (meaning themselves) did clearly see the quarrel was betwixt Christ and the Devil, betwixt Christ's seed and the Devil's. The whore of Babylon had received her deadly wound; let the Devil be her chirurgeon. Their prayers for them (the Presbyterians) should be that the Lord would pity and forgive them, in that they knew not what they did; and that He would give them a clear sight of the great work He was then, in those latter days, carrying on. Their bowels did in Christ yearn after the godly in Scotland, and the arms of their Christian love were stretched out ready to embrace them, whenever God should incline their hearts to carry on and not to gainsay and oppose His work. If however God should still suffer their eyes to be blinded, so that seeing they would not see, and their hearts to be hardened, so as to persist in gainsaying and opposing the way of the Lord, whatever misery befell their nation, either through famine or sword, would lie heavy upon them.[1]

Before the English army entered Scotland, an incident occurred which shows that if Gumble's statement that Monk was known among the soldiers as honest George Monk be true, the opinion of the soldiers must have changed from what it was at this time. At Newcastle Colonel Bright threw up his commission because the general would not give him a fortnight's time to go home to settle his private affairs.[2] When the army was about Alnwick several colonels came to the head of Colonel

---

[1] Relation of the Campaign in Scotland, pp. 331, 332, in Original Memoirs written during the Civil War; and Cromwell to the Governor of the Castle of Edinburgh, 12th Sept. 1650.

[2] Captain Hodgson's Memoirs, p. 127.

Bright's regiment, and telling the soldiers that the general
was much troubled such a regiment should want a colonel,
asked whom they would have for their colonel.   The
soldiers told them they had a good colonel, but he had
left them, and they knew not whom they might have. The
colonels asked if they would have Colonel Monk.   " Colonel
Monk ! " said some of them, " what ! to betray us ?   We
took him but not long since at Nantwich prisoner : we'll
have none of him."   The next day the colonels came
again, and asked if they would have Major-General
Lambert to be their colonel.   At which they all threw up
their hats and shouted " a Lambert ! a Lambert ! " [1] ' In
the whole of this affair, the refusal of the short leave of
absence causing the resignation of Colonel Bright, and the
proposal of Monk as his successor undoubtedly originating
with Cromwell, may be clearly seen one very remarkable
example of " weeding out the old officers and filling up
their room with turn-coat cavaliers."

Cromwell and Monk soon understood each other. Their
abilities, though very different in some points, were very
like in others.   They were both essentially men of action.
What was to be done they could do, from fighting a battle
to quelling a mutiny, from raising an army and manning a
fleet to keeping their men in efficient fighting condition by
attention to the most minute details of the commissariat,
even to furnishing their soldiers amid the bogs of Ireland
and the mountains of Scotland with a sufficient supply of
biscuit and cheese, frequently assisted by a portion of meat

---

[1] Captain Hodgson's Memoirs, pp.
139, 140. Hodgson was then an officer
in that very regiment of foot, as he
afterwards was in Lambert's regiment
of horse; for Lambert appears to have
had a regiment of horse and a regiment
of foot at the same time. See Hodgson's Memoirs, p. 140. As to the
incident related in the text, see also
Relation of the Fight at Leith, in the
same collection, p. 205.

or fish, chiefly salmon ;[1] and when better medical advice was not to be had, they had their prescriptions and remedies for sickness and wounds.   Nearly the same might be said as to the resemblance of their characters.   Their faces also bore a not inconsiderable likeness to each other.   The best original portraits[2] of both exhibit the same massive structure of countenance and head, the same look of calm intelligence and invincible resolution in the eyes and mouth. Calm and indomitable courage, and strong practical good sense characterized both alike.   But here the resemblance ends, for in Cromwell there was added an element of enthusiasm which gave to his courage more unbounded daring and to his ambition a loftier flight than suited Monk's phlegmatic temperament and unimaginative mind. For, after all, Monk did not rise above the common ranks of men.   And yet he was a sort of Cromwell—with the courage and good sense without the genius,—without that enthusiastic element and that unerring instinct telling the exact moment when a blow is to be struck, which, when combined with courage and good sense, inspire a resistless energy into a man's actions.

As regards the points of resemblance in the characters of these two men, it is also remarkable that Monk and Cromwell though both by birth gentlemen, were both characterized by a certain plainness, if not coarseness, a certain want of refinement in their tastes and habits, which not only shunned all approach to foppery but tended to the other extreme.   We cannot imagine Monk or Cromwell in

---

[1] It appears from various minutes in the Order Book of the Council of State, that salmon for the use of the troops in Ireland was purchased in Ireland at £15 per ton, a little more than three halfpence per pound. —*Order Book of the Council of State*, 25 Sept. 1649, and 23 Octob. 1649, à Meridie.   MS. State Paper Office.

[2] There were several original miniatures of Cromwell and one of Monk exhibited in the Loan Court of the South Kensington Museum in 1862.

the wildest days of their youth the sort of fine gentleman that Churchill was at the Court of Charles II., or Cæsar in the Roman Forum, when he devoted the part of his time he did not consume in pleasure to earning by his eloquence as an advocate the popularity which was to give him the command of armies and thereby the empire of the world.

It may be supposed that Monk's rejection by the soldiers of Bright's regiment would be no bar to the advancement of the man who had gained the confidence of Cromwell, not the entire confidence, for that no one possessed. Cromwell first gave Monk a regiment and then appointed him general of the ordnance.[1]

On Monday the 22nd of July Cromwell's army passed through Berwick and marched across the border. A forlorn first of dragoons[2] and then one of horse were sent forward. After these the whole army marched for Scotland over the bridge, the general's own regiment of horse and Colonel Pride's of foot leading the van. The train marched in the body of the foot.[3] On the bounds between the two kingdoms the general made " a large discourse " to the officers, "showing he spoke," says Captain Hodgson, " as a Christian and a soldier," and pointing out the inconveniences they should meet with in Scotland as to the scarcity of provisions. As to the people, he said, they would find the leading part of them to be soldiers, and they were very numerous, and at present might be unanimous. And he charged the officers to double, nay treble, their diligence, for they might be sure they had work before them.

That night they encamped at Mordington about the

---

[1] Ludlowe says that Cromwell " made up a regiment for Monk with six companies out of Sir Arthur Haselrig's regiment and six out of Colonel Fenwick's."—*Ludlowe's Memoirs*, p. 140.

4to edition. London, 1771.

[2] See p. 44 as to the difference between " horse" and " dragoons."

[3] Letter July 26 to Aug. 2, in Cromwelliana, p. 85.

house, the general and some of his principal officers being quartered in Lord Mordington's [1] house, where none were found except two or three of the inferior servants, nor any household utensils. Some of Cromwell's soldiers however had brought a little raw meat with them and became excellent cooks, a back making a dripping pan and a head-piece a porridge pot.[2] A slight incident occurred here which may be mentioned as exhibiting in Cromwell that taste for humour which, as Dr. Arnold says speaking of Hannibal, great men are seldom without. Cromwell and some of his officers were looking out of a window, and, hearing a great shout among the soldiers, they spied a soldier with a Scots kirn (or kurn, in the south of England pronounced churn) on his head. "Some of them," says Hodgson, "had been purveying abroad, and had found a vessel filled with 'Scots cream, and bringing the reversions to their tents, some got dishfuls and some hatfuls; and the cream growing low in the vessel, one would have a modest drink, and heaving up the kirn, another lifts it up, and all the cream trickles down his apparel, and his head fast in the tub; this was a merriment to the officers, as Oliver loved an innocent jest." [3]

It must not be inferred from this that Cromwell permitted plundering to be practised by his soldiers. He published a proclamation reciting that several soldiers had straggled from their colours and enforced victuals from the Scots without paying for them, and commanding them not to straggle half a mile on pain of death; and he was not a man to let his orders be disobeyed with impunity.[4] A

---

[1] Sir James Douglas, second son of William 10th Earl of Angus, was created a peer by the title of Lord Mordington, 14th Nov. 1641.— *Douglas's Peerage of Scotland.*

[2] Letters in Cromwelliana, p. 85.

[3] Captain Hodgson's Memoirs, pp. 129, 130.

[4] Whitelock, pp. 465, 466.

trooper in Colonel Whalley's regiment was sentenced by a court-martial to have his horse and arms taken from him, and to work as a pioneer for three weeks, for taking away some curtains and other things out of a Scottish gentleman's house.[1] A serjeant of Colonel Coxe's regiment was executed on a gallows on Pentland hills, there being no tree to hang him on, for being present with some soldiers of that regiment when they plundered a house, and himself taking away a cloak. Three soldiers were condemned with him, but a pardon was brought them immediately after the execution of the other.[2]

On the morning after the English army entered Scotland, a trumpeter came from the Scots Army, but, says Hodgson, to little purpose. The beacons were all lighted that night ; the men fled, and drove away their cattle.[3] Cromwell having remained at Mordington Monday night, Tuesday, and Wednesday, marched on Thursday to Cockburn's Path, or Copper's Path, as he writes it,[4] that is, to the village or small town so called, which is situated on the northern side of the pass that has given its name to the village.

It is a remark of Dr. Arnold that nothing shows more clearly the great rarity of geographical talent than the praise bestowed on Polybius as a geographer, though his

---

[1] Relation of the Fight at Leith, p. 209.

[2] Relation of the Campaign in Scotland, p. 253. See other cases of soldiers punished for violence to the country people, Whitelock, p. 468.

[3] Captain Hodgson's Memoirs, p. 130. Whitelock, p. 465. "The Border beacons," says Sir Walter Scott, "from their number and position formed a sort of telegraphic communication with Edinburgh." By the Scottish Act of Parliament 1455, c. 48, the warning of the approach of the English was to be by one bale, or faggot, two bales, or four bales ; four bales blazing beside each other were to show that the enemy are in great force. Note 9 to Canto III. of the Lay of the Last Minstrel. There was never greater need for the four bales than now, for an enemy was advancing more formidable even than Edward Longshanks with his host of archers, knights, and men-at-arms.

[4] Cromwell to the Lord President of the Council of State, July 30, 1650.

descriptions are so vague and imperfect that it is scarcely possible to understand them.[1] It is indeed a remarkable proof how little some of the most celebrated writers seem to have been aware of the importance of geography to history, that we find Sir Walter Scott describing the Lammermoor chain of hills as "a ridge of hills terminating on the sea near the town of Dunbar,"[2] and M. Guizot confounding the pass called Cockburn's Path with the field of Dunbar.[3]

The Lammermoor chain of hills rises in Edinburghshire or Mid Lothian, and stretching along the upper part that is, the part farthest from the sea, of East Lothian in Haddingtonshire, terminates on the sea, not near the town of Dunbar, but nine or ten miles south east of it, in Berwickshire, not far from the boundary between Berwickshire and Haddingtonshire, Cockburn's Path being in Berwickshire. The chain, having a strip of fertile land between it and the sea, runs in a south-eastern direction about a mile to the south or south-west of the village of Cockburn's Path, and there turns nearly at right angles to the east, that is, towards the sea, presenting to the traveller along the coast an apparently impassable barrier or wall of rock and mountain. The Lammermoor chain does not flatten itself down, like the Grampian chain, as it approaches the sea. On the contrary the sides of the Lammermoor ridge of hills are in many places very steep, and in some places form a perpendicular wall of rock. The chain is about three miles in breadth at the point where the latest London road passes it through a defile. I say the latest London road, for altogether there are three roads besides the rail-

---

[1] Arnold's History of Rome, vol. iii. note F.

[2] Sir Walter Scott's History of Scotland contained in "Tales of a Grandfather," vol. i. p. 489. Edin-

burgh, 1846.

[3] Guizot's Life of Monk—see pp. 21, 22 of the English Translation, London, 1851.

road, 1. the road called the old coast road, 2. the road that passes over the Pease Bridge, and 3. the road, the most modern of the three, that runs through the glen, or defile above mentioned. This has led to some confusion respecting the road by which Cromwell's army marched. A little careful investigation however soon clears up this confusion.

On the northern side of the Lammermoor chain of hills where it approaches the sea, there are two ravines which meet at about a quarter of a mile's distance from the sea. In each of these ravines runs a small stream or burn. These burns meet where the ravines meet, and the stream formed by their confluence is called the Pease Burn. The burn that runs through the larger and most southern of the ravines is also called the Pease Burn; and that ravine through which it runs is called the Pease Dean.[1] The burn that runs through the other, the smaller and more northern ravine, is called the Heriot Water or burn; and the ravine is called Tower Dean from an old tower, the ruins of which stand on its northern bank about a mile above the point where the two ravines meet.

The country people living in the immediate vicinity tell you that the old name of this small ruined peel or tower and of the family to which it belonged was Ravenswood, and that this family had another castle on. the sea-shore called Wolf's Crag. It is evident that the local story (it cannot be accurately called a tradition) about this ruin, which appears to have been an obscure, and, I may almost say, nameless tower, bearing no resemblance either in magnitude or position, except its being near the gorge of a pass of the Lammermoor hills, to the imaginary castle of Ravenswood, has arisen entirely out of Sir Walter Scott's

---

[1] Dean, in that part of Scotland, is   of the same kingdom.
the same word as den in other parts

romance the Bride of Lammermoor; and furnishes an instructive example of the way in which stories taken wrongly for local traditions often originate. Sir Walter Scott's romances have given rise to many similar " traditions " in various parts of Scotland, and such " traditions " may in time be transformed into history. He says himself in the Introduction to the Bride of Lammermoor:—

" The imaginary castle of Wolf's Crag has been identified by some lover of locality with that of Fast Castle. The author is not competent to judge of the resemblance betwixt the real and imaginary scene, having never seen Fast Castle except from the sea."

There is a curious old bridge near this old ruined tower, about twenty yards above the present bridge. This small old bridge, now covered with creeping plants, which is at the bottom of the ravine, only a few feet above the stream, and is only about 3 or 4 feet wide, was the only bridge across either of these ravines at the time of Cromwell's invasion; and, though it might afford a passage to horses as well as men, and might have been used by the borderer who inhabited the tower for riding across the stream and ravine, was manifestly not intended for the passage of carts or carriages. But as Cromwell had with him a train of artillery with near sixty carriages,[1] it is evident that he did not march by this road. The same reason applies with still greater force to the common assertion that he passed the other and deeper ravine at the point where the Pease Bridge now crosses it.

The depth of this other ravine called the Pease Dean, at the spot where the Pease Bridge now crosses it, is about a hundred and fifty feet, and the sides of the ravine are precipitous, indeed almost perpendicular. It is also very

---

[1] Captain Hodgson's Memoirs, p. 126.

narrow ; so that to the eye of a spectator at the rocky
bottom a little below the bridge, the deep gloomy glen,
rendered yet more sombre by the overhanging trees, shows
but a small strip of sky overhead. The lover of the
picturesque might see there almost as much to delight him
as the poet of Fitz James saw in the Trossachs' wild and
fairy glen ; the clear stream rippling along at the bottom
(for it is but a small burn) over its pebbled bed, bordered
by wild flowers, plants, and trees of various kinds and of
great beauty which cover the banks and spring from the
clefts and crevices of the rocks ; the various hues also
beautiful which the atmosphere and the weather have
painted on the rugged crags during a long series of ages ;
higher up the birch, ash, oak, and pine trees, some of them
shattered by lightning and tempest and others flinging
their boughs so as almost to meet across the chasm ;
highest of all the narrow strip of blue sky. Those deep
glens form the really beautiful parts of Scotland, scattered
as they are through all parts of the country and strangely
contrasted with the bleak landscape around. In many
parts of the country this contrast is particularly striking.
For to a person standing on the top of the bank or cliff,
often formed partly of earth partly of rock, the view
around is bleak and desolate, presenting only an expanse
of bare heathy mountainous ground. But in the narrow
sheltered glen below, at the bottom of which the stream
pursues its course, now running between two steep
precipitous banks, now flowing on beneath hazels and
alders, between banks of a more gentle slope, then
tumbling over the edge of a rock and plunging into a deep
abyss or linn, then once more emerging and flowing on
through the more open and grassy part of the glen, there
is abundance of vegetation, of grass, flowers, trees, and

plants, which in their profusion and variety of form, hue, and situation, present an agreeable and striking contrast to the bleak scene above. But I do not believe that Oliver Cromwell's love of the picturesque was such as to induce him even to descend himself to the bottom of this ravine at the point where the Pease Bridge now stands, much less to attempt,—for it could be nothing but an attempt—no power short of miraculous could have led either his artillery or his cavalry across the ravine here, —to make his army with all its artillery, horses, and carriages descend on one side and ascend on the other. The fact is, the Pease Bridge is a sight for sightseers, and those who write guide-books or hand-books for the sight-seers of the Pease Bridge, with a view of accumulating as many attractions as possible for their sight or show, have superadded to its other attractions, that this is the place where Cromwell passed the ravine and the place which he described as "the strait pass where ten men to hinder are better than forty to make their way." [1] I will now briefly state the facts of the matter.

Before the erection of the bridges, which are of comparatively modern date, the depth and precipitous banks of these ravines rendered the crossing of them a work of difficulty in all cases—in the case of an army with artillery and cavalry, an impossibility. The oldest road appears to have been made to turn or evade the difficulty, by winding down to the sea-shore, where the two ravines meet and open out somewhat. This road, called the Path, Cockburn's Path, and also the Path's Road or Peath's Road, corrupted into Pease Road, gave its name to the burn made up of the two burns; to the larger of the two ravines; and finally to a bridge built across the larger

[1] Cromwell to the Speaker, Sept. 4, 1650.

ravine in 1785–6.[1] The old coast road, the old Colbrand's
Path, now called Cockburn's Path, immediately after
crossing the burn, named from it the Path's, Peath's or
Pease Burn, in its southward course turns to the right, and
with an ascent of one foot in five ascends over the top of
the chain of hills near the point where that chain terminates at the sea.   This road was abandoned in 1786
for that by the Pease Bridge, which in its turn was superseded by the newer road by Houndwood, as the latter
must now in a great measure be by the railroad.   It is
therefore a mistake to say that Cromwell meant the chasm
where the *Pease* Bridge now is, the road to which was not
in existence then nor a hundred years after, by " the strait
pass at Copper's Path where ten men to hinder are better
than forty to make their way." [2]   Now " strait pass "
means narrow pass, a description which applies completely
to the mode in which the old coast road winds and ascends
between steep banks from the sea-shore to the upper
platform of the chain of hills, but not at all to the chasm
where the Pease Bridge now stands.

It is curious and not uninstructive to observe the difficulty of getting at the exact truth of a matter so trifling,
as this may seem to some, after a lapse of years, where new
roads have quite superseded old, but old names still
remain.   At first sight it would seem that there is no
connection between the old coast or seashore road and the
village of Cockburn's Path.   But after some investigation
you find that a footpath leading off towards the sea from
the turnpike-gate at the northern entrance of the village is
the relic of the old road which connected the village with

[1] " The Pease Bridge was built in 1785, 1786." Statistical Account of Scotland, Berwickshire, Cockburn's Path, p. 311.

[2] Cromwell to the Speaker, Sept. 4, 1650, in Relation of the Campaign in Scotland, p. 296.

the Path Road.   The path road now strikes into the new road at the railway station about a quarter of a mile north of the village.   And probably its line was formerly the same, since this point, where the Cockburn's Path railway station now is, is called Path Head, as being the place where the road called Cockburn's Path begins its gradual descent towards the sea—which fact affords further corroborative evidence that the old coast road is the road called Cockburn's Path.   The circumstance, that the only communication now between the village and this Path Road is but a footpath, might look at first as if this old road, called the Pease Road, or Path's Road, had not entered the village at all.   But this pathway, though now sought to be reduced in breadth, if not stopt up, was evidently a cartroad once, and widens into a cart-road still after passing under the railroad.   And, as it goes right out of the village, it proves the direct connection between the village and the *Pease* Road, and also proves that this road was the Cockburn's Path by which Cromwell's army marched.

This old Pease Road, proceeding from Path Head in a south-eastern direction, and descending gradually to the sea-shore about a mile and a half or two miles to the south-east of the village of Cockburn's Path, traverses the haugh, or space on a level with the sea-shore into which the two ravines having joined open, and crossing the Pease Burn, turns from the sea, and begins to ascend almost immediately with a rather steep ascent, but winding considerably ; while during the ascent, which continues for a distance not very considerable, the hills on the right and left command it.   It is here that the difficulty and danger of the pass, " where ten men to hinder are better than forty to make their way," are the greatest ; where, after passing the burn, the road or path, the *Pease* Road, winds

z

by quick turns and by a rather steep ascent among steep
green hills, through very narrow openings.

It is very remarkable that this pass closely resembles
that in which Hannibal destroyed the army of the Consul
Flaminius at the Lake Thrasymenus, or Trasimenus as it is,
I believe, more correctly written.   Polybius states that the
valley in which the Romans were caught was not the
narrow interval between the hills and the lake, but a valley
beyond that defile, and running down to the lake ; so that
the Romans when engaged in it had the lake not on their
right flank but in their rear.   Similarly an army marching
southward when engaged in the pass called Cockburn's
Path would have the sea not on their left flank, on which
it would be before they turned to ascend, but in their rear.
The word valley is perhaps a little ambiguous.   There
would however be a sort of a valley—though a steep
winding hollow way would be the more correct expression,
at least for the pass called Cockburn's Path.   The military
eye of Cromwell at once saw the importance of this pass,
but he had not the military genius to turn it to account as
Hannibal did the pass of Lake Thrasymenus.   If one
might presume to criticize, where, as Frederic said, criticism
is so easy and art so difficult, it would certainly seem that
Cromwell, instead of depending wholly for his success and
safety on a blunder of his adversary which he could hardly
have looked for, might have taken his measures so as not
only to have secured a retreat by this pass, but to have
made it a means of destroying his opponent's army.   But
Cromwell, so full of craft and so fertile in stratagem in his
political, does not appear to have possessed the same fertility in his military character.   And this distinction is, I
apprehend, when closely examined, one of deep significance ;
since, while in war craft and stratagem are legitimate

weapons, because both parties use them alike, to the best
of their ability ; in civil and political affairs they are not
legitimate weapons, because he who uses them, like a
gamester who uses packed cards or loaded dice, takes an
unfair advantage of opponents, and he will have some, if
not many such, who do not use them.

When Cromwell's scouts first came to the village of
Cockburn's Path, they fell in with three Scots, whom they
disarmed and took prisoners. These Scots alleged that
they were only countrymen, and that their ministers and
grandees had given out that the English army would kill
man, woman, and child ; and indeed had represented the
English sectaries, as they called Cromwell's army, to the
people as being "the monsters of the world." Cromwell
ordered the men's swords and other things taken from them
to be restored, and the men to be dismissed.[1] One of the
English scouts met with one of the enemy, who ran at
him with a lance, and broke it against his armour.[2] The
Scot seeing the English scout had the better, quitted his
horse, and plunged, the original dispatch says, down "a
steep hill ;" probably one of those deep and precipitous
glens or ravines, which characterize that district, probably
the glen now called Dunglass Dean, (*dean* being there used
to express what *den* does in other parts of Scotland),
where, adds the English officer who writes the account,
"our trooper could not follow him, but seized the horse."[3]

---

[1] Relation of the Fight at Leith, pp.
206, 207, Captain Hodgson's Memoirs, p. 131. Letters in Cromwelliana, pp. 83, 84, 85.

[2] A proof of the superior quality of
the defensive armour of Cromwell's
troops, and that the term "Ironsides"
was not applied without cause. There
was one horse regiment in particular

which in those Scottish wars was
called "The Brazen Wall" from their
never having been broken.

[3] Relation of the Fight at Leith, p.
207. These ravines or glens, rocky or
not, baffled the powers of description
of the English officers, most of whom
had never before seen anything of the
kind. The words used by them do not'

In the march from Mordington to Cockburn's Path the English army did not see any Scotchman in the places they passed through : but the streets were full of spectre-looking women, clothed in white flannel in a very homely manner. In Dunbar also no men were to be seen but some few decrepid ones, and boys under seven and old men above seventy years of age.[1] Cromwell published a declaration inviting all to remain in their houses without fear of molestation. At the same time he strictly enjoined his officers and soldiers not to offer the slightest violence to the persons or goods of any not immediately connected with the Scottish army. The infringement of these orders he punished with promptitude and severity.[2]

The English officers were naturally struck with the contrast between the Scottish villages and the English, particularly those of the south of England. An English village is not unfrequently spread in picturesque irregularity over a space of ground extending from half a mile to a mile or a mile and a half in length ; frequently skirting the edges of a common fringed or dotted with fine old trees, where every turn of the winding road presents some new point of beauty. The village church is a picturesque old building of stone grey with age, its old tower half covered with ivy, having in front of it perhaps an immense yew tree some 300 years old. A Scottish village on the other hand is merely a collection of cottages,—

convey any idea of the geographical character of the country which was the scene of this campaign.

[1] Relation of the Fight at Leith, pp. 207, 208. Another of the contemporary accounts says, "The people had generally deserted their habitations, some few women only were left behind ; yet we had this mercy, that their houses thus forsaken were indifferently well furnished with beer, wine, and corn, which was a very good supply to us."—*Relation of the Campaign in Scotland*, p. 232. This account does not agree with Cromwell's strict orders against plundering.

[2] Whitelock, pp. 465, 466.

at that time hovels of clay or turf,—placed close together, end to end, in rows, resembling the rows of negro cabins on a planter's estate, where nothing is left to the individual will of the tenant, but he must squat in the one case as the slave owner, in the other as the laird bids him. Whereas everything that gives beauty to an English village arises from the individual will having had nearly as much liberty to select a spot for a dwelling as the oak on the village green to shoot forth its boughs as nature bade it.   The distinction remains to this day as striking as it was then.   For where the hovels have given place to cottages built of stone, the latter form a stiff monotonous structure occupying in the same end to end rows the same ground formerly occupied by the clay hovels, without gardens or greensward between them and the dusty road, and without a village green with its scattered groups of picturesque old trees ; for land it seems, is too valuable in Scotland to be wasted on cottage gardens or village greens. The English officers were at that time probably the more struck with what they considered the barbarous poverty of Scotland, inasmuch as Scotland, besides having a nobility as old as its hills, had given to England a race of kings who declared they had a title direct from heaven. The spectacle of a Scottish village was not calculated to impress them with an idea that the condition of the people of England would be improved if they were to be governed by the Scottish king and the Scottish nobility as the people of Scotland had been governed.   And in this sense the difference between an English and Scotch village is by no means an insignificant fact.

The command of the Scottish army was held by David Leslie, a well-trained and skilful soldier, who had done more than the English accounts acknowledge towards the winning of the battle of Marston Moor, and who had defeated Montrose at Philiphaugh. But it is not quite correct to say, as Sir Walter Scott says, that David Leslie was the effective commander-in-chief in Scotland, inasmuch as it can be distinctly shown on the best authority we have on Scottish affairs at that time, Principal Baillie's " Letters and Journals," that the oligarchical Committee of Estates hampered and controlled David Leslie at Dunbar, as they had before hampered and controlled Lieut.-General Baillie at Kilsyth and Preston. Napoleon Bonaparte told the Convention when they were about to give him a colleague in his Italian campaign that he would resign if they did, and that one bad general was better than two good ones. David Leslie might have told the Committee of Estates that a bad general left alone was better than a good one controlled by Argyle and Cassilis ; and he would have better consulted his own reputation and perhaps the success of his side if he had resigned his command instead of suffering himself to be interfered with.

Leslie's dispositions, as far as they were uncontrolled, showed that he was a prudent and skilful general, and also that he was one of the few Scottish commanders who understood how to put in force the directions of what has been called the " Good King Robert's Testament." Bruce was too wise a man not to know that it would be unsafe to reckon on many Bannockburns. The sum of his testament therefore was to advise his countrymen to avoid risking great battles and to make such a use of their mountains, morasses, and deep narrow glens, that the enemy worn out with famine, fatigue, and apprehension should retreat as certainly as if routed in battle. Leslie had taken up a strong position between Edinburgh and

Leith. The right wing of his army rested upon the high grounds at the rise of the mountain called Arthur's Seat, and the left wing was posted at Leith. His lines extended from the Canongate,[1] or lower part of the old town of Edinburgh, across the Calton Hill, which was strongly fortified, to Leith which was likewise fortified. A deep trench, fortified with cannon, protected the whole line on the low ground ; while the castle built on a high and isolated perpendicular rock was at that time a place of great strength. "The guns also from Leith," says Cromwell, "scoured most parts of the line, so that they lay very strong."[2]

Cromwell finding that the Scottish army was "not to be attempted" in this strong position, and his own army having suffered considerably from such a day and night of rain as, he says, he had seldom seen, the enemy being under cover, retreated to Musselburgh for provisions supplied by a fleet which sailing along the coast accompanied the movements of his army. The provisions consisted principally of hard biscuit and cheese, and Captain Hodgson's expression is not a figurative or proverbial one when he says "About eleven o'clock we wanted our bread and cheese, and drew off towards Musselburgh."[3] Cromwell's rear was attacked as they retreated, but the Scots were repulsed, and driven within their trenches with some loss in killed and prisoners. The young king saw all this from the castle-hill,[4] and was very ill-satisfied, says Cromwell in his dispatch, to see his men do no better.[5] This incident Hume with his usual zeal to corrupt the truth of history

---

[1] Some of the Letters of the English officers call this "Cannygate street in Edinburgh." See the dispatch in the same collection with Captain Hodgson's Memoirs, p. 233.

[2] Cromwell to the Lord President of the Council of State, July 30, 1650.

[3] Captain Hodgson's Memoirs, p. 132.

[4] Relation of the Fight at Leith, p. 214.

[5] Relation of the Campaign in Scotland, p. 228.

has transformed into the king's "exerting himself in an action." The words indeed are skilfully selected. A person might in some sense be said to have "exerted himself in an action," when he walked to the top of the castle hill to look at it.[1] Or the expression "having exerted himself in an action he gained the affections of the soldiery" may be meant to apply to the following action.

Between three and four o'clock in the morning after Cromwell's retreat to Musselburgh, a body of cavalry consisting of fifteen troops, "1500, the choicest of their horse,"[2] called the Regiment of the Kirk, broke into the English lines, beat in the guards, and put a regiment of horse in some disorder. It is said that Cromwell himself in his drawers was forced to take his horse and pass over the river.[3] The English cavalry speedily forming charged the enemy, routed them, killed a great many, and took many prisoners, Major-General Montgomery being among the killed. One of those who were killed was heard to say when dying "Damn me, I'll go to my king;"[4] from

---

[1] There is not a word in Sir Edward Walker, the authority Hume cites, about the king's "exerting himself in an action." Walker's words are: "By this time the army was much increased, many Malignants and Engagers having gotten into command, his majesty high in the favour and affection of the army, which was then more evident by the soldiers having in the late action made an R. with chalk under the crown upon their arms, and generally expressing the goodness of their cause now they had the king with them." He says further, "Presently the committee" [of Estates, *i. e.* Argyle, his son Lord Lorne, Lothian, Loudon the chancellor, &c. see Walker, p. 162.] "commanded away all Malignants and Engagers and so lessened the army of 3000 or 4000 of the best men, and displaced all officers suspected, concluding then they had an army of Saints, and that they could not be beaten, for so their lying prophets daily told the people out of the pulpit," pp. 164, 165. Some men are said to be animated by a zeal for truth, others may be said to be animated by a zeal for falsehood. A lie has far more attractions for some persons than a plain fact.

[2] Relation of the Fight at Leith, p. 218. Cromwell says "15 of their most select troops." Relation of the Campaign in Scotland, p. 229.

[3] Sir Edward Walker, p. 163.

[4] Relation of the Fight at Leith, p. 219.

which and other circumstances [1] it appeared that the Kirk regiment of horse had in its ranks a good many English cavaliers. Charles's " exertions " in this action appear to have been confined to giving to each man two shillings to drink, " which made them drunk," [2] a display of " spirit and vivacity " undoubtedly better calculated to gain the affections of such troops than a long sermon on the merits of of the Solomn League and Covenant. To refute the charge of cruelty made against him by the Scots, Cromwell next day sent back the principal prisoners in his own coach, and the wounded in waggons. [3]

About the 6th of August the English army retreated to Dunbar for want of provisions, the stormy weather not permitting the ships to land their stores at Musselburgh. After giving his troops some rest Cromwell resolved to draw near to the enemy once more to try if he could bring on a battle on advantageous ground. [4] Accordingly he marched to the westward of Edinburgh, near to the eastward extremity of the Pentland Hills, that by placing his army between Edinburgh and Stirling he might inter-

---

[1] Relation of the Fight at Leith, pp. 220, 221.

[2] Relation of the Fight at Leith, p. 220 ; unless a statement of Bates, no great authority on the subject of royal prowess, be what Hume grounds his assertion on. Bates says (Part ii. p. 102) that "the pursuers had almost entered the Scots camp, had not the king's majesty, who came that morning, been happily there, and causing the cannon to be turned against the fugitives, threatened to fire upon them, if they rallied not, and drew up again in order, under the protection of the guns of the camp, that so the troops, one after another, might be received into the camp ; and that his majesty lay in his clothes all that night upon the ground

without a wink of sleep ; and that the soldiers next morning being sensible from what danger he had delivered the army, and how much he had deserved at their hands, had C. R. marked with a coal or match, some upon their hats and caps, and others on their coats, as a badge of their gratitude." But Hume does not cite Bates ; and Bates's misstatements as to Charles's conduct at the battle of Worcester are so gross that he is not to be relied on in such a matter.

[3] Whitelock, p. 467. Captain Hodgson's Memoirs, pp. 136, 137.

[4] Hodgson, p. 137. Relation of the campaign in Scotland, p. 251, et seq. in the same collection. Balfour, vol. iv. p. 39.

cept supplies, and oblige the Scots to fight him.   Leslie
immediately left his position between Edinburgh and
Leith, and took up one which covered Edinburgh to the
westward, and was protected by the ravines and water-
courses in that quarter.   Here Leslie's knowledge of the
country enabled him so dexterously to shift his positions,
as to preclude a possibility of reaching him, though Cromwell made many attempts to do so.   In one of these
Cromwell in person drew out a forlorn, and went before
them.   When he came near the enemy, one of the latter
fired a carbine ; upon which Cromwell called to him and
said if he had been one of his soldiers, he would have
cashiered him for firing at such a distance.   The man who
fired, having been with Leslie in England, said he knew the
leader of the forlorn to be Cromwell himself, and that he
had seen him in Yorkshire.   On one occasion Cromwell
appeared to be on the point of accomplishing his object ;
but as the troops advanced, a bog was found to interpose
between them and the enemy.[1]

Cromwell having tried in vain to bring the enemy to
an engagement marched towards his ships for a supply of
the wants of his army, which now began to be dispirited.
The weather had been unusually rainy and stormy, the
privations of the army had been great, sickness had broken
out, and the season was advancing.   At Musselburgh
Cromwell shipped about five hundred sick and wounded
soldiers.   It was then resolved at a general council to
march to Dunbar, and fortify that town, which, it was
thought, would, if anything could, provoke the enemy to
fight.   It was also considered that Dunbar being gar-

---

[1] Cromwell to a member of the   pp. 254, 265, 266. Captain Hodgson's
Council of State, August 31, 1650.   Memoirs, pp. 140, 141.
Relation of the Campaign in Scotland,

risoned would furnish them with accommodation for their sick men, and for receiving their recruits of horse and foot from Berwick ; and would moreover be a place for a good magazine, which they exceedingly wanted, being forced to depend upon the uncertainty of weather for landing provisions and often unable to land them, though the existence of the whole army depended upon it.[1]

Accordingly on Saturday the 31st of August, the English army marched from Musselburgh to Haddington. The Scottish army followed them within a mile and a half,[2] and as they drew near Haddington had got so close upon them, that by the time Cromwell had got the van-brigade of his horse, and his foot and artillery into their quarters, the enemy fell upon his rear and put it in some disorder, and had like to have engaged his rear brigade of horse with their whole army, had not a cloud come over the moon, and thereby, it being a misty evening, enabled him to draw off those horse to the rest of the army, which he accomplished with the loss of only three or four men. Towards midnight the Scots attacked the English quarters at the west end of Haddington, but were repulsed.[3]

Although we possess a tolerably full account of this campaign in the dispatches of Cromwell himself, and in the letters and narratives of several of his officers ; yet that account is to a certain extent incomplete and one-sided from one possessing no similar dispatches and narra-

---

[1] Cromwell to the Speaker, Sept. 4, 1650. Dunbar was hardly an exception to Cromwell's remark that the whole coast from Leith to Berwick had not one good harbour, since the harbour of Dunbar, though safe and commodious, is difficult of access.

[2] "We marched towards Dunbar, whither they pursued us close within a mile and a half : " is the expression in one of the letters. King's Pamphlets, small 4to, No. 479, article 1.

[3] Cromwell to the Speaker, Sept. 4, 1650. See also Memoirs of Captain Hodgson, p. 143 ; and Relation of the Campaign in Scotland, pp. 275, 276, in the same collection.

tives from David Leslie and his officers. The account adopted by Hume, who resembles Livy in falsehood though not in picturesque and amusing narrative, is so falsified that the truth from which it has been corrupted can now hardly be discovered even with the authentic English dispatches but without similar Scottish documents. What with national prejudices on the one hand and religious and political spirit on the other, the Scottish general and the Presbyterian ministers had as little chance of receiving justice at the hands of Walker, Clarendon, Whitelock, Burnet, Carte, and Hume, as the son of Hamilcar had of receiving it at the hands of the Roman historians. We are told by Hume, and he cites as his authorities Sir Edward Walker, page 168, and Whitelock, no page, that the clergy murmured extremely not only against their prudent general, but also against the Lord, on account of his delays in giving them deliverance.; and that they plainly told Him that, if He would not save them from the English sectaries, He should no longer be their God.[1] We are also told by the same author, and for this he cites no authority, that an advantage having offered itself on a Sunday, they hindered the general from making use of it,

---

[1] Whitelock indeed has the following passage (p. 465). " That the Scots ministers in their prayers say that, if God will not deliver them from the sectaries, He shall not be their God." But Whitelock only mentions this as a report or rumour. He does not, as he could not, say that he himself heard the Scots minister say so, or even that he had received the story from any one who had heard them. There is nothing on the subject at page 168 of Sir Edward Walker, but at page 180 Walker says " On Sunday they [the Scots] had fair opportunities to have fought him [Cromwell] but the ministers would not give way to it, because forsooth it was the Lord's day." And at page 182 he says that after the battle of Dunbar " there was great lamentation by the ministers, who now told God Almighty, it was little to them to lose their lives and estates but to him it was great loss to suffer his Elect and Chosen to be destroyed :" which if true is a pretty strong effort of fanaticism. But on such matters Walker is by no means an unexceptionable authority.

lest he should involve the nation in the guilt of sabbath-breaking. Now the incident here transformed is thus related in Cromwell's dispatch. "The next morning [Sunday] we drew into an open field, on the south side of Haddington; we not judging it safe for us to draw to the enemy upon his own ground, he being prepossessed thereof, but rather drew back to give him way to come to us, if he had so thought fit; and having waited about the space of four or five hours, to see if he would come to us, and not finding any inclination in the enemy so to do, we resolved to go, according to our first intendment, to Dunbar." [1]

Leslie had taken up his position on the higher ground to the south of the town of Haddington; and true to the principle on which he acted he was not to be induced to leave it because Cromwell wished him to do so; precisely as more than 300 years before Douglas and Randolph had laughed at the message of Edward the Third and said that when they fought it should be at their own pleasure, and not because the King of England chose to ask for a battle. If on that occasion the English army was greatly superior in numbers to the Scotch, and on the present occasion it was greatly inferior in numbers, its superiority in arms, in discipline, in veteran soldiers accustomed to victory, over the hastily raised Scottish levies convinced the prudent commander of the Scots that his only safe line of operations was the same as that recommended by Robert Bruce and so successfully pursued by Douglas and Randolph. And David Leslie, though his evil fortune which made him the victim of other men's folly has cast a cloud over his name, is the man who of all his countrymen came nearest in military skill and prudence to Bruce, Douglas, and

---

[1] Cromwell to the Speaker, Sept. 4, 1650.

Randolph, out of the long and dark catalogue of cruel yet foolish tyrants, whether kings or nobles, who pretended to be leaders in war, and for so many generations had oppressed and dishonoured Scotland.

Leslie's plan of carrying on the war was evidently fast accomplishing its work. The English army marched from Haddington towards Dunbar in such a condition that very few more such marches would have made it an easy prey to Leslie. "We staid," says Captain Hodgson, "until about ten o'clock, had been at prayer in several regiments, sent away our waggons and carriages towards Dunbar, and not long afterwards marched, a poor, shattered, hungry, discouraged army; and the Scots pursued very close that our rear-guard had much ado to secure our poor weak foot, that was not able to march up. We drew near Dunbar towards night, and the Scot ready to fall upon our rear." [1] As the English approached Dunbar, Leslie, who had hitherto hung on their rear,[2] marched to the south of a marsh, now almost entirely drained and highly cultivated, and encamped on Down Hill, a spur of the Lammermoor chain of

[1] Captain Hodgson's Memoirs, pp. 143, 144.

[2] Sir Walter Scott says (Hist. of Scotland contained in "Tales of a Grandfather," vol. i. p. 489. Edinburgh, 1846) that Leslie "moving by a shorter line than Cromwell, who was obliged to keep the coast, took possession with his army of the skirts of Lammermoor," &c. But Leslie moved by the same line as Cromwell. Leslie could not have marched among the Lammermoor hills, as this statement would imply; the ravines and other difficulties of the ground would have precluded it under the circumstances of any army but one entirely composed of infantry and those Highlanders like Montrose's. It is the more remarkable that Sir Walter Scott should have made this statement, as we are indebted to him for the excellent edition, published at Edinburgh in 1806, of the original memoirs, dispatches and letters, specially relating to Cromwell's campaign in Scotland:—nor is this the only debt which English History owes to that illustrious man, his edition of Lord Somers's Tracts (13 vols. 4to.) being the only available one, the old edition, from the want of indexes and chronological arrangement, being nearly useless. It is probable that Sir Walter may have made the statement as to Leslie's march in consequence of writing from memory.

hills, situated about two miles south-west of Dunbar. Consequently Leslie's position was between Cromwell's army and Berwick, Down Hill being about a mile on the right of the road by which Cromwell would have to march to Berwick. Leslie also sent forward a considerable party to seize the pass at Cockburn's Path.[1]

If Cromwell really intended to garrison Dunbar and fortify himself there, as he pretended in his dispatch written after his victory, there was not much need to trouble himself about the pass at Cockburn's Path being seized by Leslie, as he would depend upon receiving his supplies from England by sea. But there are some reasons[2] for concluding that the idea of garrisoning Dunbar was an after-thought put forward in his dispatch to cover the fact of his having been completely outgeneralled by David Leslie, though he had afterwards beaten Leslie's army when moved from the hill by the order of the Estates' Committee. All this seems to let in some light upon what has been considered a dark subject, Cromwell's character, moral and intellectual.

[1] Cromwell to the Speaker, Sept. 4, 1650. Captain Hodgson's Memoirs, p. 144. Relation of the Campaign in Scotland, p. 276, in the same collection.

[2] See Captain Hodgson's Memoirs, pp. 144, 145 ; and see the inconsistencies in Cromwell's Dispatch of Sept. 4, 1650, where, after writing as if he had retreated to Dunbar merely for his own convenience in having a garrison there, he speaks "of their advantages, of our weakness, of our strait." And in his letter to Sir Arthur Haselrig, governor of Newcastle, written on the second of Sept. the day before the battle, though not sent till after the battle with another letter dated September 4th, he says.

"We are upon an engagement very difficult. The enemy hath blocked up our way at the pass at Copper's Path through which we cannot get without almost a miracle. He lieth so upon the hills that we know not how to come that way without great difficulty ; and our lying here daily consumeth our men, who fall sick beyond imagination." The same letter contains further proof, in addition to the many proofs in his other letters, of his great confidence in the sagacity of Sir Henry Vane, before he found it convenient to pray to be delivered from Sir Henry Vane. He says "Let H. Vane know what I write. I would not make it public, lest danger should accrue thereby."

Cromwell's merit as a general was confined to raising
a body of troops, who were well-fed, well-disciplined, and
furnished with arms as superior to those generally used at
the time as the long shield and stabbing sword of the
Roman soldier excelled all other weapons of his time in the
work of human slaughter, and to leading on his men, thus
prepared and armed, with promptitude and daring to their
work.   But he never on any occasion—not even at this
field of Dunbar—exhibited that higher military genius
which dazzles and excites, if it does not elevate, the mind
of the reader in studying the campaigns of Hannibal and
Frederic ; and relieves the attention sick and weary with
looking at a country turned into a huge slaughter-house,
by presenting to it not the mere action of matter upon
matter, but the action of mind producing combinations so
new, so astonishing, and so powerful, that the effect is like
that of some of the great powers of Nature, and an army
is destroyed as if by a stroke of lightning.   If Cromwell
had secured in time and without awakening the suspicions
of the enemy the pass of Cockburn's Path, which has been
minutely described ; if he had taken his measures so
craftily and so skilfully as to draw on the Scots to follow
him to it, and had then destroyed them as Hannibal
destroyed the Romans at Thrasymenus ; or, such a stratagem being perhaps unlikely to succeed with so wary an
adversary as Leslie, had he escaped from the pitfall in
which he seemed to be caught by the Scottish Fabius, by
some such device of a fertile mind as that by which Hannibal escaped the toils of the Roman Fabius, he would
have owed to his own genius what, as it was, he owed to
a blunder committed by those opposed to him.   But this
merit can hardly be even here accorded to Cromwell, for
although he beat the Scots at Dunbar by the same move-

ment by which Frederic beat the French at Rosbach and the Austrians at Leuthen, Cromwell had the advantage made for him, while Frederic made it for himself. Craft, when employed against an enemy in war as Hannibal employed it, is an exercise of mind which may be fairly used by an honourable man, and also requires far greater fertility of genius than the craft which overreaches friends, which was what Cromwell excelled in, and which may be more properly called fraud. There are so many villains who owe their success both in public and private life to the same arts by which Oliver Cromwell overreached his friends and his party and made himself absolute ruler of England, Scotland, and Ireland, that it is a duty which a historian owes to truth, honesty, and morality to note carefully this part of the character of Cromwell as a general, and the light it throws on his character as a man.

Down Hill, on which Leslie had encamped, is distant, as I have said, about two miles from Dunbar. But though this spur or offshoot of the Lammermoor Hills approaches at this point so near to Dunbar, and consequently so near to the sea, the Lammermoor chain of hills does not approach the sea till it has stretched about ten miles to the south-east of Dunbar. Between the hills and the sea extends a fertile tract or strip of land, which is celebrated now for the best farming in the world, and which even then seems to have struck the English by its superior cultivation. The letters from the army state that in those parts where the army marched was the greatest plenty of corn that they ever saw and not one fallow field ; and " now," they add, marking one of the curses of war, " extremely trodden down and wasted, and the soldiers enforced to give the wheat to their horses." [1]

---

[1] Whitelock, p. 470.

Down Hill is so steep on the north and west as to be almost inaccessible. On the east it is less steep. On the south and south-east it slopes with such a gentle declivity that cavalry might charge up it. By the north-east side of the hill runs a small stream in a deep grassy glen, called Broxburn. Brocksburn, the old spelling, marks the origin of the name. Broxburn after pursuing its course for about a mile in this small glen passes through the grounds of Broxmouth-house and then joins the sea. It is impossible to understand the battle of Dunbar without understanding the nature of the ground where that battle was fought, and particularly the relative situation of Broxburn and Down Hill.

The words used in the contemporary narratives of the English officers, " a great clough," [1] " a great dyke," [2] do not by any means convey an adequate idea of the nature of the ground. For the space of about a mile, the distance between Down Hill and the point where it passes the London road and enters the park of Broxmouth-house, Broxburn runs in one of those grassy glens, or troughs, in which streams of greater or less magnitude are frequently seen in Scotland, winding about in them from one bank to the other, and leaving a large space of level ground, green sward or sand and gravel—here it is green sward—now on one side the small valley, now on the other. This small valley or glen is now pretty thickly planted with trees; but in 1650 it appears to have been only grassy,[3] not wooded. It is not only of considerable depth, some forty or fifty feet, and considerably more in width,[4] but

[1] Capt. Hodgson's Memoirs, p. 144.

[2] Relation of Cadwell, a messenger of Cromwell's army—in Carte's Ormonde Letters, vol. i. pp. 381, 382.

[3] Carte's Letters, vol. i. pp. 381, 382.

[4] Cadwell says (*Ibid.*) "about 40 or 50 feet wide, and as deep as broad '—but the width or breadth is considerably greater.

the banks are steep, except in one spot, about half a mile above the point where the burn enters the grounds of Broxmouth-house. At this spot the banks shelve or slope in such a manner as to form a sort of passage for carts. In this pass there stood a shepherd's hut which was occupied by twenty-four foot and six horse of Cromwell's army; but it was taken by Leslie the evening before the battle. It may give an idea of the size of the stream that runs somewhat rapidly down this glen, for there is a considerable fall between the foot of the hill and the sea, to mention that it is of the smallest size of those Scottish streams which contain fine trout of moderate size. At the point where the brook passes the road to Berwick and enters the grounds of Broxmouth-house, the valley or glen disappears, the high banks, that formed it, sloping or shelving down, so that the road crosses the brook without any descent on one side or ascent on the other. It was at this point and somewhat to the south of it that the principal struggle of the battle of Dunbar took place. There is one thing more that requires to be mentioned. Down Hill and the range of hills of which it forms a part do not incline towards the sea here, and consequently do not follow closely, or only for a short distance, the course of Broxburn and its little valley, but slope somewhat away from it, making with it an acute angle. Nevertheless it would appear from the reasons given by Lambert in the council of war, which will be stated presently, for the attack of Leslie's right wing, that Leslie's army was so posted as to be confined between the hill and the glen, and had not room to move freely. And even if it had room to move freely, if the movement was not made before the attack commenced, it was then too late to prevent Cromwell's attack of one flank from paralysing and destroying the whole body.

The English army had reached Dunbar on the night of Sunday the 1st of September. The next morning was very rainy and tempestuous. "Our poor army," says Captain Hodgson, "drew up about swamps and bogs, not far from Dunbar, and could not pitch a tent all that day."[1] If other evidence were wanted, Cromwell's letter to Sir Arthur Haselrig, written on that Monday the 2nd of September, the dreary day briefly described in the foregoing words of Captain Hodgson, shows that he considered himself reduced to extremities.[2] At this moment the madness, not of the Scottish ecclesiastics of the Kirk Commission, as has been so often asserted, but of the oligarchical Committee of Estates, saved him and destroyed his opponents. Baillie's words are these:—"After all tryalls, finding no maladministration on him [David Leslie] to count of, but the removal of the army from the hill the night before the rout, *which yet was a consequence of the Committee's order, contrare to his mind,* to stop the enemies' retreat, and for that end to storm Brocksmouth House as soon as possible."[3]

It is always extremely difficult to obtain a perfectly accurate statement of the numbers on each side. Crom-

[1] Captain Hodgson's Memoirs, p. 144.

[2] Cromwell to Sir Arthur Haselrig. Septr. 2, 1650.

[3] Baillie's Letters and Journals, vol. iii. p. 111. Edinburgh, 1842. Baillie adds: "On these considerations, the State unanimously did with all earnestness intreat him to keep still his charge. Against this order Warristone and, as I suppose, Sir John Cheisly did enter their dissent; I am sure Mr. James Guthrie did his, at which, as a great impertinence, many [were] offended." This Mr. James Guthrie was one of the Presbyterian preachers who showed his total want of good sense, good feeling, good manners, and common decency by "public invectives against David Leslie from the pulpit," for the loss of the battle of Dunbar. Baillie.—*Ibid.*

well's statements in his dispatch of September 4th may be considered as not very wide of the truth. He says that the enemy's numbers were "about six thousand horse, and sixteen thousand foot at least;[1] ours drawn down, as to sound men, to about seven thousand five hundred foot, and three thousand five hundred horse." But the Scots Committee of Estates had taken measures to destroy effectively any advantage they might have derived from their superiority of numbers. For they had now placed their army with its left wing resting on Down Hill and its right advanced to the place where the banks of the Broxburn valley flatten or slope down to level ground, where the road to Berwick then as now crossed the burn, where consequently their right wing lay in such a position that it might be attacked by Cromwell with an overwhelming superiority of force. That the importance of this movement in favour of the English was seen immediately by Lambert we have the authority of Captain Hodgson and of Cromwell himself; that it was seen by Cromwell we have only Cromwell's own word, which, as is too well known, is not always to be implicitly relied on. But, though there are two witnesses, Cromwell himself and Captain Hodgson, that this plan of attack was Lambert's, while that it was also Cromwell's there is no witness at all except Cromwell's own assertion, Cromwell at all events had the merit of seeing the value of it when it was suggested to him, and of putting it in execution with his usual promptitude and resolution. Nor is it to be inferred, assuming the plan to have occurred to the mind of Lambert and not to that of Cromwell, that Lambert was therefore the greater man of the two, even though it may prove him to have been a better general than Cromwell. For subsequent events abundantly proved

[1] Sir Edward Walker says they were "about 16,000 foot and 7000 horse." P. 181.

that if Lambert possessed military, he possessed no political talent : and to be a great man, a man must possess both, must be able both to lead in political affairs, and to command armies.[1] While Lambert appeared to be totally without the political element, Cromwell had enough of both elements to be pronounced a great man, though his greatness, like that of many others, was stained by crime.

On Monday the 2nd of September Cromwell wrote a note to Sir Arthur Haselrig, which shows that he considered himself reduced to extremities. The enemy had blocked up the pass at Cockburn's Path, and lay upon the hills in such a position that he could not lead his army through "without almost a miracle." Besides this, his men lying where they were " fell sick beyond imagination ; " and the numbers of the effective troops were daily diminished, a destructive flux or dysentery, a species of cholera, having attacked his army, apparently of somewhat the same kind as that which afterwards wrought such fearful destruction among the poor Scots prisoners. Under all these depressing circumstances however the English general showed not the slightest dejection of mind, and was prepared to meet any fate, whatever it might be, with an undaunted heart, and a tranquil and cheerful countenance, which kept alive in others the hope he may himself have ceased to feel. "Whatever becomes of us," he said in that note to Sir Arthur Haselrig the governor of Newcastle, "it will be well for you to get what forces you can together ; and the south to help what they can."

Thus that dreary day, Monday the 2nd of September, wore on. The 2nd of September old style is the 13th of September new style, and the sun would set at about a

---

[1] Οἵτι ις ἀμφότερα ἂν δύνωνται, καὶ   ad Philipp. πολιτιυεσ.αι καὶ στ,ατηγεῖν.   Isocrates

quarter past six. Towards evening the Scots were observed to draw down to their right wing about two-thirds of their left wing of horse, "shogging also their foot and train much to the right," that is, farther down the hill, and along the edge of the glen of Broxburn, "causing their right wing of horse to edge down towards the sea."[1] One man at least in the English army had seen this movement of the Scots with an observant eye. The sun went down behind the Lammermoor Hills amid dark and drifting clouds, and the night set in, like the day, raining and tempestuous. The rain was not however incessant; for some of the letters mention its being moonlight, at least towards morning.

Cromwell in his dispatch to the Speaker written on the 4th September says that Lambert and himself going to the Earl of Roxburgh's house [Broxmouth-house before mentioned], and observing the position which the Scots had now taken, he told Lambert that he thought it gave them an opportunity and advantage to attempt upon the enemy. To which Lambert immediately replied, that he had thought to have said the same thing. "So that it pleased the Lord," adds Cromwell, "to set this apprehension upon both our hearts at the same time. We called for Colonel Monk, and showed him the thing: and coming to our quarters at night, and demonstrating our apprehensions to some of the colonels, they also cheerfully concurred." Sir Walter Scott's statement, that Cromwell slept at the Duke of Roxburgh's house called Broxmouth and that his army was stationed in the park there, is incorrect. Broxmouth House and park are on the east side of the road to Berwick. Cromwell's army was stationed on the west side

---

[1] Cromwell to the Speaker, Sept. 4, 1650.

of that road and on the north side of Broxburn.[1]   His
train of artillery was first placed in the churchyard at
Dunbar, then brought down to a little farm-house—a little
poor Scotch farm-house, say the old pamphlets[2]—in the
middle of the field where his army was quartered.   This
farm-house was probably Cromwell's quarters where the
Council of War was held.   In addition to the above statement of Cromwell himself we have also other evidence
respecting the first suggestion of the plan of attack, which
renders the exact accuracy of Cromwell's statement at
least a little doubtful.

About nine o'clock that night a council of war was held,
and many of the colonels were for shipping the foot and
forcing a passage with the horse.   But Lambert was
against them all on that point, and gave his reasons,[3] the
principal of which were these : " First, we had great experience of the goodness of God to us, while we kept close
together ; and if we parted we lost all: Secondly, there
was no time to ship the foot, for the day would be upon
us, and we should lose all our carriages : Thirdly, we had
great advantage of them in their drawing up ; *if we beat
their right wing, we hazarded their whole army, for they
would be all in confusion, in regard they had not great
ground to traverse their regiments betwixt the mountain*

---

[1] Captain Hodgson's Memoirs, p.
144.

[2] King's Pamphlets, small 4to, No.
478, article 10.

[3] Captain Hodgson's words imply
that he was present at this Council of
war—" but honest Lambert was
against them all in that matter, he
being active the day before in observing
the disadvantage the Scots might meet
with in the position they were drawn

up in, and gave us reasons, and great
encouragement to fight."—*Memoirs,*
pp. 144, 145. The whole of Hodgson's
statement goes to show that the whole
idea of the plan of attack belonged
solely to Lambert ; and his words
" Lambert was against them all in
that matter" also seem to imply that
Cromwell himself was in favour of the
proposition for shipping the foot and
forcing a passage with the horse.

and the clough : Fourthly, they had left intervals in their bodies, upon the brink of the hill, that our horse might march a troop at once, and so the foot ; and the enemy could not wheel about, nor oppose them, but must put themselves into disorder : Lastly, our guns might have fair play at their left wing, while we were fighting their right."[1]   These reasons altered the opinion of the Council ; and one stepped up and desired that Colonel Lambert might have the conduct of the army that morning, which was granted by the general freely ;[2] and it was resolved that the attack should be begun at daybreak by six regiments of horse and three regiments and a half of foot.[3] At that time in the army of the Parliament of England a regiment of horse usually consisted of ten troops of eighty each, that is, of 800, and a regiment of foot of ten companies of 100 men each, that is, of 1000 men, but not unfrequently of twelve companies of 100 men each, that is, of 1200 men.[4]   That night the English army advanced as

[1] Captain Hodgson's Memoirs, p. 145.

[2] *Ibid.*

[3] Cromwell to the Speaker, Septr. 4, 1650.

[4] This statement is made on the authority of numerous—I might say innumerable—minutes of the MS. Order Book of the Council of State in the State Paper Office.   A regiment of horse did, however, sometimes consist of six troops of horse, and a certain proportion of dragoons.   I have stated in a former chapter the difference between horse and dragoons. Thus under date 17 November, 1649, we find this minute : "That Major Henry Cromwell shall have a commission for a regiment of horse to go over into Ireland which is to consist of six troops." Order Book of the Council of State, MS. State Paper Office.   And under date 26 Nov.

1649, two troops of dragoons are appointed to go into Ireland to complete Col. Cromwell's regiment. *Ibid.* 26 Nov. 1649. But the strength of the regiments was liable to variations according to circumstances.   Thus : " That a letter be written to the Lord General to let him know that the Council of State hath thought fit that a reducement be made of the horse of the army, and that every troop be reduced from the number of 80 to 60, except only the troops of such regiments out of which the troops are to be sent into Ireland." *Order Book of the Council of State,* 14 Nov. 1649. MS. State Paper Office. While the Resolution of the House of Commons of 11 January, 1644, sets forth that the army shall consist of 6000 horse to be divided into 10 regiments ; and of a thousand dragoons to be divided into 10 *companies;* the

close as they could to the Broxburn ravine, and placed their field pieces in position in every regiment.[1]

About half a mile above the point where the Berwick road passes Broxburn, there was, as I have said, upon the brink of the ravine a small house or shepherd's hut, and by it a shelving path where the ravine might be passed with greater facility than anywhere else, except where, as before mentioned, the Berwick road passes it. . On the morning of that day Fleetwood and Pride had stationed twenty-four foot and six horse in the hut to secure this pass. In the evening Leslie's horse drove them out, killing some and taking three prisoners, but they did not keep the pass. Leslie asked one of the prisoners if the enemy did intend to fight. He replied, "What do you think we come here for? We come for nothing else." "Soldier," said Leslie, "how will you fight when you have shipped half your men, and all your great guns?" The soldier replied, "Sir, if you please to draw down your men, you will find both men and great guns too."[2] All this might have led Leslie and his masters the Committee of Estates to be cautious in relying too much on the notion that

Order Book of the Council of State sometimes mentions dragoons as divided into *troops*. It also would seem that the same officer who is described in one place as colonel of a regiment of horse had a charge of raising and commanding dragoons. Thus on the 20th of Oct. 1649, Col. Okey is ordered to forbear to raise any more dragoons of the last 500, more than are already raised. On the 17th of Nov. 1649, it is ordered that the regiment of horse to be raised for Major Henry Cromwell shall consist of 6 troops, whereof three out of Col. Hacker's regiment, two out of Col. Okey's, and one out of Col. Harrison's. And on the 26th of Nov.

the two troops of dragoons above mentioned as appointed to go into Ireland to complete Col. Henry Cromwell's regiment are described as "of Col. Okey's regiment."—*Order Book of the Council of State.* MS. State Paper Office.

[1] King's Pamphlets, small 4to. No. 478, article 10.

[2] Carte's Letters, vol. i. p. 382. King's Pamphlets, small 4to, No. 478, art. 10. Mr. Brodie (Hist. vol. iv. p. 290 n.) cites as in corroboration of this a manuscript in the Advocate's Library. Balfour's Shorte Memories, MS. Adv. Lib.

Cromwell's situation was so desperate that he had already embarked his ordnance and part of his foot, and that he and the residue of his army would then be an easy prey. A letter from John Rushworth to the Speaker of the English Parliament, dated Dunbar, Sept. 3, 1650, explains in what way the mistake of the Scottish commander had arisen. "They were informed, as some of their prisoners confess, we had shipped our train of artillery, which was a mistake of them, for it was the 600 soldiers sick of the flux that I had shipped that morning." [1]

In fact the Scottish commanders seem to have come to the conclusion that their work was done, that, instead of the Lord's having delivered them into the hands of Cromwell, as Cromwell according to the story, as true as the story about the Duke of Wellington at Waterloo,[2] is said to have exclaimed, the Lord had delivered Cromwell and his army into their hands ; and that they had nothing more to do but sleep and take their rest that night and rise up in the morning to divide the spoil. Accordingly, somewhat past midnight the Committee of Estates proposed that they might take some rest ; and Major-General Holborne, it is said, gave order to put out all matches but two in a company. And thus, according to the same authority, in great security, the rain continuing, they made themselves shelter of the corn new reaped, and went to sleep. The horse went to forage, and many unsaddled their horses.[3] Some regiments however both of horse and foot, on the

---

[1] Old Parl. Hist. vol. xix. p. 341.

[2] The story about Cromwell's exclamation "the Lord hath delivered them into our hands" appears to be a counterpart to the melodramatic absurdity, so improbable and so uncharacteristic of the man, about the Duke of Wellington's saying at Waterloo "Up guards and at 'em." I have heard it stated on the authority of an officer who was near the Duke of Wellington at the moment, that he closed with a quick motion of his hand the telescope through which he had been watching the enemy's movements and said— "Let the line move on."

[3] Sir Edward Walker, p. 180.

extremity of the right wing of the Scots, were not unprepared when the attack began about five in the morning.
In the English army that night men were far less inclined
to sleep than to watch and pray.

At four o'clock on Tuesday morning the regiments of
horse and foot that were to begin the attack were drawn
down towards the point where the Berwick road crosses the
burn near Broxmouth-house.[1] As Lambert's regiment of foot,
to which Captain Hodgson belonged, was marching at the
head of the horse, " a cornet was at prayer in the night," [1]
and Hodgson, appointing one of his officers to take his
place, rode to hear him. " And " says the Ironside captain, " he was exceedingly carried on in the duty. I met
with so much of God in it, as I was satisfied deliverance
was at hand : and coming to my command did encourage
the poor weak soldiers, which did much affect them, which
when it came to it, indeed a little one was as David, and
the house of David as the angel of the Lord." [2]

It was five o'clock. The rain had ceased. The moon
was shining, and the dawn was beginning to appear over
the sea. Cromwell was growing impatient, for Lambert
had not come, being still busy ordering the guns along the
edge of the ravine, and the Scots by their sounding a
trumpet seemed preparing to begin the attack. At last
Lambert came not many minutes after five, and immediately
ordered Monk with his brigade of three and a half regiments of foot, whereof Cromwell's regiment of foot was
one, and his own regiment of foot, in which was Hodgson,
was another, to march about, that is, to make a detour
about Broxmouth-house towards the sea, and so to fall

---

[1] King's Pamphlets, small 4to, No.
478, art. 10. Capt. Hodgson's Memoirs, p. 146.

[2] Capt. Hodgson's Memoirs, p. 146.
Zechariah, chap. xii. v. 8.

upon the enemy's flank. In the meantime, while the brigade of foot was marching round between the house and the sea to attack the same right wing of the enemy further to the left, Lambert, Fleetwood, Whalley, and Twisleton with the six regiments of horse began the attack by charging the enemy at the pass where the Berwick road runs between Broxmouth-house and the hill.[1] The word of the Scots was "The Covenant;" that of the English, "The Lord of Hosts."[2]

We have no information in any of the narratives where David Leslie was during the battle. But as even Clarendon, while he says that David Leslie was in no degree capable of commanding in chief, admits that he was an excellent officer of horse, we may suppose that he was active in directing and probably in leading that desperate charge of the Scottish cavalry, "with lanciers in the front rank," which was made with such fury, that it drove the Ironsides back above a pistol-shot, across the hollow where the stream ran. Lanciers here must not be confounded with our modern lancers. They were the most completely armed of the cavalry of that time, wearing an iron head-piece or pot, back and breast-plates pistol and culiver proof, a buff coat between their clothes and their armour, and having a strong cut-and-thrust sword, a lance eighteen feet long,

[1] Cromwell says (Dispatch to the Speaker, Sept. 4,) that the attack though intended to be by break of day did not begin till six o'clock. But the other accounts (Carte's Letters, vol. i. p. 383, and King's Pamphlets, small 4to, No. 478, articles 7, 9, 10) and the fact that the sun (which would rise that morning about half-past 5) rose during the battle, show that it must have begun about 5 or a little after. It is remarkable that the Duke of Wellington in his dispatch to Earl Bathurst, dated Waterloo, 19th June, 1815, says, "the enemy at about 10 o'clock commenced a furious attack upon our post at Hougoumont." Gurwood's Selections from the Duke of Wellington's Dispatches, p. 858, No. 951—and in a letter to ———, Esq., dated Paris, 17 August, 1815, says, "the battle began, I believe, at 11." *Ibid.* p. 892, No. 990.

[2] Cromwell to the Speaker, Sept. 4, 1650.

and one or two pistols.   Sir Walter Scott once said to
Mr. Lockhart when near the field of Philiphaugh that he
thought it probable David Leslie had with him some of the
old soldiers of Gustavus Adolphus.   And it seems not
improbable, though, as has been shown, there were in the
Scots army no complete regiments which had served
abroad, that there were among these Scots "lanciers"
some of Gustavus's veterans.   But it was one feature of
Cromwell's troops that they could always be rallied by
officers who thoroughly understood their duty, and were
animated at once by superior intelligence and invincible
resolution   At that moment too Monk with his brigade of
foot having accomplished his detour made a furious attack
upon the extreme right[1] of the Scottish right wing ; and the
English cavalry, taking advantage of the confusion which
this created, rallied and drove the Scots lanciers back
again across the burn.   So obstinate was the resistance
made by this right wing of the Scots though exposed to
the attack of superior numbers composed of Cromwell's
best regiments, that Monk's brigade of foot was at first
overpowered and driven back. Then came that terrible charge
of Cromwell's pikemen, which made the Scots foot give
ground for three-quarters of a mile together ; the English
horse at the same time renewing their charge and driving
back the enemy.   One of the Scots regiments of foot would
not yield, though at push of pike and butt-end of the musket,
until a troop of the English horse charged from one end to
another of them.   This body of Scots foot was Lawers'
regiment of Highlanders, and their commanding officer, a
lieutenant-colonel, having been slain by a serjeant of Crom-

---

[1] It will be observed that in the
next page where Cromwell commands
his men to incline to the left, the left
of the English would be the right of
the Scots.

well's own regiment of foot ("the colonel was absent of the name of the Campbells"[1]), they stood to the push of the pike, and were all cut to pieces.

Cromwell himself came to the rear of the regiment to which Captain Hodgson belonged, and commanded them to incline to the left; "that was, to take more ground, to be clear of all bodies. And we did so," adds Hodgson, "and horse and foot were engaged all over the field; and the Scots all in confusion: and the sun appearing upon the sea, I heard Nol say, 'Now let God arise, and his enemies

---

[1] Dr. Gumble's "Life of General Monk," p. 38. It may, however, be inferred from a statement in Cromwelliana, p. 91, (Sev. Pas. in Parl., Sept. 5 to 12, "The Lord Chancellor's purse and seals taken with a book in them of their new acts signed by their declared king,") that the Colonel of Lawers' Highlanders was on some part of the field; though his "legal apprehension" kept him out of harm's way. At Dunbar the grandees fled. At Flodden, when they really were a military aristocracy, they fought and fell, for there the Scots left dead on the field their king and most of their nobility; namely, two bishops, two mitred abbots, twelve earls, thirteen lords, five eldest sons of peers, and gentlemen beyond calculation — 200 of the name of Douglas alone. And these were all slain, be it observed, not in flight (see the remarks on this subject at the end of this chapter), but in fight, many of them in the devoted but unbroken circle that fought around their king. This division of the Scots at Flodden consisted chiefly of the nobles and gentry, whose armour was so good, that the arrows made but little impression upon them. They were all on foot, and forming themselves into a circle with their spears extended on every side, they could neither be broken nor forced to retire, though the carnage among them was very great. A list of men of note killed at Dunbar is given in Balfour (vol. iv., pp. 27, 28). It contains the names of a lord of the Session, who was also one of the Committee of Estates, of six colonels, four lieutenant-colonels, a major and two ritt-masters. Not far from the door of Broxmouth House is a rough tombstone with the name of Sir William Douglas of Kirkness, one of the colonels who fell, rudely inscribed upon it. He was the only individual out of all who fell in that battle who has been honoured with such a memorial: a circumstance which may, perhaps, have given rise to the opinion announced to me by an old woman of the neighbourhood that this battle of Down Hill (as it is there called, probably to distinguish it from another battle of Dunbar fought in the year 1296) was fought between this Sir William Douglas and Oliver Crommie; which is taking as great a liberty with the great leader of the Ironsides' name as a modern French romance writer in one of his romances, has taken with his person and character.

shall be scattered ;'[1] and he following as we slowly marched, I heard him say 'I protest they run !' and then was the Scots army all in disorder and running, both right wing, and left, and main battle."[2]   The fight, says Cromwell in one letter, lasted above an hour.[3]   In another letter he says, "after a hot dispute for about an hour we routed their whole army."[4]   In answer to the ungenerous aspersions of Clarendon and others, it is sufficient to say that all the English engaged in the battle who have given any account of it state distinctly that that part of the Scots army who fought at all fought well.   The words are "a hot and stiff dispute ; the enemy made a gallant resistance and there was a very hot dispute at sword's point between our horse and theirs ;" and, as regarded the foot, "at push of pike and butt-end of musket."[5]   In

---

[1] Psalm lxviii. v. 1.

[2] Capt. Hodgson's Memoirs, pp. 147, 148.

[3] Cromwell to Richard Mayor, Esq. Sept. 4, 1650.

[4] Cromwell to Ireton. Sept. 4, 1650. The other accounts say an hour or above an hour.   "After above an hour's dispute." King's Pamphlets, small 4to, No. 478, art. 9 ;—"the dispute lasted above an hour. *Ibid*. art. 7. "After one hour's contest." King's Pamphlets, small 4to, No. 479, article 1 ;—"The dispute lasted an hour and was very hot." Cadwell, the army messenger in Carte's Letters, vol. i. p. 383.

[5] See Cromwell's Dispatches and Letters, Hodgson's Memoirs, and all the other accounts written to tell what really happened, and not what writers like Clarendon and Algernon Sidney might think fit to assert.   John Rushworth, who was there as Cromwell's secretary, says, though he is no very great authority in such a matter, "I

never beheld a more terrible charge of foot than was given by our army." Letter to the Speaker, in Old Parl. Hist. vol. xix. p. 341. "The battle was very fierce for the time, one part of their battalia stood very stiffly to it, but the rest was presently routed." *Ibid*. To those who do not know what an advocate who passes the legitimate bounds of his duty is capable of, it may seem incredible that a man in Lord Clarendon's position, for some regard for truth might be looked for from a man filling the office of Lord High Chancellor of England, the highest judicial post in the kingdom, should have made the following statement in a historical writing :—"Cromwell knew them too well to fear them on any ground, where there were no trenches or fortifications to keep him from them. Their horse did not sustain one charge ; but fled and were pursued with great execution."—*Clar. Hist*. vol. vi. p. 456, Oxford, 1826.

consequence of none of the commanders on either side having had the sagacity to adopt Gustavus Adolphus's invention of the cartridge, more work was done by the butt-end than by the muzzle of the musket through these civil wars.   And it is to be borne in mind that at that time the foot regiments being composed partly of musketeers partly of pikemen, the work had for the reason mentioned to be done chiefly by the pike and the butt-end of the musket. And the pikemen forming rather more than a third part of each regiment of foot—they were, in some cases at least, in the proportion of 400 pikemen to 600 musketeers [1]—and being generally the strongest and tallest men, were more effective than the musketeers.

Captain Hodgson expresses with accurate brevity the effect of Lambert's flank movement, which is indeed the effect of every flank · movement successfully executed. "They had routed one another, after we had done their work on their right wing." The English then moving up to the top of the hill kept the straggling parties of the enemy, that had been engaged, from rallying. So the foot threw down their arms and fled, most of them towards Dunbar, where they were surrounded and taken.

[1] Order Book of the Council of State—13 March, 164⅞. MS. State Paper Office. According to the statement of Montecuculi, the proportion on the Continent, about 1665, of pikemen to musketeers was one-third—"Aujourd'hui les regimens d'infanterie sont composés, les deux tiers de Mousquetaires et un tiers de Piquiers." Memoires de Montecuculi, I. 2. 16. And the statement in the Gentleman's Dictionary, part ii., quoted in Grose's Military Antiquities, vol. i. p. 133, is that "the pikemen used to be the third part of the company." The tallest and strongest men were generally selected for the pike ; and in France their pay was somewhat greater than that of the musketeers.   Grose, vol. i. pp. 132, 133.   The use of the pike was abolished in France by a royal ordinance in 1703.   A book on the exercise of the Foot published by royal command in 1690, contains the exercise of the pike, and the Gentleman's Dictionary published in 1705 describes the pike as a weapon formerly in use but then changed for the musket ; so that the disuse of the pike must have taken place in England some time between 1690 and 1705.   Grose, vol. i. p. 133.

Others were pursued with great slaughter as far and even farther than Haddington. About nine thousand, including many officers, were taken prisoners ; upwards of three thousand were slain.[1] Consequently either Cromwell's estimate of the numbers of the Scots army (6000 horse and 16,000 foot at least) must be greatly exaggerated, or nearly ten thousand of the Scots must have escaped from the field of battle. As Cromwell reckons the arms left behind at fifteen thousand, it is not improbable that the Scots army was not so numerous as Cromwell represented it to be, nor his own so small. He marched into Scotland with 16,354, he probably received some reinforcements while there, and he states himself his sick and wounded shipped at 500 ; while Rushworth, his secretary, writes on the 3rd Sept., 1650, "Fourteen hundred sick men have I in all sent to Berwick and Newcastle, and many hundreds are wonderful sick in the army."[2] If we add the 500 before mentioned to these 1400, instead of assuming them to be included in the 1400, we shall have the 16,350 diminished by 1900, and if we add 500 or 600 more for the sick still remaining in the army, we shall still have very nearly 14,000 men. However the " many hundreds wonderful sick in the army " mentioned by Rushworth might have amounted to far more than 500 or 600, and Cromwell in his letter to Ireton repeats his statement of 11,000, namely 3500 horse and 7500 foot, and says a

[1] Cromwell in his dispatch to the Speaker written on the day after the battle, namely, Sept. 4, 1650, says, " We believe that upon the place and near about it were about 3000 slain ; prisoners taken of their officers you have the inclosed list ; of private soldiers near 10,000." But Sir Arthur Haselrig, then governor of Newcastle, in his letter to the Committee of the Council of State, dated Oct. 31, 1650, says, "After the battle at Dunbar the Lord-General writ to me that there was about 9000 prisoners."

[2] John Rushworth to the Speaker, Dunbar, Sept. 3, 1650, in Old Parl. Hist. vol. xix. p. 341.

heavy flux had brought the army very low—from fourteen to eleven thousand.[1]

Hodgson relates what was a characteristic conclusion of the morning's work, that Cromwell made a halt and sang the hundred and seventeenth psalm.[2] He was after that busily employed in securing prisoners and baggage. The whole of the baggage and train of the Scots army containing a good store of match, powder, and ball ; and all their artillery, great and small, being about thirty guns, some of them of leather, were taken, together with near two hundred colours, which Cromwell sent to the Parliament to be hung up in Westminster Hall, where they long remained.[3]

It is certainly not easy to understand why Leslie could not bring up his left wing, and part of his centre to the support of his overmatched right wing, instead of leaving his centre and left wing to rout one another. No doubt the play of Cromwell's guns on the left wing was intended to divert their attention, but an old soldier like David Leslie must have known well the small amount of damage at that time done by artillery, which probably would not kill altogether twenty of his men, and must have been quite powerless to prevent his moving his left wing. Nor does the remark ascribed by Hodgson to Lambert that the Scots had not great ground to traverse their regiments between the mountain and the clough or ravine explain the difficulty so well as it appears to do before examining the ground. For, as I have said, Down Hill slopes somewhat away from the ravine ; and the greater part of Leslie's

[1] Cromwell to Ireton, Dunbar, 4th Sept. 1650.

[2] Captain Hodgson's Memoirs, pp. 148, 149.

[3] Cromwell to the Speaker, Sept. 4, 1650. Another letter not from Cromwell of the same date, (in the same collection, p. 275 et seq.), says—"We took all their train, being 32 pieces of ordnance, small, great, and leather guns, and all their foot colours, besides horse."

army was posted not between a ravine and a mountain but on ground which, though bounded on the west by Down Hill, on the north by the ravine, and on the east by the high road and beyond that by the park wall of Brox-mouth House, was on the south-east, the south, and south-west perfectly open and level except a gentle slope on the south-west—a slope so gentle, as before remarked, that a horse might gallop up it. Consequently there seemed to be nothing at least in the nature of the ground and the position to hinder David Leslie from bringing the whole of his left wing to the support of his right wing, instead of leaving it and his centre as he did to be routed by having the right wing driven in upon them. The inference there-fore must be, that at Dunbar David Leslie lost his head or self-possession ; an inference with which Clarendon's account of David Leslie quite agrees. Clarendon says, " The king did not believe him false ; and did always think him an excellent officer of horse, to distribute and execute orders, but in no degree capable of commanding in chief. And without doubt he was so amazed in that fatal day [Wor-cester], that he performed not the office of a general, or of any competent officer." [1]

This battle of Dunbar was the only battle in these wars (except those battles fought by Montrose), in which any considerable degree of generalship was shown. Most of the battles of this great civil war were steady pounding matches where the hostile armies drew up in parallel lines and fought till one was beaten. In order to understand the precise nature of the operation which distinguished the battle of Dunbar from the other battles of these wars it is only necessary to keep in mind the principle of what is called a flank movement—that the general who brings a

---

[1] Clar. Hist. vol. vi. pp. 515, 516. Oxford, 1826.

superior force to bear upon a particular part of the army opposed to him, and defeats that part, will probably throw into confusion and defeat the whole. At Dunbar Lambert attacked the head of the Scottish column and drove it in on its rear, pretty much as Frederic did with the French column at Rosbach, and with the flank of the Austrian line at Leuthen. It will also serve to elucidate the matter to state that the manœuvre which Frederic executed at Rosbach and still more signally at Leuthen consisted, although his own army did not amount to half that of the enemy in numbers, and herein appeared the great force of his genius, in bringing a superiority of numbers to bear upon a particular part, and by defeating that part and driving it in upon the rest, throwing into confusion and defeating the whole. This was the principle on which Frederic always acted. Thus Mitchell the English ambassador, who speaks from his own personal observation and the king's own words, says of the battle of Kolin, which Frederic lost by the failure of his intended plan, "his intention was to have flanked their right,"[1] and of the battle of Zorndorff, "the king's intention was to attack with his left the right of the enemy in flank, and to refuse his right."[2] It will be seen that the consequence

---

[1] Memoirs and Papers of Sir Andrew Mitchell, K.B. Envoy Extraordinary and Minister Plenipotentiary from the Court of Great Britain to the Court of Berlin from 1756 to 1771. London, 1850, vol. i. pp. 355, 356. "The king was then pleased to describe to me very particularly the last unhappy battle (Kolin). . . . His intention, he says, was to have flanked their right, which would have obliged them to make an alteration in their position, of which he might have profited. . . . He said his intention was

to have engaged only his left pour tourner l'ennemi, but the ardour of his troops in attacking the village had been the cause of his misfortune."

[2] Ibid. vol. i. pp. 428, 429. "As the King of Prussia thought he had gained their flank, he ordered the attack to be made by his left wing, whilst he refused his right;" and ibid. vol. ii. p. 43, "The attack began at 9 o'clock before the village of Zorndorff, which the Russians had set on fire; to the right of which there was a wood, which I believe had not been thoroughly

of this movement is to bring a superiority of force to bear
upon the enemy at a particular point—a principle, which
though anyone can see in the abstract, the application of
which in an actual campaign or battle demands a large

examined. The king's intention was
to attack with the left the right of the
enemy in flank, and to refuse the right ;
but I have since heard that we missed
of the flank, as the attack began the
moment the troops were ranged : no
care had been taken to reconnoitre the
position of the enemy." But the best
explanation of the matter is in Frederic's own account of the battle of Leuthen, where he explains the principle
of refusing one wing and attacking
with the other in flank, which he
adopted in all his battles, and of the
pains he took at Leuthen to prevent
the failure of this principle which had
happened at the battles of Prague and
Kolin. " Le projet que le Roi se pre-
parait d'executer, était de porter toute
son armée sur le flanc gauche des impé-
riaux, de faire les plus grands efforts
avec sa droite, et de refuser sa gauche
avec tant de prévoyance qu'il n'eut
point à craindre des fautes semblables
à celles qu'on avait faites à la bataille
de Prague et qui avaient causé la perte
de celle de Kolin. . . . La première
ligne reçut ordre d'avancer en échelons,
les bataillons à 50 pas de distance en
arrière les uns des autres, de sorte que
la ligne était en mouvement l'extremité de la droite se trouvait de mille
pas plus avancée que l'extremité de la
gauche, et cette disposition la mit dans
l'impossibilité de s'engager sans ordre."
Hist. de la Guerre de Sept Ans, tom. i.
p. 232 et seq. It has been sometimes
supposed that this principle was first
acted upon by Frederic and Napoleon.
The first however known to history
who applied it was Epaminondas, who
defeated by it the Spartan armies at

Leuctra and Mantinea, and thereby
raised Thebes while he lived to the
supremacy of Greece. Epaminondas
is said to have explained the principle
to the Thebans by showing them that
when the head of an adder was
destroyed, the rest of the body was
useless. "Ὁρᾶτε, ἔφη, ὅτι τὸ λοιπὸν
σῶμα ἄχρηστον, τῆς κεφαλῆς οἰχομένης."
Polyæn. ii. 3. "Frontinus," says Mr.
Grote, "mentions (Strategem. ii. 3.
2) a battle gained by Philip against the
Illyrians ; wherein observing that their
chosen troops were in the centre, he
placed his own greatest strength in his
right wing, attacked and beat their
left wing ; then came upon their
centre in flank and defeated their whole
army. The tactics employed are the
same as those of Epaminondas at
Leuctra and Mantinea ; strengthening
one wing peculiarly for the offensive ;
and keeping back the rest of the army
upon the defensive." Hist. of Greece,
vol. xi. p. 304, note. Philip resided
at Thebes from the age of 15 to that
of 18, where "the lesson,' says Mr.
Grote, " most indelible of all which
he imbibed, was derived from the
society and from the living example of
men like Epaminondas and Pelopidas."
Ibid. p. 295. It ought to be added
that, in the story told by Polyænus
above referred to, Epaminondas added
"if we break to pieces the Spartan
part" (represented by the head of the
adder) "the rest of the body consisting of their allies will be useless."
The Spartan commanders always drew
up their line of battle so that the
Spartans formed one wing of themselves. See Thucyd. v. 71.

amount not merely of military science but of military genius.

The balance of evidence goes to show that Leslie's opinion was against moving his army from Down Hill, and that he moved it in consequence of the Committee's order. But it is necessary, in justice to all parties, to bear in mind that the order was to storm Broxmouth House (where Cromwell's left was, his right extending up the north bank of Broxburn till it was opposite Leslie's left) as soon as possible. Now Leslie was probably right in his plan of keeping to his fastnesses and not trusting his raw levies—his greenhorns the king is said by one of Cromwell's officers to have called them,[1]—though superior in numbers, in an engagement on equal ground with Cromwell's veteran troops. But as Leslie obeyed the committee's order to leave his chosen position, he should also have obeyed the order to storm Broxmouth House, that is to attack Cromwell's left flank as soon as possible, which would have been immediately on leaving Down Hill. It is possible enough that with the decided superiority in quality of Cromwell's troops, Leslie might have failed even though he had made the attack instead of allowing Cromwell to make it, but he would have had a chance of success which he had not, as it was, for the following reasons, for which I am indebted to the kindness of a military friend, and which I therefore print as a quotation.

" The only explanation apparently that can be given for David Leslie's allowing himself to be outflanked is one common to every battle lost and won by the same process ; namely, that, to use Jomini's expression, Cromwell had the advantage of the ' initiative : ' which means that if a

---

[1] Relation of the Fight at Leith, p. 214.

bold stroke is made at any part of the enemy's line, the chances are that the aggressive movement is well on the road towards completion before the enemy can sufficiently detect the object to put into effect his counteracting defensive movement. If it were not for this, the movement of outflanking could never be effected at all, for if the attacked party is supposed to know of the intended movement from the very beginning,[1] and to execute a flank movement at the right time and in the right direction, the result will be that it will find itself outflanking the assailants. In this way the battle of Dunbar wants no supposition of Leslie's army being cramped for room to make it intelligible; any more than the battle of Leuthen wants such a supposition.

"With regard to the effect of the fire of the English artillery in preventing Leslie from moving, I do not think that any fire of artillery will stop a movement, unless in the case of a powerful artillery firing grape at close quarters. The Russian artillery fire at Inkerman, though a perfect hell upon earth when you had to stand it for hour after hour, would not for a moment have checked a movement with fresh troops. And as to the idea of Cromwell's pop-guns, which I will engage did not kill twenty men

---

[1] The battle of Pharsalia affords an example of a flank movement on the part of Pompey so executed as to prove advantageous to his opponent and not to himself. Pompey had placed nearly all his cavalry in his left wing with the design of outflanking and over-powering Cæsar's right wing, where was the tenth legion in which Cæsar was accustomed to take his station in action. Cæsar, perceiving this, drew six cohorts from the reserve and placed them in the rear of the tenth legion with orders not to let the enemy see them; but, as soon as the cavalry advanced, to run through the intervals of the tenth legion and not to throw their javelins but to push upwards and wound the eyes and faces of the horsemen, who prided themselves on their good looks and fine clothes. The Roman fine gentlemen of that time went down before Cæsar's plebeian veterans as those of a date some 1700 years later did before Cromwell's. — See Cæsar, Bell. Civ. iii. 89, 93, and Plutarch, Life of Pompeius, c. 69.

during the action, hindering any one from moving, I do not think it is tenable at all.

" It often strikes one, reading the history of battles won by the flank movement, that the losing party has made surprisingly little attempt to retrieve the day by bringing up his centre and unengaged flank to the point attacked. This apparent sluggishness is, I think, susceptible of two explanations.   One lies in the length of time required for the transmission of orders and the movement of troops. The other lies in the constitution of the human mind ; in the mental paralysis which seizes a man of ordinary stamp in any great crisis, and which is apt to render a commander incapable of using the resources still at his disposal, just in proportion as the need to use them becomes urgent. This mental infirmity, I am inclined to think, has more to do with the conduct, or rather non-conduct, of battles than is often supposed.   A man who has not seen war with his own eyes is apt to criticise a battle as he would a game at chess.   One party, he argues, has made a move ; why does not the other party make the counteracting move ? It is because human weakness stands in the way ; because the urgent necessity for action has frightened him out of the power of making any move at all.   It is not necessary to attribute anything like disreputable cowardice to the commander exhibiting this sort of indecision.   He may be, on the contrary, a man of what may fairly be called decided courage ; one who, though he cannot make a movement to save his life, will stand to be cut down with the utmost resolution.   It is not impossible that Leslie may have had a touch of the weakness I have referred to. And I suspect that it was chiefly in the opposite turn of mind that Cromwell's strength lay ; he could do *something*, and do it boldly."

Cromwell himself had with his characteristic good sense told the House of Commons at the end of the second year of the war, that he would recommend to their prudence not to insist upon any complaint or oversight of any commander-in-chief upon any occasion whatsoever ; adding this reason for his recommendation, "for as I must acknowledge myself guilty of oversights, so I know they can rarely be avoided in military affairs." [1]   It is instructive to compare with this the terms in which Lord Clarendon and Mrs. Hutchinson speak of military affairs, of which their knowledge was about equal.   The lawyer and the lady are equally profuse of their scorn and reprobation for brave men when the chances of war have gone against them.   But the considerations suggested by the remark of Cromwell above quoted in exculpation of the Scottish commander do not in any degree exculpate those who then administered the government of Scotland, and over-ruled the commander of the Scottish army.

In the long black catalogue of disasters brought upon Scotland during a period of five hundred years by rulers whom .God in His wrath had sent to be her curse, her scourge, and her shame, there is none greater or more shameful than this rout of Dunbar, rendered yet more galling and made to bear a pre-eminence of hardship and infamy by the treatment which the prisoners met with from the victors.   In a letter to the Council of State, ordered to be printed and published by the English Parliament, 8th Nov. 1650, Sir Arthur Haselrig, governor of Newcastle, states that after the battle at Dunbar the lord-general wrote to him that there were about nine thousand prisoners, and that he had set at liberty all those that were wounded, and, as he thought, disabled for future

---

[1] Parl. Hist. vol. iii. pp. 326, 327.

service, in number five thousand one hundred. The rest
the general sent towards Newcastle, conducted to Berwick
by Major Hobson, and from Berwick to Newcastle by some
foot of the garrison of Berwick and a troop of horse. It
is stated on other authority that the Scots were driven
like turkeys by the English soldiers, and went along
cursing their king and clergy for insnaring them in
misery.[1] I have shown that they had been dragged from
their homes and driven by force into the ranks by their
native oppressors, their lairds and lords. It is further
stated in Haselrig's letter to the Council of State that the
officers that marched with them to Berwick were neces-
sitated to kill about thirty, fearing the loss of them all,
for they fell down in great numbers, and said they were
not able to march from fatigue, wounds, and want of food.
It is further stated that the officers in command of the
guard brought their prisoners far in the night, so that
doubtless many ran away. When they came to Morpeth,
the prisoners, being put into a large walled garden, ate up
raw cabbages, leaves, and roots, "so many that the very
seed, and labour at fourpence a day, was valued at nine
pounds; which cabbage as I conceive," proceeds Haselrig,
"they having fasted, as they themselves said, near eight
days, poisoned their bodies; for, as they were coming
from thence to Newcastle, some died by the wayside; and
when they came to Newcastle, I put them into the greatest
church in the town; and the next morning when I sent
them to Durham, about seven score were sick, and not
able to march, and three died that night, and some fell
down in their march from Newcastle to Durham and died."
The royalist writers accuse Haselrig of starving the

---

[1] Whitelock, p. 470.

prisoners.[1]   On the other hand there is a statement in Whitelock to the effect that the Scottish soldiers had been starved by their own officers before the battle, and that they had been at least comparatively well fed by the governor of Berwick. This statement is that the governor of Berwick gave to each Scotch prisoner for one day three biscuits and a pottle of pease, which they said was more than their own officers gave them in three days together.[2]

When the prisoners came to Durham, they were told off into the great cathedral church, and their number was found to be only three thousand. The disease, dysentery, still increasing among them, the sick were removed out of the cathedral church to the bishop's castle. Abundance of wholesome food was now supplied to them ; and medicine, nurses, and medical attendance were provided for the sick and wounded. Notwithstanding all this, they still continued to die with frightful rapidity, many who were apparently healthy and had not at all been sick, suddenly dying, without any other apparent cause but that they were all infected and that the strength of some held out longer, so that when the governor wrote his letter, that is, made his report to the Council of State, about sixteen hundred were dead and buried. The report among other things states, " They were so unruly, sluttish, and nasty, that it is not to be believed ; they acted rather like beasts than men ; so that the marshal was allowed forty men to

[1] Bates (Part ii. p. 106) tells the story in his way, which, as may be supposed, differs a good deal from Haselrig's. "The prisoners," says Bates, "after the wounded, sick, and weak, and those that were of no value were set at liberty, are sent to Newcastle in England ; where by the governor Haselrig many of them were starved, having nothing to eat but green cabbage-leaves and oats in a small proportion. The more robust that outlived this diet are condemned to the sugar-mills, and by the English are transported to the West Indies."

[2] Whitelock, p. 470.

cleanse and sweep them every day." Other accounts state
that the countrymen were much enslaved to their lords,
and the people very poor, and barbarous and dirty, washing
their linen not above once a month and their hands and
faces not above once a year.[1] It would seem that at that
time the Highlanders, at least those serving in Leslie's
army, were not distinguished from the Lowlanders by any
peculiar dress, for the report says :—"there are about
500 sick in the castle, and about 600 yet in health in the
cathedral, most of which are in probability Highlanders,
they being hardier than the rest, and other means to distinguish them we have not." Whether the Highlanders or
Lowlanders were the chief aggressors in the following
revolting cruelties I will not presume to say. "Some were
killed by themselves [by the prisoners]; for they were
exceeding cruel one towards another. If a man was perceived to have any money, it was two to one but he was
killed before morning, and robbed ; and if any had good
clothes, he that wanted, if he was able, would strangle
him, and put on his clothes."[2]

· Now as this passage has been edited without comment
by Sir Walter Scott, who possessed the command of the
Advocates' Library and all the best sources of information
for disproving it if he considered it false or improbable, I
greatly fear that it must be considered as too true a tale.
When we reflect that the Scottish Government professed to
have undertaken this war for the glory of God and the
purity of the Christian religion, of which they declared
themselves to be not only the best but the sole judges and
champions, can any satire of the most severe satirist who

[1] Whitelock, p. 468.
[2] Sir Arthur Haselrig to the Committee of the Council of State—in the
same collection with Captain Hodgson's
Memoirs—p. 343—edited with notes
by Walter Scott, Edinburgh, 1806.

ever lashed the follies and vices of mankind exceed the
intensity of reprobation conveyed by the simple fact here
stated ? Here were kings, nobles, and priests, or presbyters,
if they prefer the term, who had been, as they declared,
set over a nation by Almighty God to lead them and feed
them, to govern them and teach them and preach to them ;
—and what had they done ? Preaching indeed they had
given in plenty ; but how had they taught them ? After
a thousand years under the religion of the Church of Rome,
and a hundred years under that of the Kirk of Scotland,
here was the vast bulk of a nation still in that state of
primæval barbarism where " there is continual fear and
danger of violent death, and the life of man, solitary, poor,
nasty, brutish and short." They had shorn their flock
indeed, but they had neither fed them, nor led them, for it
will not be denied that true Presbyterians of some
shade or other composed the bulk of the army of
the Covenanted Kirk and Covenanted Oligarchy of Scotland.   But all this cruelty, barbarity, and wretchedness
of the people were the natural consequence of a reformation consecrated by grillades of the trustees of church
lands by the nobles, and of a clergy dependent on such
nobles for every morsel of bread they ate.   There can be
little doubt that the people at large were worse off since
those lands out of which they received at least some pit-
tance of food had been violently and lawlessly seized to
swell the pride, luxury, insolence, and other vices of the
feudal oligarchy.   If Scotland had continued a separate
and independent kingdom, and her aristocracy or oligarchy
had been suffered to run out its full career, there can be
little doubt but the nobility of Scotland would have had a
similar fate to that of the nobility of France.   It would
have terminated its career at the lanterne or the guillotine.

But the union with England saved it from such a fate ; and as a reward for ages of tyranny, cruelty, and crime, has made it the wealthiest oligarchy that the world ever saw, operating in the same way as if the union of England with a larger kingdom had given to the English king the absolute ownership of every acre of land over which before he had only the rights of suzerain.[1]

The miserable remnant of the unfortunate Scottish prisoners, those who had escaped the sword, pestilence, and famine, the cruelty of the English Government destined to a fate hitherto unknown in Christian warfare. The Long Parliament of England transported to the English settlements in America men who had borne arms by order of their own lords which they could not disobey, and there sold them for slaves.

When we regard the barbarities perpetrated by the Irish in Ireland against the English settlers, and by Montrose and his Irish and Highlanders in Scotland ; when we regard the treatment of the people of Scotland by their native

---

[1] Certain Roman families were observed to keep up a uniform character of pride and cruelty through successive generations. Some families in the Scottish aristocracy, as probably in all aristocracies, might lay claim to the same pre-eminence as the Claudii. It is within the memory of the present generation that certain members of the Scottish nobility, whose ancestors had pre-eminently distinguished themselves, not by great deeds done against their country's enemies, which might help to reconcile that country to the pride of those "of whom herself was proud," but by the rapacious cruelty of robbers, were remarked for a combination of pride, cruelty, and insolence which seemed rather to belong to robbers of the darkest and most barbarous ages than to British noblemen of the 19th century. But they did after their kind, and it is astonishing how long the characteristics of a race will remain in the blood. One can partly understand (what to those accustomed to the decency and humanity which have now long prevailed in England is absolutely unintelligible), from what one has heard of the effect produced on the minds of a generally *canny* and sober-minded people by those men's deeds and demeanour, how a people may get exasperated by a long series of provocations to a state of phrenzy like that in which the Parisian populace hanged De Foulon at the lanterne and tore out the heart of Berthier before it had ceased to beat.

oppressors, and the treatment of the Scottish prisoners by the English parliament; and call to remembrance the chivalrous humanity of Robert Bruce on certain memorable occasions towards the weak and helpless, we seem almost forced to the conclusion that civilisation had retrograded instead of advancing in the course of those three hundred and thirty years from the beginning of the 14th till the middle of the 17th century.

With regard to the 5000 prisoners who were dismissed by Cromwell as being disabled, it is stated in Whitelock "that the general sent home upon their paroles 5000 of the prisoners being wounded, old men and boys, the men housekeepers forced out of their houses to take arms, and 2100 of them died by the way."[1] This sufficiently shows of what materials a great part of the Scottish army was composed ; and it also shows what sort of treatment the unfortunate people of Scotland then met with from their rulers, who dragged from their homes to be starved, ill-used, and finally butchered, boys and old men, under and above the age fit for military service. Under such circumstances it required no very great effort of administrative genius to improve the condition of the great body of the people of Scotland, as it was improved under the government of the English Parliament, and afterwards under that of Cromwell, and his lieutenant Monk.

At the battle of Dunbar the Scottish generals seem to have distinguished themselves, if by nothing else, by their speed in running away. Leven hasted to Edinburgh, and after him David Leslie, who mustered about 1300 horse.[2] Thence with their king and Committee of Estates, as their oligarchical parliament was called, they retreated to Stirling, where they perhaps hoped to be able to make a stand by

[1] Whitelock, p. 471.　　　　　[2] Whitelock, p. 471.

defending the passes of the Forth, and for that purpose forcing more unhappy old men and boys from their homes to be slaughtered in defence of civil and ecclesiastical tyranny. But with such a king and such a nobility it is evident what the end would be.

An act was passed by the English parliament for a day of public thanksgiving for the victory over the Scots. It was also ordered that the colours taken at Preston and Dunbar should be hung up in Westminster Hall, and that medals of gold and silver should be given to the soldiery in remembrance of God's mercy and of their valour and victory.[1]

After the battle of Dunbar, the major general (Lambert) marched to Haddington, while Cromwell stayed behind with two regiments to order affairs at Dunbar, where he had already distributed pease and wheat among the poor people to the value of £240 out of the supply sent from London to the army. But, as has been shown, either from inability or oversight, in ordering the destination of the prisoners whom he sent to England, he seems to have left the feeding of them unprovided for. He then marched to Edinburgh and Leith, whence the enemy had drawn all their forces towards Stirling and Perth.[2]

Edinburgh Castle and almost all the other strong places on the south side of the Forth were soon surrendered to the English. It was believed that there was more money, plate, and rich household stuff in Edinburgh Castle than in any other part of Scotland, the inhabitants of Edinburgh having carried their property thither for safe custody. One of the articles of surrender provided, with respect to all the goods in the castle belonging to any person whatsoever,

---

[1] Whitelock, *ibid.*—Parl. Hist. vol. iii. pp. 1355, 1356.   [2] Whitelock, pp. 468, 471.

that an edict be proclaimed to the people about Edinburgh to come, own, and receive their own ; and if any be at a far distance or dead, that a place be provided in the town of Edinburgh for keeping the same till they be owned ; and, after owning, the owners may have liberty to carry them where they please. And such was the discipline of Cromwell's soldiers, that they did not in the least interrupt the inhabitants in removing their goods, or take a single article. " So that," says the report, " considering the impregnable strength of the place, the great loss of men we must have had, in case we had stormed it (if we had carried it that way which was almost impossible,) and the love of the people, which we now have gained by this civil usage, it was the best course that could have been taken ; and if it were put in the balance would not appear to be of much less consequence than the defeat at Down Hill near Dunbar." [1] The articles however were not concluded and settled till the 19th of December, and on the 24th of December the Scottish garrison marched out, in conformity with the fifth article, " with their arms and baggage, with drums beating and colours flying, matches lighted at both ends, and ball in their mouths, as they usually are wont to march, and all their goods, with a free conduct to Brunt Island in Fife." [2] But by reason of the great winds the soldiers that came out of the Castle could not get over to Fife immediately, but were forced to stay in Leith that night with a guard.[3]

The English army, having stayed in Edinburgh and Leith six or seven days for rest and refreshment, marched towards Stirling. On the 18th of September when they had

<hr />

[1] The Articles of the Rendition of Edinburgh Castle to the Lord-General Cromwell, in the same collection with Captain Hodgson's Memoirs, p. 347 et seq. originally published by authority of the English Parliament.

[2] *Ibid.* p. 353.

[3] *Ibid.* p. 351.

advanced to within a mile of Stirling, a letter was drawn up to be sent to Stirling, requiring the surrender of that place.[1] A trumpeter was sent with this letter. A gentleman ou foot, with a pike in his hand, met the trumpeter and told him he must return back, for they would not let him come in or receive his letter.· In the afternoon of the same day, a trumpeter came from Stirling to the English army about the release of prisoners, desiring that they might be released upon ransom. To this Cromwell wrote in answer that they came not thither to make merchandize of men, or to get a gain to themselves, but for the service and security of the Commonwealth of England. Preparations were then made to storm the place, ladders and all things necessary being provided for that purpose; but by reason of several disadvantages, particularly the strength of the castle, it was thought fit to retreat.[1] And, as the dispatches express it, the work of the English now was "to stand still and see salvation wrought for them; this nation [the Scottish] being destined for ruin, which makes them thus to divide amongst themselves when an enemy is in their bowels."[2] Of this there could not be a stronger proof than the report that upon news of the victory at Dunbar being brought to the king, he thanked God that he was so rid of the Scots, and said the kirk might now see their error in prohibiting him to be in person with their army, and keeping out the English and the rest of his followers.[3]

In fact the Scots were now divided into four parties. Some of those who have been before described as the strict or rigid Presbyterians were in their present extremity disposed to relax the extreme rigour of their exclusive doc-

---

[1] Relation of the Campaign in Scotland, in the same collection with Captain Hodgson's Memoirs, pp. 315-318.

[2] Ibid. p. 336.
[3] Whitelock, p. 472.

trines, and to admit into the army by way of reinforcing it such of the moderate Presbyterians or Engagers, and even of the Royalists or Malignants, as were inclined to make a formal confession of their former errors.   Now this caused a division of the strict Presbyterians into two parts, which may be called the strict and the more strict or stricter.   The stricter Presbyterians, in particular the Presbyterians of the western counties, may be also styled the democratic as distinguished from the aristocratic Presbyterians, the root of whose Presbyterianism was the plunder of the church lands. Of these democratic Presbyterians or Remonstrators, as they were called, there assembled an army of about four thou- sand men under Colonels Kerr and Strachan.   They were resolved to oppose both the king's forces, and the forces of the parliament of England.   After some fights between Major General Lambert and them, the leaders, says Captain Hodgson, "came in to us, and desired protection, and proved very faithful."[1]   That their political opinions did not differ much from those of the English Parliament ap- pears from a declaration of their Commissioners sent to the English head-quarters.   The purport of this declaration is that they will not own the interest of king and lords; that, as to the executive part of the kingly power, they do not think it fit the king should be admitted to it, until he had given better satisfaction to their kirk; that his father was justly put to death for his acts of tyranny, though there might be some miscarriages in the way; that the Commissioners and kirk had done very ill in provoking the English, but the English Parliament were much to blame for sending an army to make an invasion, to proceed to blood before they gave them warning.[2]

The dispatches of the English officers make frequent

[1] Captain Hodgson's Memoirs, pp. 149, 150.

[2] Relation of the Campaign in Scot- land, p. 334.

mention of what they term the robberies and murders committed by "those villanous moss-troopers." This term, though formerly appropriated to the freebooters of the Borders, the English applied to all the small bands of men who lurked among the mountains and morasses, and took every advantage which the nature of the country abound-·ing in difficult passes afforded them to annoy the English troops, and cut off small parties, or straggling soldiers. But the rigid discipline of Cromwell's troops, and the stern promptitude with which redress was exacted, furnished those moss-troopers and their abettors with some experience which was new to them. Thus we read of a letter to the sheriff of Cumberland, "to be speeded away to Mr. John Scott, bailiff and brother to the lord of Buccleugh, for de-manding restitution upon his tenants, the moss-troopers, for the horses by them stolen the night we quartered in their country; since which promises have been made of restitution; and we doubt not to receive it very suddenly, or else to take satisfaction another way ourselves."[1] And again, "Major Browne hath with a party of horse pos-sessed a strong house, not far from Dalkeith, called Dal-houz [Dalhousie], it was suspected to have been an har-bour for those villanous moss-troopers who murdered some of our men, that were either straggling or going for pro-visions."[2]

There is one feature of the battle of Dunbar, which as having probably led to the unjust imputations of Clarendon and others, on the courage of the Scots, may require some explanation. Though by Cromwell's own account in his letter to the Speaker, "the enemy made a gallant resist-ance, and there was a very hot dispute at sword's point

---

[1] Relation of the Campaign in Scot-land, p. 327.   [2] *Ibid.* pp. 333, 334.

between our horse and theirs;" and as regarded the foot
"at push of pike and butt-end of musket;" yet he says of
Dunbar, "I do not believe we have lost 20 men." This
however is probably an understatement. For another letter
from head-quarters says—"we lost not 40 men—no officer
but Major Rooksby, who died of his wounds next day;—
Captain Lloyd sorely wounded." Also at the battle of
Worcester Cromwell says "it was as stiff a contest for 4 or
5 hours, as ever I have seen, yet I do not think we have lost
200 men." It is possible that neither Lord Clarendon nor
Mrs. Hutchinson ever heard of the battle of Bannockburn.
If they had, the fact that at Bannockburn thirty thousand
English, including 200 knights and 700 esquires were left
dead upon the field,[1] while the loss of the Scots in the
battle was as small in proportion as that of the English at
Dunbar, might have led them to pause before making their
imputations upon the courage of the Scots. The explanation of this great disproportion between the loss of the
conquered and of the conquerors at Bannockburn and Dunbar is that at both those times, as in ancient warfare, battles
not being determined by artillery and musketry, and the
defensive armour being then of at least some avail, it was
not till one side had turned their backs, that the carnage
commenced. It is stated that at the battle of Pharsalia
Cæsar lost 200 men, at that of Thapsus 50, at that of
Munda (as stiff a business, Cæsar said, like Cromwell at
Worcester, as ever he had seen) a thousand; while the loss
of his enemies at Pharsalia was estimated at 15,000,[2] at
Thapsus at 10,000,[3] at Munda at 30,000, "et si quid

---

[1] Tytler's History of Scotland, vol. i.
pp. 314, 319.

[2] Cæsar, De Bello Civili, iii. 99.

[3] This is the statement in the book
De Bello Africano (c. 86) of which

Hirtius, who served under Cæsar in the
Gallic war, is generally supposed to be
the author. Plutarch's statement is
50,000.—*Life of C. Cæsar*, c. 53.

amplius." [1]   And in all these cases it was Romans opposed
to Romans.   The disproportion between the loss of the
conquerors and that of the conquered at Cannæ is still more
striking.[2]   These facts will be sufficient to show, the mode of
warfare being the same or nearly so, that nothing could be
more illogical, to say no more, than the inferences of some
English writers against the Scottish troops, the unfortunate
men slaughtered at Dunbar and Worcester, or reserved for
a worse fate, to perish of sheer starvation, or be sold for
slaves, a somewhat different treatment from that which the
conquered after the battle of Pharsalia received from the
conqueror who freely forgave all who had borne arms
against him.   The return made for that magnanimous
clemency did not perhaps encourage the English Parliament to follow that example.   Notwithstanding Cæsar's
humanity, he could not always succeed in giving quarter.
Thus at Thapsus, in spite of his earnest entreaties to his
soldiers to spare them, many Romans were slaughtered after
they had thrown down their arms and begged for quarter.[3]
The facts above stated, however, when the armies opposed to
each other were both composed of the best soldiers of the
ancient world, will show that the disproportion between the
numbers of the slain on the two sides arose simply from the
mode of warfare and not from the side that had the vastly
disproportioned number of slain having, as Clarendon says
of the Scots at Dunbar, fled without fighting.   It is indeed
true that the larger proportion of the Scots had no op-

[1] See the book De Bello Hispanico,
(c. 31)—attributed by some to C.
Oppius, another friend of Cæsar.

[2] There are some interesting remarks
on the causes of this disproportion in
a book published at Paris in 1836
under the title "Précis des Guerres de
Jules César, par NAPOLEON, écrit à
l'Ile de St. Hélène sous la dictée de
l'Empereur, par M. Marchand"—
which bears considerable marks of
authenticity.

[3] De Bello Afric. c. 85. "Ii omnes
Scipionis milites, quum fidem Cæsaris
implorarent, inspectante ipso Cæsare,
et a militibus deprecante, eis uti par-
cerent, ad unum sunt interfecti."

portunity of fighting, having been thrown into irretrievable confusion, as I have shown, by the combined operation of the nature of the ground and of their right wing being driven in upon them, so that they necessarily "routed one another."

I have in a note in a former page referred to the battle of Flodden, as a battle fought at a time when the Scottish nobility were a military aristocracy. That battle is remarkable as a battle in which, though fought as in ancient warfare, the disproportion between the numbers of the slain on the two sides was less than in any of the battles above mentioned ; for the loss of the English was about five thousand men, that of the Scots about twice that number. The cause was, that the main division of the Scots commanded by the king in person could not be broken. Night fell without the battle's being absolutely decided. But during the night the remnant of the Scottish army drew off " in silent despair " from the bloody field on which they left their king and nearly all their nobility. And yet, according to Lord Clarendon and other writers of his time, the Scots were a nation of cowards. There is another point in which the battle of Dunbar forms a strong contrast with the battle of Flodden. At Dunbar it was a regiment of Highlanders that fought the most obstinately. At Flodden the Highlanders who formed one division of the Scottish army, being annoyed by the volleys of the English arrows, broke their ranks, and were routed with great slaughter ; which circumstance was the principal cause of the disproportion between the loss of the Scots and that of the English in that battle.

ALBEMARLE STREET, LONDON,
November, 1863.

MR. MURRAY'S
GENERAL LIST OF WORKS.

ALBERT (PRINCE). THE PRINCIPAL SPEECHES AND
ADDRESSES of H.R.H. THE PRINCE CONSORT; with an Introduction giving some Outlines of his Character. Portrait. 8vo.
10s. 6d.

ABBOTT'S (REV. J.) Philip Musgrave; or, Memoirs of a Church of
England Missionary in the North American Colonies. Post 8vo. 2s.

ABERCROMBIE'S (JOHN) Enquiries concerning the Intellectual
Powers and the Investigation of Truth. 16th Edition. Fcap. 8vo. 6s. 6d.

———————————— Philosophy of the Moral Feelings. 12th Edition.
Fcap. 8vo. 4s.

ACLAND'S (REV. CHARLES) Popular Account of the Manners and
Customs of India. Post 8vo. 2s.

ÆSOP'S FABLES. A New Translation. With Historical
Preface. By Rev. THOMAS JAMES. With 100 Woodcuts, by TENNIEL
and WOLF. 50th Thousand. Post 8vo. 2s. 6d.

AGRICULTURAL (THE) JOURNAL. Of the Royal Agricultural
Society of England. 8vo. Published half-yearly.

AIDS TO FAITH : a Series of Essays. By various Writers. Edited
by WILLIAM THOMSON, D.D., Lord Archbishop of York. 8vo. 9s.

CONTENTS.

Rev. H. L. MANSEL—On Miracles.
BISHOP FITZGERALD—Christian Evidences.
REV. DR. MCCAUL—On Prophecy.
Rev. F. C. COOK — Ideology and Subscription.
Rev. DR. MCCAUL—Mosaic Record of Creation.

Rev. GEORGE RAWLINSON—The Pentateuch.
ARCHBISHOP THOMSON—Doctrine of the Atonement.
Rev. HAROLD BROWNE—On Inspiration.
BISHOP ELLICOTT—Scripture and its Interpretation.

AMBER-WITCH (THE). The most interesting Trial for Witchcraft ever known. Translated from the German by LADY DUFF
GORDON. Post 8vo. 2s.

ARMY LIST (MONTHLY) Published by Authority. Fcap. 8vo. 1s. 6d.

ARTHUR'S (LITTLE) History of England. By LADY CALLCOTT.
120th Thousand. With 20 Woodcuts. Fcap. 8vo. 2s. 6d.

ATKINSON'S (MRS.) Recollections of Tartar Steppes and their
Inhabitants. With Illustrations. Post 8vo. 12s.

AUNT IDA'S Walks and Talks; a Story Book for Children. By
a LADY. Woodcuts. 16mo. 5s.

AUSTIN'S (JOHN) LECTURES ON JURISPRUDENCE ; or, the Philosophy
of Positive Law. 3 Vols. 8vo. 39s.

——————— (SARAH) Fragments from German Prose Writers.
With Biographical Notes. Post 8vo. 10s.

B

BARBAULD'S (Mrs) Hymns in Prose for Children. With 112 Original Designs by Barnes, Wimperis, Coleman, and Kennedy. Engraved by Cooper. Small 4to.

BARROW'S (Sir John) Autobiographical Memoir, including Reflections, Observations, and Reminiscences at Home and Abroad. From Early Life to Advanced Age. Portrait. 8vo. 16s.

———————— Voyages of Discovery and Research within the Arctic Regions, from 1818 to the present time. 8vo. 15s.

———————— Life and Voyages of Sir Francis Drake. With numerous Original Letters. Post 8vo. 2s.

BATES' (H. W.) Naturalist on the River Amazons during eleven years of Adventure and Travel. *Second Edition.* Illustrations. 2 Vols. Post 8vo.

BEES AND FLOWERS. Two Essays. By Rev. Thomas James. Reprinted from the "Quarterly Review." Fcap. 8vo. 1s. each.

BELL'S (Sir Charles) Mechanism and Vital Endowments of the Hand as evincing Design. *Sixth Edition.* Woodcuts. Post 8vo. 6s.

BENEDICT'S (Jules) Sketch of the Life and Works of Felix Mendelssohn-Bartholdy. *Second Edition.* 8vo. 2s. 6d.

BERTHA'S Journal during a Visit to her Uncle in England. Containing a Variety of Interesting and Instructive Information. *Seventh Edition.* Woodcuts. 12mo.

BIRCH'S (Samuel) History of Ancient Pottery and Porcelain : Egyptian, Assyrian, Greek, Roman, and Etruscan. With 200 Illustrations. 2 Vols. Medium 8vo. 42s.

BLUNT'S (Rev. J. J.) Principles for the proper understanding of the Mosaic Writings, stated and applied, together with an Incidental Argument for the truth of the Resurrection of our Lord. Being the Hulsean Lectures for 1832. Post 8vo. 6s. 6d.

———————— Undesigned Coincidences in the Writings of the Old and New Testament, an Argument of their Veracity : containing the Books of Moses, Historical and Prophetical Scriptures, and the Gospels and Acts. *8th Edition.* Post 8vo. 6s.

———————— History of the Church in the First Three Centuries. *Third Edition.* Post 8vo. 7s. 6d.

———————— Parish Priest; His Duties, Acquirements and Obligations. *Fourth Edition.* Post 8vo. 7s. 6d.

———————— Lectures on the Right Use of the Early Fathers. *Second Edition.* 8vo. 15s.

———————— Plain Sermons Preached to a Country Congregation. *Second Edition.* 3 Vols. Post 8vo. 7s. 6d. each.

———————— Literary Essays, reprinted from the Quarterly Review. 8vo. 12s.

BLACKSTONE'S COMMENTARIES on the Laws of England. Adapted to the present state of the law. By R. Malcolm Kerr, LL.D. *Third Edition.* 4 Vols. 8vo. 63s.

———————————————————————— For Students. Being those Portions which relate to the British Constitution and the Rights of Persons. Post 8vo. 9s.

BLAKISTON'S (CAPT.) Narrative of the Expedition sent to explore the Upper Waters of the Yang-Tsze. Illustrations. 8vo. 18s.

BLOMFIELD'S (BISHOP) Memoir, with Selections from his Correspondence. By his Son. 2nd Edition. Portrait, 2 Vols. post 8vo. 18s.

BOOK OF COMMON PRAYER. Illustrated with Coloured Borders, Initial Letters, and Woodcuts. A new edition. 8vo.

BORROW'S (GEORGE) Bible in Spain; or the Journeys, Adventures, and Imprisonments of an Englishman in an Attempt to circulate the Scriptures in the Peninsula. 3 Vols. Post 8vo. 27s.; or Popular Edition, 16mo, 3s. 6d.

———— Zincali, or the Gipsies of Spain; their Manners, Customs, Religion, and Language. 2 Vols. Post 8vo. 18s.; or Popular Edition, 16mo, 3s. 6d.

———— Lavengro; The Scholar—The Gipsy—and the Priest. Portrait. 3 Vols. Post 8vo. 30s.

———— Romany Rye; a Sequel to Lavengro. Second Edition. 2 Vols. Post 8vo. 21s.

———— Wild Wales: its People, Language, and Scenery. 3 Vols. Post 8vo. 30s.

BOSWELL'S (JAMES) Life of Samuel Johnson, LL.D. Including the Tour to the Hebrides. Edited by Mr. CROKER. Portraits. Royal 8vo. 10s.

BRACE'S (C. L.) History of the Races of the Old World. Designed as a Manual of Ethnology. Post 8vo. 9s.

BRAY'S (MRS.) Life of Thomas Stothard, R.A. With Personal Reminiscences. Illustrated with Portrait and 60 Woodcuts of his chief works. 4to.

BREWSTER'S (SIR DAVID) Martyrs of Science, or the Lives of Galileo, Tycho Brahe, and Kepler. Fourth Edition. Fcap. 8vo. 4s. 6d.

———— More Worlds than One. The Creed of the Philosopher and the Hope of the Christian. Eighth Edition. Post 8vo. 6s.

———— Stereoscope: its History, Theory, Construction, and Application to the Arts and to Education. Woodcuts. 12mo. 5s. 6d.

———— Kaleidoscope: its History, Theory, and Construction, with its application to the Fine and Useful Arts. Second Edition. Woodcuts. Post 8vo. 5s. 6d.

BRINE'S (Capt.) Narrative of the Rise and Progress of the Taeping Rebellion in China. Plans. Post 8vo. 10s. 6d.

BRITISH ASSOCIATION REPORTS. 8vo. York and Oxford, 1831-32, 13s. 6d. Cambridge, 1833, 12s. Edinburgh, 1834, 15s. Dublin, 1835, 13s. 6d. Bristol, 1836, 12s. Liverpool, 1837, 16s. 6d. Newcastle, 1838, 15s. Birmingham, 1839, 13s. 6d. Glasgow, 1840, 15s. Plymouth, 1841, 13s. 6d. Manchester, 1842, 10s. 6d. Cork, 1843, 12s. York, 1844, 20s. Cambridge, 1845, 12s. Southampton, 1846, 15s. Oxford, 1847, 18s. Swansea, 1848, 9s. Birmingham, 1849, 10s. Edinburgh, 1850, 15s. Ipswich, 1851, 16s. 6d. Belfast, 1852, 15s. Hull, 1853, 10s. 6d. Liverpool, 1854, 18s. Glasgow, 1855, 15s.; Cheltenham, 1856, 18s.; Dublin, 1857, 15s.; Leeds, 1858, 20s. Aberdeen, 1859, 15s. Oxford, 1860. Manchester, 1861. 15s.

BRITISH CLASSICS. A New Series of Standard English
Authors, printed from the most correct text, and edited with elucida-
tory notes. Published occasionally in demy 8vo. Volumes, varying in
price.

Already Published.

GOLDSMITH'S WORKS. Edited by Peter Cunningham, F.S.A.
Vignettes. 4 Vols. 30*s.*

GIBBON'S DECLINE AND FALL OF THE ROMAN EMPIRE.
Edited by William Smith, LL.D. Portrait and Maps. 8 Vols. 60*s.*

JOHNSON'S LIVES OF THE ENGLISH POETS. Edited by Peter
Cunningham, F.S.A. 3 Vols. 22*s.* 6*d.*

BYRON'S POETICAL WORKS. Edited, with Notes. 6 vols. **45***s.*

In Preparation.

WORKS OF POPE. With Life, Introductions, and Notes, by Rev. Whitwell Elwin. Portrait.

HUME'S HISTORY OF ENGLAND. Edited, with Notes.

LIFE AND WORKS OF SWIFT. Edited by John Forster.

BROUGHTON'S (Lord) Journey through Albania and other
Provinces of Turkey in Europe and Asia, to Constantinople, 1809—10.
Third Edition. Illustrations. 2 Vols. 8vo. 30*s.*

———————— Visits to Italy. *3rd Edition.* 2 vols. Post 8vo. 18*s.*

BUBBLES FROM THE BRUNNEN OF NASSAU. By an Old
Man. *Sixth Edition.* 16mo. 5*s.*

BUNYAN (John) and Oliver Cromwell. Select Biographies. By
Robert Southey. Post 8vo. 2*s.*

BUONAPARTE'S (Napoleon) Confidential Correspondence with his
Brother Joseph, sometime King of Spain. *Second Edition.* 2 vols. 8vo.
26*s.*

BURGHERSH'S (Lord) Memoir of the Operations of the Allied
Armies under Prince Schwarzenberg and Marshal Blucher during the
latter end of 1813—14. 8vo. 21*s.*

———————— Early Campaigns of the Duke of Wellington in
Portugal and Spain. 8vo. 8*s.* 6*d.*

BURGON'S (Rev. J. W.) Memoir of Patrick Fraser Tytler.
Second Edition. Post 8vo. 9*s.*

———————— Letters from Rome, written to Friends at Home.
Illustrations. Post 8vo. 12*s.*

BURN'S (Lieut.-Col.) French and English Dictionary of Naval
and Military Technical Terms. *Fourth Edition.* Crown 8vo. 15*s.*

BURNS' (Robert) Life. By John Gibson Lockhart. Fifth
Edition. Fcap. 8vo. 3*s.*

BURR'S (G. D.) Instructions in Practical Surveying, Topogra-
phical Plan Drawing, and on sketching ground without Instruments.
Third Edition. Woodcuts. Post 8vo. 7*s.* 6*d.*

BUTTMAN'S LEXILOGUS; a Critical Examination of the
Meaning of numerous Greek Words, chiefly in Homer and Hesiod.
Translated by Rev. J. R. Fishlake. *Fifth Edition.* 8vo. 12*s.*

BUXTON'S (Sir Fowell) Memoirs. With Selections from his
Correspondence. By his Son. Portrait. *Fifth Edition.* 8vo. 16*s.*
Abridged Edition, Portrait. Fcap. 8vo. 2*s.* 6*d.*

BYRON'S (LORD) Life, Letters, and Journals. By THOMAS MOORE. Plates. 6 Vols. Fcap. 8vo. 18s.

———— Life, Letters, and Journals. By THOMAS MOORE. Portraits. Royal 8vo. 9s.

———— Poetical Works. Portrait. 6 Vols. 8vo. 45s.

———— Poetical Works. Plates. 10 Vols. Fcap. 8vo. 30s.

———— Poetical Works. 8 Vols. 24mo. 20s.

———— Poetical Works. Plates. Royal 8vo. 9s.

———— Poetical Works. Portrait. Crown 8vo. 6s.

———— Childe Harold. With 80 Engravings. Small 4to. 21s.

———— Childe Harold. With 30 Vignettes. 12mo. 6s.

———— Childe Harold. 16mo. 2s. 6d.

———— Childe Harold. Vignettes. 16mo. 1s.

———— Childe Harold. Portrait. 16mo. 6d.

———— Tales and Poems. 24mo. 2s. 6d.

———— Miscellaneous. 2 Vols. 24mo. 5s.

———— Dramas and Plays. 2 Vols. 24mo. 5s.

———— Don Juan and Beppo. 2 Vols. 24mo. 5s.

———— Beauties. Selected from his Poetry and Prose. Portrait, Fcap. 8vo. 3s. 6d.

CARNARVON'S (LORD) Portugal, Gallicia, and the Basque Provinces. From Notes made during a Journey to those Countries. *Third Edition.* Post 8vo. 3s. 6d.

———————— Recollections of the Druses of Lebanon. With Notes on their Religion. *Third Edition.* Post 8vo. 5s. 6d.

CAMPBELL'S (LORD) Lives of the Lord Chancellors and Keepers of the Great Seal of England. From the Earliest Times to the Death of Lord Eldon in 1838. *Fourth Edition.* 10 Vols. Crown 8vo. 6s. each.

———————— Lives of the Chief Justices of England. From the Norman Conquest to the Death of Lord Tenterden. *Second Edition.* 3 Vols. 8vo. 42s.

———————— Shakspeare's Legal Acquirements Considered. 8vo. 5s. 6d.

———————— Life of Lord Chancellor Bacon. Fcap. 8vo. 2s. 6d.

———————— (GEORGE) Modern India. A Sketch of the System of Civil Government. With some Account of the Natives and Native Institutions. *Second Edition.* 8vo. 16s.

———————— India as it may be. An Outline of a proposed Government and Policy. 8vo. 12s.

———————— (THOS.) Short Lives of the British Poets. With an Essay on English Poetry. Post 8vo. 3s. 6d.

CALVIN'S (JOHN) Life. With Extracts from his Correspondence. By THOMAS H. DYER. Portrait. 8vo. 15s.

CALLCOTT'S (LADY) Little Arthur's History of England. 130th *Thousand.* With 20 Woodcuts. Fcap. 8vo. 2s. 6d.

CASTLEREAGH (THE) DESPATCHES, from the commencement
of the official career of the late Viscount Castlereagh to the close of his
life. Edited by the MARQUIS OF LONDONDERRY. 12 Vols. 8vo. 14s.each.

CATHCART'S (SIR GEORGE) Commentaries on the War in Russia
and Germany, 1812-13. Plans. 8vo. 14s.

———————— Military Operations in Kaffraria, which led to the
Termination of the Kaffir War. *Second Edition*. 8vo. 12s.

CAVALCASELLE (G. B.). Notices of the Lives and Works of
the Early Flemish Painters. Woodcuts. Post 8vo. 12s.

CHAMBERS' (G. F.) Handbook of Descriptive and Practical
Astronomy. Illustrations. Post 8vo. 12s.

CHANTREY (SIR FRANCIS). Winged Words on Chantrey's Wood-
cocks. Edited by JAS. P. MUIRHEAD. Etchings. Square 8vo. 10s. 6d.

CHARMED ROE (THE) ; or, The Story of the Little Brother and
Sister. By OTTO SPECKTER. Plates. 16mo. 5s.

CHURTON'S (ARCHDEACON) Gongora. An Historical Essay on the
Age of Philip III. and IV. of Spain. With Translations. Portrait.
2 Vols. Small 8vo. 15s.

CLAUSEWITZ'S (CARL VON) Campaign of 1812, in Russia.
Translated from the German by LORD ELLESMERE. Map. 8vo. 10s. 6d.

CLIVE'S (LORD) Life. By REV. G. R. GLEIG, M.A. Post 8vo. 3s. 6d.

COBBOLD'S (REV. R. H.) Pictures of the Chinese drawn by a
Native Artist, described by a Foreign Resident. With 24 Plates.
Crown 8vo. 9s.

COLCHESTER (THE) PAPERS. The Diary and Correspondence
of Charles Abbott, Lord Colchester, Speaker of the House of Commons,
1802-1817. Edited by HIS SON. Portrait. 3 Vols. 8vo. 42s.

COLERIDGE'S (SAMUEL TAYLOR) Table-Talk. *Fourth Edition.*
Portrait. Fcap. 8vo. 6s.

———————— (HENRY NELSON) Introductions to the Greek
Classic Poets. *Third Edition.* Fcap. 8vo. 5s. 6d.

———————— (SIR JOHN) on Public School Education, with
especial reference to Eton. *Third Edition.* Fcap. 8vo. 2s.

COLONIAL LIBRARY. [See Home and Colonial Library.]

COOK'S (Rev. F. C.) Sermons Preached at Lincoln's Inn Chapel,
and on Special Occasions. 8vo.

COOKERY (MODERN DOMESTIC). Founded on Principles of Economy
and Practical Knowledge, and adapted for Private Families. By a
Lady. *New Edition.* Woodcuts. Fcap. 8vo. 5s.

CORNWALLIS (THE) Papers and Correspondence during the
American War,—Administrations in India,—Union with Ireland, and
Peace of Amiens. Edited by CHARLES ROSS. *Second Edition.* 3 Vols.
8vo. 63s.

COWPER'S (MARY COUNTESS) Diary while Lady of the Bedchamber
to Caroline Princess of Wales. Portrait. 8vo.

CRABBE'S (REV. GEORGE) Life, Letters, and Journals. By his SON.
Portrait. Fcap. 8vo. 3s.

———————— Poetical Works. With his Life. Plates. 8 Vols.
Fcap. 8vo. 24s.

———————— Life and Poetical Works. Plates. Royal 8vo. 7s.

CROKER'S (J. W.) Progressive Geography for Children. *Fifth Edition.* 18mo. 1s. 6d.

———— Stories for Children, Selected from the History of England. *Fifteenth Edition.* Woodcuts. 16mo. 2s. 6d.

———— Boswell's Life of Johnson. Including the Tour to the Hebrides. Portraits. Royal 8vo. 10s.

———— LORD HERVEY's Memoirs of the Reign of George the Second, from his Accession to the death of Queen Caroline. Edited with Notes. *Second Edition.* Portrait. 2 Vols. 8vo. 21s.

———— Essays on the Early Period of the French Revolution. 8vo. 15s.

———— Historical Essay on the Guillotine. Fcap. 8vo. 1s.

CROMWELL (OLIVER) and John Bunyan. By ROBERT SOUTHEY. Post 8vo. 2s.

CROWE'S (J. A.) Notices of the Early Flemish Painters; their Lives and Works. Woodcuts. Post 8vo. 12s.

———— AND CAVALCASELLE'S History of Painting in Italy, from 2nd to 16th Century. Derived from Historical Researches as well as inspection of the Works of Art in that Country. Illustrations. 2 Vols. 8vo.

CUNNINGHAM'S (ALLAN) Poems and Songs. Now first collected and arranged, with Biographical Notice. 24mo. 2s. 6d.

———— (CAPT. J. D.) History of the Sikhs. From the Origin of the Nation to the Battle of the Sutlej. *Second Edition.* Maps. 8vo. 15s.

CURETON (REV. W.) Remains of a very Ancient Recension of the Four Gospels in Syriac, hitherto unknown in Europe. Discovered, Edited, and Translated. 4to. 21s.

CURTIUS' (PROFESSOR) Student's Greek Grammar, for the use of Colleges and the Upper Forms. Translated under the Author's revision. Edited by DR WM. SMITH. Post 8vo. 7s. 6d.

———— Smaller Greek Grammar for the use of the Middle and Lower Forms, abridged from the above. 12mo. 3s 6d.

CURZON'S (HON. ROBERT) Visits to the Monasteries of the Levant. *Fourth Edition.* Woodcuts. Post 8vo. 15s.

———— ARMENIA AND ERZEROUM. A Year on the Frontiers of Russia, Turkey, and Persia. *Third Edition.* Woodcuts. Post 8vo. 7s. 6d.

CUST'S (GENERAL) Annals of the Wars of the 18th & 19th Centuries. 9 Vols. Fcap. 8vo. 5s. each.

DARWIN'S (CHARLES) Journal of Researches into the Natural History of the Countries visited during a Voyage round the World. Post 8vo. 9s.

———— Origin of Species by Means of Natural Selection; or, the Preservation of Favoured Races in the Struggle for Life. Post 8vo. 14s.

———— Fertilization of Orchids through Insect Agency, and as to the good of Intercrossing. Woodcuts. Post 8vo. 9s.

DAVIS'S (NATHAN) Visit to the Ruined Cities of Numidia and Carthaginia. Illustrations. 8vo. 16s.

DAVY'S (SIR HUMPHRY) Consolations in Travel; or, Last Days of a Philosopher. *Fifth Edition.* Woodcuts. Fcap. 8vo. 6s.

———— Salmonia; or, Days of Fly Fishing. *Fourth Edition.* Woodcuts. Fcap. 8vo. 6s.

DELEPIERRE'S (OCTAVE) History of Flemish Literature and its celebrated Authors. From the Twelfth Century to the present Day. 8vo. 9s.

DENNIS' (GEORGE) Cities and Cemeteries of Etruria. Plates. 2 Vols. 8vo. 42s.

DIXON'S (HEPWORTH) Story of the Life of Lord Bacon. Portrait. Fcap. 8vo. 7s. 6d.

DOG-BREAKING; the Most Expeditious, Certain, and Easy Method, whether great excellence or only mediocrity be required. By LIEUT.-COL. HUTCHINSON. Third Edition. Woodcuts. Post 8vo. 9s.

DOMESTIC MODERN COOKERY. Founded on Principles of Economy and Practical Knowledge, and adapted for Private Families. New Edition. Woodcuts. Fcap. 8vo. 5s.

DOUGLAS'S (GENERAL SIR HOWARD) Life and Adventures; From Notes, Conversations, and Correspondence. By S. W. FULLOM. Portrait. 8vo. 15s.

———— On the Theory and Practice of Gunnery. 5th Edition. Plates. 8vo. 21s.

———— Military Bridges, and the Passages of Rivers in Military Operations. Third Edition. Plates. 8vo. 21s.

———— Naval Warfare with Steam. Second Edition. 8vo. 8s. 6d.

———— Modern Systems of Fortification, with special reference to the Naval, Littoral, and Internal Defence of England. Plans. 8vo. 12s.

DRAKE'S (SIR FRANCIS) Life, Voyages, and Exploits, by Sea and Land. By JOHN BARROW. Third Edition. Post 8vo. 2s.

DRINKWATER'S (JOHN) History of the Siege of Gibraltar, 1779-1783. With a Description and Account of that Garrison from the Earliest Periods. Post 8vo. 2s.

DU CHAILLU'S (PAUL B.) EQUATORIAL AFRICA, with Accounts of the Gorilla, the Nest-building Ape, Chimpanzee, Crocodile, &c. Illustrations. 8vo. 21s.

DUDLEY'S (EARL OF) Letters to the late Bishop of Llandaff. Second Edition. Portrait. 8vo. 10s. 6d.

DUFFERIN'S (LORD) Letters from High Latitudes, being some Account of a Yacht Voyage to Iceland, &c., in 1856. Fourth Edition. Woodcuts. Post 8vo. 9s.

DYER'S (THOMAS H.) Life and Letters of John Calvin. Compiled from authentic Sources. Portrait. 8vo. 15s.

———— History of Modern Europe, from the taking of Constantinople by the Turks to the close of the War in the Crimea. Vols. 1 & 2. 8vo. 30s.

EASTLAKE'S (SIR CHARLES) Italian Schools of Painting. From the German of KUGLER. Edited, with Notes. Third Edition. Illustrated from the Old Masters. 2 Vols. Post 8vo. 30s.

EASTWICK'S (E. B.) Handbook for Bombay and Madras, with Directions for Travellers, Officers, &c. Map. 2 Vols. Post 8vo. 24s.

EDWARDS' (W. H.) Voyage up the River Amazon, including a Visit to Para. Post 8vo. 2s.

ELDON'S (LORD) Public and Private Life, with Selections from his Correspondence and Diaries. By HORACE TWISS. *Third Edition.* Portrait. 2 Vols. Post 8vo. 21s.

ELLIS (REV. W.) Visits to Madagascar, including a Journey to the Capital, with notices of Natural History, and Present Civilisation of the People. *Fifth Thousand.* Map and Woodcuts. 8vo. 16s.

—— (MRS.) Education of Character, with Hints on Moral Training. Post 8vo. 7s. 6d.

ELLESMERE'S (LORD) Two Sieges of Vienna by the Turks. Translated from the German. Post 8vo. 2s.

———— Second Campaign of Radetzky in Piedmont. The Defence of Temeswar and the Camp of the Ban. From the German. Post 8vo. 6s. 6d.

———— Campaign of 1812 in Russia, from the German of General Carl Von Clausewitz. Map. 8vo. 10s. 6d.

———— Poems. Crown 4to. 24s.

———— Essays on History, Biography, Geography, and Engineering. 8vo. 12s.

ELPHINSTONE'S (HON. MOUNTSTUART) History of India—the Hindoo and Mahomedan Periods. *Fourth Edition.* Map. 8vo. 18s.

ENGEL'S (CARL) Music of the Most Ancient Nations; particularly of the Assyrians, Egyptians, and Hebrews; with Special Reference to the Discoveries in Western Asia and in Egypt. Illustrated. 8vo.

ENGLAND (HISTORY OF) from the Peace of Utrecht to the Peace of Versailles, 1713—83. By LORD MAHON. *Library Edition,* 7 Vols. 8vo. 93s.; or *Popular Edition,* 7 Vols. Post 8vo. 35s.

———— From the First Invasion by the Romans, down to the 14th year of Queen Victoria's Reign. By MRS. MARKHAM. 118th *Edition.* Woodcuts. 12mo. 6s.

ENGLISHWOMAN IN AMERICA. Post 8vo. 10s. 6d.

ERSKINE'S (ADMIRAL) Journal of a Cruise among the Islands of the Western Pacific, including the Fejees, and others inhabited by the Polynesian Negro Races. Plates. 8vo. 16s.

ESKIMAUX and English Vocabulary, for Travellers in the Arctic Regions. 16mo. 3s. 6d.

ESSAYS FROM "THE TIMES." Being a Selection from the LITERARY PAPERS which have appeared in that Journal. *Seventh Thousand.* 2 vols. Fcap. 8vo. 8s.

EXETER'S (BISHOP OF) Letters to the late Charles Butler, on the Theological parts of his Book of the Roman Catholic Church; with Remarks on certain Works of Dr. Milner and Dr. Lingard, and on some parts of the Evidence of Dr. Doyle. *Second Edition.* 8vo. 16s.

FALKNER'S (FRED.) Muck Manual for the Use of Farmers. A Treatise on the Nature and Value of Manures. *Second Edition.* Fcap. 8vo. 5s.

FAMILY RECEIPT-BOOK. A Collection of a Thousand Valuable and Useful Receipts. Fcap. 8vo. 5s. 6d.

FANCOURT'S (Col.) History of Yucatan, from its Discovery to the Close of the 17th Century. With Map. 8vo. 10s. 6d.

FARRAR'S (Rev. A. S.) Sermons on Science in Theology. 8vo. 9s.

———— Critical History of Free Thought in reference to the Christian Religion. Being the Bampton Lectures, 1832. 8vo. 16s.

———— (F. W.) Origin of Language, based on Modern Researches. Fcap. 8vo. 5s.

FEATHERSTONHAUGH'S (G. W.) Tour through the Slave States of North America, from the River Potomac to Texas and the Frontiers of Mexico. Plates. 2 Vols. 8vo. 26s.

FELLOWS' (Sir Charles) Travels and Researches in Asia Minor, more particularly in the Province of Lycia. *New Edition.* Plates. Post 8vo. 9s.

FERGUSSON'S (James) Palaces of Nineveh and Persepolis Restored : an Essay on Ancient Assyrian and Persian Architecture. Woodcuts. 8vo. 16s.

———— Rock-Cut Temples of India, described with 75 Photographs taken on the Spot. By Major Gill. Medium 8vo. 1

———— Handbook of Architecture. Being a Concise and Popular Account of the Different Styles prevailing in all Ages and Countries in the World. With 850 Illustrations. 8vo. 26s.

———— History of the Modern Styles of Architecture, completing the above work. With 312 Illustrations. 8vo. 31s. 6d.

FERRIER'S (T. P.) Caravan Journeys in Persia, Afghanistan, Herat, Turkistan, and Beloochistan, with Descriptions of Meshed, Balk, and Candahar, &c. *Second Edition.* Map. 8vo. 21s.

———— History of the Afghans. Map. 8vo. 21s.

FISHER'S (Rev. George) Elements of Geometry, for the Use of Schools. *Fifth Edition.* 18mo. 1s. 6d.

———— First Principles of Algebra, for the Use of Schools. *Fifth Edition.* 18mo. 1s. 6d.

FLOWER GARDEN (The). An Essay. By Rev. Thos. James. Reprinted from the "Quarterly Review." Fcap. 8vo. 1s.

FORBES' (C. S.) Iceland ; its Volcanoes, Geysers, and Glaciers. Illustrations. Post 8vo. 14s.

FORD'S (Richard) Handbook for Spain, Andalusia, Ronda, Valencia, Catalonia, Granada, Gallicia, Arragon, Navarre, &c. *Third Edition.* 2 Vols. Post 8vo. 30s.

———— Gatherings from Spain. Post 8vo. 3s. 6d.

FORSTER'S (John) Arrest of the Five Members by Charles the First. A Chapter of English History re-written. Post 8vo. 12s.

———— Debates on the Grand Remonstrance, 1641. With an Introductory Essay on English freedom under the Plantagenet and Tudor Sovereigns. *Second Edition.* Post 8vo. 12s.

———— Oliver Cromwell, Daniel De Foe, Sir Richard Steele, Charles Churchill, Samuel Foote. Biographical Essays. *Third Edition.* Post 8vo. 12s.

FORSYTH'S (William) New Life of Cicero. Post. 8vo.

FORTUNE'S (ROBERT) Narrative of Two Visits to the Tea Countries of China, between the years 1843-52, with full Descriptions of the Tea Plant. *Third Edition.* Woodcuts. 2 Vols. Post 8vo. 18s.

———— Chinese,— Inland,— on the Coast,— and at Sea. 1853-56. Woodcuts. 8vo. 16s.

———— Yedo and Peking. Being a Journey to the Capitals of Japan and China. With Notices of the Agriculture and Trade of those Countries, Illustrations. 8vo. 15s.

FRANCE (HISTORY OF). From the Conquest by the Gauls to the Death of Louis Philippe. By Mrs. MARKHAM. 56th Thousand. Woodcuts. 12mo. 6s.

FRENCH (THE) in Algiers; The Soldier of the Foreign Legion— and the Prisoners of Abd-el-Kadir. Translated by Lady DUFF GORDON. Post 8vo. 2s.

GALTON'S (FRANCIS) Art of Travel; or, Hints on the Shifts and Contrivances available in Wild Countries. *Third Edition.* Woodcuts. Post 8vo. 7s. 6d.

GEOGRAPHICAL (THE) Journal. Published by the Royal Geographical Society of London. 8vo.

GERMANY (HISTORY OF). From the Invasion by Marius, to the present time. By Mrs. MARKHAM. *Fifteenth Thousand.* Woodcuts. 12mo. 6s.

GIBBON'S (EDWARD) History of the Decline and Fall of the Roman Empire. *A New Edition.* Preceded by his Autobiography. Edited, with Notes, by Dr. WM. SMITH. Maps. 8 Vols. 8vo. 60s.

———— (The Student's Gibbon); Being an Epitome of the above work, incorporating the Researches of Recent Commentators. By Dr. WM. SMITH. *Ninth Thousand.* Woodcuts. Post 8vo. 7s. 6d.

GIFFARD'S (EDWARD) Deeds of Naval Daring; or, Anecdotes of the British Navy. New Edition. Fcap. 8vo. 3s. 6d.

GOLDSMITH'S (OLIVER) Works. A New Edition. Printed from the last editions revised by the Author. Edited by PETER CUNNINGHAM. Vignettes. 4 Vols. 8vo. 30s. (Murray's British Classics.)

GLADSTONE'S (RIGHT HON. W. E.) Financial Statements of 1853, 60, and 63; also his Speeches on Tax-Bills, 1861, and on Charities, 1863. 8vo.

GLEIG'S (REV. G. R.) Campaigns of the British Army at Washington and New Orleans. Post 8vo. 2s.

———— Story of the Battle of Waterloo. Post 8vo. 3s. 6d.

———— Narrative of Sale's Brigade in Affghanistan. Post 8vo. 2s.

———— Life of Robert Lord Clive. Post 8vo. 3s. 6d.

———— Life and Letters of Sir Thomas Munro. Post 8vo 3s. 6d.

GORDON'S (SIR ALEX. DUFF) Sketches of German Life, and Scenes from the War of Liberation. From the German. Post 8vo. 3s. 6d.

———— (LADY DUFF) Amber-Witch: A Trial for Witchcraft. From the German. Post 8vo. 2s.

———— French in Algiers. 1. The Soldier of the Foreign Legion. 2. The Prisoners of Abd-el-Kadir. From the French. Post 8vo. 2s.

GOUGER'S (HENRY) Personal Narrative of Two Years' Imprisonment in Burmah. *Second Edition.* Woodcuts. Post 8vo. 12s.

GRENVILLE (THE) PAPERS. Being the Public and Private
Correspondence of George Grenville, including his PRIVATE DIARY.
Edited by W. J. SMITH. 4 Vols. 8vo. 16s. each.

GREY'S (SIR GEORGE) Polynesian Mythology, and Ancient
Traditional History of the New Zealand Race. Woodcuts. Post
8vo. 10s. 6d.

GROTE'S (GEORGE) History of Greece. From the Earliest Times
to the close of the generation contemporary with the death of Alexander
the Great. *Fourth Edition.* Maps. 8 vols. 8vo. 112s.

———————— (MRS.) Memoir of Ary Scheffer. Post 8vo. 8s. 6d.

———————— Collected Papers. 8vo. 10s. 6d.

HALLAM'S (HENRY) Constitutional History of England, from the
Accession of Henry the Seventh to the Death of George the Second.
Seventh Edition. 3 Vols. 8vo. 30s.

———————— History of Europe during the Middle Ages.
Tenth Edition. 3 Vols. 8vo. 30s.

———————— Literary History of Europe, during the 15th, 16th and
17th Centuries. *Fourth Edition.* 3 Vols. 8vo. 36s.

———————— Literary Essays and Characters. Selected from the
last work. Fcap. 8vo. 2s.

———————— Historical Works. History of England,—Middle Ages
of Europe,—Literary History of Europe. 10 Vols. Post 8vo. 6s. each.

———————— (ARTHUR) Remains; in Verse and Prose. With Preface, Memoir, and Portrait. Fcap. 8vo. 7s. 6d.

HAMILTON'S (JAMES) Wanderings in North Africa. Post 8vo. 12s.

HART'S ARMY LIST. (*Quarterly and Annually.*) 8vo. 10s. 6d.
and 21s.

HANNAH'S (Rev. Dr.) Bampton Lectures for 1863; the Divine
and Human Elements in Holy Scripture. 8vo.

HAY'S (J. H. DRUMMOND) Western Barbary, its wild Tribes and
savage Animals. Post 8vo. 2s. -

HEAD'S (SIR FRANCIS) Horse and his Rider. Woodcuts. Post 8vo. 5s.

———————— Rapid Journeys across the Pampas. Post 8vo. 2s.

———————— Descriptive Essays. 2 Vols. Post 8vo. 18s.

———————— Bubbles from the Brunnen of Nassau. 16mo. 5s.

———————— Emigrant. Fcap. 8vo. 2s. 6d.

———————— Stokers and Pokers; or, N.-Western Railway. Post
8vo. 2s.

———————— Defenceless State of Great Britain. Post 8vo. 12s.

———————— Faggot of French Sticks. 2 Vols. Post 8vo. 12s.

———————— Fortnight in Ireland. Map. 8vo. 12s.

———————— (SIR EDMUND) Shall and Will; or, Future Auxiliary
Verbs. Fcap. 8vo. 4s.

HAND-BOOK—TRAVEL-TALK. English, German, French, and Italian. 18mo. 3s. 6d.

———— NORTH GERMANY, HOLLAND, BELGIUM, and the Rhine to Switzerland. Map. Post 8vo. 10s.

————KNAPSACK GUIDE TO BELGIUM AND THE RHINE. Post 8vo. (In the Press.)

———— SOUTH GERMANY, Bavaria, Austria, Styria, Salzberg, the Austrian and Bavarian Alps, the Tyrol, Hungary, and the Danube, from Ulm to the Black Sea. Map. Post 8vo. 10s.

———— KNAPSACK GUIDE TO THE TYROL. Post 8vo. (In the Press.)

———— PAINTING. German, Flemish, and Dutch Schools. Edited by DR. WAAGEN. Woodcuts. 2 Vols. Post 8vo. 24s.

———— LIVES OF THE EARLY FLEMISH PAINTERS, with Notices of their Works. By CROWE and CAVALCASELLE. Illustrations. Post 8vo. 12s.

———— SWITZERLAND, Alps of Savoy, and Piedmont. Maps. Post 8vo. 9s.

———— KNAPSACK GUIDE TO SWITZERLAND. Post 8vo. (In the Press.)

———— FRANCE, Normandy, Brittany, the French Alps, the Rivers Loire, Seine, Rhone, and Garonne, Dauphiné, Provence, and the Pyrenees. Maps. Post 8vo. 10s.

———— KNAPSACK GUIDE TO FRANCE. Post 8vo. (In the Press.)

———— PARIS AND ITS ENVIRONS. Map. Post 8vo. (Nearly Ready.)

———— SPAIN, Andalusia, Ronda, Granada, Valencia, Catalonia, Gallicia, Arragon, and Navarre. Maps. 2 Vols. Post 8vo. 30s.

———— PORTUGAL, LISBON, &c. Map. Post 8vo.

———— NORTH ITALY, Piedmont, Liguria, Venetia, Lombardy, Parma, Modena, and Romagna. Map. Post 8vo. 12s.

———— CENTRAL ITALY, Lucca, Tuscany, Florence, The Marches, Umbria, and the Patrimony of St. Peter's. Map. Post 8vo. 10s.

———— ROME AND ITS ENVIRONS. Map. Post 8vo. 9s.

———— SOUTH ITALY, Two Sicilies, Naples, Pompeii, Herculaneum, and Vesuvius. Map. Post 8vo. 10s.

———— KNAPSACK GUIDE TO ITALY AND ROME. 1 Vol. Post 8vo. (In Preparation.) ·

———— SICILY, Palermo, Messina, Catania, Syracuse, Etna, and the Ruins of the Greek Temples. Map. Post 8vo. (In the Press.)

———— PAINTING. The Italian Schools. From the German of KUGLER. Edited by Sir CHARLES EASTLAKE, R.A. Woodcuts. 2 Vols. Post 8vo. 30s.

———— LIVES OF THE EARLY ITALIAN PAINTERS, AND PROGRESS OF PAINTING IN ITALY, from CIMABUE to BASSANO. By Mrs. JAMESON. Woodcuts. Post 8vo. 12s.

———— DICTIONARY OF ITALIAN PAINTERS. By A LADY. Edited by RALPH WORNUM. With a Chart. Post 8vo. 6s. 6d.

HAND-BOOK—GREECE, the Ionian Islands, Albania, Thessaly, and Macedonia. Maps. Post 8vo. 15s.

———— TURKEY, Malta, Asia Minor, Constantinople, Armenia, Mesopotamia, &c. Maps. Post 8vo. (*In the Press.*)

———— EGYPT, Thebes, the Nile, Alexandria, Cairo, the Pyramids, Mount Sinai, &c. Map. Post 8vo. 15s.

———— SYRIA & PALESTINE, Peninsula of Sinai, Edom, and Syrian Desert. Maps. 2 Vols. Post 8vo. 24s.

———— BOMBAY AND MADRAS. Map. 2 Vols. Post 8vo. 24s.

———— DENMARK, Norway and Sweden. Maps. Post 8vo. 15s.

———— RUSSIA, The Baltic and Finland. Maps. Post 8vo. 12s.

———— MODERN LONDON. A Complete Guide to all the Sights and Objects of Interest in the Metropolis. Map. 16mo. 3s. 6d.

———— WESTMINSTER ABBEY. Woodcuts. 16mo. 1s.

———— KENT AND SUSSEX, Canterbury, Dover, Ramsgate, Sheerness, Rochester, Chatham, Woolwich, Brighton, Chichester, Worthing, Hastings, Lewes, Arundel, &c. Map. Post 8vo. 10s.

———— SURREY, HANTS, Kingston, Croydon, Reigate, Guildford, Winchester, Southampton, Portsmouth, and Isle of Wight. Maps. Post 8vo. 7s. 6d.

———— BERKS, BUCKS, AND OXON, Windsor, Eton, Reading, Aylesbury, Uxbridge, Wycombe, Henley, the City and University of Oxford, and the Descent of the Thames to Maidenhead and Windsor. Map. Post 8vo. 7s. 6d.

———— WILTS, DORSET, AND SOMERSET, Salisbury, Chippenham, Weymouth, Sherborne, Wells, Bath, Bristol, Taunton, &c. Map. Post 8vo. 7s. 6d.

———— DEVON AND CORNWALL, Exeter, Ilfracombe, Linton, Sidmouth, Dawlish, Teignmouth, Plymouth, Devonport, Torquay, Launceston, Truro, Penzance, Falmouth, &c. Maps. Post 8vo. 7s. 6d.

———— NORTH AND SOUTH WALES, Bangor, Carnarvon, Beaumaris, Snowdon, Conway, Menai Straits, Carmarthen, Pembroke, Tenby, Swansea, The Wye, &c. Maps. 2 Vols. Post 8vo. 12s.

———— CATHEDRALS OF ENGLAND—Southern Division, Winchester, Salisbury, Exeter, Wells, Chichester, Rochester, Canterbury. With 110 Illustrations. Vols. Crown 8vo. 24s.

———— CATHEDRALS OF ENGLAND—Eastern Division, Oxford, Peterborough, Norwich, Ely, and Lincoln. With 90 Illustrations. Crown 8vo. 18s.

———— CATHEDRALS OF ENGLAND—Western Division, Bristol, Gloucester, Hereford, Worcester, and Lichfield. Illustrations. Crown 8vo.

———— FAMILIAR QUOTATIONS. From English Authors. *Third Edition.* Fcap. 8vo. 5s.

HEBER'S (BISHOP) Journey through India. *Twelfth Edition.* 2 Vols. Post 8vo. 7*s.*

———— Poetical Works. *Sixth Edition.* Portrait. Fcap. 8vo. 6*s.*

———— Sermons Preached in England. *Second Edition.* 8vo.

———— Hymns for Church Service. 16mo. 2*s.*

HEIRESS (THE) in Her Minority; or, The Progress of Character. By the Author of "BERTHA'S JOURNAL." 2 Vols. 12mo. 18*s.*

HERODOTUS. A New English Version. Edited, with Notes and Essays, historical, ethnographical, and geographical. By Rev. G. RAWLINSON, assisted by SIR HENRY RAWLINSON and SIR J. G. WILKINSON. *Second Edition.* Maps and Woodcuts. 4 Vols. 8vo. 48*s.*

HERVEY'S (LORD) Memoirs of the Reign of George the Second, from his Accession to the Death of Queen Caroline. Edited, with Notes, by MR. CROKER. *Second Edition.* Portrait. 2 Vols. 8vo. 21*s.*

HESSEY (REV. DR.). Sunday—Its Origin, History, and Present Obligations. Being the Bampton Lectures for 1860. *Second Edition.* 8vo. 16*s.*

HICKMAN'S (WM.) Treatise on the Law and Practice of Naval Courts-Martial. 8vo. 10*s.* 6*d.*

HILLARD'S (G. S.) Six Months in Italy. 2 Vols. Post 8vo. 16*s.*

HOLLWAY'S (J. G.) Month in Norway. Fcap. 8vo. 2*s.*

HONEY BEE (THE). An Essay. By REV. THOMAS JAMES. Reprinted from the "Quarterly Review." Fcap. 8vo. 1*s.*

HOOK'S (DEAN) Church Dictionary. *Eighth Edition.* 8vo. 16*s.*

———— (THEODORE) Life. By J. G. LOCKHART. Reprinted from the "Quarterly Review." Fcap. 8vo. 1*s.*

HOOKER'S (Dr. J. D.) Himalayan Journals; or, Notes of an Oriental Naturalist in Bengal, the Sikkim and Nepal Himalayas, the Khasia Mountains, &c. *Second Edition.* Woodcuts. 2 Vols. Post 8vo. 18s.

HOPE'S (A. J. BERESFORD) English Cathedral of the Nineteenth Century. With Illustrations. 8vo. 12*s.*

HORACE (Works of). Edited by DEAN MILMAN. With 300 Woodcuts. Crown 8vo. 21*s.*

———— (Life of). By DEAN MILMAN. Woodcuts, and coloured Borders. 8vo. 9*s.*

HUME'S (DAVID) History of England, from the Invasion of Julius Cæsar to the Revolution of 1688. Abridged for Students. Correcting his errors, and continued to 1858. *Twenty-fifth Thousand.* Woodcuts. Post 8vo. 7*s.* 6*d.*

HUTCHINSON (COL.) on the most expeditious, certain, and easy Method of Dog-Breaking. *Third Edition.* Woodcuts. Post 8vo. 9*s.*

HUTTON'S (H. E.) Principia Græca; an Introduction to the Study of Greek. Comprehending Grammar, Delectus, and Exercise-book, with Vocabularies. *Third Edition.* 12mo. 3*s.* 6*d.*

HOME AND COLONIAL LIBRARY. A Series of Works adapted for all circles and classes of Readers, having been selected for their acknowledged interest and ability of the Authors. Post 8vo. Published at 2s. and 3s. 6d. each, and arranged under two distinctive heads as follows :—

CLASS A.
HISTORY, BIOGRAPHY, AND HISTORIC TALES.

1. SIEGE OF GIBRALTAR. By JOHN DRINKWATER. 2s.

2. THE AMBER-WITCH. By LADY DUFF GORDON. 2s.

3. CROMWELL AND BUNYAN. By ROBERT SOUTHEY. 2s.

4. LIFE OF SIR FRANCIS DRAKE. By JOHN BARROW.

5. CAMPAIGNS AT WASHINGTON. By REV. G. R. GLEIG. 2s.

6. THE FRENCH IN ALGIERS. By LADY DUFF GORDON. 2s.

7. THE FALL OF THE JESUITS. 2s.

8. LIVONIAN TALES. 2s.

9. LIFE OF CONDE. By LORD MAHON. 3s. 6d.

10. SALE'S BRIGADE. By REV. G. R. GLEIG. 2s.

11. THE SIEGES OF VIENNA. By LORD ELLESMERE. 2s.

12. THE WAYSIDE CROSS. By CAPT. MILMAN. 2s.

13. SKETCHES OF GERMAN LIFE. By SIR A. GORDON. 3s. 6d.

14. THE BATTLE OF WATERLOO. By REV. G. R. GLEIG. 3s. 6d.

15. AUTOBIOGRAPHY OF STEFFENS. 2s.

16. THE BRITISH POETS. By THOMAS CAMPBELL. 3s. 6d.

17. HISTORICAL ESSAYS. By LORD MAHON. 3s. 6d.

18. LIFE OF LORD CLIVE. By REV. G. R. GLEIG. 3s. 6d.

19. NORTH - WESTERN RAILWAY. By SIR F. B. HEAD. 2s.

20. LIFE OF MUNRO. By REV. G. R. GLEIG. 3s. 6d.

CLASS B.
VOYAGES, TRAVELS, AND ADVENTURES.

1. BIBLE IN SPAIN. By GEORGE BORROW. 3s. 6d.

2. GIPSIES OF SPAIN. By GEORGE BORROW. 3s. 6d.

3 & 4. JOURNALS IN INDIA. By BISHOP HEBER. 2 Vols. 7s.

5. TRAVELS IN THE HOLY LAND. By IRBY and MANGLES. 2s.

6. MOROCCO AND THE MOORS. By J. DRUMMOND HAY. 2s.

7. LETTERS FROM THE BALTIC. By a LADY. 2s.

8. NEW SOUTH WALES. By MRS. MEREDITH. 2s.

9. THE WEST INDIES. By M. G. LEWIS. 2s.

10. SKETCHES OF PERSIA. By SIR JOHN MALCOLM. 3s. 6d.

11. MEMOIRS OF FATHER RIPA. 2s.

12 & 13. TYPEE AND OMOO. By HERMANN MELVILLE. 2 Vols. 7s.

14. MISSIONARY LIFE IN CANADA. By REV. J. ABBOTT. 2s.

15. LETTERS FROM MADRAS. By a LADY. 2s.

16. HIGHLAND SPORTS. By CHARLES ST. JOHN. 3s. 6d.

17. PAMPAS JOURNEYS. By SIR F. B. HEAD. 2s.

18. GATHERINGS FROM SPAIN. By RICHARD FORD. 3s. 6d.

19. THE RIVER AMAZON. By W. H. EDWARDS. 2s.

20. MANNERS & CUSTOMS OF INDIA. By REV. C. ACLAND. 2s.

21. ADVENTURES IN MEXICO. By G. F. RUXTON. 3s. 6d.

22. PORTUGAL AND GALLICIA. By LORD CARNARVON. 3s. 6d.

23. BUSH LIFE IN AUSTRALIA. By REV. H. W. HAYGARTH. 2s.

24. THE LIBYAN DESERT. By BAYLE ST. JOHN. 2s.

25. SIERRA LEONE. By a LADY. 3s. 6d.

⁎ Each work may be had separately.

IRBY AND MANGLES' Travels in Egypt, Nubia, Syria, and the Holy Land. Post 8vo. 2s.

JAMES' (Rev. Thomas) Fables of Æsop. A New Translation, with Historical Preface. With 100 Woodcuts by Tenniel and Wolf. *Thirty-eighth Thousand.* Post 8vo. 2s. 6d.

JAMESON'S (Mrs.) Lives of the Early Italian Painters, from Cimabue to Bassano, and the Progress of Painting in Italy. *New Edition.* With Woodcuts. Post 8vo. 12s.

JESSE'S (Edward) Scenes and Occupations of Country Life. *Third Edition.* Woodcuts. Fcap. 8vo. 6s.

———— Gleanings in Natural History. *Eighth Edition.* Fcap. 8vo. 6s.

JOHNSON'S (Dr. Samuel) Life. By James Boswell. Including the Tour to the Hebrides. Edited by the late Mr. Croker. Portraits. Royal 8vo. 10s.

———————— Lives of the most eminent English Poets. Edited by Peter Cunningham. 3 vols. 8vo. 22s. 6d. (Murray's British Classics.)

JOURNAL OF A NATURALIST. Woodcuts. Post 8vo. 9s 6d.

JOWETT (Rev. B.) on St. Paul's Epistles to the Thessalonians, Galatians, and Romans. *Second Edition.* 2 Vols. 8vo. 30s.

KEN'S (Bishop) Life. By A Layman. *Second Edition.* Portrait. 2 Vols. 8vo. 18s.

———— Exposition of the Apostles' Creed. Extracted from his "Practice of Divine Love." Fcap. 1s. 6d.

———— Approach to the Holy Altar. Extracted from his " Manual of Prayer" and "Practice of Divine Love." Fcap. 8vo. 1s. 6d.

KING'S (Rev. S. W.) Italian Valleys of the Alps; a Tour through all the Romantic and less-frequented "Vals" of Northern Piedmont. Illustrations. Crown 8vo. 18s.

———— (Rev. C. W.) Antique Gems; their Origin, Use, and Value, as Interpreters of Ancient History, and as illustrative of Ancient Art. Illustrations. 8vo. 42s.

KING EDWARD VIth's Latin Grammar; or, an Introduction to the Latin Tongue, for the Use of Schools. *Sixteenth Edition.* 12mo. 3s. 6d.

———————————————— First Latin Book; or, the Accidence, Syntax, and Prosody, with an English Translation for the Use of Junior Classes. *Fourth Edition.* 12mo. 2s. 6d.

KIRK'S (J. Foster) History of Charles the Bold, Duke of Burgundy. Portrait. 2 Vols. 8vo.

KUGLER'S Italian Schools of Painting: Edited, with Notes, by
SIR CHARLES EASTLAKE. *Third Edition.* Woodcuts. 2 Vols. Post
8vo. 30s.

——————— German, Dutch, and Flemish Schools of Painting.
Edited, with Notes, by DR. WAAGEN. *Second Edition.* Woodcuts. 2
Vols. Post 8vo. 24s.

LABARTE'S (M. JULES) Handbook of the Arts of the Middle Ages
and Renaissance. With 200 Woodcuts. 8vo. 18s.

LATIN GRAMMAR (KING EDWARD VITH'S). For the Use of
Schools. *Sixteenth Edition.* 12mo. 3s. 6d.

——————— First Book (KING EDWARD VITH'S); or, the Accidence,
Syntax, and Prosody, with English Translation for Junior Classes.
Fourth Edition. 12mo. 2s. 6d.

LAYARD'S (A. H.) Nineveh and its Remains. Being a Narrative of Researches and Discoveries amidst the Ruins of Assyria.
With an Account of the Chaldean Christians of Kurdistan; the Yezedis,
or Devil-worshippers; and an Enquiry into the Manners and Arts of
the Ancient Assyrians. *Sixth Edition.* Plates and Woodcuts. 2 Vols.
8vo. 36s.

——————————————— Nineveh and Babylon; being the Result
of a Second Expedition to Assyria. *Fourteenth Thousand.* Plates.
8vo. 21s. Or *Fine Paper,* 2 Vols. 8vo. 30s.

——————— Popular Account of Nineveh. *15th Edition.* With
Woodcuts. Post 8vo. 5s.

LEAKE'S (COL.) Topography of Athens, with Remarks on its
Antiquities. *Second Edition.* Plates. 2 Vols. 8vo. 30s.

——————— Travels in Northern Greece. Maps. 4 Vols. 8vo. 60s.

——————— Disputed Questions of Ancient Geography. Map.
8vo. 6s. 6d.

——————— Numismata Hellenica, and Supplement. Completing
a descriptive Catalogue of Twelve Thousand Greek Coins, with
Notes Geographical and Historical. With Map and Appendix. 4to.
63s.

——————— Peloponnesiaca. 8vo. 15s.

——————— Degradation of Science in England. 8vo. 3s. 6d.

LESLIE'S (C. R.) Handbook for Young Painters. With Illustrations. Post 8vo. 10s. 6d.

——————— Autobiographical Recollections, with Selections
from his Correspondence. Edited by TOM TAYLOR. Portrait. 2 Vols.
Post 8vo. 18s.

——————— Life of Sir Joshua Reynolds. With an Account
of his Works, and a Sketch of his Cotemporaries. By TOM TAYLOR.
2 Vols. 8vo. (*In the Press.*)

LETTERS FROM THE BALTIC. By a LADY. Post 8vo. 2s.

——————— MADRAS. By a LADY. Post 8vo. 2s.

——————— SIERRA LEONE. By a LADY. Post 8vo. 3s. 6d.

LEWIS' (Sir G. C.) Essay on the Government of Dependencies.
8vo. 12s.

———— Glossary of Provincial Words used in Herefordshire and
some of the adjoining Counties. 12mo. 4s. 6d.

———— (Lady Theresa) Friends and Contemporaries of the
Lord Chancellor Clarendon, illustrative of Portraits in his Gallery.
With a Descriptive Account of the Pictures, and Origin of the Collec-
tion. Portraits. 3 Vols. 8vo. 42s.

———— (M. G.) Journal of a Residence among the Negroes in the
West Indies. Post 8vo. 2s.

LIDDELL'S (Dean) History of Rome. From the Earliest Times
to the Establishment of the Empire. With the History of Literature
and Art. 2 Vols. 8vo. 28s.

———————— Student's History of Rome. Abridged from the
above Work. 25th Thousand. With Woodcuts. Post 8vo. 7s. 6d.

LINDSAY'S (Lord) Lives of the Lindsays; or, a Memoir of the
Houses of Crawfurd and Balcarres. With Extracts from Official Papers
and Personal Narratives. Second Edition. 3 Vols. 8vo. 24s.

————————Report of the Claim of James, Earl of Crawfurd and
Balcarres, to the Original Dukedom of Montrose, created in 1488.
Folio. 15s.

————————— Scepticism; a Retrogressive Movement in Theology
and Philosophy. 8vo. 9s.

LISPINGS from LOW LATITUDES; or, the Journal of the Hon.
Impulsia Gushington. Edited by Lord Dufferin. With 24 Plates,
4to. 21s.

LITTLE ARTHUR'S HISTORY OF ENGLAND. By Lady
Callcott. 120th Thousand. With 20 Woodcuts. Fcap. 8vo. 2s. 6d.

LIVINGSTONE'S (Rev. Dr.) Popular Account of his Missionary
Travels in South Africa. Illustrations. Post 8vo. 6s.

LIVONIAN TALES. By the Author of "Letters from the
Baltic." Post 8vo. 2s.

LOCKHART'S (J. G.) Ancient Spanish Ballads. Historical and
Romantic. Translated, with Notes. Illustrated Edition. 4to. 21s. Or,
Popular Edition, Post 8vo. 2s. 6d.

———————— Life of Robert Burns. Fifth Edition. Fcap. 8vo. 3s.

LONDON'S (Bishop of) Dangers and Safeguards of Modern
Theology. Containing Suggestions to the Theological Student under
present difficulties. Second Edition. 8vo. 9s.

LOUDON'S (Mrs.) Instructions in Gardening for Ladies. With
Directions and Calendar of Operations for Every Month. Eighth
Edition. Woodcuts. Fcap. 8vo. 5s.

———————— Modern Botany; a Popular Introduction to the
Natural System of Plants. Second Edition. Woodcuts. Fcap. 8vo. 6s.

LOWE'S (Sir Hudson) Letters and Journals, during the Captivity
of Napoleon at St. Helena. By William Forsyth. Portrait. 3 Vols.
8vo. 45s.

LUCAS' (Samuel) Secularia; or, Surveys on the Main Stream of History. 8vo. 12s.

LUCKNOW: A Lady's Diary of the Siege. *Fourth Thousand.* Fcap. 8vo. 4s. 6d.

LYELL'S (Sir Charles) Principles of Geology; or, the Modern Changes of the Earth and its Inhabitants considered as illustrative of Geology. *Ninth Edition.* Woodcuts. 8vo. 18s.

———— Visits to the United States, 1841-46. *Second Edition.* Plates. 4 Vols. Post 8vo. 24s.

———— Geological Evidences of the Antiquity of Man. *Second Edition.* Illustrations. 8vo. 14s.

MAHON'S (Lord) History of England, from the Peace of Utrecht to the Peace of Versailles, 1713—83. *Library Edition,* 7 Vols. 8vo. 93s. *Popular Edition,* 7 Vols. Post 8vo. 35s.

———— " Forty-Five ; " a Narrative of the Rebellion in Scotland. Post 8vo. 3s.

———— History of British India from its Origin till the Peace of 1783. Post 8vo. 3s. 6d.

———— Spain under Charles the Second; 1690 to 1700. *Second Edition.* Post 8vo. 6s. 6d.

———— Life of William Pitt, with Extracts from his MS. Papers. *Second Edition.* Portraits. 4 Vols. Post 8vo. 42s.

———— Condé, surnamed the Great. Post 8vo. 3s. 6d.

———— Belisarius. *Second Edition.* Post 8vo. 10s. 6d.

———— Historical and Critical Essays. Post 8vo. 3s. 6d.

———— Miscellanies. *Second Edition.* Post 8vo. 5s. 6d.

———— Story of Joan of Arc. Fcap. 8vo. 1s.

———— Addresses. Fcap. 8vo. 1s.

McCLINTOCK'S (Capt. Sir F. L.) Narrative of the Discovery of the Fate of Sir John Franklin and his Companions in the Arctic Seas. *Twelfth Thousand.* Illustrations. 8vo. 16s.

McCULLOCH'S (J. R.) Collected Edition of Ricardo's Political Works. With Notes and Memoir. *Second Edition.* 8vo. 16s.

MAINE (H. Sumner) on Ancient Law: its Connection with the Early History of Society, and its Relation to Modern Ideas. *Second Edition.* 8vo. 12s.

MALCOLM'S (Sir John) Sketches of Persia. *Third Edition.* Post 8vo. 3s. 6d.

MANSEL (Rev. H. L.) Limits of Religious Thought Examined. Being the Bampton Lectures for 1858. *Fourth Edition.* Post 8vo. 7s. 6d.

MANTELL'S (Gideon A.) Thoughts on Animalcules; or, the Invisible World, as revealed by the Microscope. *Second Edition.* Plates. 16mo. 6s.

MANUAL OF SCIENTIFIC ENQUIRY, Prepared for the Use of Officers and Travellers. By various Writers. Edited by Sir J. F. Herschel and Rev. R. Main. *Third Edition.* Maps. Post 8vo. 9s. (*Published by order of the Lords of the Admiralty.*)

MARKHAM'S (MRS.) History of England. From the First Invasion by the Romans, down to the fourteenth year of Queen Victoria's Reign. 156th Edition. Woodcuts. 12mo. 6s.

———————— History of France. From the Conquest by the Gauls, to the Death of Louis Philippe. Sixtieth Edition. Woodcuts. 12mo. 6s.

———————— History of Germany. From the Invasion by Marius, to the present time. Fifteenth Edition. Woodcuts. 12mo. 6s.

———————— History of Greece. From the Earliest Times to the Roman Conquest. By Dr. WM. SMITH. Woodcuts. 16mo. 3s. 6d.

———————— History of Rome, from the Earliest Times to the Establishment of the Empire. By DR. WM. SMITH. Woodcuts. 16mo. 3s. 6d.

———————— (CLEMENTS, R.) Travels in Peru and India, for the purpose of collecting Cinchona Plants, and introducing Bark into India. Maps and Illustrations. 8vo. . 16s.

MARKLAND'S (J. H.) Reverence due to Holy Places. Third Edition. Fcap. 8vo. 2s.

MARRYAT'S (JOSEPH) History of Modern and Mediæval Pottery and Porcelain. With a Description of the Manufacture. Second Edition. Plates and Woodcuts. 8vo. 31s. 6d.

———————— (HORACE) Jutland, the Danish Isles, and Copenhagen. Illustrations. 2 Vols. Post 8vo. 24s.

———————— Sweden and Isle of Gothland. Illustrations. 2 Vols. Post 8vo. 28s.

MATTHIÆ'S (AUGUSTUS) Greek Grammar for Schools. Abridged from the Larger Grammar. By Blomfield. Ninth Edition. Revised by EDWARDS. 12mo. 3s.

MAUREL'S (JULES) Essay on the Character, Actions, and Writings of the Duke of Wellington. Second Edition. Fcap. 8vo. 1s. 6d.

MAXIMS AND HINTS on Angling and Chess. By RICHARD PENN. Woodcuts. 12mo. 1s.

MAYNE'S (R. C.) Four Years in British Columbia and Vancouver Island. Its Forests, Rivers, Coasts, and Gold Fields, and Resources for Colonisation. Illustrations. 8vo. 16s.

MELVILLE'S (HERMANN) Typee and Omoo; or, Adventures amongst the Marquesas and South Sea Islands. 2 Vols Post 8vo. 7s.

MENDELSSOHN'S Life. By JULES BENEDICT. 8vo. 2s. 6d.

MEREDITH'S (MRS. CHARLES) Notes and Sketches of New South Wales. Post 8vo. 2s.

———————— Tasmania, during a Residence of Nine Years. Illustrations. 2 Vols. Post 8vo. 18s.

MERRIFIELD (MRS.) on the Arts of Painting in Oil, Miniature, Mosaic, and Glass; Gilding, Dyeing. and the Preparation of Colours and Artificial Gems. 2 Vols. 8vo. 30s.

MESSIAH (THE): A Narrative of the Life, Travels, Death, Resurrection, and Ascension of our Blessed Lord. BY A LAYMAN. Author of the "Life of Bishop Ken." Map. 8vo. 18s.

MILLS' (ARTHUR) India in 1858 ; A Summary of the Existing
Administration—Political, Fiscal, and Judicial. *Second Edition*. Map.
8vo. 10s. 6d.

MILMAN'S (DEAN) History of Christianity, from the Birth of
Christ to the Abolition of Paganism in the Roman Empire. *New
Edition*. 3 Vols. 8vo. 36s.

———————————— Latin Christianity ; including that
of the Popes to the Pontificate of Nicholas V. *Second Edition*. 6 Vols.
8vo. 72s.

———————————— the Jews, from the Earliest Period,
brought down to Modern Times. 3 Vols. 8vo. 36s.

————— Character and Conduct of the Apostles considered as
an Evidence of Christianity. 8vo. 10s. 6d.

————— Life and Works of Horace. With 300 Woodcuts.
2 Vols. Crown 8vo. 30s.

————— Poetical Works. Plates. 3 Vols. Fcap. 8vo. 18s.

————— Fall of Jerusalem. Fcap. 8vo. 1s.

————— (CAPT. E. A.) Wayside Cross. A Tale of the Carlist
War. Post 8vo. 2s.

MILNES' (R. MONCKTON, LORD HOUGHTON) Selections from Poetical
Works. Fcap. 8vo.

MODERN DOMESTIC COOKERY. Founded on Principles of
Economy and Practical Knowledge, and adapted for Private Families.
New Edition. Woodcuts. Fcap. 8vo. 5s.

MONASTERY AND THE MOUNTAIN CHURCH. By Author
of " Sunlight through the Mist." Woodcuts. 16mo. 4s.

MOORE'S (THOMAS) Life and Letters of Lord Byron. Plates.
6 Vols. Fcap. 8vo. 18s.

————— Life and Letters of Lord Byron. Portraits. Royal
8vo. 9s.

MOTLEY'S (J. L.) History of the United Netherlands : from the
Death of William the Silent to the Synod of Dort. Embracing the
English-Dutch struggle against Spain; and a detailed Account of the
Spanish Armada. Portraits. 2 Vols. 8vo. 30s.

MOUHOT'S (HENRI) Siam Cambojia, and Lao ; a Narrative of
Travels and Discoveries. Illustrations. 8vo.

MOZLEY'S (REV. J. B.) Treatise on Predestination. 8vo. 14s.

————— Primitive Doctrine of Baptismal Regeneration. 8vo. 7s.6d.

MUCK MANUAL (The) for Farmers. A Practical Treatise on the
Chemical Properties of Manures. By FREDERICK FALKNER. *Second
Edition*. Fcap. 8vo. 5s.

MUNDY'S (GEN.) Pen and Pencil Sketches during a Tour
in India. *Third Edition*. Plates. Post 8vo. 7s. 6d.

————— (ADMIRAL) Account of the Italian Revolution, with
Notices of Garibaldi, Francis II., and Victor Emmanuel. Post 8vo. 12s.

MUNRO'S (GENERAL SIR THOMAS) Life and Letters. By the REV.
G. R. GLEIG. Post 8vo. 3s. 6d.

MURCHISON'S (SIR RODERICK) Russia in Europe and the Ural Mountains. With Coloured Maps, Plates, Sections, &c. 2 Vols. Royal 4to.

———————— Siluria; or, a History of the Oldest Rocks containing Organic Remains. *Third Edition.* Map and Plates. 8vo. 42*s.*

MURRAY'S RAILWAY READING. For all classes of Readers.

[*The following are published:*]

WELLINGTON. By LORD ELLESMERE. 6*d.*
NIMROD ON THE CHASE. 1*s.*
ESSAYS FROM "THE TIMES." 2 Vols. 8*s.*
MUSIC AND DRESS. 1*s.*
LAYARD'S ACCOUNT OF NINEVEH. 5*s.*
MILMAN'S FALL OF JERUSALEM. 1*s.*
MAHON'S "FORTY-FIVE." 3*s.*
LIFE OF THEODORE HOOK. 1*s.*
DEEDS OF NAVAL DARING. 2 Vols. 5*s.*
THE HONEY BEE. 1*s.*
JAMES' ÆSOP'S FABLES. 2*s.* 6*d.*
NIMROD ON THE TURF. 1*s.* 6*d.*
OLIPHANT'S NEPAUL. 2*s.* 6*d.*
ART OF DINING. 1*s.* 6*d.*
HALLAM'S LITERARY ESSAYS. 2*s.*

MAHON'S JOAN OF ARC. 1*s.*
HEAD'S EMIGRANT. 2*s.* 6*d.*
NIMROD ON THE ROAD. 1*s.*
WILKINSON'S ANCIENT EGYPTIANS. 12*s.*
CROKER ON THE GUILLOTINE. 1*s.*
HOLLWAY'S NORWAY. 2*s.*
MAUREL'S WELLINGTON. 1*s.* 6*d.*
CAMPBELL'S LIFE OF BACON. 2*s.* 6*d.*
THE FLOWER GARDEN. 1*s.*
LOCKHART'S SPANISH BALLADS. 2*s.* 6*d.*
LUCAS ON HISTORY. 6*d.*
BEAUTIES OF BYRON. 3*s.*
TAYLOR'S NOTES FROM LIFE. 2*s.*
REJECTED ADDRESSES. 1*s.*
PENN'S HINTS ON ANGLING. 1*s.*

MUSIC AND DRESS. Reprinted from the "Quarterly Review." Fcap. 8vo. 1*s.*

NAPIER'S (SIR WM.) English Battles and Sieges of the Peninsular War. *Third Edition.* Portrait. Post 8vo. 10*s.* 6*d.*

———————— Life and Letters. Edited by H. A. BRUCE, M.P. Portraits. 2 Vols. Crown 8vo.

———————— Life of General Sir Charles Napier; chiefly derived from his Journals and Letters. *Second Edition.* Portraits. 4 Vols. Post 8vo. 48*s.*

NAUTICAL ALMANACK. Royal 8vo. 2*s.* 6*d.* (*Published by Authority.*)

NAVY LIST (Quarterly). (*Published by Authority.*) Post 8vo. 2*s.* 6*d.*

NELSON (ROBERT), Memoir of his Life and Times. By Rev. C. T. SECRETAN, M.A. Portrait. 8vo. 10*s.* 6*d.*

NEWBOLD'S (LIEUT.) Straits of Malacca, Penang, and Singapore. 2 Vols. 8vo. 26*s.*

NEWDEGATE'S (C. N.) Customs' Tariffs of all Nations; collected and arranged up to the year 1855. 4to. 30*s.*

NICHOLLS' (SIR GEORGE) History of the English Poor-Laws. 2 Vols. 8vo. 28*s.*

———————— Irish and Scotch Poor-Laws. 2 Vols. 8vo. 26*s.*

———————— (Rev. H. G.) Historical Account of the Forest of Dean. Woodcuts, &c. Post 8vo. 10*s.* 6*d.*

———————— Personalities of the Forest of Dean, its successive Officials, Gentry, and Commonalty. Post 8vo. 3*s.* 6*d.*

NICOLAS' (SIR HARRIS) Historic Peerage of England. Exhibiting the Origin, Descent, and Present State of every Title of Peerage which has existed in this Country since the Conquest. By WILLIAM COURTHOPE. 8vo. 30*s.*

NIMROD On the Chace—The Turf—and The Road. Reprinted from the "Quarterly Review." Woodcuts. Fcap. 8vo. 3*s.* 6*d.*

O'CONNOR'S (R.) Field Sports of France ; or, Hunting, Shooting, and Fishing on the Continent. Woodcuts. 12mo. 7s. 6d.

OXENHAM'S (Rev. W.) English Notes for Latin Elegiacs ; designed for early Proficients in the Art of Latin Versification, with Prefatory Rules of Composition in Elegiac Metre. *Fourth Edition.* 12mo. 3s. 6d.

PAGET'S (John) Hungary and Transylvania. With Remarks on their Condition, Social, Political, and Economical. *Third Edition.* Woodcuts. 2 Vols. 8vo. 18s.

PARIS' (Dr.) Philosophy in Sport made Science in Earnest ; or, the First Principles of Natural Philosophy inculcated by aid of the Toys and Sports of Youth. *Ninth Edition.* Woodcuts. Post 8vo. 7s. 6d.

PEEL'S (Sir Robert) Memoirs. Edited by Earl Stanhope and Mr. Cardwell. 2 Vols. Post 8vo. 7s. 6d. each.

PENN'S (Richard) Maxims and Hints for an Angler and Chess-player. *New Edition.* Woodcuts. Fcap. 8vo. 1s.

PENROSE'S (F. C.) Principles of Athenian Architecture, and the Optical Refinements exhibited in the Construction of the Ancient Buildings at Athens, from a Survey. With 40 Plates. Folio. 5l. 5s.

PERCY'S (John, M.D.) Metallurgy ; or, the Art of Extracting Metals from their Ores and adapting them to various purposes of Manufacture. *First Division* — Fuel, Fire-Clays, Copper, Zinc, and Brass. Illustrations. 8vo. 21s.

———— Iron and Steel, forming the *Second Division* of the above Work. Illustrations. 8vo.

PHILLIPP (Charles Spencer March) On Jurisprudence. 8vo. 12s.

PHILLIPS' (John) Memoirs of William Smith, the Geologist. Portrait. 8vo. 7s. 6d.

———— Geology of Yorkshire, The Coast, and Limestone District. Plates. 4to. Part I., 20s.—Part II., 30s.

———— Rivers, Mountains, and Sea Coast of Yorkshire. With Essays on the Climate, Scenery, and Ancient Inhabitants. *Second Edition*, Plates. 8vo. 15s.

PHILPOTT'S (Bishop) Letters to the late Charles Butler, on the Theological parts of his "Book of the Roman Catholic Church ;" with Remarks on certain Works of Dr. Milner and Dr. Lingard, and on some parts of the Evidence of Dr. Doyle. *Second Edition.* 8vo. 16s.

POPE'S (Alexander) Life and Works. *A New Edition.* Containing nearly 500 unpublished Letters. Edited with a New Life, Introductions and Notes. By Rev. Whitwell Elwin. Portraits. 8vo. (*In the Press.*)

PORTER'S (Rev. J. L.) Five Years in Damascus. With Travels to Palmyra, Lebanon and other Scripture Sites. Map and Woodcuts. 2 Vols. Post 8vo. 21s.

———— Handbook for Syria and Palestine : including an Account of the Geography, History, Antiquities, and Inhabitants of these Countries, the Peninsula of Sinai, Edom, and the Syrian Desert. Maps. 2 Vols. Post 8vo. 24s.

PRAYER-BOOK (The Illustrated), with 1000 Illustrations of Borders, Initials, Vignettes, &c. Medium 8vo.

PRECEPTS FOR THE CONDUCT OF LIFE. Extracted from the Scriptures. *Second Edition.* Fcap. 8vo. 1s.

PRINSEP'S (JAS.) Essays on Indian Antiquities, Historic, Numismatic, and Palæographic, with Tables. Edited by EDWARD THOMAS. Illustrations. 2 Vols. 8vo. 52s. 6d.

PROGRESS OF RUSSIA IN THE EAST. An Historical Summary. Map. 8vo. 6s. 6d.

PUSS IN BOOTS. With 12 Illustrations. By OTTO SPECKTER. Coloured, 16mo. 2s. 6d.

QUARTERLY REVIEW (THE). 8vo. 6s.

RAWLINSON'S (REV. GEORGE) Herodotus. A New English. Version. Edited with Notes and Essays. Assisted by SIR HENRY RAWLINSON and SIR J. G. WILKINSON. *Second Edition.* Maps and Woodcut. 4 Vols. 8vo. 48s.

———— Historical Evidences of the truth of the Scripture Records stated anew, the Bampton Lectures for 1859. *Second Edition.* 8vo. 14s.

———— History, Geography, and Antiquities of the Five Great Monarchies of the Ancient World. Illustrations. 8vo.

Vol. I., Chaldæa and Assyria. 16s. Vols. II. and III., Babylon, Media, and Persia.

REJECTED ADDRESSES (THE). By JAMES AND HORACE SMITH. Fcap. 8vo. 1s., or *Fine Paper,* Portrait, fcap. 8vo. 5s.

REYNOLDS' (SIR JOSHUA) His Life and Times. From Materials collected by the late C. R. LESLIE, R.A. Edited by TOM TAYLOR. Portraits and Illustrations. 2 Vols. 8vo.

RICARDO'S (DAVID) Political Works. With a Notice of his Life and Writings. By J. R. M'CULLOCH. *New Edition.* 8vo. 16s.

RIPA'S (FATHER) Memoirs during Thirteen Years' Residence at the Court of Peking. From the Italian. Post 8vo. 2s.

ROBERTSON'S (CANON) History of the Christian Church, From the Apostolic Age to the Concordat of Worms, A.D. 1123. *Second Edition.* 3 Vols. 8vo. 38s.

———— Life of Becket. Illustrations. Post 8vo. 9s.

ROBINSON'S (REV. DR.) Biblical Researches in the Holy Land. Being a Journal of Travels in 1838, and of Later Researches in 1852. Maps. 3 Vols. 8vo. 36s.

ROMILLY'S (SIR SAMUEL) Memoirs and Political Diary. By his Sons. *Third Edition.* Portrait. 2 Vols. Fcap. 8vo. 12s.

ROSS'S (SIR JAMES) Voyage of Discovery and Research in the Southern and Antarctic Regions, 1839-43. Plates. 2 Vols. 8vo. 36s.

ROWLAND'S (DAVID) Manual of the English Constitution; Its Rise, Growth, and Present State. Post 8vo. 10s. 6d.

———— Laws of Nature the Foundation of Morals. Post 8vo

RUNDELL'S (MRS.) Domestic Cookery, adapted for Private Families. *New Edition.* Woodcuts. Fcap. 8vo. 5s.

RUSSELL'S (J. RUTHERFURD, M.D.) Art of Medicine—Its History and its Heroes. Portraits. 8vo. 14s.

RUSSIA; A Memoir of the Remarkable Events which attended the Accession of the Emperor Nicholas. By BARON M. KORFF. 8vo. 10s. 6d.

RUXTON'S (George F.) Travels in Mexico; with Adventures among the Wild Tribes and Animals of the Prairies and Rocky Mountains. Post 8vo. 3s. 6d.

SALE'S (Lady) Journal of the Disasters in Affghanistan. Post 8vo. 12s.

———— (Sir Robert) Brigade in Affghanistan. With an Account of the Defence of Jellalabad. By Rev. G. R. Gleig. Post 8vo. 2s.

SANDWITH'S (Humphry) Siege of Kars. Post 8vo. 3s. 6d.

SCOTT'S (G. Gilbert) Secular and Domestic Architecture, Present and Future. Second Edition. 8vo. 9s.

———— (Master of Baliol) Sermons Preached before the University of Oxford. Post 8vo. 8s. 6d.

SCROPE'S (G. P.) Geology and Extinct Volcanoes of Central France. Second Edition. Illustrations. Medium 8vo. 30s.

SELF-HELP. With Illustrations of Character and Conduct. By Samuel Smiles. 50th Thousand. Post 8vo. 6s.

SENIOR'S (N. W.) Suggestions on Popular Education. 8vo. 9s.

SHAFTESBURY (Lord Chancellor); Memoirs of his Early Life. With his Letters, &c. By W. D. Christie. Portrait. 8vo. 10s. 6d.

SHAW'S (T. B.) Student's Manual of English Literature. Edited, with Notes and Illustrations, by Dr. Wm. Smith. Post 8vo. 7s. 6d.

SIERRA LEONE; Described in Letters to Friends at Home. By A Lady. Post 8vo. 3s. 6d.

SIMMONS on Courts-Martial. 5th Edition. 8vo. 14s.

SMILES' (Samuel) Lives of British Engineers; from the Earliest Period to the Death of Robert Stephenson; with an account of their Principal Works, and a History of Inland Communication in Britain. Portraits and Illustrations. 3 Vols. 8vo. 63s.

———— Industrial Biography: Iron-Workers and Tool Makers. Post 8vo. 7s. 6d.

———— Story of George Stephenson's Life. Woodcuts. Post 8vo. 6s.

———— Self-Help. With Illustrations of Character and Conduct. Post 8vo. 6s.

———— Workmen's Earnings, Savings, and Strikes. Fcap. 8vo. 1s. 6d.

SOMERVILLE'S (Mary) Physical Geography. Fifth Edition. Portrait. Post 8vo. 9s.

———————— Connexion of the Physical Sciences. Ninth Edition. Woodcuts. Post 8vo. 9s.

SOUTH'S (John F.) Household Surgery; or, Hints on Emergencies. Seventeenth Thousand. Woodcuts. Fcp. 8vo. 4s. 6d.

SMITH'S (DR. WM.) Dictionary of the Bible; its Antiquities, Biography, Geography, and Natural History. Illustrations. 3 Vols. 8vo. 105s.

———— Greek and Roman Antiquities. *2nd Edition.* Woodcuts. 8vo. 42s.

———————————— Biography and Mythology. Woodcuts. 3 Vols. 8vo. 5l. 15s. 6d.

———————————— Geography. Woodcuts. 2 Vols. 8vo. 30s.

——————— Latin-English Dictionary. *9th Thousand.* 8vo. 21s.

——————— Classical Dictionary. 10th *Thousand.* Woodcuts. 8vo. 18s.

——————— Smaller Classical Dictionary. *20th Thousand.* Woodcuts. Crown 8vo. 7s. 6d.

——————————— Dictionary of Antiquities. 20th *Thousand.* Woodcuts. Crown 8vo. 7s. 6d.

——————————— Latin-English Dictionary. *25th Thousand.* 12mo. 7s. 6d.

——————— Latin-English Vocabulary; for those reading Phædrus, Cornelius Nepos, and Cæsar. *Second Edition.* 12mo. 3s. 6d.

——————— Principia Latina—Part I. Containing a Grammar, Delectus, and Exercise Book, with Vocabularies. *3rd Edition.* 12mo. 3s. 6d.

——————————— Part II. A Reading-book, containing Mythology, Geography, Roman Antiquities, and History. With Notes and Dictionary. *Second Edition.* 12mo. 3s. 6d.

——————————— Part III. A Latin Poetry Book. Containing:—Hexameters and Pentameters; Eclogæ Ovidianæ; Latin Prosody. 12mo. 3s. 6d.

——————————— Part IV. Latin Prose Composition. Containing Rules of Syntax, with copious Examples, Explanations of Synonyms, and a systematic course of Exercises on the Syntax. 12mo. 3s. 6d.

——————————— Græca; a First Greek Course. A Grammar, Delectus, and Exercise-book, with Vocabularies. By H. E. HUTTON, M.A. *3rd Edition.* 12mo. 3s. 6d.

——————— Student's Greek Grammar. By Professor CURTIUS. Post 8vo. 7s. 6d.

——————————— Latin Grammar. Post 8vo. 7s. 6d.

——————— Smaller Greek Grammar. Abridged from the above. 12mo. 3s. 6d.

——————————— Latin Grammar. Abridged from the above. 12mo. 3s. 6d.

STANLEY'S (CANON) History of the Eastern Church. *Second Edition.* Plans. 8vo. 16s.

——————— Jewish Church. From ABRAHAM TO SAMUEL. *Second Edition.* Plans. 8vo. 16s.

——————— Sermons on Evangelical and Apostolical Teaching. *Second Edition.* Post 8vo. 7s. 6d.

——————— St. Paul's Epistles to the Corinthians. *Second Edition.* 8vo. 18s.

——————— Historical Memorials of Canterbury. *Third Edition.* Woodcuts. Post 8vo. 7s. 6d.

——————— Sinai and Palestine, in Connexion with their History. *Sixth Edition.* Map. 8vo. 16s.

——————— Bible in the Holy Land. Being Extracts from the above work. *Second Edition.* Woodcuts. Fcp. 8vo. 2s. 6d.

——————— ADDRESSES AND CHARGES OF BISHOP STANLEY. With Memoir. *Second Edition.* 8vo. 10s. 6d.

STANLEY'S (Canon) Sermons Preached during the Tour of H.R.H. the Prince of Wales in the East, with Notices of some of the Places Visited. 8vo. 9s.

SOUTHEY'S (Robert) Book of the Church. *Seventh Edition.* Post 8vo. 7s. 6d.

———— Lives of Bunyan and Cromwell. Post 8vo. 2s.

SPECKTER'S (Otto) Puss in Boots. With 12 Woodcuts. Square 12mo. 1s. 6d. plain, or 2s. 6d. coloured.

———————— Charmed Roe; or, the Story of the Little Brother and Sister. Illustrated. 16mo.

ST. JOHN'S (Charles) Wild Sports and Natural History of the Highlands. Post 8vo. 3s. 6d.

———————— (Bayle) Adventures in the Libyan Desert and the Oasis of Jupiter Ammon. Woodcuts. Post 8vo. 2s.

STANHOPE'S (Earl) Life of William Pitt. With Extracts from his M.S. Papers. *Second Edition.* Portraits. 2 Vols. Post 8vo. 42s.

———————— Miscellanies. *Second Edition.* Post 8vo. 5s. 6d.

STEPHENSONS' (George and Robert) Lives. Forming the Third Volume of Smiles' "Lives of British Engineers." Portrait and Illustrations. 8vo. 21s.

STOTHARD'S (Thos.) Life. With Personal Reminiscences. By Mrs. Bray. With Portrait and 60 Woodcuts. 4to. 21s.

STREET'S (G. E.) Brick and Marble Architecture of Italy in the Middle Ages. Plates. 8vo. 21s.

STUDENT'S HUME. A History of England from the Invasion of Julius Cæsar to the Revolution of 1688. Based on the Work by David Hume. Continued to 1858. *Twenty-fifth Thousand.* Woodcuts. Post 8vo. 7s. 6d.
   *** A Smaller History of England. 12mo. 3s. 6d.

———————— HISTORY OF FRANCE; From the Earliest Times to the Establishment of the Second Empire, 1852. Edited by Dr. Wm. Smith. Woodcuts. Post 8vo. 7s. 6d.

———————— HISTORY OF GREECE; from the Earliest Times to the Roman Conquest. With the History of Literature and Art. By Wm. Smith, LL.D. 25th Thousand. Woodcuts. Crown 8vo. 7s. 6d. (Questions. 2s.)
   *** A Smaller History of Greece. 12mo. 3s. 6d.

———————— HISTORY OF ROME; from the Earliest Times to the Establishment of the Empire. With the History of Literature and Art. By H. G. Liddell, D.D. 25th Thousand. Woodcuts. Crown 8vo. 7s. 6d.
   *** A Smaller History of Rome. 12mo. 3s. 6d.

———————— GIBBON; an Epitome of the History of the Decline and Fall of the Roman Empire. Incorporating the Researches of Recent Commentators. 9th Thousand. Woodcuts. Post 8vo. 7s. 6d.

———————— MANUAL OF ANCIENT GEOGRAPHY. By Rev. W. L. Bevan, M. A. Edited by Dr. Wm. Smith. Woodcuts. Post 8vo. 7s. 6d.

———————————— THE ENGLISH LANGUAGE. By George P. Marsh. Edited by Dr. Wm. Smith. Post 8vo. 7s. 6d.

———————————— ENGLISH LITERATURE. By T. B. Shaw. Edited by Dr. Wm. Smith Post 8vo. 7s. 6d.

SWIFT'S (Jonathan) Life, Letters, Journals, and Works. By John Forster. 8vo. (*In Preparation.*)

SYME'S (Professor) Principles of Surgery. *5th Edition.* 8vo. 14s.

TAIT'S (Bishop) Dangers and Safeguards of Modern Theology. 8vo. 9s.

TAYLOR'S (Henry) Notes from Life. Fcap. 8vo. 2s.

THOMSON'S (Archbishop) Lincoln's Inn Sermons. 8vo. 10s. 6d.

———— (Dr.) New Zealand. Illustrations. 2 Vols. Post 8vo. 24s.

THREE-LEAVED MANUAL OF FAMILY PRAYER; arranged so as to save the trouble of turning the Pages backwards and forwards. Royal 8vo. 2s.

TOCQUEVILLE'S (M. de) State of France before the Revolution, 1789, and on the Causes of that Event. Translated by Henry Reeve, 8vo. 14s.

TRANSACTIONS OF THE ETHNOLOGICAL SOCIETY OF LONDON. New Series; Vols. I. and II. 8vo.

TREMENHEERE'S (H. S.) Political Experience of the Ancients, in its bearing on Modern Times. Fcap. 8vo. 2s. 6d.

TRISTRAM'S (H. B.) Great Sahara. Illustrations. Post 8vo. 15s.

TWISS' (Horace) Public and Private Life of Lord Chancellor Eldon, with Selections from his Correspondence. Portrait. *Third Edition.* 2 Vols. Post 8vo. 21s.

TYNDALL'S (John) Glaciers of the Alps. With an account of Three Years' Observations and Experiments on their General Phenomena. Woodcuts. Post 8vo. 14s.

TYTLER'S (Patrick Fraser) Memoirs. By Rev. J. W. Burgon, M.A. 8vo. 9s.

VAUGHAN'S (Rev. Dr.) Sermons preached in Harrow School. 8vo. 10s. 6d.

VENABLES' (Rev. R. L.) Domestic Scenes in Russia. Post 8vo. 5s.

VOYAGE to the Mauritius. By Author of "Paddiana." Post 8vo. 9s. 6d.

WAAGEN'S (Dr.) Treasures of Art in Great Britain. Being an Account of the Chief Collections of Paintings, Sculpture, Manuscripts, Miniatures, &c. &c., in this Country. Obtained from Personal Inspection during Visits to England. 4 Vols. 8vo.

WALKS AND TALKS. A Story-book for Young Children. By Aunt Ida. With Woodcuts. 16mo. 5s.

WALSH'S (Sir John) Practical Results of the Reform Bill of 1832. 8vo. 5s. 6d.

WATT'S (James) Life. With Selections from his Private and Public Correspondence. By James P. Muirhead, M.A. *Second Edition.* Portrait. 8vo. 16s.

———— Origin and Progress of his Mechanical Inventions. By J. P. Muirhead. Plates. 3 Vols. 8vo. 45s.

WELLINGTON'S (THE DUKE OF) Despatches during his various
Campaigns. Compiled from Official and other Authentic Documents. By
COL. GURWOOD, C.B. 8 Vols. 8vo. 21s. each.

———————— Supplementary Despatches, and other Papers.
Edited by his SON. Vols. I. to IX. 8vo. 20s. each.

———————— Selections from his Despatches and General
Orders. By COLONEL GURWOOD. 8vo. 18s.

———————— Speeches in Parliament. 2 Vols. 8vo. 42s.

WILKINSON'S (SIR J. G.) Popular Account of the Private Life,
Manners, and Customs of the Ancient Egyptians. *New Edition.*
Revised and Condensed. With 500 Woodcuts. 2 Vols. Post 8vo. 12s.

———————— Dalmatia and Montenegro; with a Journey to
Mostar in Hertzegovina, and Remarks on the Slavonic Nations. Plates
and Woodcuts. 2 Vols. 8vo. 42s.

———————— Handbook for Egypt.—Thebes, the Nile, Alexandria, Cairo, the Pyramids, Mount Sinai, &c. Map. Post 8vo. 15s.

———————— On Colour, and on the Necessity for a General
Diffusion of Taste among all Classes; with Remarks on laying out
Dressed or Geometrical Gardens. With Coloured Illustrations and
Woodcuts. 8vo. 18s.

———————— (G. B.) Working Man's Handbook to South Australia; with Advice to the Farmer, and Detailed Information for the
several Classes of Labourers and Artisans. Map. 18mo. 1s. 6d.

WILSON'S (BISHOP DANIEL,) Life, with Extracts from his
Letters and Journals. By Rev. JOSIAH BATEMAN. *Second Edition.*
Illustrations. Post 8vo. 9s.

———————— (GENL. SIR ROBERT) Secret History of the French
Invasion of Russia, and Retreat of the French Army, 1812. *Second
Edition.* 8vo. 15s.

———————— Private Diary of Travels, Personal Services, and
Public Events, during Missions and Employments in Spain, Sicily,
Turkey, Russia, Poland, Germany, &c. 1812-14. 2 Vols. 8vo. 26s.

———————— Autobiographical Memoirs. Containing an Account of
his Early Life down to the Peace of Tilsit. Portrait. 2 Vols. 8vo.
26s.

WOOD'S (LIEUT.) Voyage up the Indus to the Source of the
River Oxus, by Kabul and Badakhshan. Map. 8vo. 14s.

WORDSWORTH'S (CANON) Journal of a Tour in Athens and
Attica. *Third Edition.* Plates. Post 8vo. 8s. 6d.

———————— Pictorial, Descriptive, and Historical Account
of Greece, with a History of Greek Art, by G. SCHARF, F.S.A. *New
Edition.* With 600 Woodcuts. Royal 8vo. 28s.

WORNUM (RALPH). A Biographical Dictionary of Italian Painters:
with a Table of the Contemporary Schools of Italy. By a LADY.
Post 8vo. 6s. 6d.

YOUNG'S (DR. THOS.) Life and Miscellaneous Works, edited by DEAN
PEACOCK and JOHN LEITCH. Portrait and Plates. 4 Vols. 8vo. 15s. each.

BRADBURY AND EVANS, PRINTERS, WHITEFRIARS.

Lightning Source UK Ltd.
Milton Keynes UK
UKHW011623160119
335572UK00012B/982/P